BIG IDEAS MATH®

RED ACCELERATED

Record and Practice Journal

- Activity Recording Journal
- Activity Manipulatives
- Extra Practice Worksheets
- Fair Game Review Worksheets
- Glossary

Erie, Pennsylvania

ISBN 13: 978-1-60840-301-1
ISBN 10: 1-60840-301-7

23456789-VLP-16 15 14 13 12

Contents

Contents

Contents

Contents

Contents

Contents

Contents

Contents

Name____ Date__________

1.6 The Coordinate Plane

For use with Activity 1.6

Essential Question How can you use ordered pairs to locate points in a coordinate plane?

1 EXAMPLE: Plotting Points in a Coordinate Plane

Plot the ordered pairs. Connect the points to make a picture. Color the picture when you are done.

1(4, 12)	**2**(9, 9)	**3**(12, 4)	**4**(12, –3)	**5**(10, –9)
6(9, –10)	**7**(7, –9)	**8**(2, –11)	**9**(–1, –11)	**10**(–3, –10)
11(–4, –8)	**12**(–11, –10)	**13**(–12, –9)	**14**(–11, –8)	**15**(–11, –6)
16(–12, –5)	**17**(–11, –4)	**18**(–4, –6)	**19**(–3, –3)	**20**(–4, 0)
21(–8, 2)	**22**(–8, 3)	**23**(–5, 8)	**24**(–1, 11)	

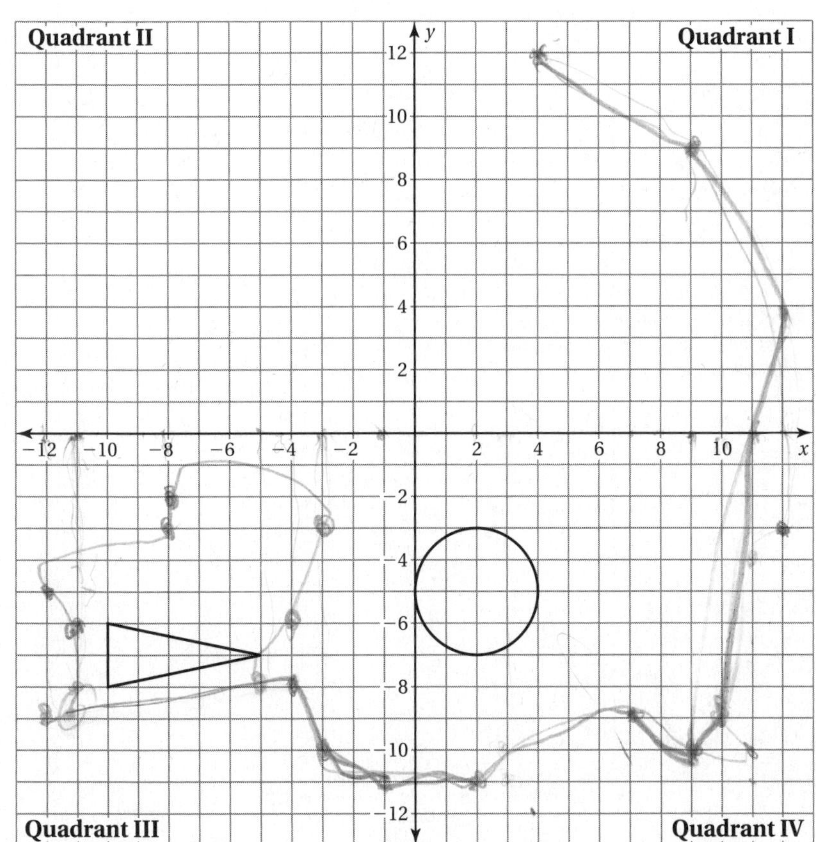

Name ______________________________ Date __________

2 ACTIVITY: Plotting Points in a Coordinate Plane

Work with a partner.

Plot the ordered pairs. Connect the points to make a picture. Describe and color the picture when you are done.

1(6, 9)	**2**(4, 11)	**3**(2, 12)	**4**(0, 11)	**5**(–2, 9)
6(–6, 2)	**7**(–9, 1)	**8**(–11, –3)	**9**(–7, 0)	**10**(–5, –1)
11(–5, –5)	**12**(–4, –8)	**13**(–6, –10)	**14**(–3, –9)	**15**(–3, –10)
16(–4, –11)	**17**(–4, –12)	**18**(–3, –11)	**19**(–2, –12)	**20**(–2, –11)
21(–1, –12)	**22**(–1, –11)	**23**(–2, –10)	**24**(–2, –9)	**25**(1, –9)
26(2, –8)	**27**(2, –10)	**28**(1, –11)	**29**(1, –12)	**30**(2, –11)
31(3, –12)	**32**(3, –11)	**33**(4, –12)	**34**(4, –11)	**35**(3, –10)
36(3, –8)	**37**(4, –6)	**38**(6, 0)	**39**(9, –3)	**40**(9, –1)
41(8, 1)	**42**(5, 3)	**43**(3, 6)	**44**(3, 7)	**45**(4, 8)

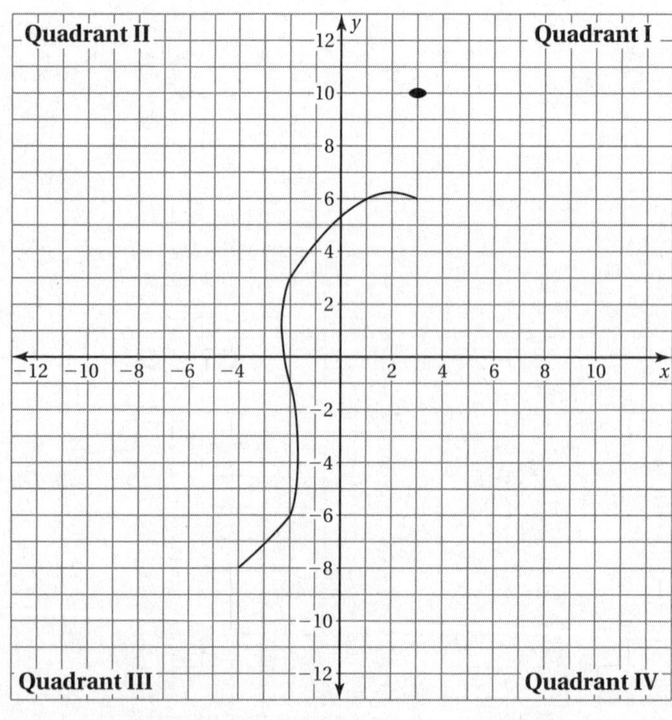

What Is Your Answer?

3. **IN YOUR OWN WORDS** How can you use ordered pairs to locate points in a coordinate plane?

4. Make up your own "dot-to-dot" picture. Use at least 20 points. Your picture should have at least two points in each quadrant.

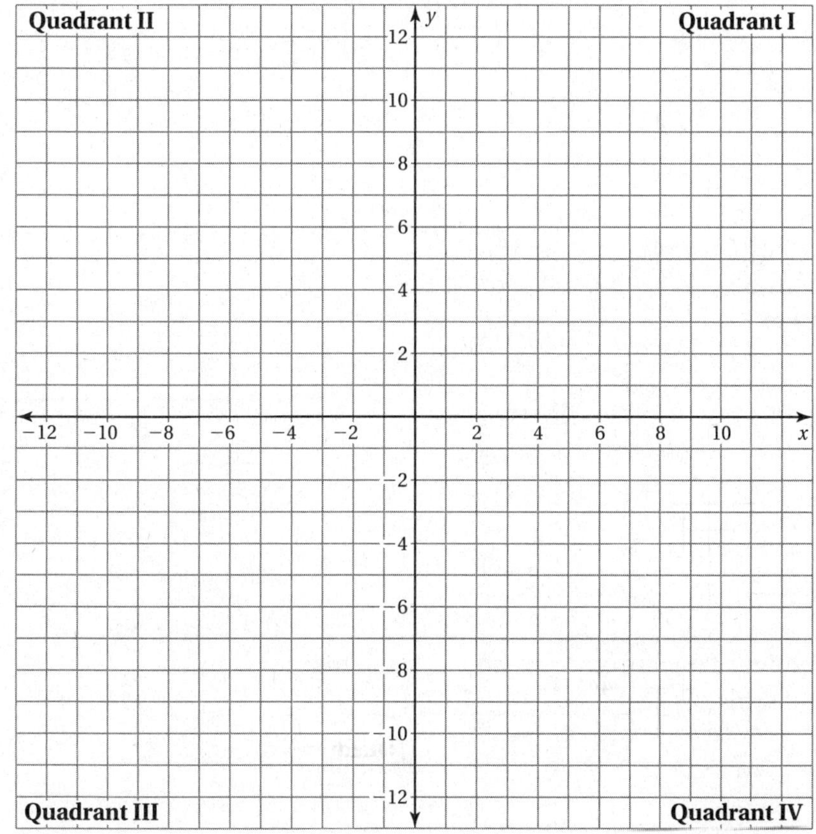

Name ______________________________ Date __________

1.6 Practice

For use after Lesson 1.6

Plot the ordered pair in the coordinate plane. Describe the location of the point.

1. $A(8, 4)$

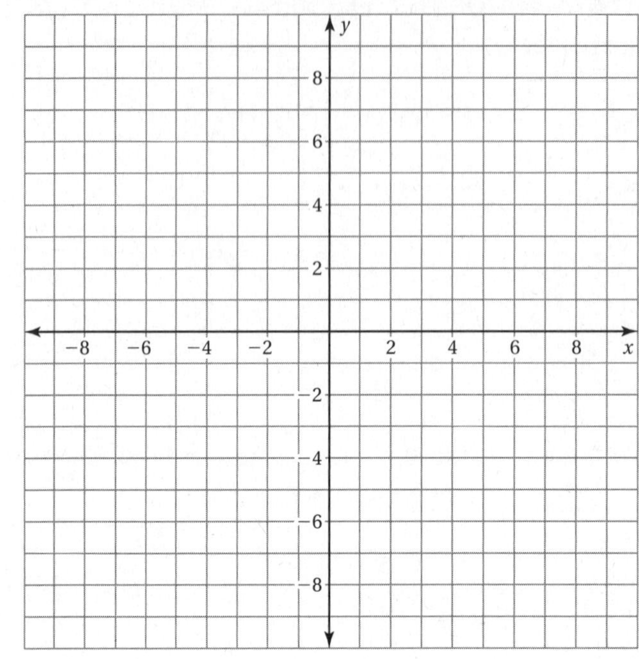

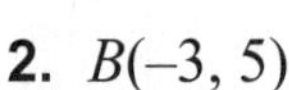

2. $B(-3, 5)$

3. $C(-2, -2)$

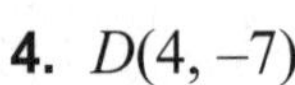

4. $D(4, -7)$

5. $E(-6, -5)$

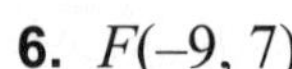

6. $F(-9, 7)$

7. The coordinates of three vertices of a rectangle are shown in the figure. What are the coordinates of the fourth vertex?

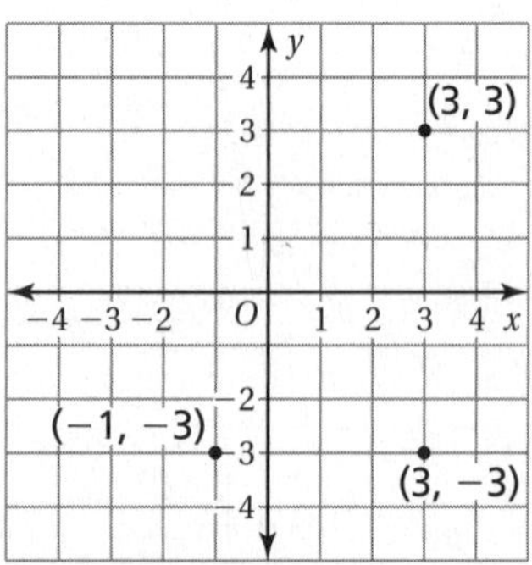

8. Your house is located at $(-4, 3)$, which is 4 blocks west and 3 blocks north of the center of town. To get from your house to the mall, you walk 7 blocks east and 4 blocks south.

a. What ordered pair corresponds to the location of the mall?

b. Is your house or the mall closer to the center of town? Explain.

Name________________________________ Date__________

Chapter 2 Fair Game Review

Write the decimal as a fraction.

1. 0.26

2. 0.79

3. 0.571

4. 0.846

Write the fraction as a decimal.

5. $\frac{3}{8}$

6. $\frac{4}{10}$

7. $\frac{11}{16}$

8. $\frac{17}{20}$

9. A quarterback completed 0.6 of his passes during a game. Write the decimal as a fraction.

Name ________________________________ Date ________

Chapter 2

Fair Game Review (continued)

Evaluate the expression.

10. $\frac{1}{8} + \frac{1}{9}$

11. $\frac{2}{3} + \frac{9}{10}$

12. $\frac{7}{12} - \frac{1}{4}$

13. $\frac{6}{7} - \frac{4}{5}$

14. $\frac{5}{9} \bullet \frac{1}{3}$

15. $\frac{8}{15} \bullet \frac{3}{4}$

16. $\frac{7}{8} \div \frac{11}{16}$

17. $\frac{3}{10} \div \frac{2}{5}$

18. You have 8 cups of flour. A recipe calls for $\frac{2}{3}$ cup of flour. Another recipe calls for $\frac{1}{4}$ cup of flour. How much flour do you have left after making the recipes?

Name____ Date__________

2.1 Rational Numbers

For use with Activity 2.1

Essential Question How can you use a number line to order rational numbers?

A **rational number** is a number that can be written as a ratio of two integers.

$2 = \frac{2}{1}$ $\quad -3 = \frac{-3}{1}$ $\quad -\frac{1}{2} = \frac{-1}{2}$ $\quad 0.25 = \frac{1}{4}$

1 ACTIVITY: Ordering Rational Numbers

Work in groups of five. Order the numbers from least to greatest.

a. $-0.5, 1.25, -\frac{1}{3}, 0.5, -\frac{5}{3}$

- Make a number line on the floor using masking tape and a marker.

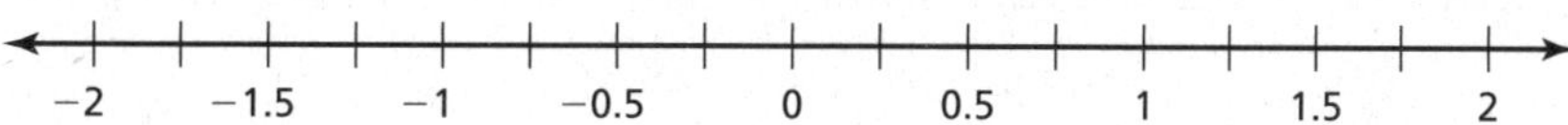

- Write the numbers on pieces of paper. Then each person should choose one piece of paper.
- Stand on the location of your number on the number line.
- Use your positions to order the numbers from least to greatest.

  The numbers from least to greatest are

  ______, ______, ______, ______, and ______.

b. $-\frac{7}{4}, 1.1, \frac{1}{2}, -\frac{1}{10}, -1.3$

c. $-\frac{1}{4}, 2.5, \frac{3}{4}, -1.7, -0.3$

d. $-1.4, -\frac{3}{5}, \frac{9}{2}, \frac{1}{4}, 0.9$

e. $\frac{9}{4}, 0.75, -\frac{5}{4}, -0.8, -1.1$

Name ______________________________ Date __________

2.1 Rational Numbers (continued)

2 ACTIVITY: The Game of Math Card War

Preparation:

- Cut index cards to make 40 playing cards.*
- Write each number in the table on a card.

$-\frac{3}{2}$	$\frac{3}{10}$	$-\frac{3}{4}$	-0.6	1.25	-0.15	$\frac{5}{4}$	$\frac{3}{5}$	-1.6	-0.3
$\frac{3}{20}$	$\frac{8}{5}$	-1.2	$\frac{19}{10}$	0.75	-1.5	$-\frac{6}{5}$	$-\frac{3}{5}$	1.2	0.3
1.5	1.9	-0.75	-0.4	$\frac{3}{4}$	$-\frac{5}{4}$	-1.9	$\frac{2}{5}$	$-\frac{3}{20}$	$-\frac{19}{10}$
$\frac{6}{5}$	$-\frac{3}{10}$	1.6	$-\frac{2}{5}$	0.6	0.15	$\frac{3}{2}$	-1.25	0.4	$-\frac{8}{5}$

To Play:

- Play with a partner.
- Deal 20 cards to each player face-down.
- Each player turns one card face-up. The player with the greater number wins. The winner collects both cards and places them at the bottom of his or her cards.
- Suppose there is a tie. Each player lays three cards face-down, then a new card face-up. The player with the greater of these new cards wins. The winner collects all ten cards and places them at the bottom of his or her cards.
- Continue playing until one player has all the cards. This player wins the game.

*Cut-outs are available in the back of the Record and Practice Journal.

Name____________________ Date__________

2.1 Rational Numbers (continued)

What Is Your Answer?

3. **IN YOUR OWN WORDS** How can you use a number line to order rational numbers? Give an example.

The numbers are in order from least to greatest. Fill in the blank spaces with rational numbers.

4. $-\frac{1}{2}$, ☐, $\frac{1}{3}$, ☐, $\frac{7}{5}$, ☐

5. $-\frac{5}{2}$, ☐, -1.9, ☐, $-\frac{2}{3}$, ☐

6. $-\frac{1}{3}$, ☐, -0.1, ☐, $\frac{4}{5}$, ☐

7. -3.4, ☐, -1.5, ☐, 2.2, ☐

Name ______________________________ Date ________

2.1 Practice
For use after Lesson 2.1

Write the rational number as a decimal.

1. $-\frac{9}{10}$

2. $-4\frac{2}{3}$

3. $1\frac{7}{16}$

Write the decimal as a fraction or mixed number in simplest form.

4. -0.84

5. 5.22

6. -1.716

Order the numbers from least to greatest.

7. $\frac{1}{5}, 0.1, -\frac{1}{2}, -0.25, 0.3$

8. $-1.6, \frac{5}{2}, -\frac{7}{8}, 0.9, -\frac{6}{5}$

9. $-\frac{2}{3}, \frac{5}{9}, 0.5, -1.3, -\frac{10}{3}$

10. Relative to ground level, a black garden ant digs $-20\frac{7}{9}$ feet and a red harvester ant digs $-20\frac{39}{50}$ feet. Which ant is closer to ground level?

11. The table shows the position of each runner relative to when the first place finisher crossed the finish line. Who finished in second place? Who finished in fifth place?

Runner	A	B	C	D	E	F
Meters	-1.264	$-\frac{5}{4}$	-1.015	-0.480	$-\frac{14}{25}$	$-\frac{13}{8}$

Name____ Date__________

2.2 Adding and Subtracting Rational Numbers

For use with Activity 2.2

Essential Question How does adding and subtracting rational numbers compare with adding and subtracting integers?

1 ACTIVITY: Adding and Subtracting Rational Numbers

Work with a partner. Use a number line to find the sum or difference.

a. $2.7 + (-3.4)$

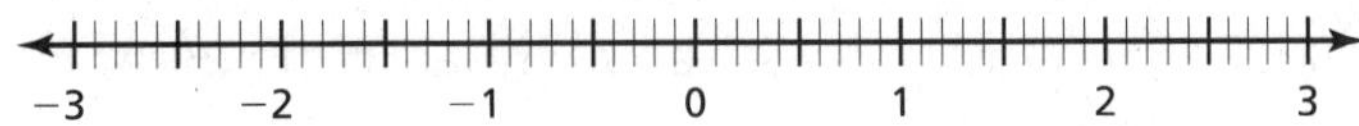

b. $\frac{3}{10} + \left(-\frac{9}{10}\right)$

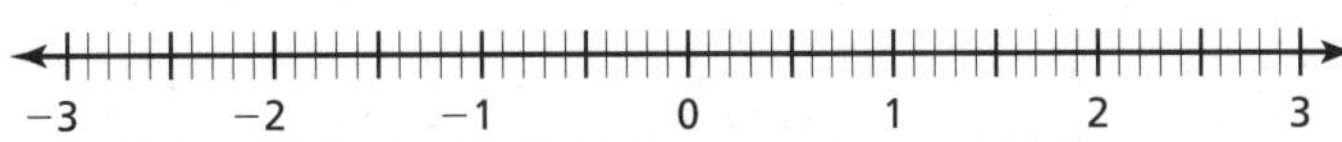

c. $-\frac{6}{10} - 1\frac{3}{10}$

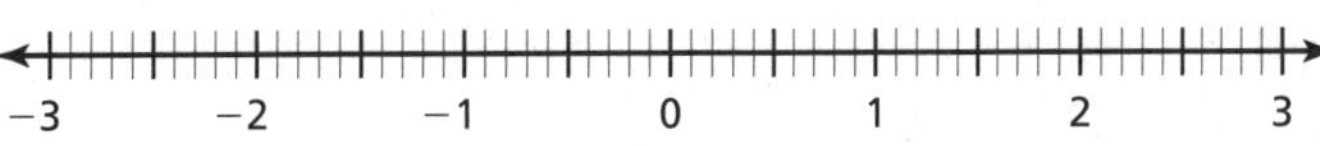

d. $1.3 + (-3.4)$

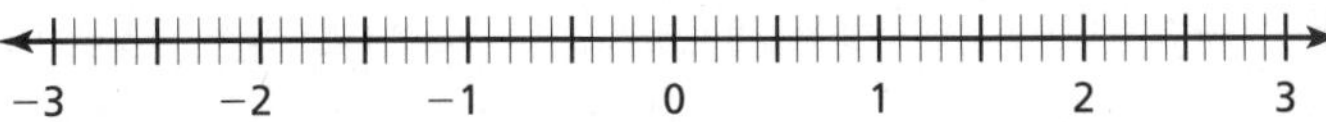

e. $-1.9 - 0.8$

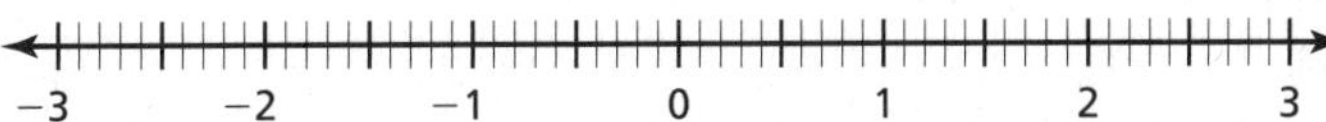

2.2 Adding and Subtracting Rational Numbers (continued)

2 ACTIVITY: Adding and Subtracting Rational Numbers

Work with a partner. Write the numerical expression shown on the number line. Then find the sum or difference.

a.

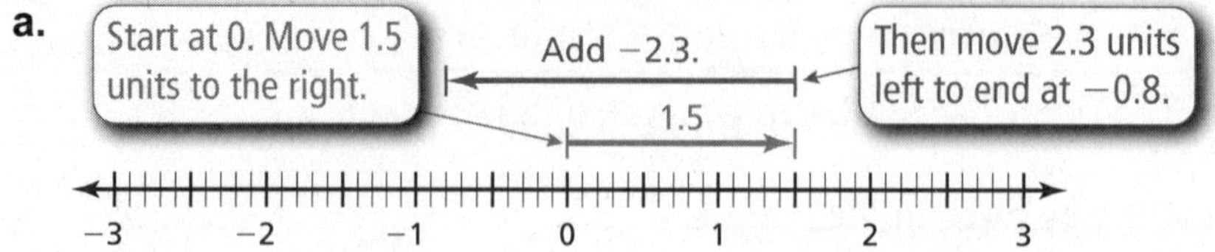

b.

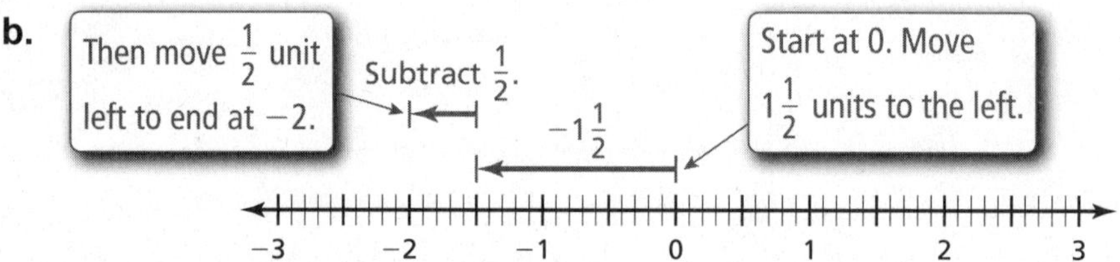

3 ACTIVITY: Financial Literacy

Work with a partner. The table shows the balance in a checkbook.

- Deposits and interest are amounts added to the account.
- Amounts shown in parentheses are taken from the account.

Date	Check #	Transaction	Amount	Balance
--	--	Previous Balance	--	100.00
1/02/2009	124	Groceries	(34.57)	
1/06/2009		Check deposit	875.50	
1/11/2009		ATM withdrawal	(40.00)	
1/14/2009	125	Electric company	(78.43)	
1/17/2009		Music store	(10.55)	
1/18/2009	126	Shoes	(47.21)	
1/20/2009		Check deposit	125.00	
1/21/2009		Interest	2.12	
1/22/2009	127	Cell phone	(59.99)	

Name____ Date__________

2.2 Adding and Subtracting Rational Numbers (continued)

You can find the balance in the second row two different ways.

$100.00 - 34.57 = 65.43$ Subtract 34.57 from 100.00.

$100.00 + (-34.57) = 65.43$ Add –34.57 to 100.00.

a. Complete the balance column of the table on the previous page.

b. How did you find the balance in the tenth row?

c. Use a different way to find the balance in part (b).

What Is Your Answer?

4. IN YOUR OWN WORDS How does adding and subtracting rational numbers compare with adding and subtracting integers? Give an example.

PUZZLE **Find a path through the table so that the numbers add up to the sum. You can move horizontally or vertically.**

5. Sum: $\frac{3}{4}$

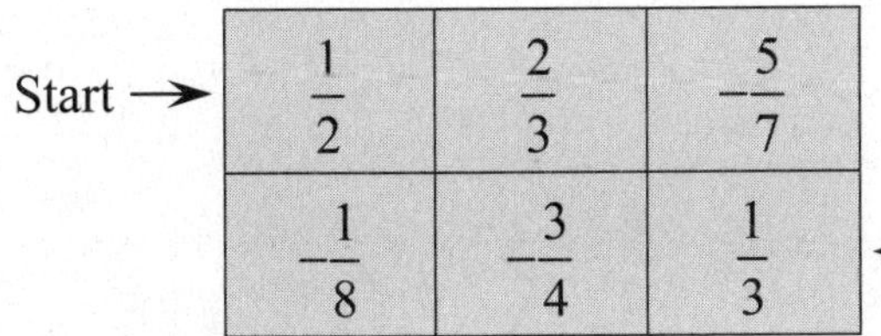

Start →

$\frac{1}{2}$	$\frac{2}{3}$	$-\frac{5}{7}$
$-\frac{1}{8}$	$-\frac{3}{4}$	$\frac{1}{3}$

← End

6. Sum: –0.07

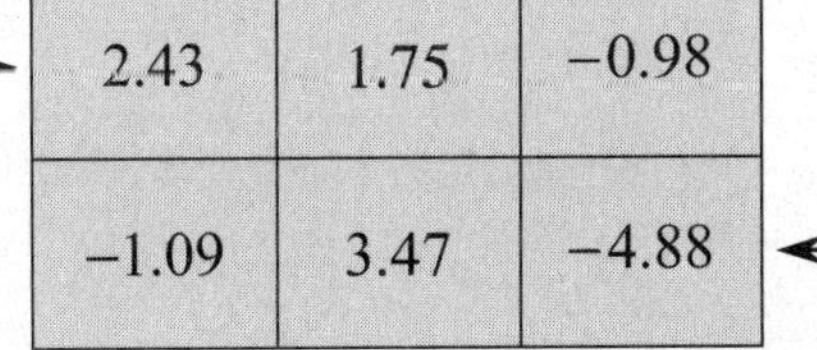

Start →

2.43	1.75	–0.98
–1.09	3.47	–4.88

← End

Name ______________________________ Date __________

2.2 Practice
For use after Lesson 2.2

Add or subtract. Write fractions in simplest form.

1. $-\frac{4}{5} + \frac{3}{20}$

2. $-8 + \left(-\frac{6}{7}\right)$

3. $1\frac{2}{15} + \left(-3\frac{1}{2}\right)$

4. $-\frac{1}{6} - \frac{5}{12}$

5. $\frac{9}{10} - 3$

6. $5\frac{3}{4} - \left(-4\frac{5}{6}\right)$

7. $0.46 + (-0.642)$

8. $0.13 - 5.7$

9. $-2.57 - (-3.48)$

10. Tubs of ice cream are delivered to a store at a temperature of 36.7°F. The ice cream is stored in a –40°F freezer. When a tub is brought out of the freezer, its temperature is 22.2°F. Write the difference between the temperatures of the ice cream after the ice cream is in the freezer and before it is in the freezer.

11. Before a race, you start $4\frac{5}{8}$ feet behind your friend. At the halfway point, you are $3\frac{2}{3}$ feet ahead of your friend. What is the change in distance between you and your friend from the beginning of the race?

Name______________________________ Date__________

2.3 Multiplying and Dividing Rational Numbers

For use with Activity 2.3

Essential Question How can you use operations with rational numbers in a story?

1 EXAMPLE: Writing a Story

Write a story that uses addition, subtraction, multiplication, or division of rational numbers. Draw pictures for your story.

There are many possible stories. Here is an example.

24 Lemons	-$11.75
5 cups sugar	-$1.50
30 plastic glasses	-$1.50
18 sales ($0.50 each)	$9.00
PROFIT	-$5.75

Lauryn decides to earn some extra money. She sets up a lemonade stand. To get customers, she uses big plastic glasses and makes a sign saying "All you can drink for 50¢!"

Lauryn can see that her daily profit is negative. But, she decides to keep trying. After one week, she has the same profit each day.

Sunday	Monday	Tuesday	Wednesday	Thursday	Friday	Saturday
-$5.75	-$5.75	-$5.75	-$5.75	-$5.75	-$5.75	-$5.75

Lauryn is frustrated. Her daily profit for the first week is

$$7(-5.75) = (-5.75) + (-5.75) + (-5.75) + (-5.75) + (-5.75) + (-5.75) + (-5.75)$$
$$= -40.25.$$

She realizes that she has too many customers who are drinking a second and even a third glass of lemonade. So, she decides to try a new strategy. Soon, she has a customer. He buys a glass of lemonade and drinks it.

He hands the empty glass to Lauryn and says "*That was great. I'll have another glass.*" Today, Lauryn says "*That will be 50¢ more, please.*" The man says "*But, you only gave me one glass and the sign says 'All you can drink for 50¢!'*" Lauryn replies, "*One glass IS all you can drink for 50¢.*"

With her new sales strategy, Lauryn starts making a profit of $8.25 per day. Her profit for the second week is

$$7(8.25) = (8.25) + (8.25) + (8.25) + (8.25) + (8.25) + (8.25) + (8.25) = 57.75.$$

Her profit for the two weeks is $-40.25 + 57.75 = \$17.50$. So, Lauryn has made some money. She decides that she is on the right track.

Name ______________________________ Date __________

2.3 Multiplying and Dividing Rational Numbers (continued)

2 ACTIVITY: Writing a Story

Work with a partner. Write a story that uses addition, subtraction, multiplication, or division of rational numbers.

- At least one of the numbers in the story has to be negative and *not* an integer.
- Draw pictures to help illustrate what is happening in the story.
- Include the solution of the problem in the story.

If you are having trouble thinking of a story, here are some common uses of negative numbers.

- A profit of –\$15 is a loss of \$15.
- An elevation of –100 feet is a depth of 100 feet below sea level.
- A gain of –5 yards in football is a loss of 5 yards.
- A score of –4 in golf is 4 strokes under par.
- A balance of –\$25 in your checking account means the account is overdrawn by \$25.

Name________________________________ Date__________

What Is Your Answer?

3. **IN YOUR OWN WORDS** How can you use operations with rational numbers in a story? You already used rational numbers in your story. Describe another use of a negative rational number in a story.

PUZZLE Read the cartoon. Fill in the blanks using 4s or 8s to make the equation true.

"Dear Mom, I'm in a hurry. To save time I won't be typing any 4's or 8's."

4. $\left(-\frac{1}{\square}\right) + \left(-\frac{1}{\square}\right) = -\frac{1}{\square}$

5. $\left(-\frac{1}{\square}\right) \times \left(-\frac{1}{\square}\right) = \frac{1}{6\square}$

6. $1.\square \times \left(-0.\square\right) = -1.\square\square$

7. $\left(-\frac{3}{\square}\right) \div \left(\frac{3}{\square}\right) = -\frac{1}{2}$

8. $-4.\square \div 2 = -2.\square$

Name ______________________________ Date __________

2.3 Practice
For use after Lesson 2.3

Multiply or divide. Write fractions in simplest form.

1. $-\frac{8}{9}\left(-\frac{18}{25}\right)$

2. $-4\left(\frac{9}{16}\right)$

3. $-3\frac{3}{7} \times 2\frac{1}{2}$

4. $-\frac{2}{3} \div \frac{5}{9}$

5. $\frac{7}{13} \div (-2)$

6. $-5\frac{5}{8} \div \left(-4\frac{7}{12}\right)$

7. $-1.39 \times (-6.8)$

8. $-10 \div 0.22$

9. $-12.166 \div (-1.54)$

10. In a game of tug of war, your team changes $-1\frac{3}{10}$ feet in position every 10 seconds. What is your change in position after 30 seconds?

11. The table shows the change of gas prices over a month's time. What is the mean change?

Week	Change
1	−\$0.06
2	+\$0.10
3	−\$0.08
4	+\$0.02

Name______________________________ Date__________

2.3b Practice

For use after Lesson 2.3b

Evaluate the expression. Explain each step.

1. $4 + 5 + (-4)$

2. $(5.3 + 2.5) + 4.7$

3. $-2.1 + (2.1 - 4)$

4. $5 \bullet 8 \bullet \frac{1}{5}$

5. $12\left(\frac{1}{6} \bullet 2\right)$

6. $\frac{1}{3}\left(3 \bullet \frac{3}{2}\right)$

7. A beryllium atom has positively-charged protons and negatively-charged electrons. The sum of the charges gives the charge of the beryllium atom. Find the charge of the atom.

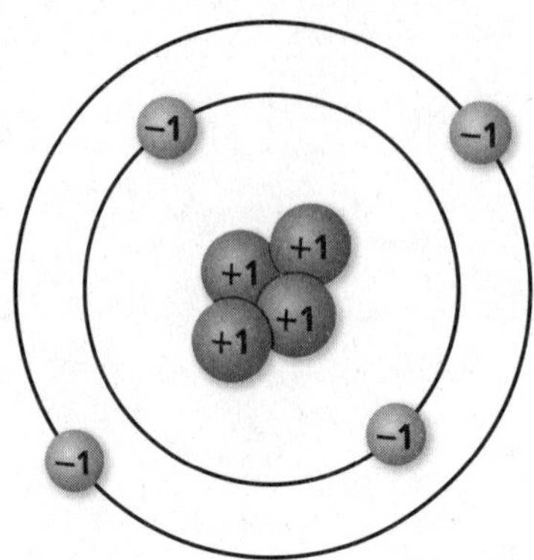

8. The table shows ways to gain and lose points in a card game. List a series of at least three events that results in 0 points.

Event	Points	Event	Points
Win a bid of 6	+60	Lose a bid of 10	−100
Lose a bid of 2	−20	Win a bid of 4	+40
Win a bid of 10	+100	Lose a bid of 6	−60
Lose a bid of 4	−40	Win a bid of 2	+20

Name____________________ Date__________

2.4 Solving Equations Using Addition or Subtraction
For use with Activity 2.4

Essential Question How can you use inverse operations to solve an equation?

1 EXAMPLE: Using Addition to Solve an Equation

Use algebra tiles to model and solve $x - 3 = -4$.

Model the equation $x - 3 = -4$.
Draw a sketch of your tiles.

To get the green tile by itself, remove the red tiles on the left side by adding three yellow tiles to each side.

Remove the "zero pairs" from each side.
Draw a sketch of the remaining tiles.

The remaining tiles show the value of x.

x = −7

2 EXAMPLE: Using Addition to Solve an Equation

Use algebra tiles to model and solve $-5 = n + 2$.

−5 = −3 + 2

________ $= n$ or $n =$ ________

Name ______________________________ Date __________

3 ACTIVITY: Solving Equations Using Algebra Tiles

Work with a partner. Use algebra tiles to model and solve the equation.

a. $y + 10 = -5$

b. $p - 7 = -3$

c. $-15 = t - 5$

d. $8 = 12 + z$

4 ACTIVITY: Writing and Solving Equations

Work with a partner. Write an equation shown by the algebra tiles. Then solve.

a.

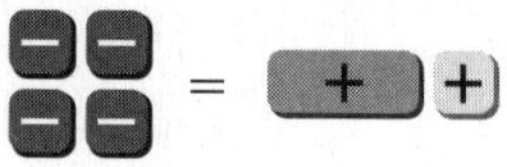

b.

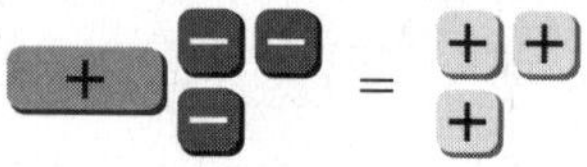

c.

d.

Name____ Date__________

What Is Your Answer?

5. Decide whether the statement is *true* or *false*. Explain your reasoning.

a. In an equation, any letter can be used as a variable. ____________

b. The goal in solving an equation is to get the variable by itself. ____________

c. In the solution, the variable always has to be on the left side of the equal sign. ____________

d. If you add a number to one side, you should add it to the other side. ____________

6. **IN YOUR OWN WORDS** How can you use inverse operations to solve an equation without algebra tiles? Give two examples.

7. What makes the cartoon funny?

"Dear Sir: Yesterday you said $x = 2$. Today you are saying $x = 3$. Please make up your mind."

8. The word *variable* comes from the word *vary*. For example, the temperature in Maine varies a lot from winter to summer. Write two other English sentences that use the word *vary*.

Name ______________________________ Date __________

2.4 Practice

For use after Lesson 2.4

Solve the equation. Check your solution.

1. $y + 12 = -26$
2. $15 + c = -12$
3. $-16 = d + 21$
4. $n + 12.8 = -0.3$
5. $1\frac{1}{8} = g - 4\frac{2}{5}$
6. $-5.47 + k = -14.19$

Write the verbal sentence as an equation. Then solve.

7. 42 less than x is -50.
8. 32 is the sum of a number z and 9.
9. A clothing company makes a profit of \$2.3 million. This is \$4.1 million more than last year. What was the profit last year?
10. A drop on a wooden roller coaster is $-98\frac{1}{2}$ feet. A drop on a steel roller coaster is $100\frac{1}{4}$ feet lower than the drop on the wooden roller coaster. What is the drop on the steel roller coaster?

Name____ Date__________

2.5 Solving Equations Using Multiplication or Division

For use with Activity 2.5

Essential Question How can you use multiplication or division to solve an equation?

1 ACTIVITY: Using Division to Solve an Equation

Work with a partner. Use algebra tiles to model and solve the equation.

a. $3x = -12$

Model the equation $3x = -12$. Draw a sketch of your tiles.

Your goal is to get one green tile by itself. Because there are three green tiles, divide the red tiles into three equal groups.

Keep one of the groups. This shows the value of x. Draw a sketch of the remaining tiles.

$x =$ ________.

b. $2k = -8$

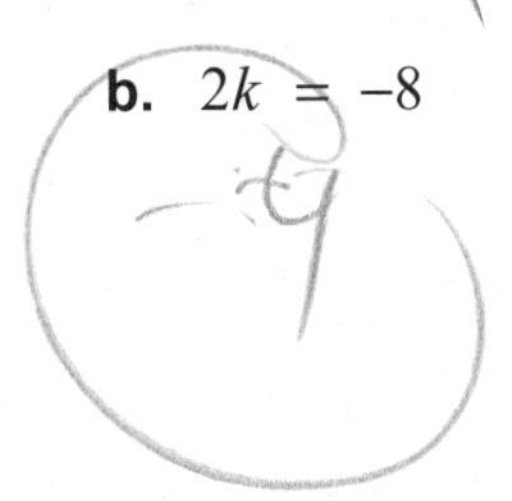

c. $-15 = 3t$

d. $-20 = 5m$

e. $4h = -16$

Name ______________________________ Date __________

2 ACTIVITY: Writing and Solving Equations

Work with a partner. Write an equation shown by the algebra tiles. Then solve.

a.

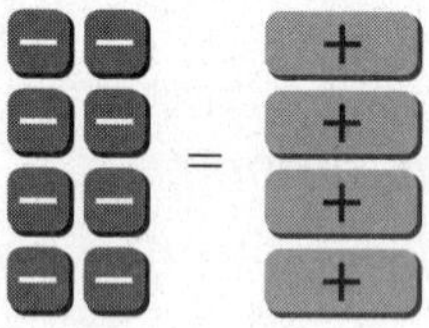

b.

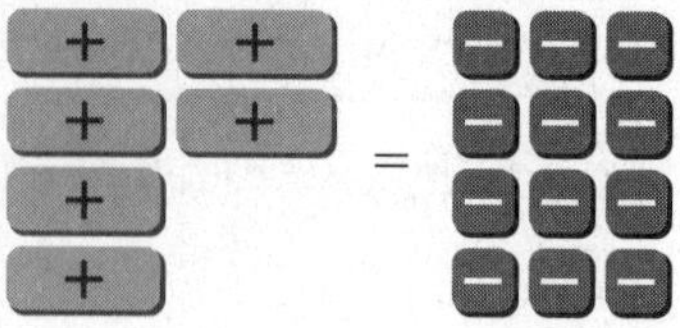

c.

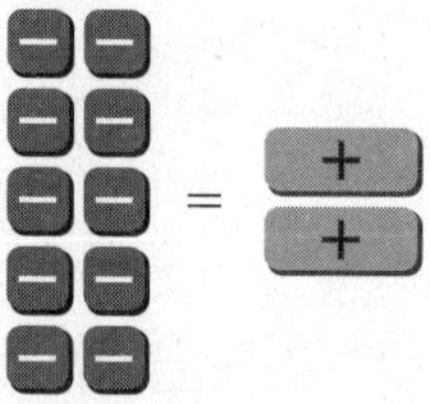

d.

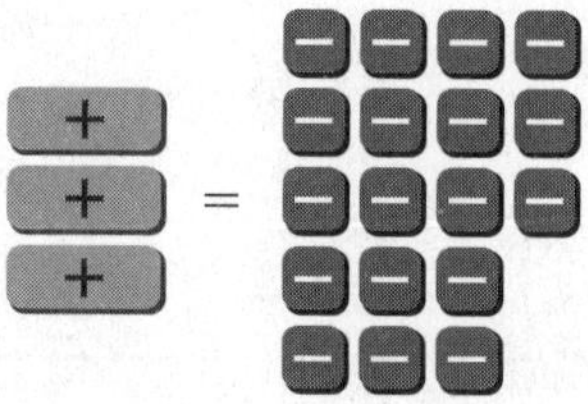

3 ACTIVITY: The Game of Math Card War

Preparation:

- Cut index cards to make 40 playing cards.*
- Write each equation in the table on the next page on the card.

*Cut-outs are available in the back of the Record and Practice Journal.

Name______________________________ Date__________

2.5b Practice

For use after Lesson 2.5b

Identify the terms and like terms in the expression.

1. $3x + 4 - 7x - 6$

2. $-9 + 2.5y - 0.7y + 6.4y$

Simplify the expression.

3. $5a - 2a + 9$

4. $\frac{5}{8}y + 7 - \frac{7}{8}y + \frac{1}{8}y$

5. $m - \frac{1}{6} - 4m + \frac{5}{6}$

6. $2.3w - 7 + 8.1 - 3w$

7. $7(d - 1) + 2$

8. $5(p + 2) + 6(-3 - p)$

Name ______________________________ Date __________

2.5b Practice (continued)

Write an expression in simplest form that represents the perimeter of the polygon.

9. 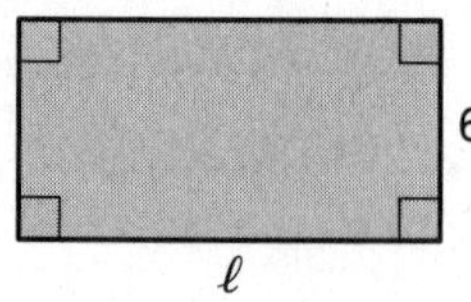

10. 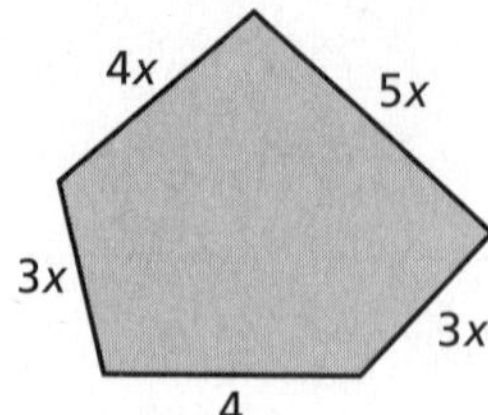

11. 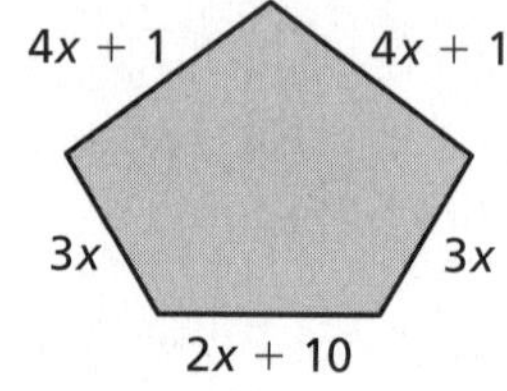

12. Write an expression in simplest form that represents the cost for shampooing and cutting w women's hair and m men's hair.

	Women	Men
Cut	\$15	\$7
Shampoo	\$5	\$2

13. On a hike, each hiker carries the items shown. Write an expression in simplest form that represents the weight carried by x hikers.

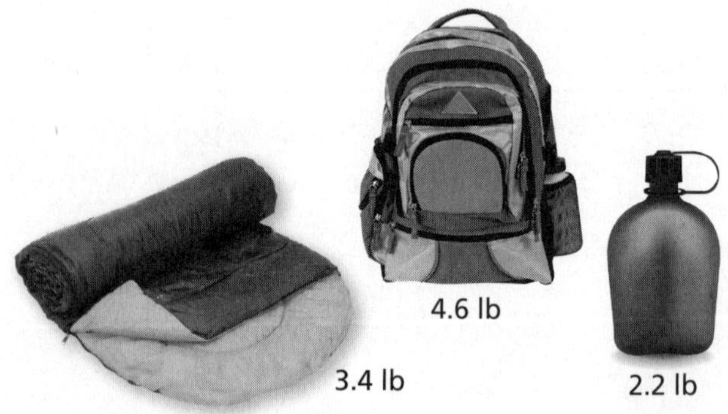

Name____ Date__________

2.6 Solving Two-Step Equations

For use with Activity 2.6

Essential Question In a two-step equation, which step should you do first?

1 EXAMPLE: Solving a Two-Step Equation

Use algebra tiles to model and solve $2x - 3 = -5$.

Model the equation $2x - 3 = -5$.
Draw a sketch of your tiles.

Remove the three red tiles on the left side by adding __________ yellow tiles to each side.

Because there are two green tiles, divide the red tiles into __________ equal groups.

Keep one of the groups. This shows the value of x.
Draw a sketch of the remaining tiles.

$x =$ _________.

2 EXAMPLE: The Math Behind the Tiles

Solve $2x - 3 = -5$ without using algebra tiles. Describe each step. Which step is first, adding 3 to each side or dividing each side by 2?

$x =$ _____. The first step is ________________________________.

3 ACTIVITY: Solving Equations Using Algebra Tiles

Work with a partner.

- **Write an equation shown by the algebra tiles.**
- **Use algebra tiles to model and solve the equation.**
- **Check your answer by solving the equation without using algebra tiles.**

a. 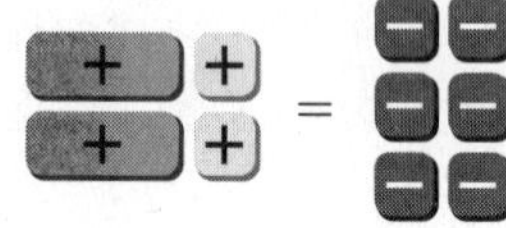

b. 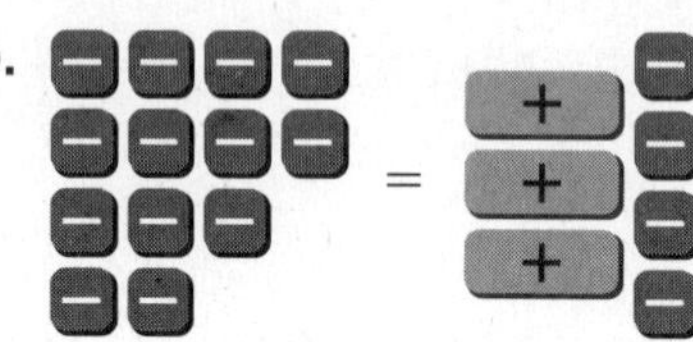

4 ACTIVITY: Working Backwards

Work with a partner.

a. Your friend pauses a video game to get a drink. You continue the game. You double the score by saving a princess. Then you lose 75 points because you do not collect the treasure. You finish the game with –25 points. How many points did you start with?

One way to solve the problem is to work backwards. To do this, start with the end result and retrace the events.

You started the game with ____________ points.

2.6 Solving Two-Step Equations (continued)

b. You triple your account balance by making a deposit. Then you withdraw \$127.32 to buy groceries. Your account is now overdrawn by \$10.56. By working backwards, find your account balance before you made the deposit.

What Is Your Answer?

5. **IN YOUR OWN WORDS** In a two-step equation, which step should you do first? Give four examples.

6. Solve the equation $2x - 75 = -25$. How do your steps compare with the strategy of working backwards in Activity 4?

Name ______________________________ Date __________

2.6 Practice

For use after Lesson 2.6

Solve the equation. Check your solution.

1. $3a - 5 = -14$

2. $10 = -2c + 22$

3. $18 = -5b - 17$

4. $-12 = -8z + 12$

5. $1.3n - 0.03 = -9$

6. $-\frac{5}{11}h + \frac{7}{9} = \frac{2}{9}$

7. It costs \$34.95 to rent a jet ski for four hours plus \$15.75 for each additional hour. You have \$100. Can you rent the jet ski for 8 hours? Explain.

8. The length of a rectangle is 3 meters less than twice its width.

a. Write an equation to find the length of the rectangle.

b. The length of the rectangle is 11 meters. What is the width of the rectangle?

Name____ Date__________

2.6b Practice
For use after Lesson 2.6b

Solve the inequality. Graph the solution.

1. $b - 4 < 8$

2. $-9.6 \le z - 2.1$

3. $16 + c \ge 14$

4. $9 > y + \frac{3}{4}$

5. $\frac{x}{6} \le -12$

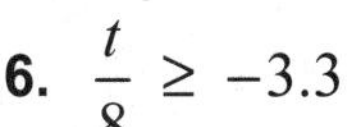

6. $\frac{t}{8} \ge -3.3$

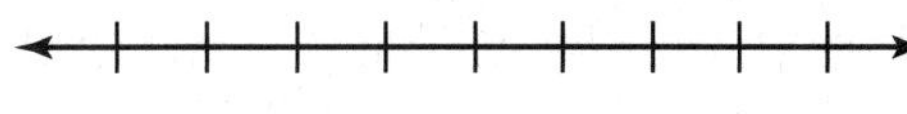

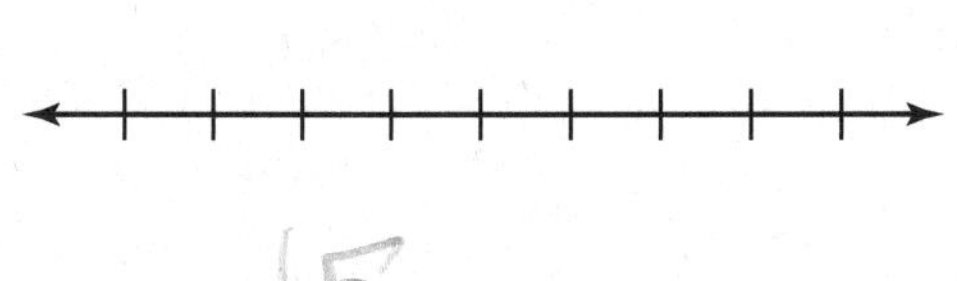

7. $5n < 75$

8. $4f > -48$

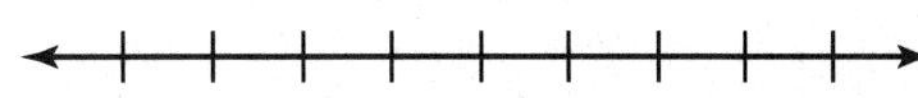

9. $-\frac{m}{6} < 1.2$

10. $-\frac{k}{2} \le -\frac{1}{2}$

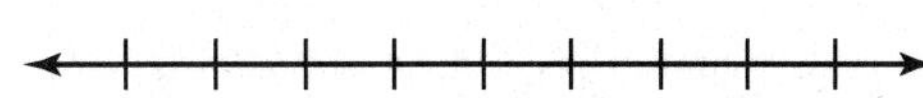

Name ______________________________ Date __________

2.6b Practice (continued)

11. $-15a > -60$

12. $-8p \geq 17.6$

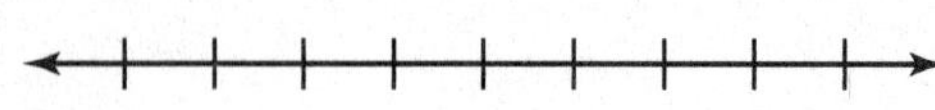

13. $2x - 5 \leq 23$

14. $-\frac{1}{4}(p - 12) > -2$

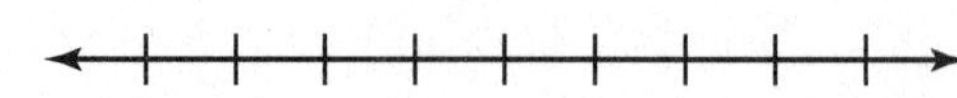

15. A dog's water container holds at most 20 quarts.

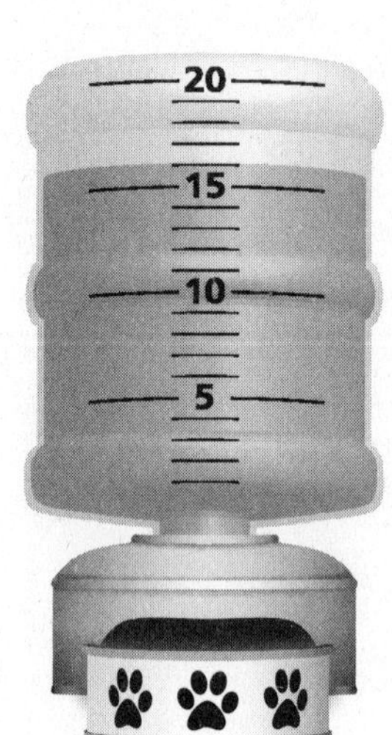

a. Which inequality shows how much water w your dog has drunk? Solve the inequality.

$w + 16 \geq 20$	$w + 16 \leq 20$

b. Interpret the solution to part (a).

16. To win a trivia game, you need at least 60 points. Each question is worth 4 points. So far, you have earned 24 points.

a. Write and solve an inequality that represents the number of questions you need to answer correctly to win the game.

b. Graph the solution in part (a). Will you have won the game after correctly answering 6 more questions? 10 more questions? Explain.

Name______________________________ Date__________

Chapter 3 Fair Game Review

Simplify.

1. $\frac{3}{18}$

2. $\frac{4}{6}$

3. $\frac{12}{60}$

4. $\frac{14}{28}$

5. $\frac{16}{36}$

6. $\frac{40}{50}$

Are the fractions equivalent?

7. $\frac{3}{8} \stackrel{?}{=} \frac{6}{11}$

8. $\frac{4}{10} \stackrel{?}{=} \frac{16}{40}$

9. $\frac{22}{32} \stackrel{?}{=} \frac{11}{16}$

10. $\frac{63}{72} \stackrel{?}{=} \frac{7}{9}$

11. You see 58 birds while on a bird watching tour. Of those birds, you see 12 hawks. Write and simplify the fraction of hawks you see.

Name ________________________________ Date __________

Chapter 3

Fair Game Review (continued)

Convert.

12. 12 feet = 4 yards

13. 28 quarts = 7 gallons

14. 48 inches = 4 feet

15. 10,000 pounds = 5 tons

16. 9 pints = 18 cups

17. 80 pounds = 1280 ounces

18. 5 yards = 180 inches

1 ft = 12 inches
3 ft = 1 yard = 12 x 3 = 36 inch
5 yard = 5 x 36 = 180 inches

19. 28 ounces = 1.75 pounds

20. You buy three gallons of fruit punch for a party. How many cups will that serve?

48 Cups

Name______________________________ Date__________

3.1 Ratios and Rates
For use with Activity 3.1

Essential Question How do rates help you describe real-life problems?

1 ACTIVITY: Finding Reasonable Rates

Work with a partner.

a. Match each description with a verbal rate.

b. Match each verbal rate with a numerical rate.

c. Give a reasonable numerical rate for each description. Then give an unreasonable rate.

Description	Verbal Rate	Numerical Rate
Your pay rate for washing cars	inches per month	$\frac{\square \text{ m}}{\text{sec}}$; $\frac{\square \text{ m}}{\text{sec}}$
The average rainfall in a rain forest	pounds per acre	$\frac{\square \text{ people}}{\text{yr}}$; $\frac{\square \text{ people}}{\text{yr}}$
Your average driving rate along an interstate	meters per second	$\frac{\square \text{ lb}}{\text{acre}}$; $\frac{\square \text{ lb}}{\text{acre}}$
The growth rate for the length of a baby alligator	people per year	$\frac{\square \text{ mi}}{\text{h}}$; $\frac{\square \text{ mi}}{\text{h}}$
Your running rate in a 100-meter dash	dollars per hour	$\frac{\square \text{ in.}}{\text{yr}}$; $\frac{\square \text{ in.}}{\text{yr}}$
The population growth rate of a large city	dollars per year	$\frac{\square \text{ in.}}{\text{mo}}$; $\frac{\square \text{ in.}}{\text{mo}}$
The average pay rate for a professional athlete	miles per hour	$\frac{\$\square}{\text{h}}$; $\frac{\$\square}{\text{h}}$
The fertilization rate for an apple orchard	inches per year	$\frac{\$\square}{\text{yr}}$; $\frac{\$\square}{\text{yr}}$

Name ______________________________ Date __________

3.1 Ratios and Rates (continued)

2 ACTIVITY: Unit Analysis

Work with a partner. Some real-life problems involve the product of an amount and a rate. Find each product. List the units.

a. $6\text{ h} \times \frac{\$12}{\text{h}}$ 72

b. $6\text{ mo} \times \frac{\$700}{\text{mo}}$ 4200

c. $10\text{ gal} \times \frac{22\text{ mi}}{\text{gal}}$

d. $9\text{ lb} \times \frac{\$3}{\text{lb}}$

e. $13\text{ min} \times \frac{60\text{ sec}}{\text{min}}$

3 ACTIVITY: Writing a Story

Work with a partner.

- Think of a story that compares two different rates.
- Write the story.
- Draw pictures for the story.

What Is Your Answer?

4. **RESEARCH** Use newspapers, the Internet, or magazines to find examples of salaries. Try to find examples of each of the following ways to write salaries.

   a. dollars per hour **b.** dollars per month **c.** dollars per year

5. **IN YOUR OWN WORDS** How do rates help you describe real-life problems? Give two examples.

6. To estimate the annual salary for a given hourly pay rate, multiply by 2 and insert "000" at the end. **Sample:** \$10 per hour is about \$20,000 per year.

   a. Explain why this works. Assume the person is working 40 hours a week.

   b. Estimate the annual salary for an hourly pay rate of \$8 per hour.

   c. You earn \$1 million per month. What is your annual salary?

   d. Why is thc cartoon funny?

"We had someone apply for the job. He says he would like \$1 million a month, but will settle for \$8 an hour."

Name ______________________________ Date __________

3.1 Practice

For use after Lesson 3.1

Write the ratio as a fraction in simplest form.

1. 8 to 14

2. 36 even : 12 odd

3. 42 vanilla to 48 chocolate

Find the unit rate.

4. \$2.50 for 5 ounces

5. 15 degrees in 2 hours

6. 183 miles in 3 hours

Use the table to find the rate.

7.

Boxes	0	1	2	3
Pounds	0	30	60	90

8.

Notebooks	0	5	10	15
Dollars	0	9.45	18.90	28.35

9. A laser printer prints 360 pages in 30 minutes. What is the printing rate in pages per minute?

10. A clothing store sells four shirts for \$60.00. The next week, the store runs a special that is buy three shirts for \$19.50 each, get the fourth free. Which is the better buy?

11. You create 15 centerpieces for a party in 5 hours.

a. What is the unit rate?

b. How long will it take you to make 42 centerpieces?

Name____ Date__________

3.2 Slope

For use with Activity 3.2

Essential Question How can you compare two rates graphically?

1 ACTIVITY: Comparing Unit Rates

Work with a partner. The table shows the maximum speeds of several animals.

a. Find the missing speeds. Round your answers to the nearest tenth.

b. Which animal is fastest? Which animal is slowest?

c. Explain how you convert between the two units of speed.

Animal	Speed (miles per hour)	Speed (feet per second)
Antelope	61.0	
Black Mamba Snake		29.3
Cheetah		102.6
Chicken		13.2
Coyote	43.0	
Domestic Pig		16.0
Elephant		36.6
Elk		66.0
Giant Tortoise	0.2	
Giraffe	32.0	
Gray Fox		61.6
Greyhound	39.4	
Grizzly Bear		44.0
Human		41.0
Hyena	40.0	
Jackal	35.0	
Lion		73.3
Peregrine Falcon	200.0	
Quarter Horse	47.5	
Spider		1.76
Squirrel	12.0	
Thomson's Gazelle	50.0	
Three-Toed Sloth		0.2
Tuna	47.0	

Name ______________________________ Date __________

2 ACTIVITY: Comparing Two Rates Graphically

Work with a partner. A cheetah and a Thomson's gazelle are running at constant speeds.

a. Find the missing distances.

	Cheetah	Gazelle
Time (seconds)	**Distance (feet)**	**Distance (feet)**
0	0	0
1	102.6	
2		
3		
4		
5		
6		
7		

b. Use the table to complete the line graph for each animal.

c. Which graph is steeper? The speed of which animal is greater?

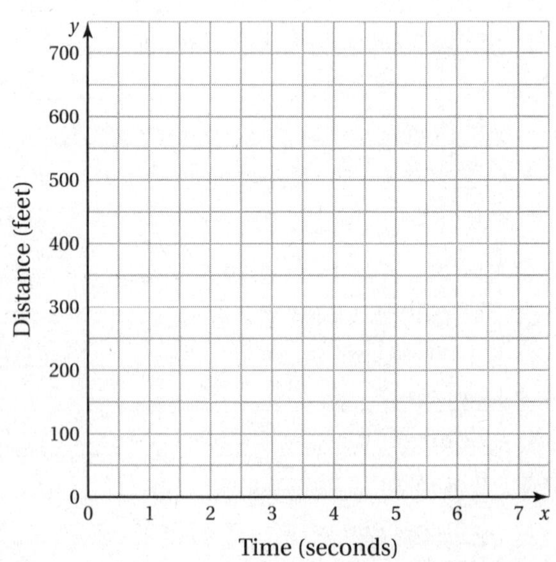

What Is Your Answer?

3. **IN YOUR OWN WORDS** How can you compare two rates graphically? Explain your reasoning. Give some examples with your answer.

4. Choose 10 animals from Activity 1.

   a. Make a table for each animal similar to the table in Activity 2.

   b. Sketch a graph of the distances for each animal.

   c. Compare the steepness of the 10 graphs. What can you conclude?

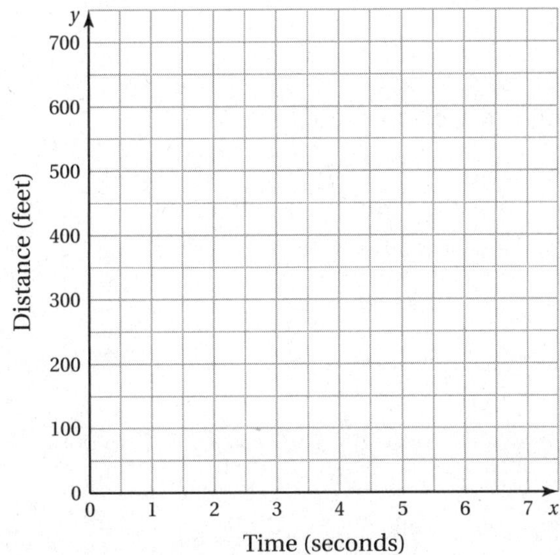

Name ______________________________ Date __________

3.2 Practice

For use after Lesson 3.2

Find the slope of the line.

1.

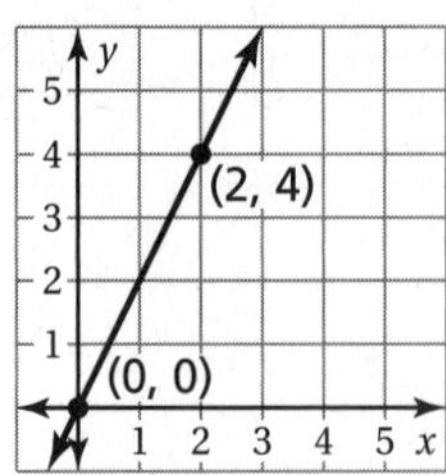

2.

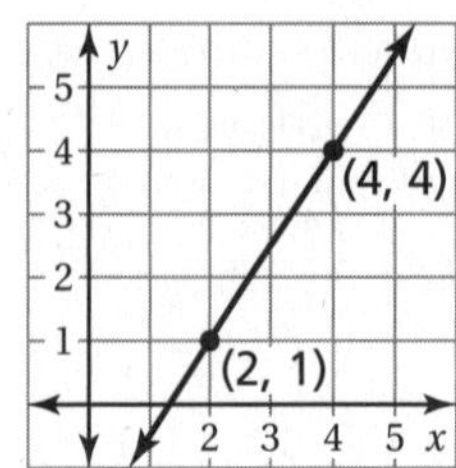

3.

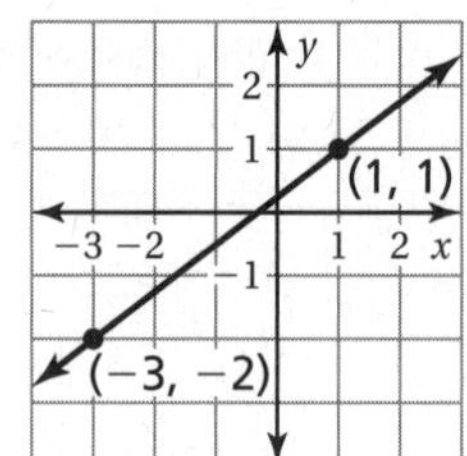

Graph the data. Then find the slope of the line through the points.

4.

Minutes, *x*	0	1	3	5
Pages, *y*	0	1.5	4.5	7.5

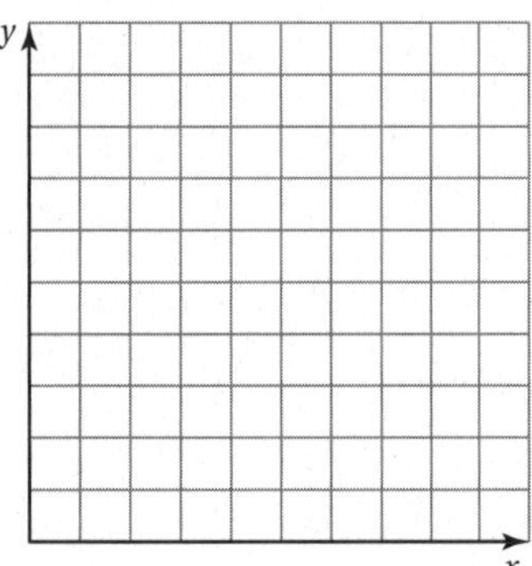

5.

Miles, *x*	0	1	2	3
Calories, *y*	0	135	270	405

6. By law, the maximum slope of a wheelchair ramp is $\frac{1}{12}$.

   a. A ramp is designed that is 4 feet high and has a horizontal length of 50 feet. Does this ramp meet the law? Explain.

   b. What could be adjusted on an unacceptable ramp so that it meets the law?

Name______________________________ Date__________

3.3 Proportions

For use with Activity 3.3

Essential Question How can proportions help you decide when things are "fair"?

1 ACTIVITY: Determining Proportions

Work with a partner. Tell whether the two ratios are equivalent. If they are not equivalent, change the second day to make the ratios equivalent. Explain your reasoning.

a. On the first day, you pay \$5 for 2 boxes of popcorn. The next day, you pay \$7.50 for 3 boxes.

First Day

$$\frac{\$5.00}{\$7.50} \stackrel{?}{=} \frac{2 \text{ boxes}}{3 \text{ boxes}}$$

Next Day

b. On the first day, it takes you 3 hours to drive 135 miles. The next day, it takes you 5 hours to drive 200 miles.

First Day

$$\frac{3 \text{ h}}{5 \text{ h}} \stackrel{?}{=} \frac{135 \text{ mi}}{200 \text{ mi}}$$

Next Day

c. On the first day, you walk 4 miles and burn 300 calories. The next day, you walk 3 miles and burn 225 calories.

First Day

$$\frac{4 \text{ mi}}{3 \text{ mi}} \stackrel{?}{=} \frac{300 \text{ cal}}{225 \text{ cal}}$$

Next Day

d. On the first day, you download 5 songs and pay \$2.25. The next day, you download 4 songs and pay \$2.00.

First Day

$$\frac{5 \text{ songs}}{4 \text{ songs}} \stackrel{?}{=} \frac{\$2.25}{\$2.00}$$

Next Day

3.3 Proportions (continued)

2 ACTIVITY: Checking a Proportion

Work with a partner.

a. It is said that "one year in a dog's life is equivalent to seven years in a human's life." Explain why Newton thinks he has a score of 105 points. Did he solve the proportion correctly?

$$\frac{1 \text{ year}}{7 \text{ years}} \stackrel{?}{=} \frac{15 \text{ points}}{105 \text{ points}}$$

"I got 15 on my online test. That's 105 in dog points! Isn't that an A+?"

b. If Newton thinks his score is 98 points, how many points does he actually have? Explain your reasoning.

3 ACTIVITY: Determining Fairness

Work with a partner. Write a ratio for each sentence. If they are equal, then the answer is "It is fair." If they are not equal, then the answer is "It is not fair." Explain your reasoning.

a. You pay \$184 for 2 tickets to a concert. & I pay \$266 for 3 tickets to the same concert. ➡ **Is this fair?**

b.

You get 75 points for answering 15 questions correctly.	&	I get 70 points for answering 14 questions correctly.

→ **Is this fair?**

c.

You trade 24 football cards for 15 baseball cards.	&	I trade 20 football cards for 32 baseball cards.

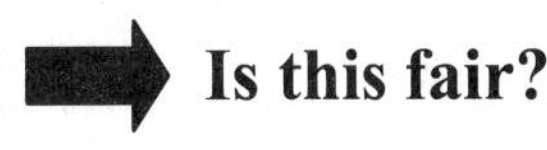

What Is Your Answer?

4. Find a recipe for something you like to eat. Then show how two of the ingredient amounts are proportional when you double or triple the recipe.

5. **IN YOUR OWN WORDS** How can proportions help you decide when things are "fair?" Give an example.

Name ______________________________ Date ________

3.3 Practice

For use after Lesson 3.3

Tell whether the ratios form a proportion.

1. $\frac{1}{5}, \frac{5}{15}$

2. $\frac{2}{3}, \frac{12}{18}$

3. $\frac{15}{2}, \frac{4}{30}$

4. $\frac{56}{21}, \frac{8}{3}$

5. $\frac{5}{8}, \frac{62.5}{100}$

6. $\frac{17}{20}, \frac{90.1}{106}$

7. $\frac{3.2}{4}, \frac{16}{24}$

8. $\frac{34}{50}, \frac{6.8}{10}$

Tell whether the two rates form a proportion.

9. 28 points in 3 games;
112 points in 12 games

10. 32 notes in 4 measures;
12 notes in 2 measures

11. You can type 105 words in two minutes. Your friend can type 210 words in four minutes. Are these rates proportional? Explain.

12. You make punch for a party. The ratio of ginger ale to fruit juice is 8 cups to 3 cups. You decide to add 4 more cups of ginger ale. How many more cups of fruit juice do you need to add to keep the correct ratio? Explain.

Name____ Date__________

3.4 Writing Proportions

For use with Activity 3.4

Essential Question How can you write a proportion that solves a problem in real life?

1 ACTIVITY: Writing Proportions

Work with a partner. A rough rule for finding the correct bat length is "The bat length should be half of the batter's height." So, a 62-inch tall batter uses a bat that is 31 inches long. Write a proportion to find the bat length for each given batter height.

a. 58 inches **b.** 60 inches **c.** 64 inches

2 ACTIVITY: Bat Lengths

Work with a partner. Here is a more accurate table for determining the bat length for a batter. Find all of the batter heights for which the rough rule in Activity 1 is exact.

Weight of Batter (pounds)	Height of Batter (inches)							
	45–48	49–52	53–56	57–60	61–64	65–68	69–72	Over 72
Under 61	28	29	29					
61–70	28	29	30	30				
71–80	28	29	30	30	31			
81–90	29	29	30	30	31	32		
91–100	29	30	30	31	31	32		
101–110	29	30	30	31	31	32		
111–120	29	30	30	31	31	32		
121–130	29	30	30	31	32	33	33	
131–140	30	30	31	31	32	33	33	
141–150	30	30	31	31	32	33	33	
151–160	30	31	31	32	32	33	33	33
161–170		31	31	32	32	33	33	34
171–180				32	33	33	34	34
Over 180					33	33	34	34

3.4 Writing Proportions (continued)

3 ACTIVITY: Checking a Proportion

Work with a partner. The batting average of a baseball player is the number of "hits" divided by the number of "at bats."

$$\text{Batting Average} = \frac{\text{Hits } (H)}{\text{At Bats } (A)}$$

A player whose batting average is 0.250 is said to be "batting 250."

$$\frac{20 \text{ hits}}{80 \text{ at bats}} = 0.250 = \frac{250 \text{ hits}}{1000 \text{ at bats}}$$

Actual hits → 20 hits

Actual at bats → 80 at bats

Batting average → 0.250

Batting 250 out of 1000 → $\frac{250 \text{ hits}}{1000 \text{ at bats}}$

Write a proportion to find how many hits *H* a player needs to achieve the given batting average. Then solve the proportion.

a. 50 times at bat
batting average is 0.200.

b. 84 times at bat
batting average is 0.250.

c. 80 times at bat
batting average is 0.350.

d. 1 time at bat
batting average is 1.000.

What Is Your Answer?

4. IN YOUR OWN WORDS How can you write a proportion that solves a problem in real life?

5. Two players have the same batting average.

	At Bats	Hits	Batting Average
Player 1	132	45	
Player 2	132	45	

Player 1 gets four hits in the next five at bats. Player 2 gets three hits in the next three at bats.

a. Who has the higher batting average?

b. Does this seem fair? Explain your reasoning.

Name ______________________________ Date __________

3.4 Practice
For use after Lesson 3.4

Write a proportion to find how many points a student needs to score on the test to get the given score.

1. Test worth 50 points; test score of 84%

2. Test worth 75 points; test score of 96%

Use the table to write a proportion.

3.

	Trip 1	Trip 2
Miles	104	78
Gallons	4	g

4.

	Tree 1	Tree 2
Inches	15	x
Years	4	3

Solve the proportion.

5. $\frac{1}{3} = \frac{x}{12}$

6. $\frac{5}{9} = \frac{25}{y}$

7. $\frac{26}{z} = \frac{13}{22}$

8. $\frac{b}{30} = \frac{2.6}{1.5}$

9. A local Humane Society houses 300 animals. The ratio of cats to all animals is 7 : 15.

a. Write a proportion that gives the number of cats c.

b. How many cats are in the Humane Society?

10. Your school buys 30 graphing calculators for $1822.50. Write and solve a proportion that gives the cost c of buying 120 calculators.

Name____ Date__________

3.5 Solving Proportions

For use with Activity 3.5

Essential Question How can you use ratio tables and cross products to solve proportions in science?

1 ACTIVITY: Solving a Proportion in Science

SCIENCE Scientists use *ratio tables* to determine the amount of a compound (like salt) that is dissolved in a solution. Work with a partner to show how scientists use cross products to determine the unknown quantity in a ratio.

a. Sample: Salt Water

Salt Water	1 L	3 L
Salt	250 g	x g

I liter 3 liter

There are ______ grams of salt in the 3-liter solution.

b. White Glue Solution

Water	$\frac{1}{2}$ cup	1 cup
White Glue	$\frac{1}{2}$ cup	x cups

c. Borax Solution

Borax	1 tsp	2 tsp
Water	1 cup	x cups

Name ______________________________ Date __________

3.5 Solving Proportions (continued)

d. Slime (see recipe)

Borax Solution	$\frac{1}{2}$ cup	1 cup
White Glue Solution	y cups	x cups

Recipe for **SLIME**

1. Add ½ cup of water and ½ cup white glue. Mix thoroughly. This is your white glue solution.
2. Add a couple drops of food coloring to the glue solution. Mix thoroughly.
3. Add 1 teaspoon of borax to 1 cup of water. Mix thoroughly. This is your borax solution (about 1 cup).
4. Pour the borax solution and the glue solution into a separate bowl.
5. Place the slime that forms in a plastic bag and squeeze the mixture repeatedly to mix it up.

2 ACTIVITY: The Game of Criss Cross

Preparation:

- Cut index cards to make 48 playing cards.
- Write each number on a card.
  1, 1, 1, 2, 2, 2, 3, 3, 3, 4, 4, 4, 5, 5, 5, 6, 6, 6, 7, 7, 7, 8, 8, 8, 9, 9, 9, 10, 10, 10, 12, 12, 12, 13, 13, 13, 14, 14, 14, 15, 15, 15, 16, 16, 16, 18, 20, 25
- Make a copy of the game board.

To Play:

- Play with a partner.
- Deal 8 cards to each player.
- Begin by drawing a card from the remaining cards. Use four of your cards to try and form a proportion.
- Lay the four cards on the game board. If you form a proportion, say "Criss Cross" and you earn 4 points. Place the four cards in a discard pile. Now it is your partner's turn.
- If you cannot form a proportion, then it is your partner's turn.
- When the original pile of cards is empty, shuffle the cards in the discard pile and start again.
- The first player to reach 20 points wins.

Name______________________________________ Date__________

What Is Your Answer?

3. **IN YOUR OWN WORDS** How can you use ratio tables and cross products to solve proportions in science? Give an example.

4. **PUZZLE** Use each number once to form three proportions.

1	2	10	4	12	20
15	5	16	6	8	3

Name ______________________________ Date __________

3.5 Practice

For use after Lesson 3.5

Solve the proportion using multiplication.

1. $\dfrac{a}{40} = \dfrac{3}{10}$

2. $\dfrac{6}{11} = \dfrac{c}{77}$

3. $\dfrac{b}{65} = \dfrac{7}{13}$

Solve the proportion using the Cross Products Property.

4. $\dfrac{k}{6} = \dfrac{8}{16}$

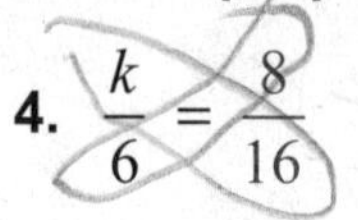

5. $\dfrac{5.4}{7} = \dfrac{27}{h}$

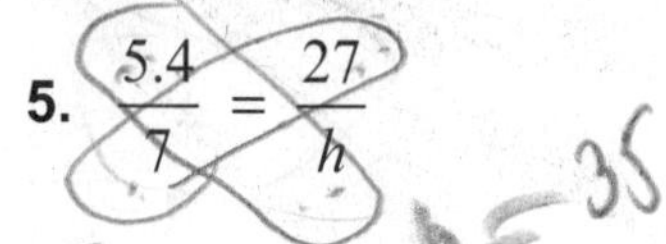

6. $\dfrac{15}{n} = \dfrac{20}{8}$

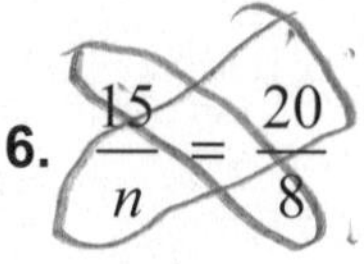

Solve the proportion.

7. $\dfrac{5}{2} = \dfrac{4x}{8}$

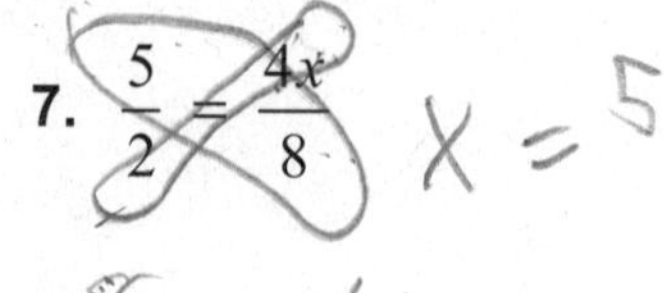

8. $\dfrac{8}{11} = \dfrac{4}{y + 2}$

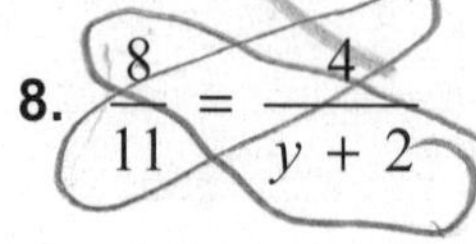

9. $\dfrac{3}{z - 1} = \dfrac{9}{15}$

10. A cell phone company charges \$5 for 250 text messages. How much does the company charge for 300 text messages?

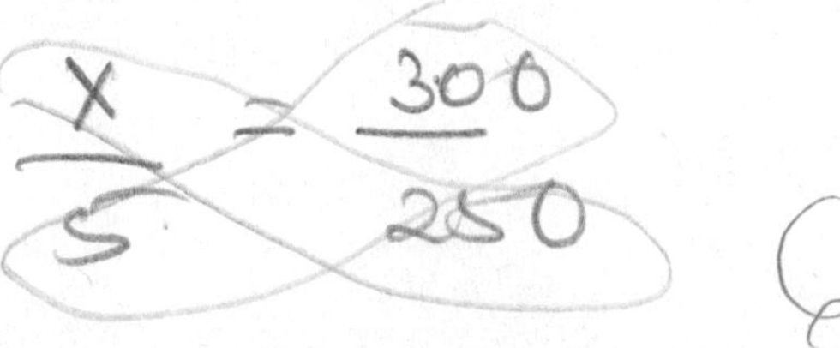

11. There are 84 players on a football team. The ratio of offensive players to defensive players is 4 to 3. How many offensive players are on the team?

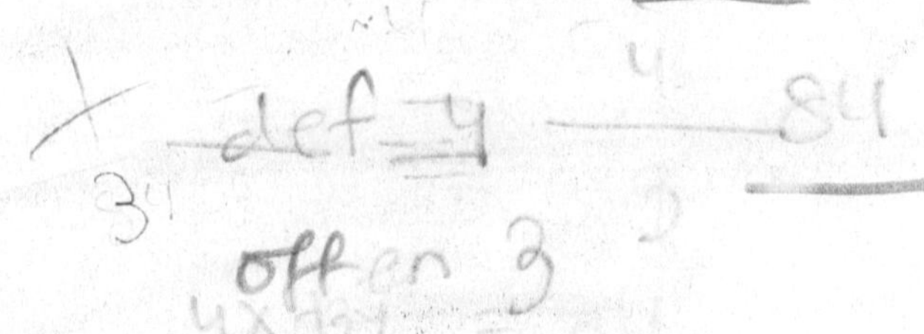

Name______________________________ Date__________

3.6 Converting Measures Between Systems

For use with Activity 3.6

Essential Question How can you compare lengths between the customary and metric systems?

1 ACTIVITY: Customary Measure History

Work with a partner.

a. Match the measure of length with its historical beginning.

Length	*Historical Beginning*
Inch	The length of a human foot.
Foot	The width of a human thumb.
Yard	The distance a human can walk in 1000 paces (two steps).
Mile	The distance from a human nose to the end of an outstretched human arm.

b. Use a ruler to measure your thumb, arm, and foot. How do your measurements compare to your answers from part (a)? Are they close to the historical measures?

You already know how to convert measures within the customary and metric systems.

Equivalent Customary Lengths

1 ft = 12 in. 1 yd = 3 ft 1 mi = 5280 ft

Equivalent Metric Lengths

1 m = 1000 mm 1 m = 100 cm 1 km = 1000 m

You will learn how to convert between the two systems.

Converting Between Systems

1 in. ≈ 2.54 cm

1 mi ≈ 1.6 km

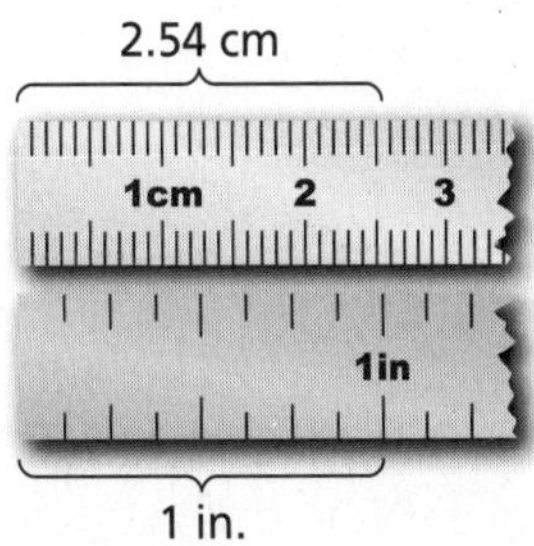

Name ______________________________ Date __________

3.6 Converting Measures Between Systems (continued)

2 ACTIVITY: Comparing Measures

Work with a partner. Answer each question. Explain your answer. Use a diagram in your explanation.

	Metric	*Customary*
a. Car Speed: Which is faster?	80 km/h	60 mi/h
b. Trip Distance: Which is farther?	200 km	200 mi
c. Human Height: Who is taller?	180 cm	5 ft 8 in.
d. Wrench Width: Which is wider?	8 mm	5/16 in.
e. Swimming Pool Depth: Which is deeper?	1.4 m	4 ft
f. Mountain Elevation: Which is higher?	2000 m	7000 ft
g. Room Width: Which is wider?	3.5 m	12 ft

What Is Your Answer?

3. **IN YOUR OWN WORDS** How can you compare lengths between the customary and metric systems? Give examples with your description.

4. **HISTORY** The meter and the metric system originated in France. In 1791, the French Academy of Sciences was instructed to create a new system of measurement. This new system would be based on powers of 10.

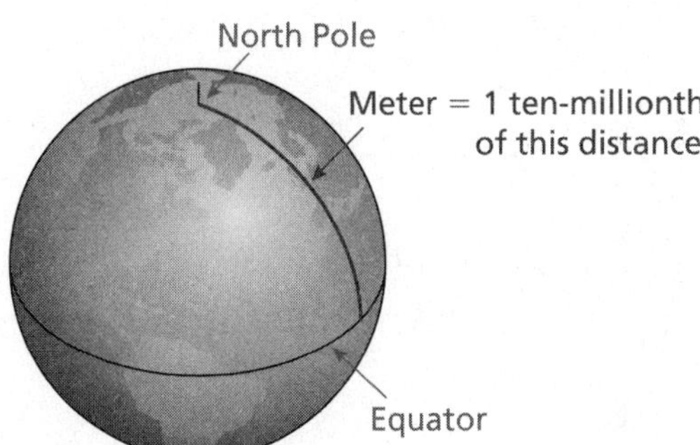

The fundamental units of this system would be based on natural values that were unchanging. The French Academy of Sciences decided to find the length of an imaginary arc that began at the North Pole and ended at the equator.

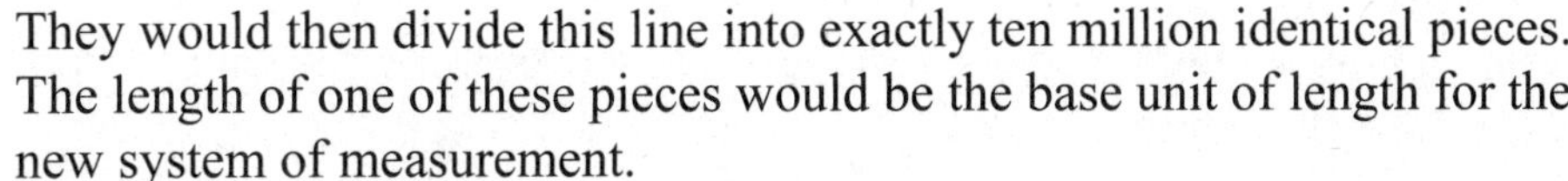

They would then divide this line into exactly ten million identical pieces. The length of one of these pieces would be the base unit of length for the new system of measurement.

a. Find the distance around Earth in meters.

b. Find the distance around Earth in kilometers.

5. Find the distance around Earth in miles.

Name ____ Date __________

3.6 Practice

For use after Lesson 3.6

Complete the statement using a ratio. Round to the nearest hundredth, if necessary.

1. 10 mi ≈ _______ km **2.** 15 kg ≈ _______ lb **3.** 6 qt ≈ _______ L

Complete the statement using < or >.

4. 11 in. _______ 22 cm

5. 12 kg _______ 500 oz

6. 8 gal _______ 25 L

7. 10 m _______ 30 ft

Complete the statement. Round to the nearest hundredth, if necessary.

8. 60 mi/h ≈ _______ km/h

9. 6 ft/sec ≈ _______ cm/sec

10. 52 gal/min ≈ _______ L/min

11. 5 kg/day ≈ _______ oz/day

12. One lap around a high school track is 400 meters. How many laps do you run around the track if you run 2 miles?

13. A doctor prescribes 200 milligrams of medicine for a patient. How many ounces of medicine is the patient taking?

14. The lightest weight class for young men competing in freestyle wrestling is from 29 kilograms to 32 kilograms. What is the range of the weight class in pounds?

Name_______________________________ Date__________

3.7 Direct Variation
For use with Activity 3.7

Essential Question How can you use a graph to show the relationship between two variables that vary directly? How can you use an equation?

1 ACTIVITY: Math in Literature

Gulliver's Travels was written by Jonathan Swift and published in 1725. Gulliver was shipwrecked on an island in Lilliput, where the people were only 6 inches tall. When the Lilliputians decided to make a shirt for Gulliver, a Lilliputian tailor stated that he could determine Gulliver's measurements by simply measuring the distance around Gulliver's thumb. He said "Twice around the thumb equals once around the wrist. Twice around the wrist is once around the neck. Twice around the neck is once around the waist."

Work with a partner. Use the tailor's statement to complete the table.

Thumb, t	Wrist, w	Neck, n	Waist, x
0 in.	0 in.		
1 in.	2 in.		
2 in.	4 in.		
3 in.	6 in.		
4 in.	8 in.		
5 in.	10 in.		

Name ____________________ Date ________

2 EXAMPLE: Drawing a Graph

Use the information from Activity 1 to draw a graph of the relationship between the distance around the thumb *t* and the distance around the wrist *w*.

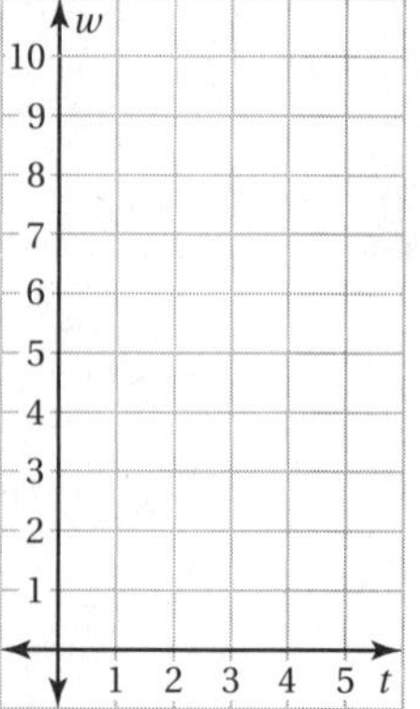

Use the table to write ordered pairs. Then plot the ordered pairs.

What do you notice about the graph?

This type of relationship is called **direct variation**. You can write an equation to describe the relationship between t and w.

$w = 2t$ Wrist is twice thumb.

3 ACTIVITY: Drawing a Graph

Work with a partner. Use the information from Activity 1 to draw a graph of the relationship. Write an equation that describes the relationship between the two variables.

a. Thumb t and neck n

$n = \square\, t$

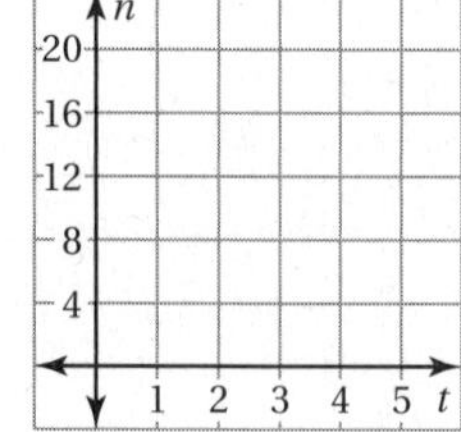

b. Wrist w and waist x

$x = \square\, w$

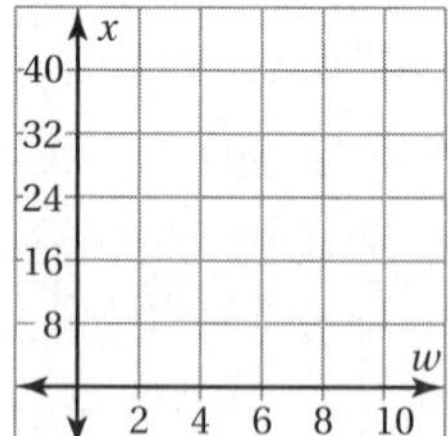

3.7 Direct Variation (continued)

c. Wrist w and thumb t

$$t = \square\, w$$

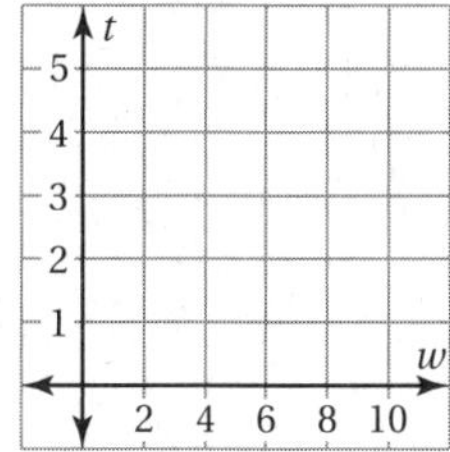

d. Waist x and wrist w

$$w = \square\, x$$

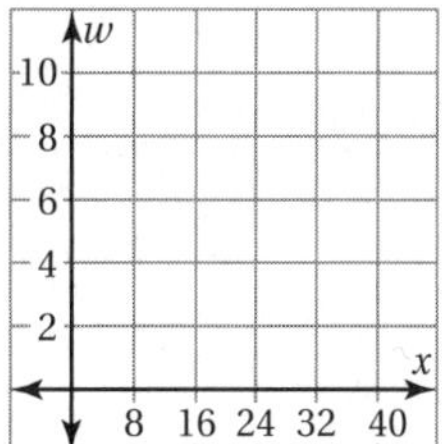

What Is Your Answer?

4. IN YOUR OWN WORDS How can you use a graph to show the relationship between two variables that vary directly? How can you use an equation?

5. Give a real-life example of two variables that vary directly.

6. Work with a partner. Use string to find the distance around your thumb, wrist, and neck. Do your measurements agree with those of the tailor in *Gulliver's Travels*? Explain your reasoning.

Name ______________________________ Date __________

3.7 Practice

For use after Lesson 3.7

Tell whether x and y show direct variation. Explain your reasoning.

1.

x	1	2	3	4
y	3	6	9	12

2.

x	–1	0	1	2
y	1	3	7	13

3.

x	0	2	4	6
y	8	5	2	–1

4. $y + 2 = x$

5. $3y = x$

6. $\dfrac{y}{x} = 4$

The variables x and y vary directly. Use the values to write an equation that relates x and y.

7. $y = 8; x = 2$

8. $y = 14, x = 16$

9. $y = 25, x = 35$

10. The table shows the cups c of dog food needed to feed a dog that weighs p pounds. Tell whether p and c show direct variation.

Pounds, p	10	20	40	70
Food, c	$\frac{3}{4}$	$1\frac{1}{4}$	2	$2\frac{3}{4}$

11. Write a direct variation equation that relates x tires to y cars.

12. Tell whether h and m show direct variation. If so, write an equation of direct variation.

Hours, h	1	2	4	5
Miles, m	60.5	121	242	302.5

Name______________________________ Date__________

3.7b Practice

For use after Lesson 3.7b

Interpret each plotted point in the graph of the proportional relationship.

1.

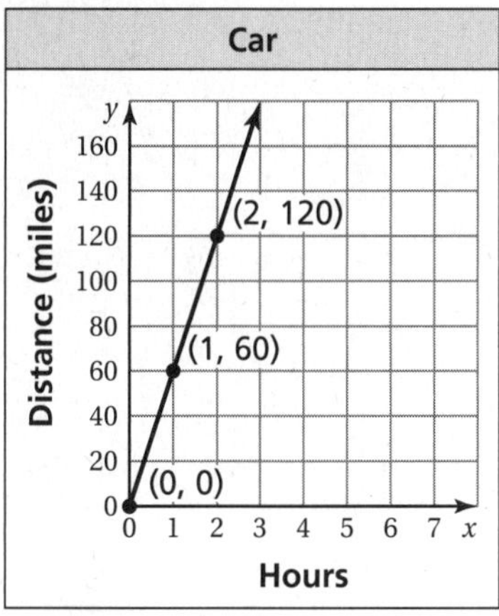

2.

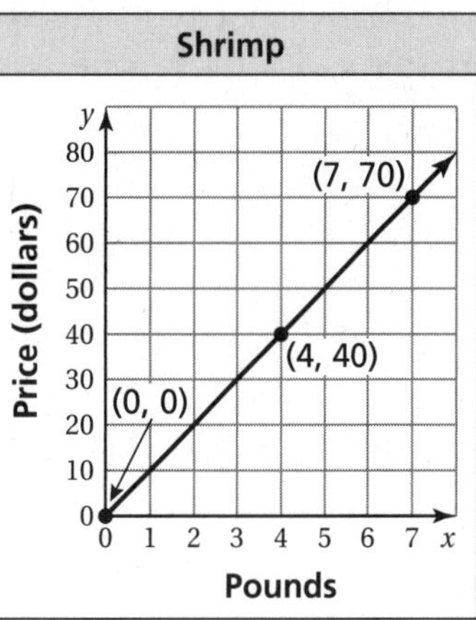

3.

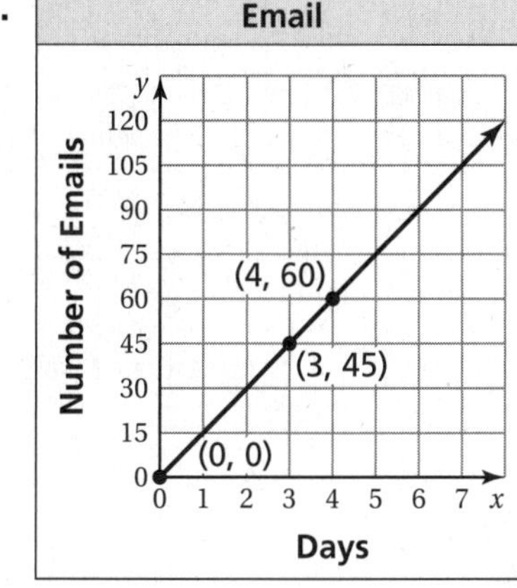

4.

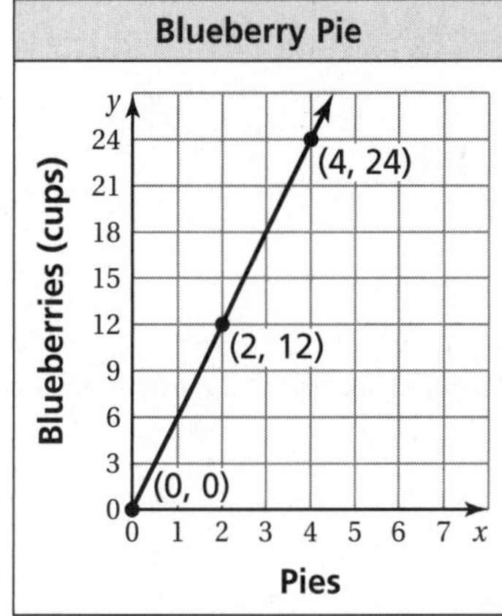

Name ____ Date __________

3.7b **Practice (continued)**

5. The graph shows that the tips of two waiters are proportional to the costs of meals.

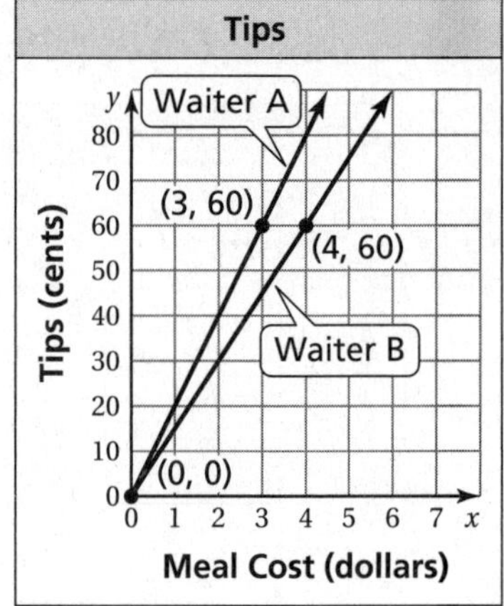

   a. Express the tip rate for each waiter as a percent.

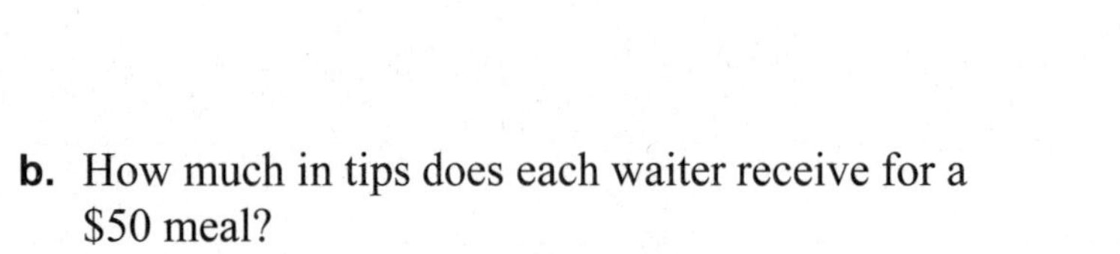

   b. How much in tips does each waiter receive for a \$50 meal?

6. The graph shows that the commissions of two salesmen are proportional to the amount of sales.

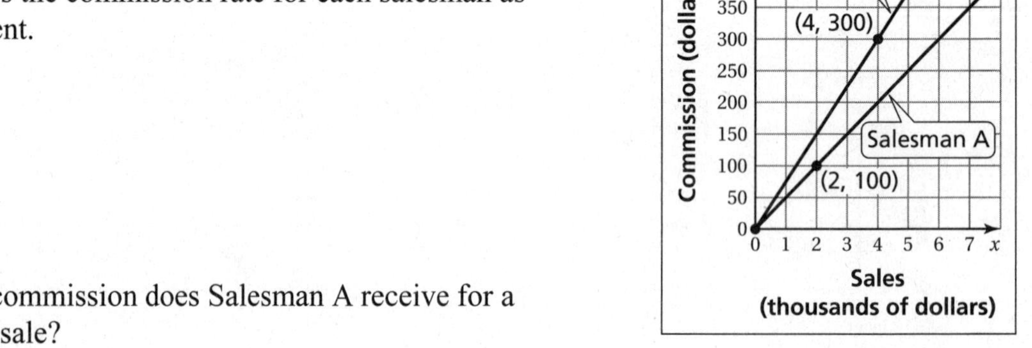

   a. Express the commission rate for each salesman as a percent.

   b. What commission does Salesman A receive for a \$5000 sale?

   c. How much less commission does Salesman A receive than Salesman B for a \$5000 sale?

Name______________________________ Date__________

3.8 Inverse Variation

For use with Activity 3.8

Essential Question How can you recognize when two variables are inversely proportional?

1 ACTIVITY: Comparing the Height and the Base

Work with a partner.

a. There are nine ways to arrange 36 square blocks to form a rectangle. Here are two ways. Draw the other seven ways.

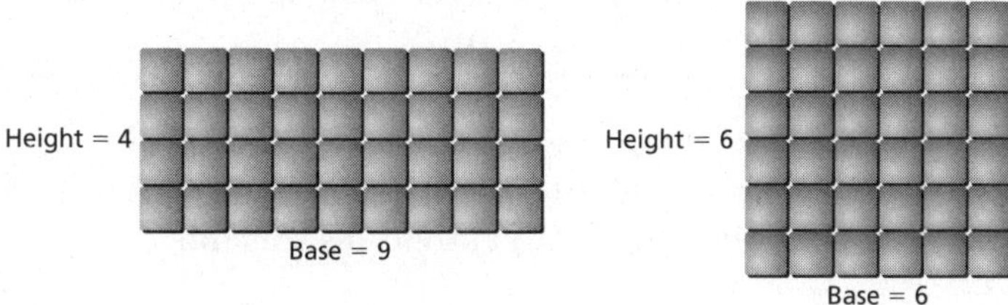

b. Order the nine ways according to height. Record your results in the table.

Height, h	Base, b	Area, A

c. Look at the first and second columns of the table. Complete each sentence.

- When the height increases, the base ____________________.
- When the height decreases, the base ____________________.

In Activity 1, the relationship between the height and base is an example of **inverse variation**. You can describe the relationship with an equation.

$$h = \frac{36}{b} \qquad h \text{ and } b \text{ are inversely proportional.}$$

2 ACTIVITY: Comparing Direct and Inverse Variation

Work with a partner. Discuss each description. Tell whether the two variables are examples of *direct variation* or *inverse variation*. Use a table to explain your reasoning. Write an equation that relates the variables.

a. You bring 200 cookies to a party. Let n represent the number of people at the party and c represent the number of cookies each person receives.

b. You work at a restaurant for 20 hours. Let r represent your hourly pay rate and p represent the total amount you earn.

c. You are going on a 240-mile trip. Let t represent the number of hours driving and s represent the speed of the car.

What Is Your Answer?

3. **IN YOUR OWN WORDS** How can you recognize when two variables are inversely proportional? Explain how a table can help you recognize inverse variation.

4. **SCIENCE** The *wing beat frequency* of a bird is the number of times per second the bird flaps its wings.

Hummingbird

Mallard Duck

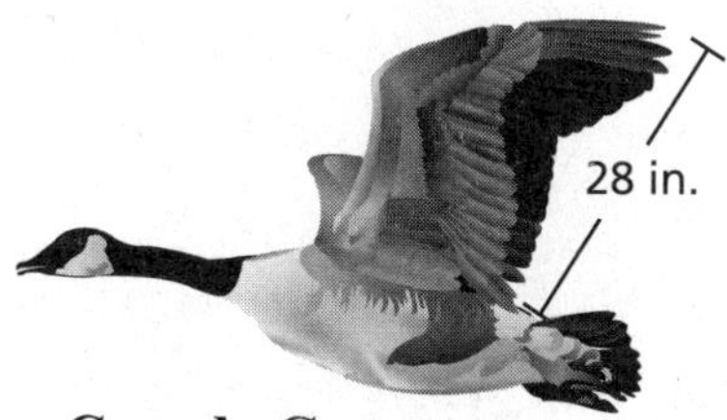

Canada Goose

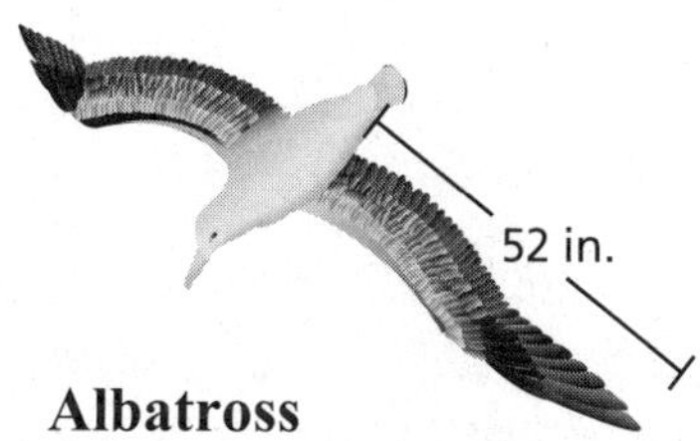

Albatross

Which of the following seems true? Explain your reasoning.

- Wing length and wing beat frequency are directly proportional.
- Wing length and wing beat frequency are inversely proportional.
- Wing length and wing beat frequency are unrelated.

5. **SCIENCE** Think of an example in science where two variables are inversely proportional.

Name ______________________________________ Date __________

3.8 Practice

For use after Lesson 3.8

Tell whether x and y show *direct variation, inverse variation,* or *neither.* Explain your reasoning.

1. $2y = 3x + 1$ **2.** $\frac{y}{5} = \frac{6}{x}$ **3.** $\frac{y}{x} = 4$ **4.** $xy = 2$

The variables x and y vary inversely. Write an equation relating x and y.

5.

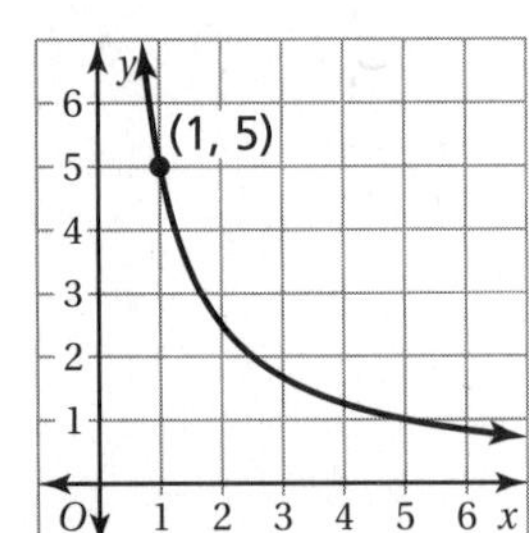

6.

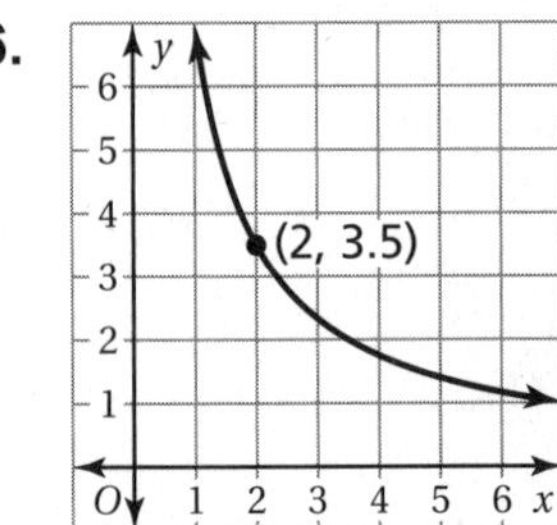

7. You have 1.5 pounds of spaghetti. When you make dinner for four people, each person is served 6 ounces of spaghetti.

a. Complete the table. Does the serving size s vary inversely with the number of people p? If so, write an equation relating s and p.

People, p	Serving Size, s
2	
4	6
6	

b. How much spaghetti will each person receive if you are serving five people?

Name____ Date__________

Chapter 4 Fair Game Review

What percent of the model is shaded?

1.

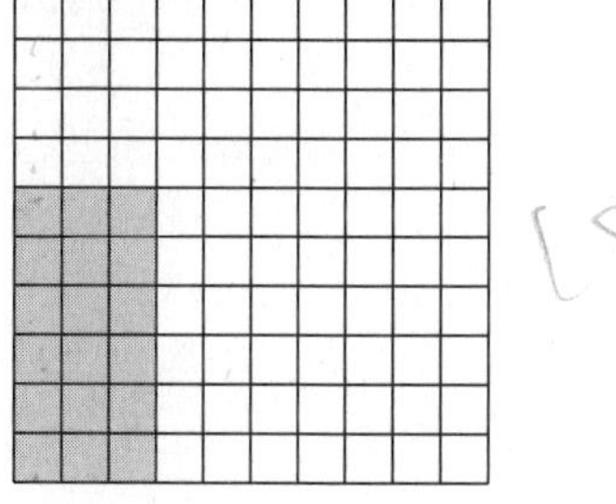

2.

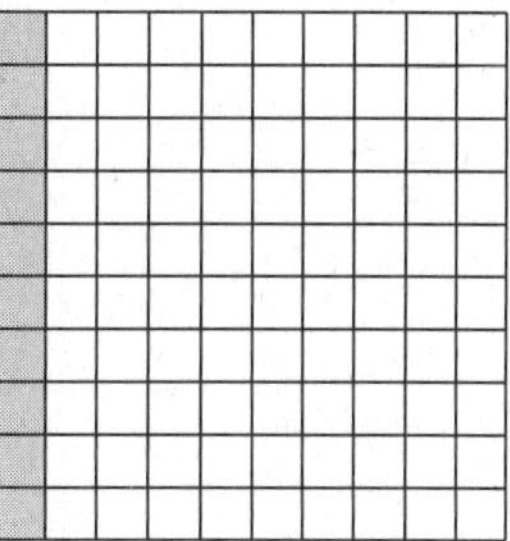

3.

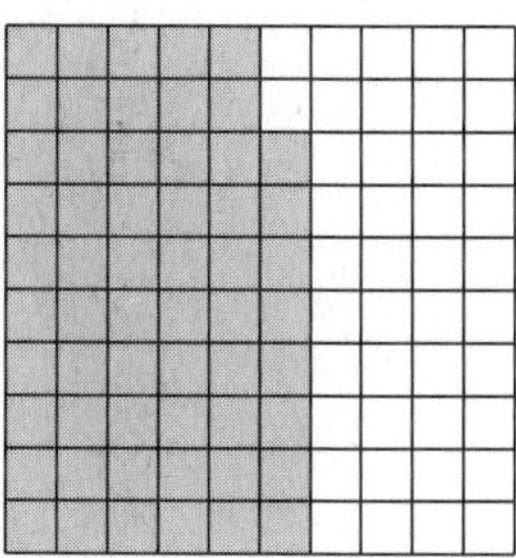

4.

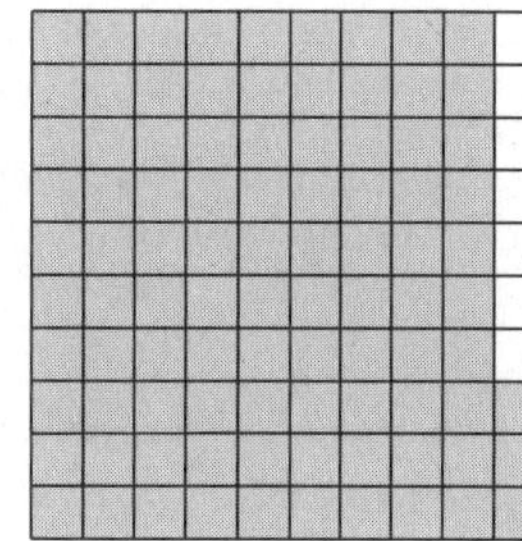

Write the fraction as a decimal or the decimal as a fraction.

5. $\frac{5}{8}$

6. $\frac{21}{40}$

7. 0.26

8. 0.79

9. In your class, 0.65 of the students are wearing sneakers. What fraction of students are wearing sneakers?

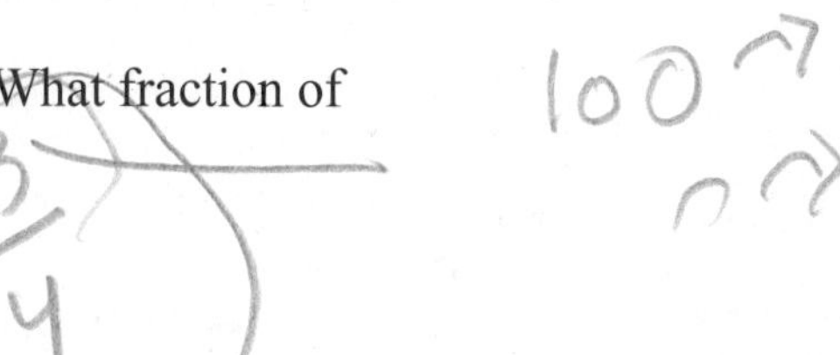

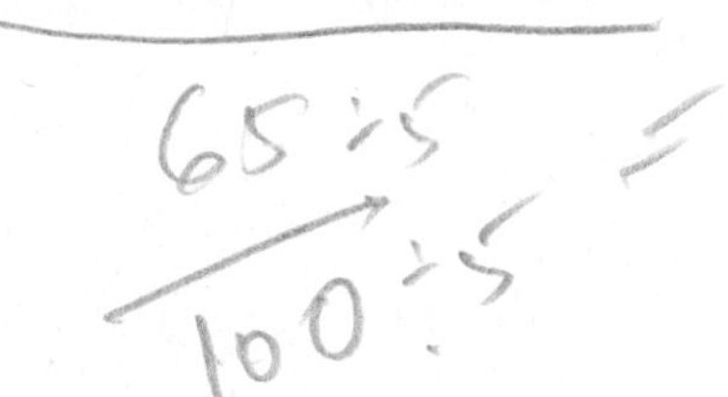

Name ______________________________ Date __________

Fair Game Review (continued)

Write the fraction as a percent or the percent as a fraction.

10. $\frac{13}{20}$

11. $\frac{47}{50}$

12. 52%

13. 31%

Write the decimal as a percent or the percent as a decimal.

14. 0.06

15. 0.84

16. 22%

17. 191%

Complete the table.

	Percent	Decimal	Fraction
18.	45%		
19.		0.73	
20.			$\frac{3}{10}$

Name____ Date__________

4.1 The Percent Equation

For use with Activity 4.1

Essential Question How can you use models to estimate percent questions?

1 ACTIVITY: Estimating a Percent

Work with a partner. Estimate the locations of 50%, 75%, 40%, 6%, and 65% on the model. 50% is done for you.

0% 50% 100%

2 ACTIVITY: Estimating a Part of a Number

The statement "25% of 12 is 3" has three numbers. In real-life problems, any one of these can be unknown.

Part → $\frac{3}{12} = 0.25 = 25\%$ ← Percent

Whole →

Which number is missing?	Question	Type of Question
______	What is 25% of 12?	Find a part of a number.
______	3 is what percent of 12?	Find a percent.
______	3 is 25% of what?	Find a percent.

Work with a partner. Estimate the answer to each question using a model.

a. What number is 50% of 30?

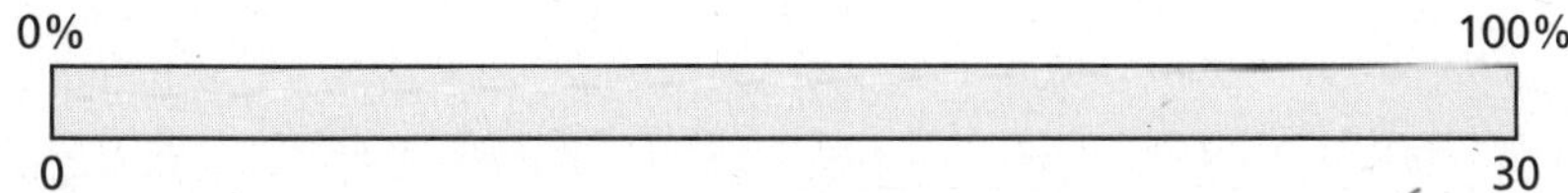

Name ______________________ Date __________

4.1 The Percent Equation (continued)

b. What number is 75% of 30?

c. What number is 40% of 30?

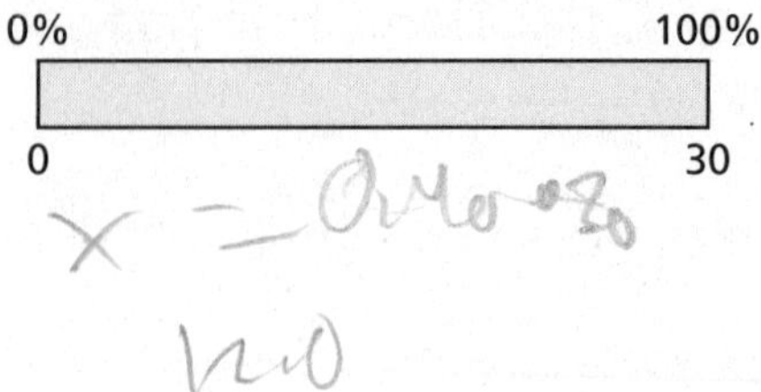

d. What number is 6% of 30?

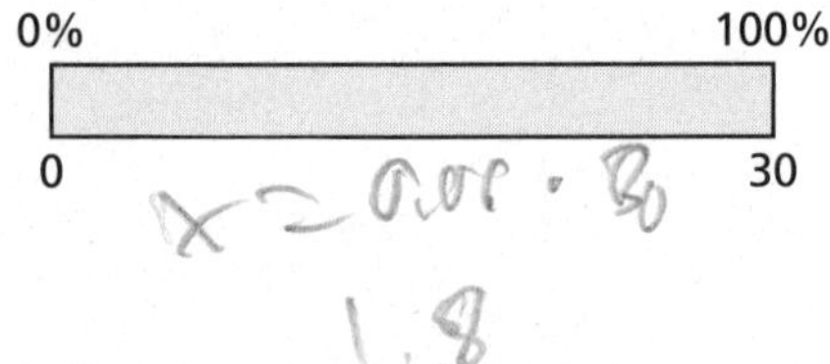

e. What number is 65% of 30?

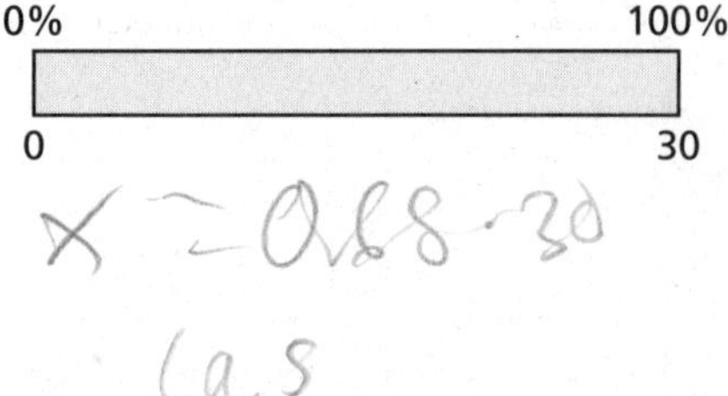

3 ACTIVITY: Estimating a Percent

Work with a partner. Estimate the answer to the question using a model.

a. 15 is what percent of 75?

b. 5 is what percent of 20?

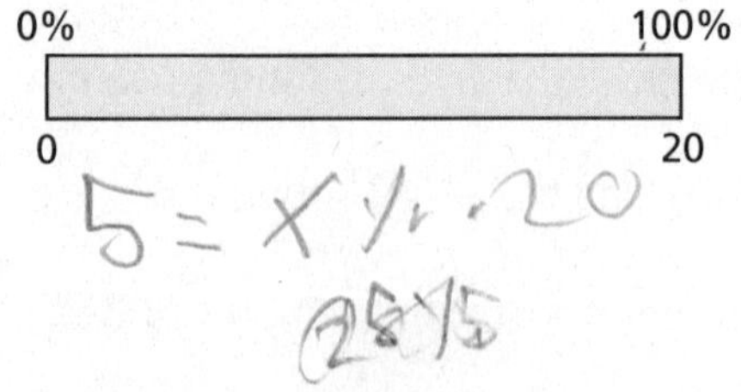

c. 18 is what percent of 40?

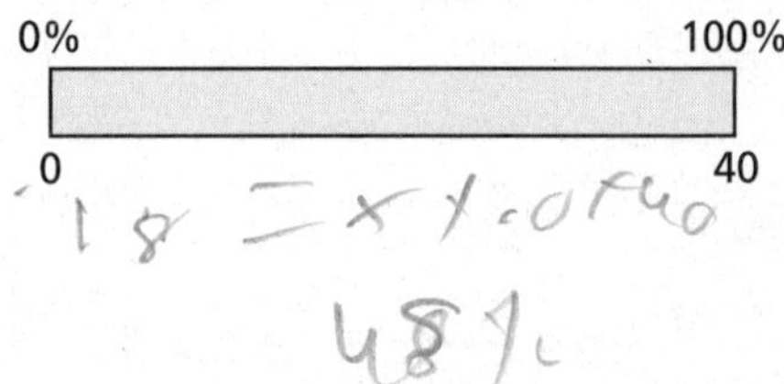

d. 50 is what percent of 80?

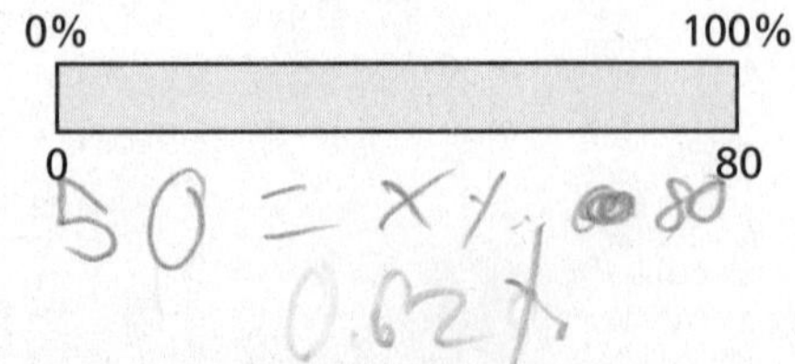

e. 75 is what percent of 50?

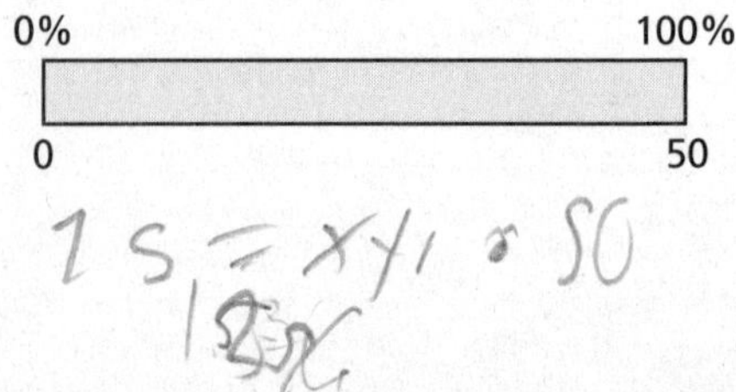

4.1 The Percent Equation (continued)

4 ACTIVITY: Estimating a Percent

Work with a partner. Estimate the answer to the question using a model.

a. 24 is $33\frac{1}{3}\%$ of what number?

0% 100%

b. 13 is 25% of what number?

0% 100%

c. 110 is 20% of what number?

0% 100%

d. 75 is 75% of what number?

0% 100%

e. 81 is 45% of what number?

0% 100%

What Is Your Answer?

5. IN YOUR OWN WORDS How can you use models to estimate percent questions? Give examples to support your answer.

Name ______________________________ Date __________

4.1 Practice

For use after Lesson 4.1

Write and solve an equation to answer the question.

1. 40% of 60 is what number?

2. 17 is what percent of 50?

3. 38% of what number is 57?

4. 44% of 25 is what number?

5. 52 is what percent of 50?

6. 150% of what number is 18?

7. You put 60% of your paycheck into your savings account. Your paycheck is $235. How much money do you put in your savings account?

8. You made lemonade and iced tea for a school fair. You made 15 gallons of lemonade and 60% is gone. About 52% of the iced tea is gone. The ratio of gallons of lemonade to gallons of iced tea was 3 : 2.

a. How many gallons of lemonade are left?

b. How many gallons of iced tea did you make?

c. About how many gallons of iced tea are left?

Name_______________________________ Date__________

4.2 Percents of Increase and Decrease

For use with Activity 4.2

Essential Question What is a percent of decrease? What is a percent of increase?

1 ACTIVITY: Percent of Decrease

Each year in the Columbia River Basin, adult salmon swim up river to streams to lay eggs and hatch their young.

To go up river, the adult salmon use fish ladders. But, to go down the river, the young salmon must pass through several dams.

There are electric turbines at each of the eight dams on the main stem of the Columbia and Snake Rivers. About 88% of the young salmon pass through these turbines unharmed.

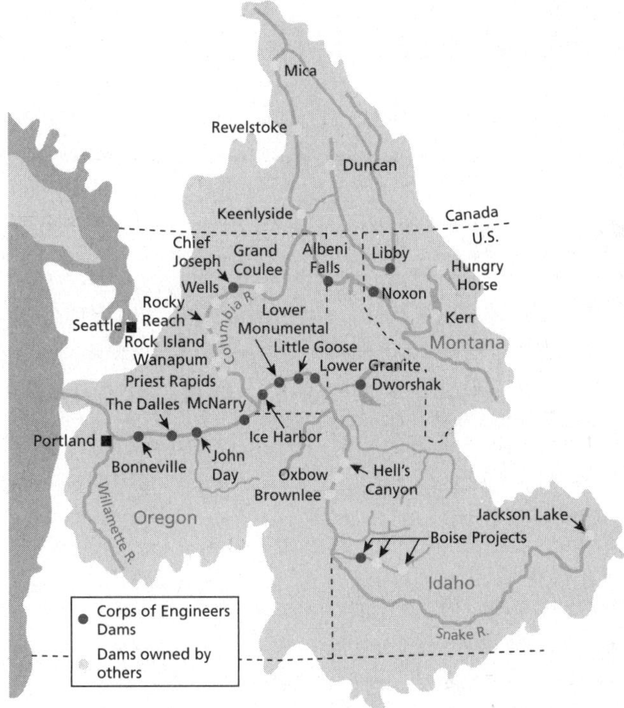

Complete the table to show the number of young salmon that make it through the dams.

Dam	0	1	2	3	4	5	6	7	8
Salmon	1000								

Name ______________________________ Date __________

Use the table you made on the previous page to complete the bar graph.

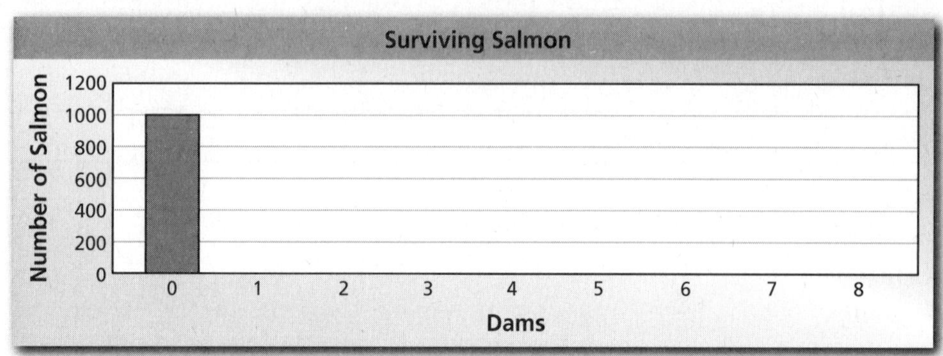

2 ACTIVITY: Percent of Increase

From 2000 to 2006, the population of Florida increased about 2% each year. Complete the table and the bar graph using this pattern. Predict the population for 2015.

2006 Population 18,000,000

For 2007:

$$2\% \text{ of } 18{,}000{,}000 = 0.02 \bullet 18{,}000{,}000$$
$$= 360{,}000$$

$$18{,}000{,}000 + 360{,}000 = 18{,}360{,}000$$

2006 Population → 18,000,000; Increase → 360,000; 2007 Population → 18,360,000

Year	Population
2006	18,000,000
2007	18,360,000
2008	
2009	
2010	
2011	
2012	
2013	
2014	
2015	

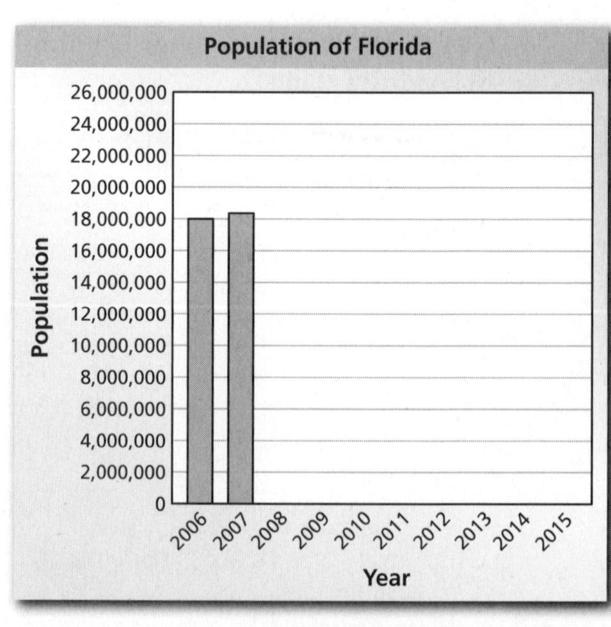

What Is Your Answer?

3. In Activity 1, by what percent does the number of young salmon decrease with each dam?

4. Describe real-life examples of a percent of decrease and a percent of increase.

5. **IN YOUR OWN WORDS** What is a percent of decrease? What is a percent of increase?

Name ____________________ Date ________

4.2 Practice

For use after Lesson 4.2

Identify the percent of change as an *increase* or *decrease*. Then find the percent of change. Round to the nearest tenth of a percent, if necessary.

1. 25 points to 50 points

2. 125 invitations to 75 invitations

3. 32 pages to 28 pages

4. 7 players to 10 players

Find the new amount.

5. 120 books increased by 55%

6. 80 members decreased by 65%

7. One week, 72 people got a speeding ticket. The next week, only 36 people got a speeding ticket. What is the percent of change in speeding tickets?

8. The number of athletes participating in the Paralympics rose from 130 athletes in 1952 to 3806 athletes in 2004. What is the percent of change? Round your answer to the nearest tenth of a percent.

Name____ Date __________

4.3 Discounts and Markups

For use with Activity 4.3

Essential Question How can you find discounts and markups efficiently?

1 ACTIVITY: Comparing Discounts

Work with a partner. The same pair of sneakers is on sale at three stores. Which one is the best buy?

a. Regular Price: $45

b. Regular Price: $49

c. Regular Price: $39

a.

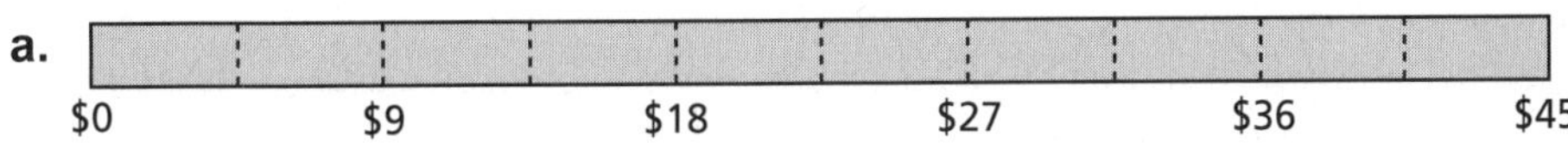

b.

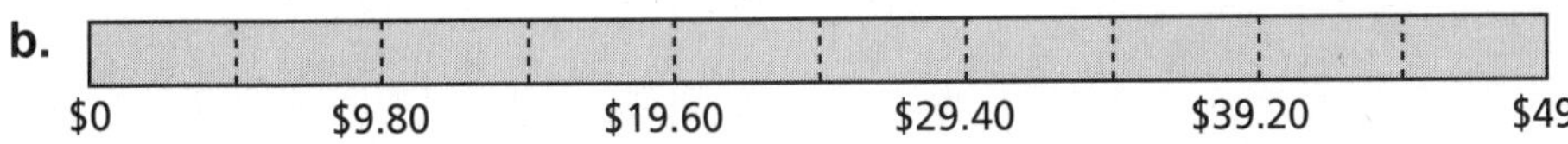

c.

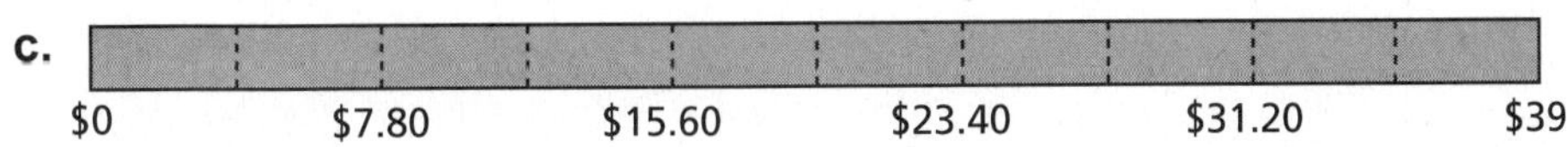

Name ______________________________ Date __________

4.3 Discounts and Markups (continued)

2 ACTIVITY: Finding the Original Price

Work with a partner. You buy a shirt that is on sale for 30% off. You pay $22.40. Your friend wants to know the original price of the shirt. How can your friend find the original price?

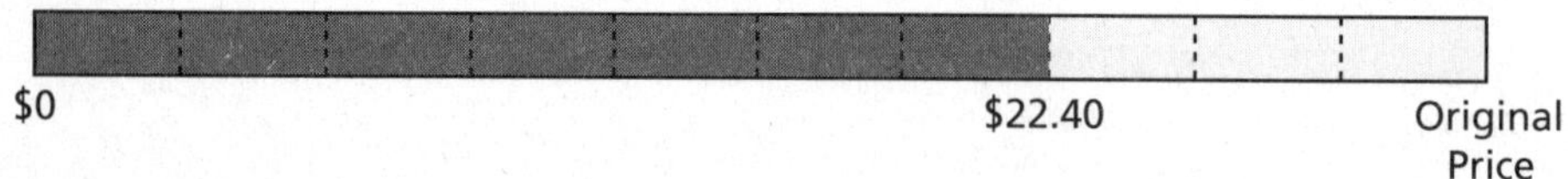

3 ACTIVITY: Calculating Markup

You own a small jewelry store. You increase the price of jewelry by 125%.

Work with a partner. Use a model to estimate the selling price of the jewelry. Then use a calculator to find the selling price.

a. Your cost is $250.

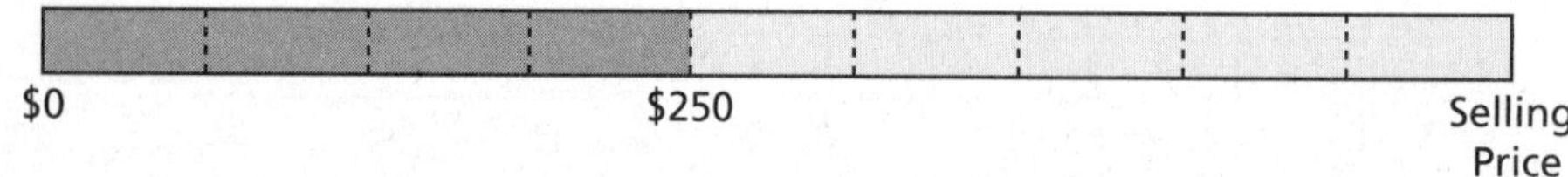

Name________________________________ Date__________

4.3 Discounts and Markups (continued)

b. Your cost is \$50.

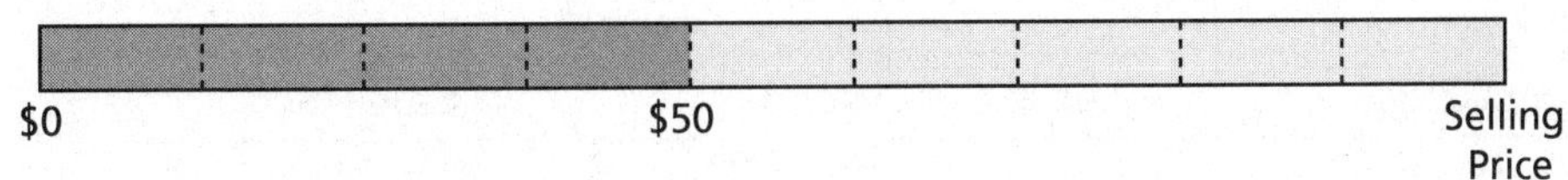

c. Your cost is \$20.

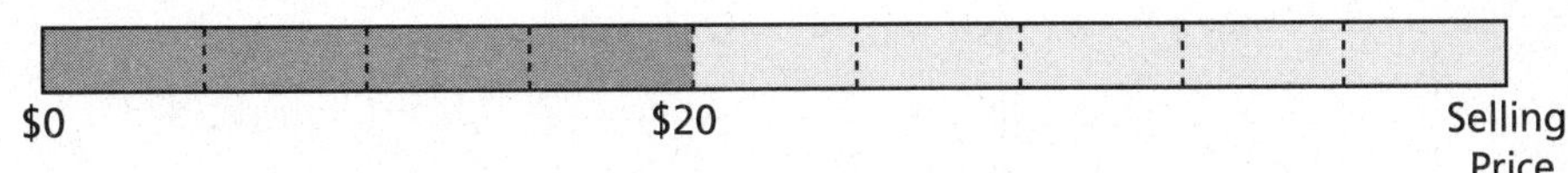

What Is Your Answer?

4. IN YOUR OWN WORDS How can you find discounts and markups efficiently? Give examples of each.

Name ______________________________ Date __________

4.3 Practice

For use after Lesson 4.3

Complete the table.

	Original Price	Percent of Discount	Sale Price
1.	$20	20%	
2.	$95	35%	
3.		75%	$55.50
4.		40%	$78

Find the cost to store, percent of markup, or selling price.

5. Cost to store: $20
Markup: 15%
Selling price: ?

6. Cost to store: ?
Markup: 80%
Selling Price: $100.80

7. Cost to store: $110
Markup: ?
Selling price: $264

8. A store buys an item for $10. To earn a profit of $25, what percent does the store need to markup the item?

9. Your dinner at a restaurant costs $13.65 after you use a coupon for a 25% discount. You leave a tip for $3.00.

a. How much was your dinner before the discount?

b. You tip your server based on the price before the discount. What percent tip did you leave? Round your answer to the nearest tenth of a percent.

Name______________________________ Date__________

4.4 Simple Interest
For use with Activity 4.4

Essential Question How can you find the amount of simple interest earned on a savings account? How can you find the amount of interest owed on a loan?

Simple interest is money earned on a savings account or an investment. It can also be money you pay for borrowing money.

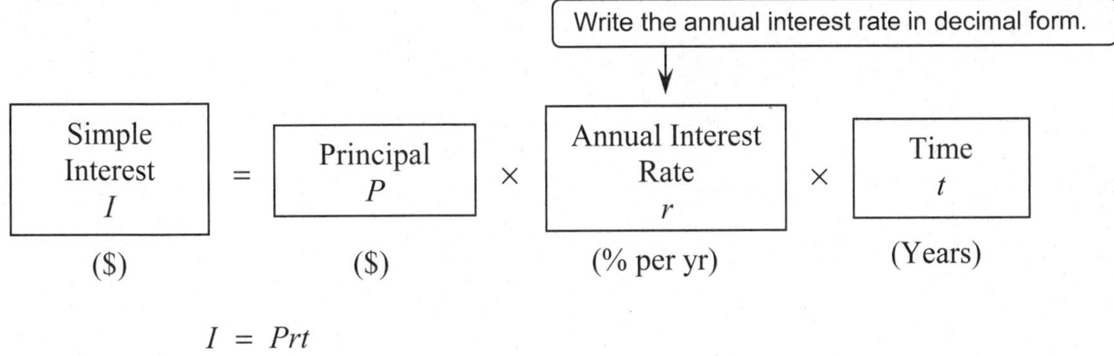

$$I = Prt$$

1 ACTIVITY: Finding Simple Interest

Work with a partner. You put \$100 in a savings account. The account earns 6% simple interest per year. (a) Find the interest earned and the balance at the end of 6 months. (b) Complete the table. Then make a bar graph that shows how the balance grows in 6 months.

a. $I = Prt$

b.

Time	Interest	Balance
0 month		
1 month		
2 months		
3 months		
4 months		
5 months		
6 months		

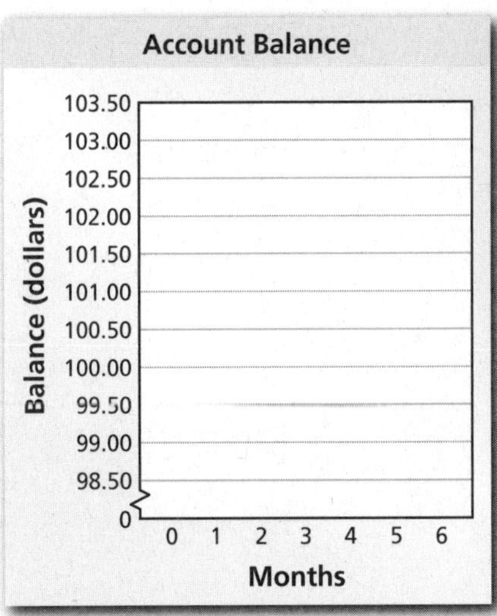

2 ACTIVITY: Financial Literacy

Work with a partner. Use the following information to write a report about credit cards. In the report, describe how a credit card works. Include examples that show the amount of interest paid each month on a credit card.

U.S. Credit Card Data

- A typical family in the United States owes about $5000 in credit card debt.
- A typical credit card interest rate is 18% to 20% per year. This is called the annual percentage rate.

3 ACTIVITY: The National Debt

Work with a partner. In 2010, the United States owed about $10 trillion in debt. The interest rate on the national debt is about 3% per year.

a. Write $10 trillion in decimal form. How many zeros does this number have?

b. How much interest does the United States pay each year on its national debt?

c. How much interest does the United States pay each day on its national debt?

d. The United States has a population of about 300 million people. Estimate the amount of interest that each person pays per year toward interest on the national debt.

What Is Your Answer?

4. IN YOUR OWN WORDS How can you find the amount of simple interest earned on a savings account? How can you find the amount of interest owed on a loan? Give examples with your answer.

Name ______________________ Date ________

4.4 Practice
For use after Lesson 4.4

An account earns simple interest. (a) Find the interest earned. (b) Find the balance of the account.

1. \$400 at 7% for 3 years

2. \$1200 at 5.6% for 4 years

Find the annual simple interest rate.

3. $I = \$18$, $P = \$200$, $t = 18$ months

4. $I = \$310$, $P = \$1000$, $t = 5$ years

Find the amount of time.

5. $I = \$60$, $P = \$750$, $r = 4\%$

6. $I = \$825$, $P = \$2500$, $r = 5.5\%$

7. You put \$500 in a savings account. The account earns \$15.75 simple interest in 6 months. What is the annual interest rate?

8. You put \$1000 in an account. The simple interest rate is 4.5%. After a year, you put in another \$550. What is your total interest after 2 years from the time you opened the account?

Name____ Date__________

Chapter 5 Fair Game Review

Find the perimeter or circumference.

1. 7 ft, 3 ft, 20 ft, 1 ft

2. 1 in., 5 in., 4 in., 12 in.

3. 11 cm

4. 12 in., 15 in., 15 in., 10 in., 12 in.

5. 6 mm

6. 10 in., 6 in., 9 in., 17 in.

7. A restaurant sets up tables for a party in a U-shape. What is the perimeter of the tables?

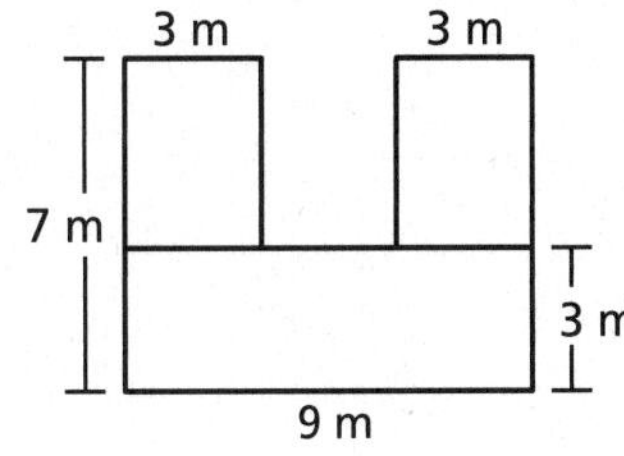

Name ______________________________ Date __________

Chapter 5 Fair Game Review (continued)

Solve the proportion.

8. $\frac{x}{20} = \frac{4}{5}$

9. $\frac{6}{x} = \frac{9}{12}$

10. $\frac{4}{9} = \frac{5}{x}$

11. $\frac{2x}{21} = \frac{2}{7}$

12. $\frac{18}{5x} = \frac{3}{5}$

13. $\frac{9}{10} = \frac{108}{10x}$

14. A flower shop sells a dozen roses for \$25. How much does it cost to buy 18 roses?

Name____ Date__________

5.1 Identifying Similar Figures
For use with Activity 5.1

Essential Question How can you use proportions to help make decisions in art, design, and magazine layouts?

Original Photograph

In a computer art program, when you click and drag on a side of a photograph, you distort it.

But when you click and drag on a corner of the photograph, it remains proportional to the original.

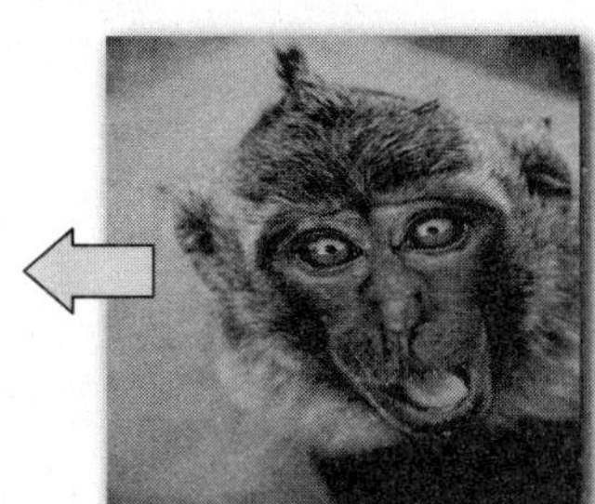
Distorted

Distorted

Proportional

1 ACTIVITY: Reducing Photographs

Work with a partner. You are trying to reduce the photograph to the indicated size for a nature magazine. Can you reduce the photograph to the indicated size without distorting or cropping? Explain your reasoning.

a.

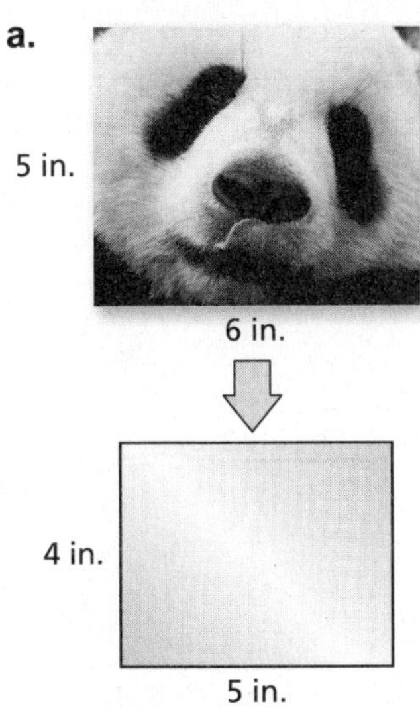

b.

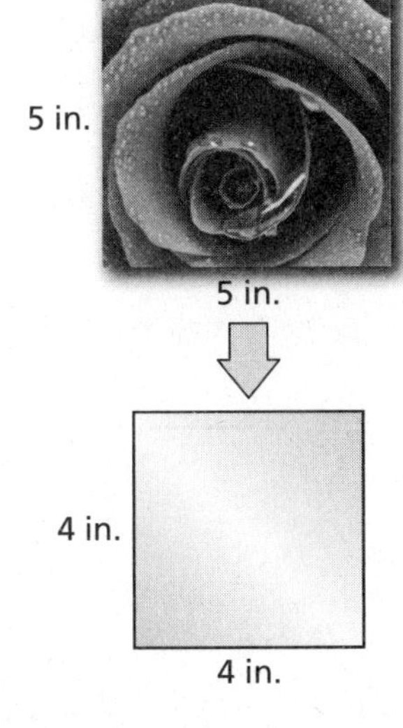

c.

2 ACTIVITY: Proportional Designs

Work with a partner.

a. Tell whether the new designs are proportional to the original design. Explain your reasoning.

Original	**Design 1**	**Design 2**
8, 8, 7	7, 7, 6	$6\frac{6}{7}$, $6\frac{6}{7}$, 6

b. Draw two designs that are proportional to the given design. Make one bigger and one smaller. Label the sides of the designs with their lengths.

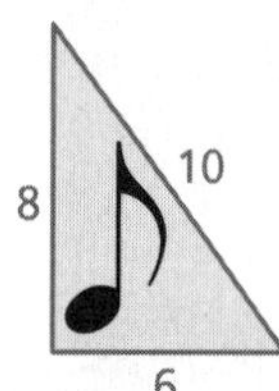

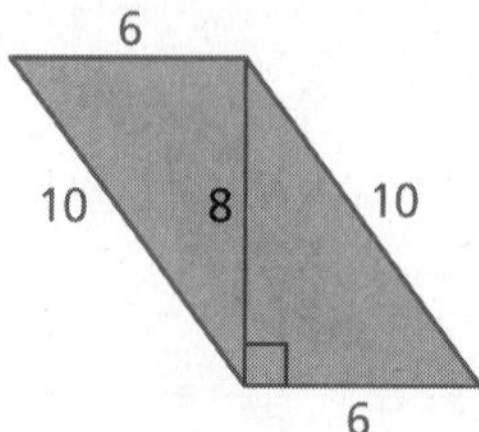

Name____ Date__________

What Is Your Answer?

3. **IN YOUR OWN WORDS** How can you use proportions to help make decisions in art, design, and magazine layouts? Give two examples.

4. **a.** Use a computer art program to draw two rectangles that are proportional to each other.

   b. Print the two rectangles on the same piece of paper.

   c. Use a centimeter ruler to measure the length and width of each rectangle. Record your measurements here.

"I love this statue. It seems similar to a big statue I saw in New York."

   d. Find the following ratios. What can you conclude?

$$\frac{\text{Length of Larger}}{\text{Length of Smaller}} \qquad \frac{\text{Width of Larger}}{\text{Width of Smaller}}$$

Name ______________________________ Date ________

5.1 Practice
For use after Lesson 5.1

Name the corresponding angles and the corresponding sides of the similar figures.

1.
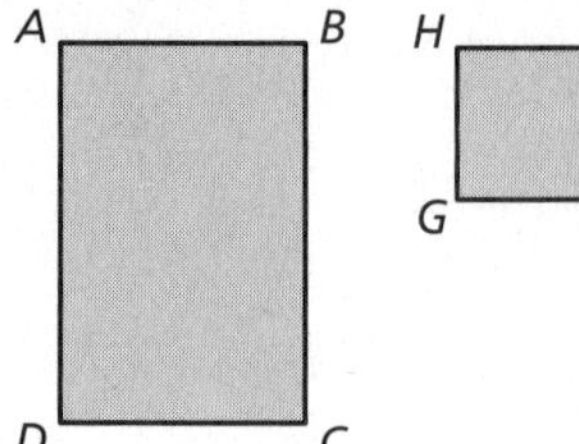

2.
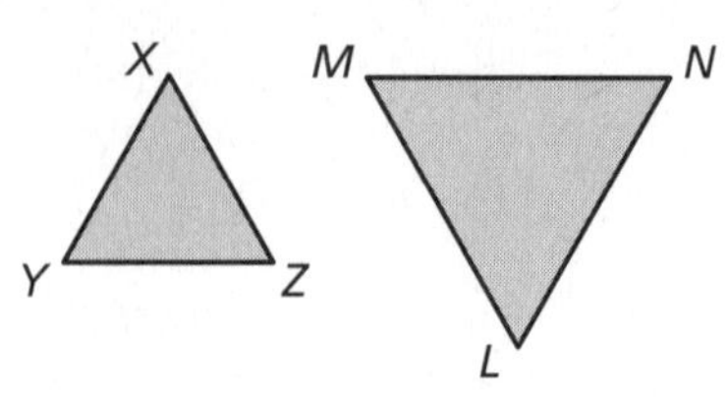

Tell whether the two figures are similar. Explain your reasoning.

3.
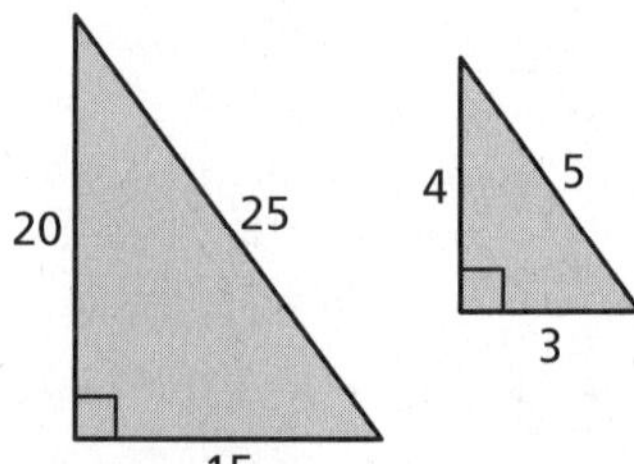

4.
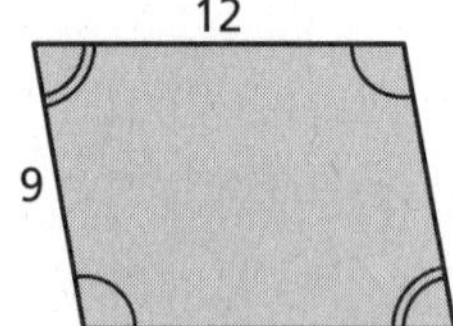

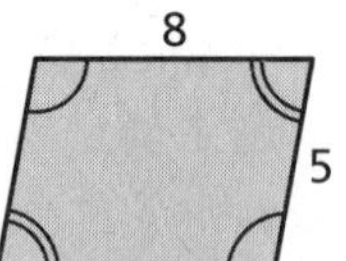

5. In your classroom, a dry erase board is 8 feet long and 4 feet wide. Your teacher makes individual dry erase boards for you to use at your desk that are 11.5 inches long and 9.5 inches wide. Are the boards similar?

6. You have a 4 x 6 photo of you and your friend.

a. You order a 5 x 7 print of the photo. Is the new photo similar to the original?

b. You enlarge the original photo to three times its size on your computer. Is the new photo similar to the original?

Name______________________________ Date__________

5.2 Perimeters and Areas of Similar Figures

For use with Activity 5.2

Essential Question How do changes in dimensions of similar geometric figures affect the perimeters and areas of the figures?

ACTIVITY: Comparing Perimeters and Areas

Work with a partner. Use pattern blocks to make a figure whose dimensions are 2, 3, and 4 times greater than those of the original figure. Find the perimeter *P* and area *A* of each larger figure.

a. Square

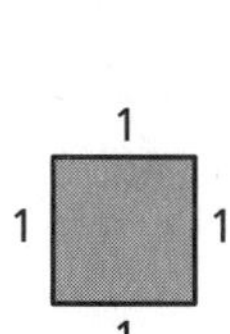

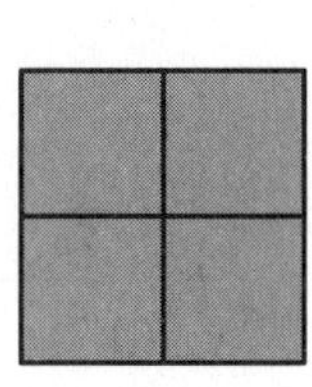

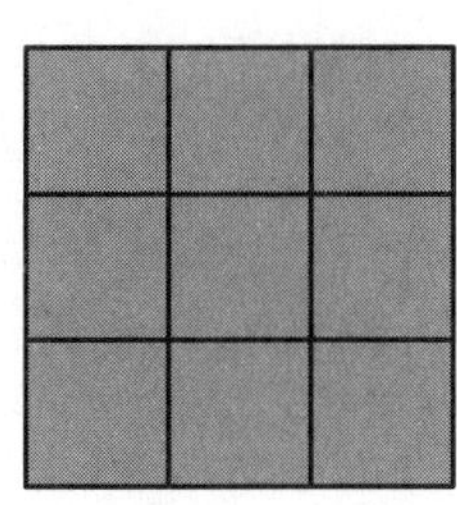

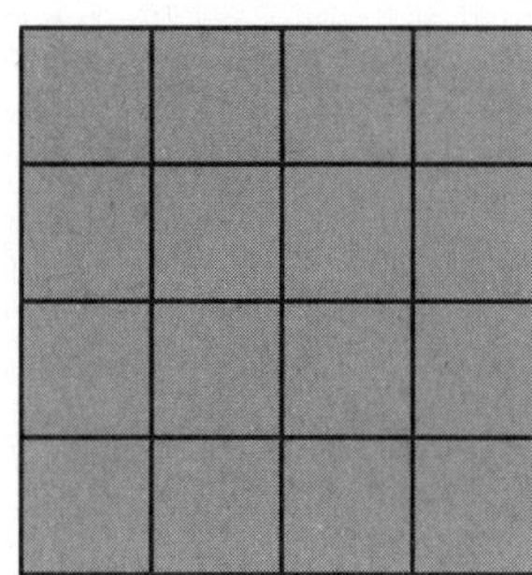

$P = 4$ $\quad P =$ ______ $\quad P =$ ______ $\quad P =$ ______

$A = 1$ $\quad A =$ ______ $\quad A =$ ______ $\quad A =$ ______

b. Triangle

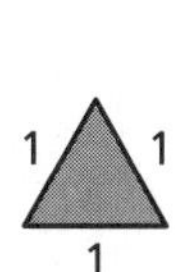

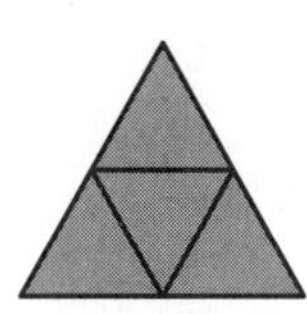

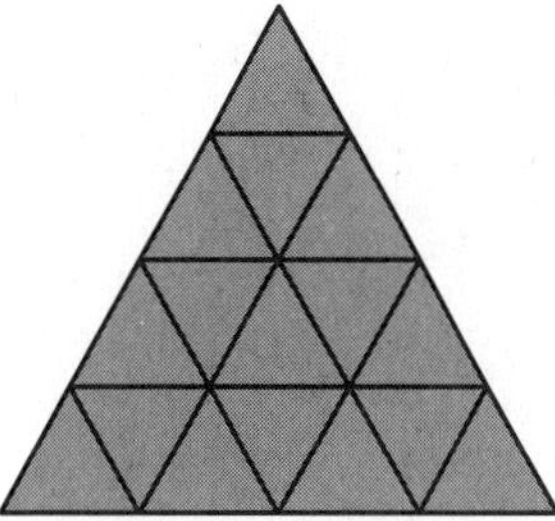

$P = 3$ $\quad P =$ ______ $\quad P =$ ______ $\quad P =$ ______

$A = B$ $\quad A =$ ______ $\quad A =$ ______ $\quad A =$ ______

c. Rectangle

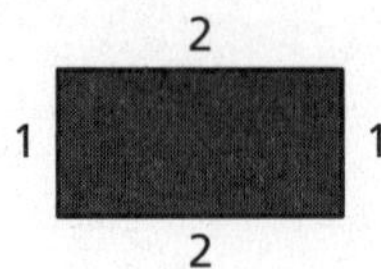

$P = 6$

$A = 2$

d. Parallelogram

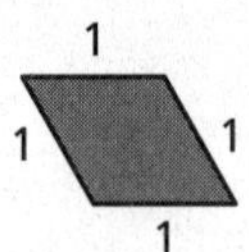

$P = 4$

$A = C$

2 ACTIVITY: Finding Patterns for Perimeters

Work with a partner. Complete the table for the perimeters of the figures in Activity 1. Describe the pattern.

Figure	Original Side Lengths	Double Side Lengths	Triple Side Lengths	Quadruple Side Lengths
	$P = 4$			
	$P = 3$			
	$P = 6$			
	$P = 4$			

Name ______________________________ Date __________

5.2 Perimeters and Areas of Similar Figures (continued)

3 ACTIVITY: Finding Patterns for Areas

Work with a partner. Complete the table for the areas of the figures in Activity 1. Describe the pattern.

Figure	Original Side Lengths	Double Side Lengths	Triple Side Lengths	Quadruple Side Lengths
(square)	$A = 1$			
(triangle)	$A = B$			
(rectangle)	$A = 2$			
(parallelogram)	$A = C$			

What Is Your Answer?

4. **IN YOUR OWN WORDS** How do changes in dimensions of similar geometric figures affect the perimeters and areas of the figures?

Name ______________________________ Date ________

5.2 Practice

For use after Lesson 5.2

The two figures are similar. Find the ratios (shaded to nonshaded) of the perimeters and of the areas.

1.

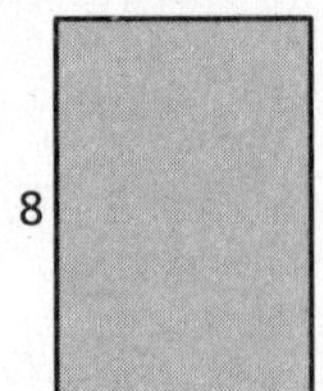

2.

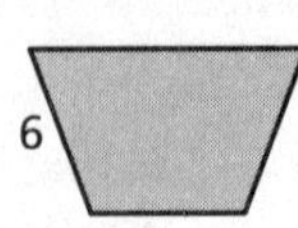

3.

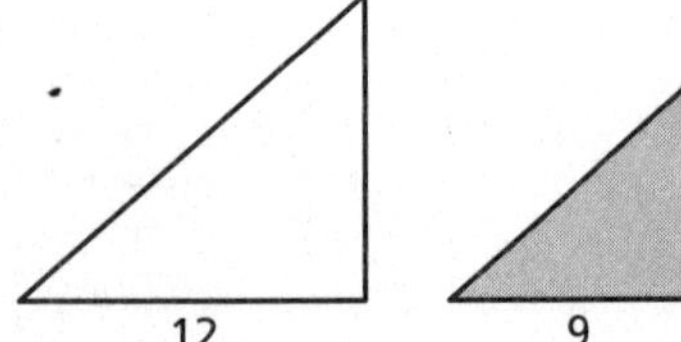

4.

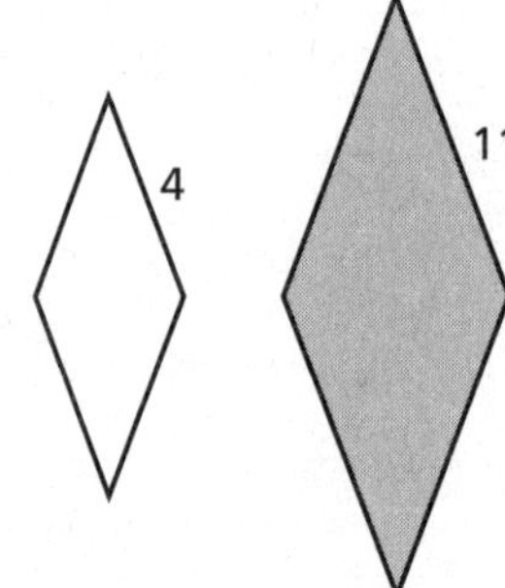

5. You buy two picture frames that are similar. The ratio of the corresponding side lengths is 4 : 5. What is the ratio of the areas?

6. Rectangle A is similar to Rectangle B. What is the ratio of the perimeter of Rectangle A to the perimeter of Rectangle B?

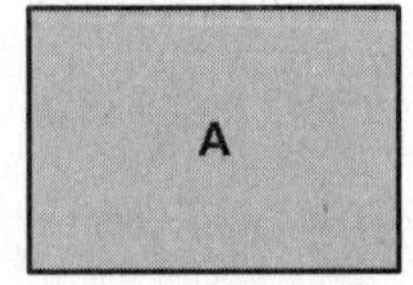

Name____ Date__________

5.3 Finding Unknown Measures in Similar Figures

For use with Activity 5.3

Essential Question What information do you need to know to find the dimensions of a figure that is similar to another figure?

1 ACTIVITY: Drawing and Labeling Similar Figures

Work with a partner. You are given the rectangle. Find another rectangle that is similar and has one side from $(-1, -6)$ to $(5, -6)$. Label the vertices.

a.

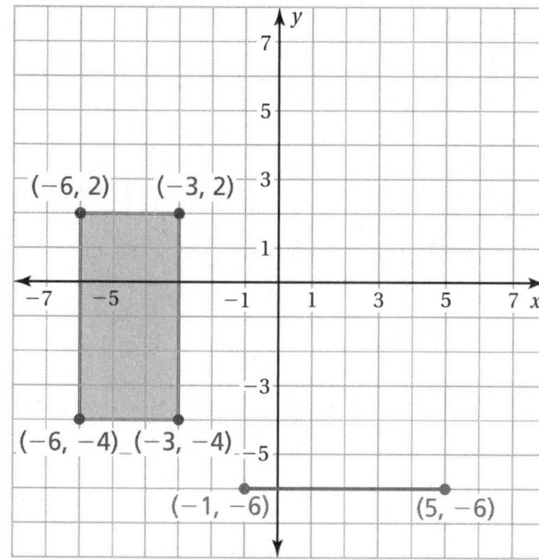

You can see that the two rectangles are similar by showing that ratios of corresponding sides are equal. Complete the steps below. Are the two rectangles above similar?

$$\frac{\text{Shaded Length}}{\text{Unshaded Length}} \stackrel{?}{=} \frac{\text{Shaded Width}}{\text{Unshaded Length}}$$

$$\frac{\text{change in } y}{\text{change in } y} \stackrel{?}{=} \frac{\text{change in } x}{\text{change in } x}$$

$$\frac{\square}{\square} = \frac{\square}{\square}$$

Name ______________________________ Date __________

b. There are three other rectangles that are similar to the shaded rectangle and have the given side.

- Draw each one. Label the vertices of each.

- Show that each is similar to the original shaded rectangle.

2 ACTIVITY: Reading a Map

Work with a partner.

a. The rectangles are similar. Find the length of the larger rectangle. Explain your reasoning.

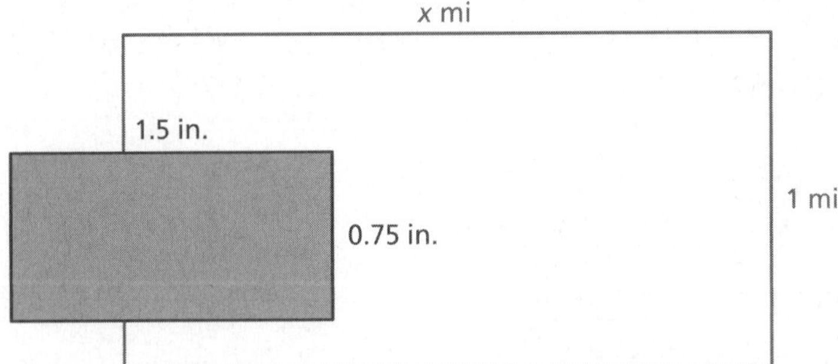

Name______________________________ Date__________

b. The distance marked by the vertical line on the map is 1 mile. Find the distance marked by the horizontal line. Explain your reasoning.

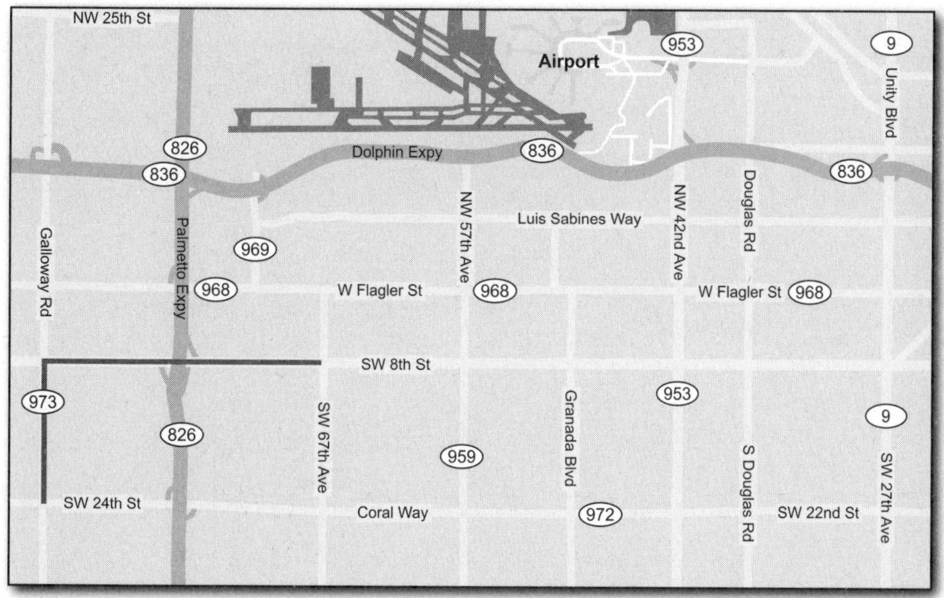

What Is Your Answer?

3. **IN YOUR OWN WORDS** What information do you need to know to find the dimensions of a figure that is similar to another figure? Give some examples using two rectangles.

4. When you know the length and width of one rectangle and the length of a similar rectangle, can you always find the missing width? Why or why not?

Name ______________________ Date ________

5.3 Practice

For use after Lesson 5.3

The polygons are similar. Find the value of x.

1.

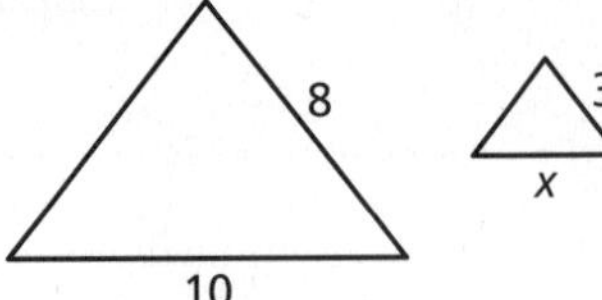

2.

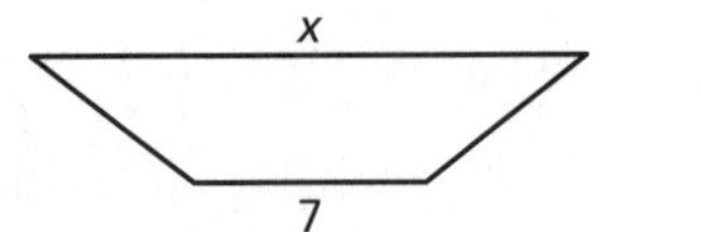

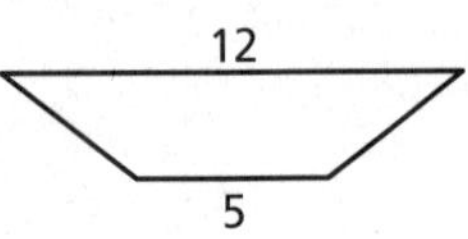

3.

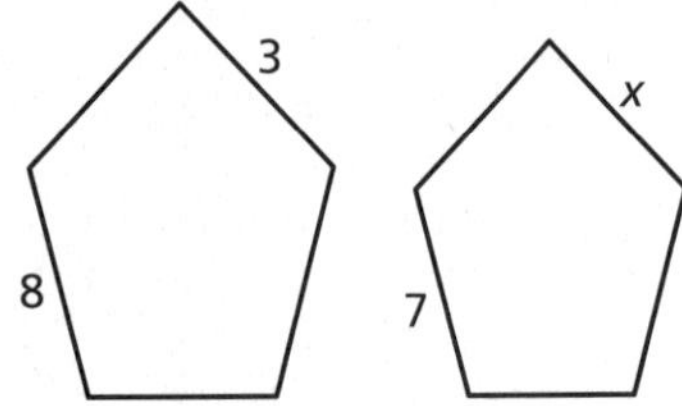

4. The ratio of the perimeters is 2 : 5.

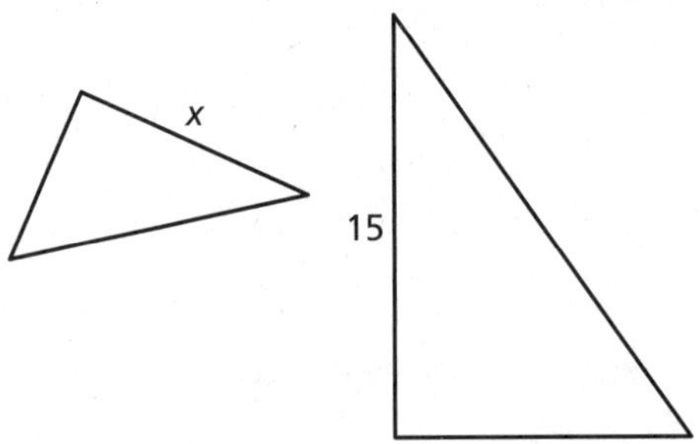

5. A tree casts a shadow that is 50 feet long. A 4-foot person casts a shadow that is 10 feet long. How tall is the tree?

6. A cookie sheet is 12 inches wide and has a perimeter of 52 inches. You buy a similar cookie sheet that is 15 inches wide. What is its perimeter?

Name ____________________ Date __________

5.4 Scale Drawings

For use with Activity 5.4

Essential Question How can you use a scale drawing to estimate the cost of painting a room?

1 ACTIVITY: Making Scale Drawings

Work with a partner. You have decided that your classroom needs to be painted. Start by making a scale drawing of each of the four walls.

- **Measure each of the walls.**
- **Measure the locations and dimensions of parts that will *not* be painted.**
- **Decide on a scale for your drawings.**
- **Make a scale drawing of each of the walls.**

Sample: Wall #1

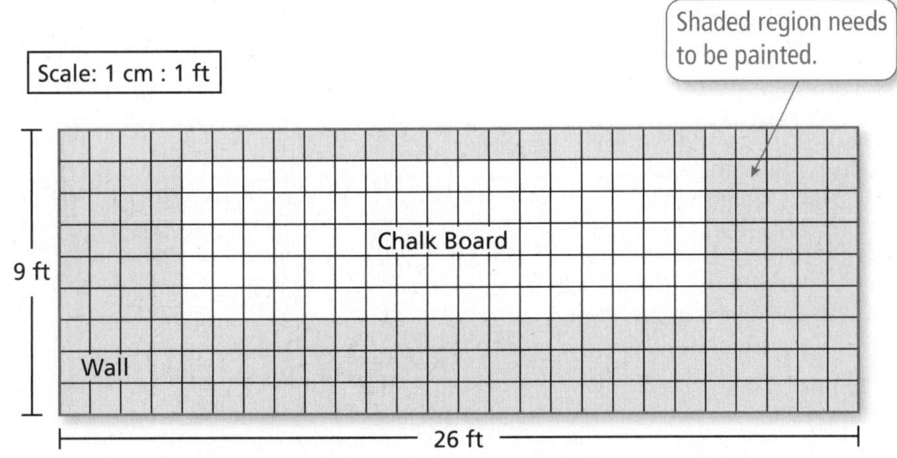

- **For each wall, find the area of the part that needs to be painted.**

Dimensions		***Area***
Dimensions of the wall	9 ft by 26 ft	$9 \times 26 = 234$ sq ft
Dimensions of the part that will *not* be painted	5 ft by 17 ft	$5 \times 17 = 85$ sq ft
Area of painted part		$234 - 85 = 149$ sq ft

2 ACTIVITY: Using Scale Drawings

Work with a partner.

You are using a paint that covers 200 square feet per gallon. Each wall will need two coats of paint.

Interior latex paint	$40 per gallon
Roller, pan, and brush set	$12

a. Find the total area of the walls in your classroom that need to be painted.

b. Find the amount of paint you need to buy.

c. Estimate the total cost of painting your classroom.

What Is Your Answer?

3. **IN YOUR OWN WORDS** How can you use a scale drawing to estimate the cost of painting a room?

4. Use a scale drawing to estimate the cost of painting another room, such as your bedroom or another room in your house.

5. Look at some maps in your school library or on the Internet. Make a list of the different scales used on the maps.

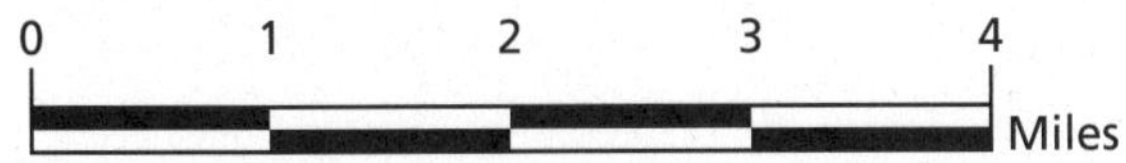

"I don't get it. According to this map, we only have to drive $8\frac{1}{2}$ inches."

6. When you view a map on the Internet, how does the scale change when you zoom out? How does the scale change when you zoom in?

Name ______________________________ Date __________

5.4 Practice
For use after Lesson 5.4

Find the missing dimension. Use the scale factor 1 : 8.

Item	Model	Actual
1. Statue	Height: 168 in.	Height: ________ ft
2. Painting	Width: ________ cm	Width: 200 m
3. Alligator	Height: ________ in.	Height: 6.4 ft
4. Train	Length: 36.5 in.	Length: ________ ft

5. The diameter of the moon is 2160 miles. A model has a scale of 1 in. : 150 mi. What is the diameter of the model?

6. A map has a scale of 1 in. : 4 mi.

a. You measure 3 inches between your house and the movie theater. How many miles is it from your house to the movie theater?

b. It is 17 miles to the mall. How many inches is that on the map?

Name____ Date__________

5.4b Practice

For use after Lesson 5.4b

1. The city park diagram has a scale of 1 cm : 50 yd. Find the actual area of the park.

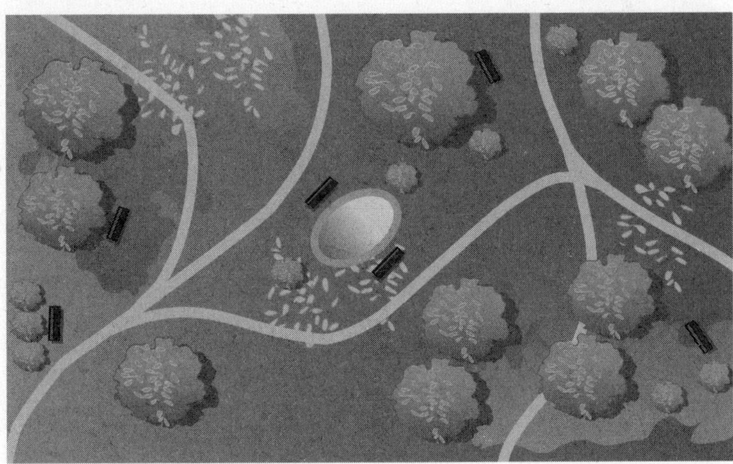

2. The stained glass window diagram has a scale of 1 cm : 2 ft. Find the actual area of the window.

Name ______________________ Date ________

5.4b Practice (continued)

Recreate the scale drawing of a Mexican flag so that it has the given scale.

1 in. : 4 ft

3. 1 in. : 2 ft

4. 1 in. : 8 ft

Name____ Date__________

5.5 Translations

For use with Activity 5.5

Essential Question How can you use translations to make a tessellation?

When you slide a tile it is called a **translation**. When tiles can be used to cover a floor with no empty spaces, the collection of tiles is called a *tessellation*.

1 ACTIVITY: Describing Tessellations

Work with a partner. Can you make the pattern by using a translation of single tiles that are all of the same shape and design? If so, outline the single tile.

a. Sample:

Tile Pattern

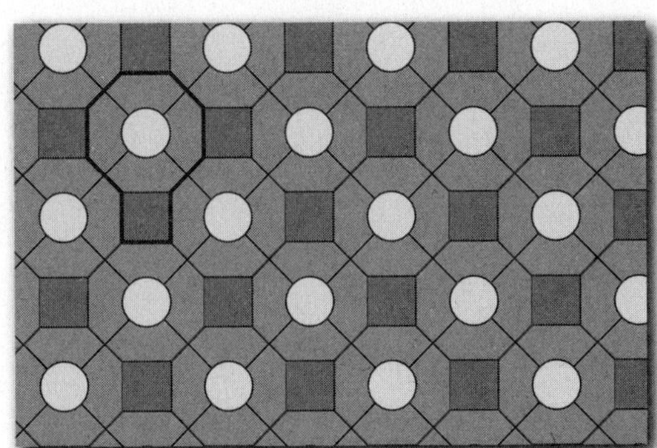

Single Tiles

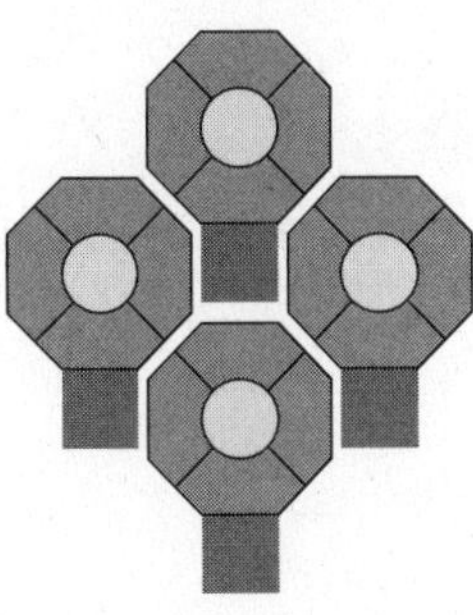

b.

c.

d. 

e. 

2 ACTIVITY: Tessellations and Basic Shapes

Work with a partner.

a. Which pattern blocks can you use to make a tessellation?

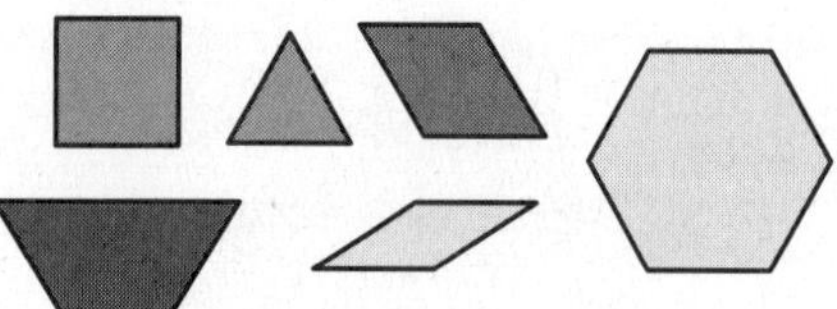

b. For each pattern block you listed in part (a), draw the tessellation.

c. Can you make the tessellation using only translations, or do you have to rotate or flip the pattern blocks?

3 ACTIVITY: Designing Tessellations

Work with a partner. Design your own tessellation. Use one of the basic shapes from Activity 2.

Sample:

Start with a square.

Cut a design out of one side.

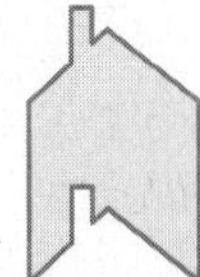

Tape it to the other side to make your pattern.

- **Use your pattern and translations to make your tessellation.**
- **Color the tessellation.**

What Is Your Answer?

4. **IN YOUR OWN WORDS** How can you use translations to make a tessellation? Give an example.

5. Draw any parallelogram. Does it tessellate? Is it true that any parallelogram can be translated to make a tessellation? Explain why.

Name ______________________ Date ________

5.5 Practice

For use after Lesson 5.5

Tell whether the shaded figure is a translation of the nonshaded figure.

1. 

2. 

3. 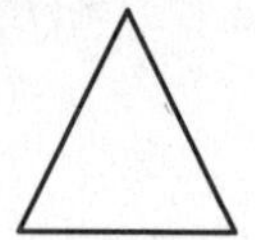

4. Translate the figure 4 units left and 1 unit down. What are the coordinates of the image?

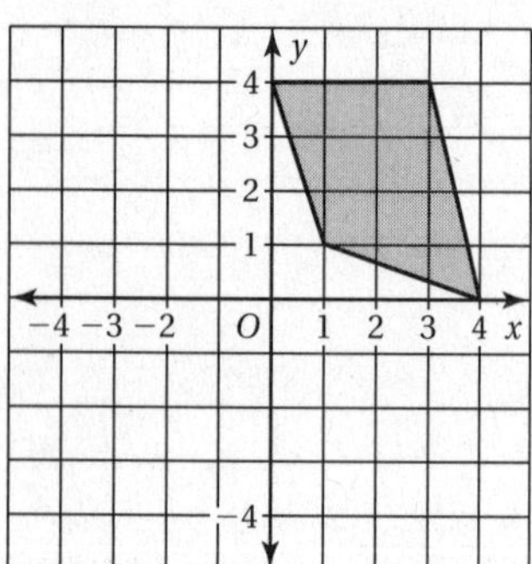

5. Translate the triangle 5 units right and 4 units up. What are the coordinates of the image?

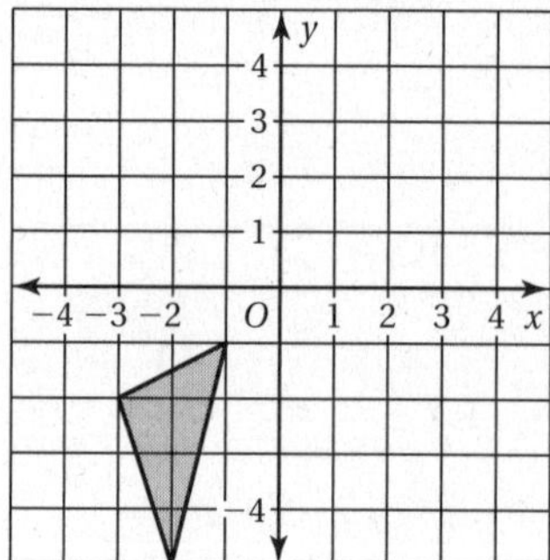

6. A rectangle is translated 3 units left and 4 units down. Then the image is translated 6 units right and 1 unit up. Write a translation of the original rectangle to the ending position.

7. Describe the translation from the shaded figure to the nonshaded figure.

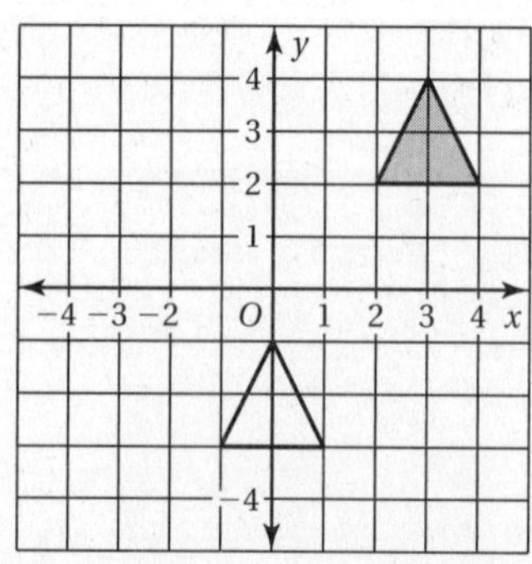

Name______________________________ Date__________

5.6 Reflections

For use with Activity 5.6

Essential Question How can you use reflections to classify a frieze pattern?

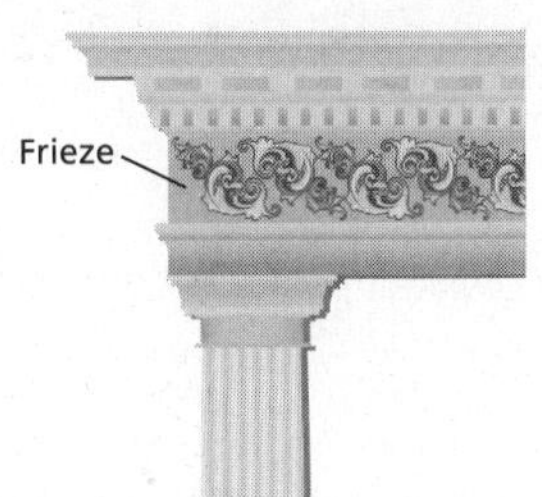

A *frieze* is a horizontal band that runs at the top of a building. A frieze is often decorated with a design that repeats.

- All frieze patterns are translations of themselves.
- Some frieze patterns are reflections of themselves.

1 EXAMPLE: Frieze Patterns

Is the frieze pattern a reflection of itself when folded horizontally? vertically?*

- Fold (reflect) on the horizontal axis. The pattern coincides.

- Fold (reflect) on the vertical axis. The pattern coincides.

The frieze pattern is a reflection of itself when it is folded horizontally *and* vertically.

2 ACTIVITY: Frieze Patterns and Reflections

Work with a partner. Is the frieze pattern a reflection of itself when folded *horizontally*, *vertically*, or *neither*?

a.

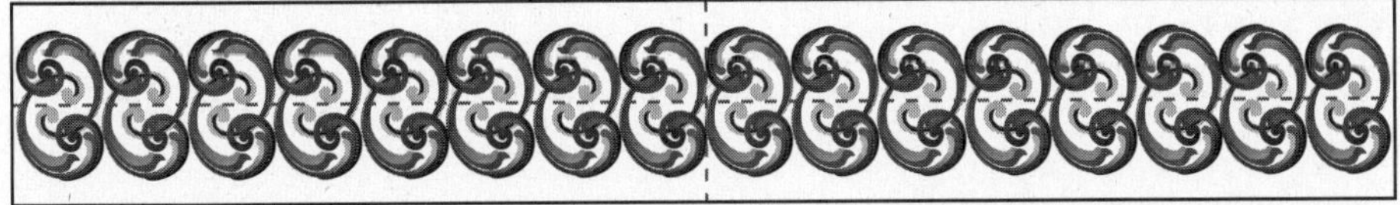

*Cut-outs are available in the back of the Record and Practice Journal.

Name ______________________________ Date __________

5.6 Reflections (continued)

b. 

c. 

d. 

e.

f. 

What Is Your Answer?

3. Draw a frieze pattern that is a reflection of itself when folded horizontally.

4. Draw a frieze pattern that is a reflection of itself when folded vertically.

5. Draw a frieze pattern that is not a reflection of itself when folded horizontally or vertically.

6. **IN YOUR OWN WORDS** How can you use reflections to classify a frieze pattern?

Name ______________________ Date ________

5.6 Practice
For use after Lesson 5.6

Tell whether the shaded figure is a reflection of the nonshaded figure.

1. 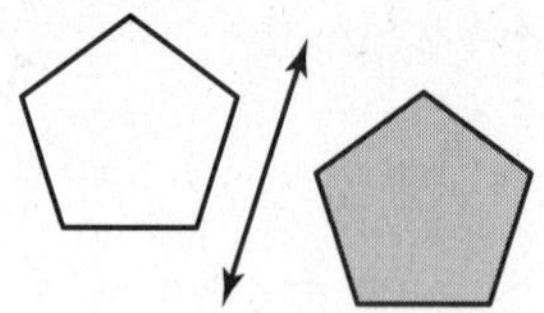

2. 

3. 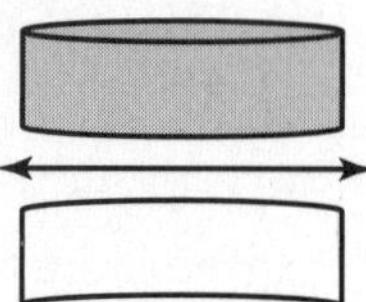

Find the coordinates of the figure after reflecting in the *x*-axis.

4. $A(1, 2), B(3, 3), C(0, 4)$

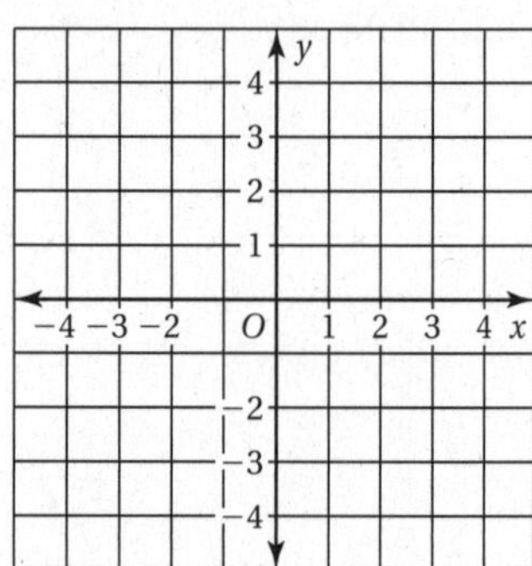

5. $W(4, 2), X(3, 4), Y(1, 3), Z(3, 1)$

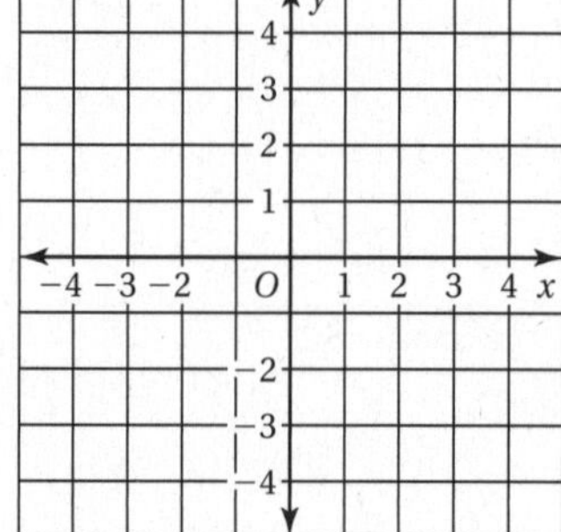

Find the coordinates of the figure after reflecting in the *y*-axis.

6. $J(3, 4), K(4, 0), L(2, 3)$

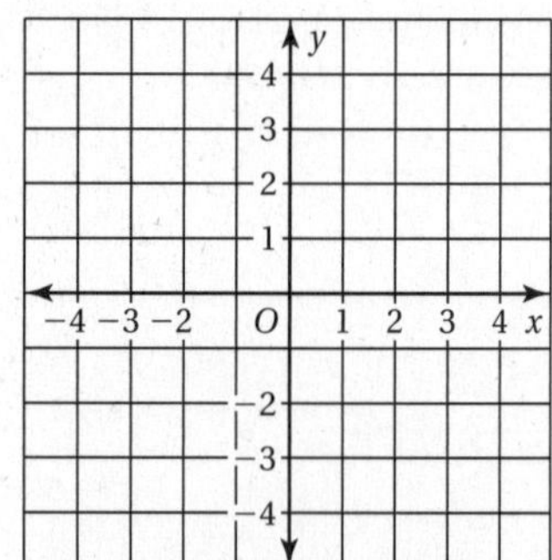

7. $M(2, 2), N(2, 3), P(3, 3), Q(4, 1)$

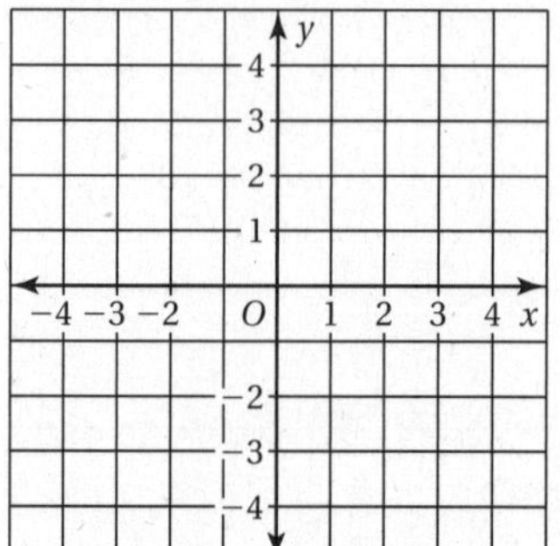

8. In a pinball game, if you perfectly reflect the ball off of the wall, will the ball hit the bonus target?

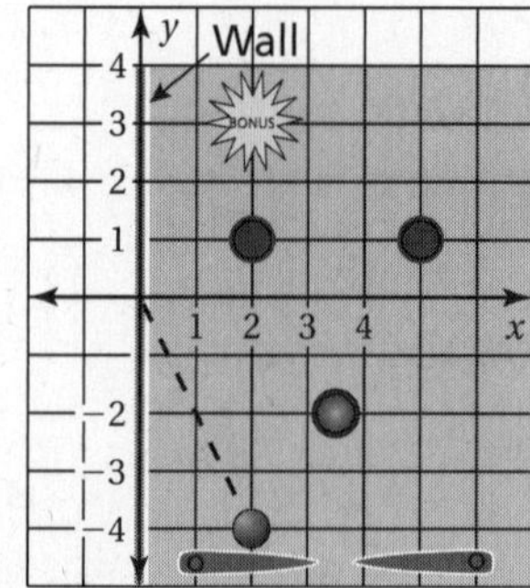

Name____ Date__________

5.7 Rotations

For use with Activity 5.7

Essential Question What are the three basic ways to move an object in a plane?

1 ACTIVITY: Three Basic Ways to Move Things

There are three basic ways to move objects on a flat surface.

1. Translate the object.

2. Reflect the object.

3. Rotate the object.

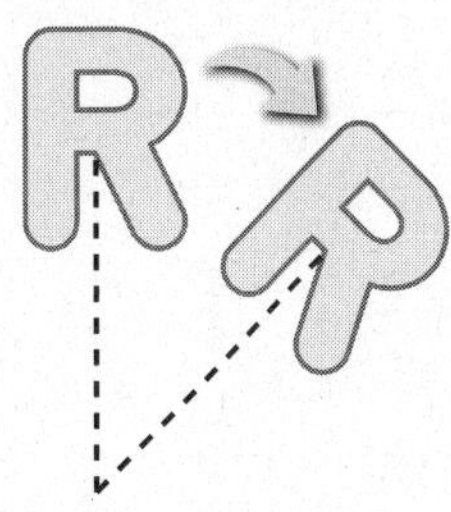

Work with a partner.

- Cut out a paper triangle that is the same size as the shaded triangle shown.*
- Decide how you can move the shaded triangle to make each nonshaded triangle.
- Is each move a *translation*, a *reflection*, or a *rotation*?

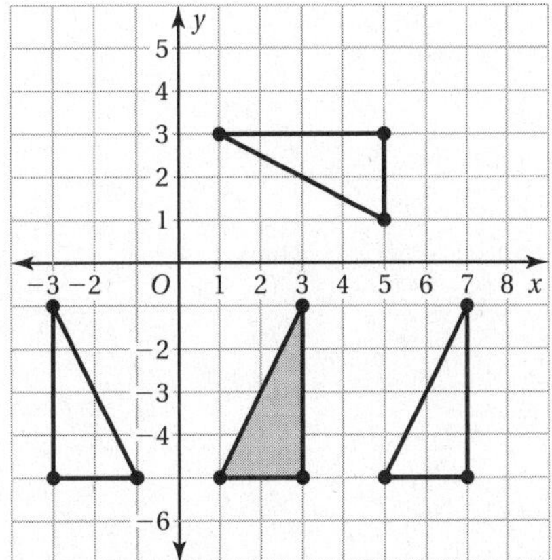

- Draw four other nonshaded triangles in a coordinate plane. Describe how you can move the shaded triangle to make each nonshaded triangle.

*Cut-outs are available in the back of the Record and Practice Journal.

Name ______________________________ Date __________

5.7 Rotations (continued)

2 ACTIVITY: Tessellating a Plane

Work with a partner.

a. Describe how the figure labeled 1 in each diagram can be moved to make the other figures.

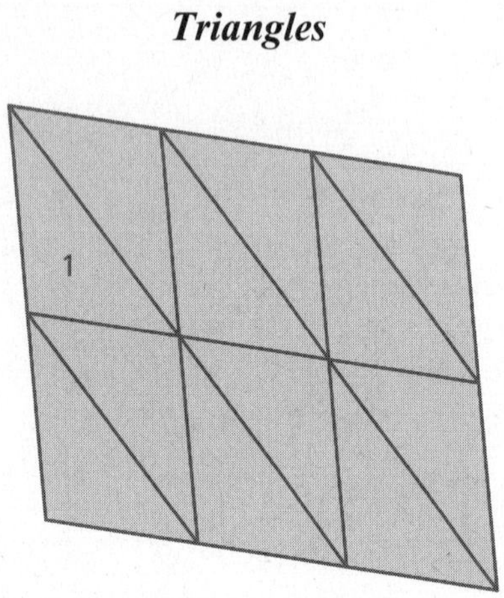

Triangles

1

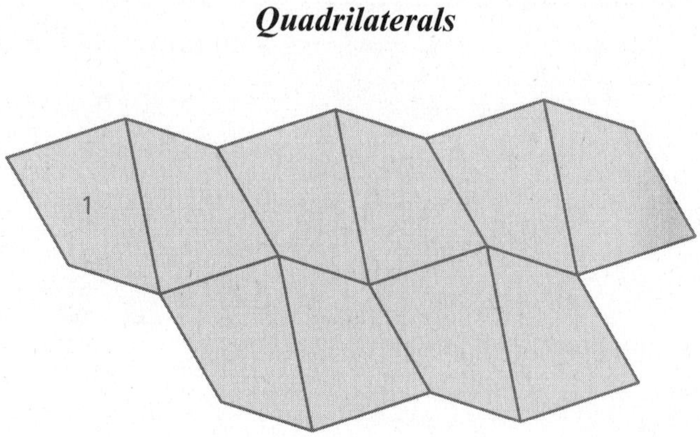

Quadrilaterals

1

b. EXPERIMENT Will *any* triangle tessellate? Conduct an experiment to gather information to help form your conclusion. Draw a triangle. Cut it out. Then use it to trace other triangles so that you cover the plane with triangles that are all the same shape.

c. **EXPERIMENT** Will *any* quadrilateral tessellate? Conduct an experiment to gather information to help form your conclusion. Draw a quadrilateral. Cut it out. Then use it to trace other quadrilaterals so that you cover the plane with quadrilaterals that are all the same shape.

What Is Your Answer?

3. **IN YOUR OWN WORDS** What are the three basic ways to move an object in a plane? Draw an example of each.

"Dear Sub Shop: Why do you put the cheese on the subs so some parts have double coverage and some have none?"

"My suggestion is that you use the tessellation property of triangles for even cheese coverage."

Name ______________________________ Date __________

5.7 Practice

For use after Lesson 5.7

Tell whether the shaded figure is a rotation of the nonshaded figure about the origin. If so, give the angle and the direction of rotation.

1.

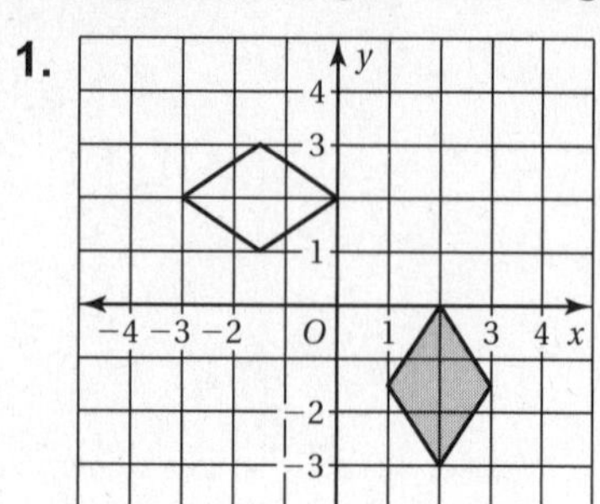

2.

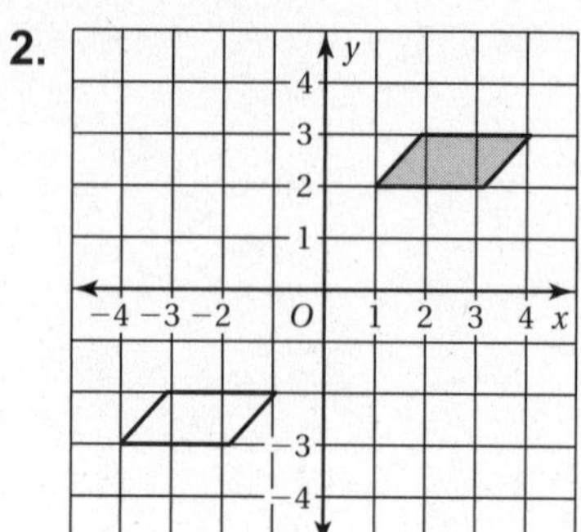

The vertices of a triangle are $A(1, 1)$, $B(3, 1)$, and $C(3, 4)$. Rotate the triangle as described. Find the coordinates of the image.

3. $90°$ clockwise about the origin

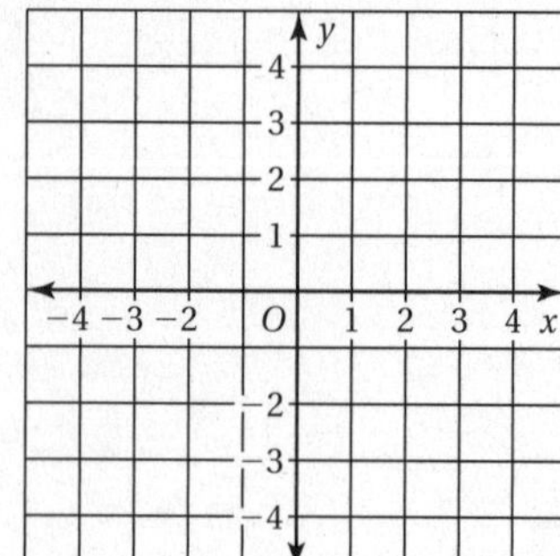

4. $270°$ counterclockwise about vertex A

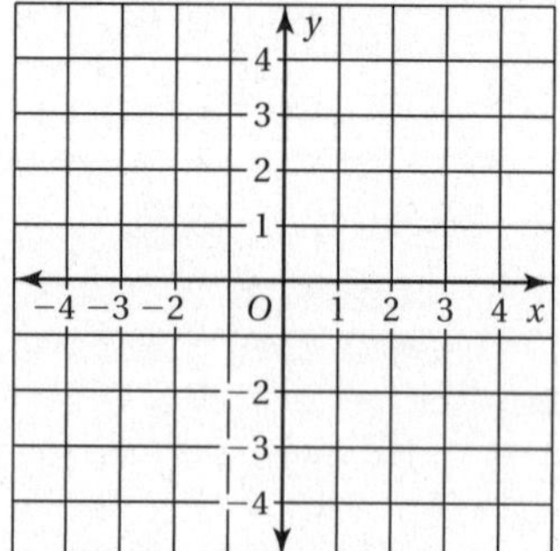

5. A triangle is rotated $180°$ about the origin. Its image is reflected in the x-axis. The vertices of the final triangle are $(-4, -4)$, $(-2, -4)$, and $(-3, -1)$. What are the vertices of the original triangle?

Name____ Date__________

Chapter 6

Fair Game Review

Find the area.

1.

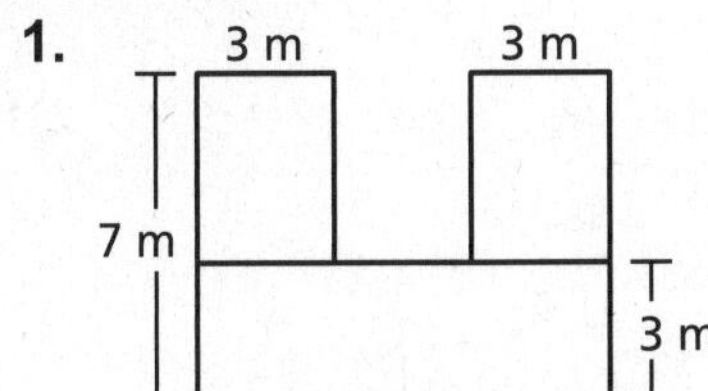

2.

5 m

14 m

3.

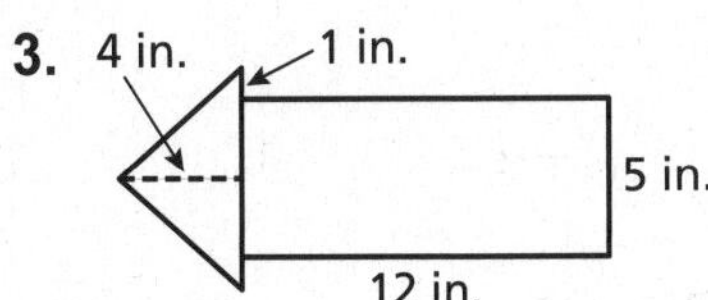

4.

12 in.

9 in.

7 in. 12 in.

5.

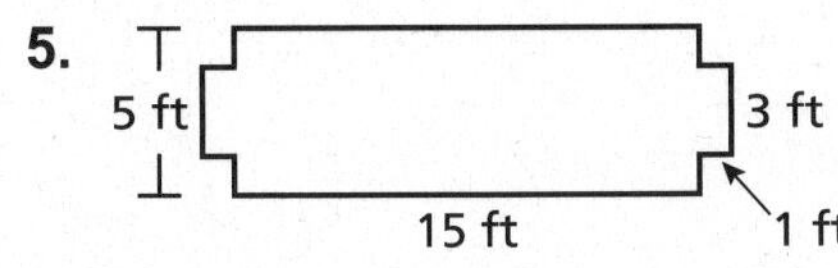

6.

10 in.

4 in.

8 in.

17 in.

7. You are putting carpet in 2 rooms of your house. The carpet costs $1.48 per square foot. How much docs it cost to put carpet in the rooms?

10 ft

18 ft

12 ft

10 ft

Name ______________________________ Date __________

Fair Game Review (continued)

Find the area.

8. 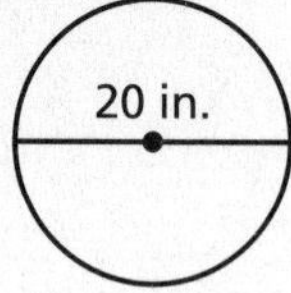

9. 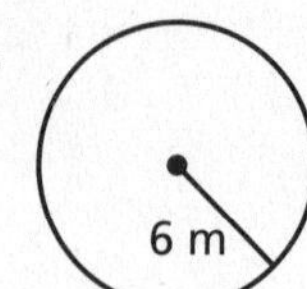

10. 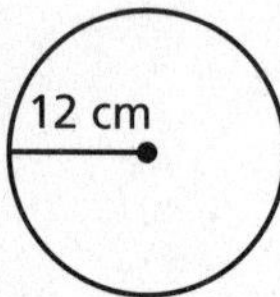

11. 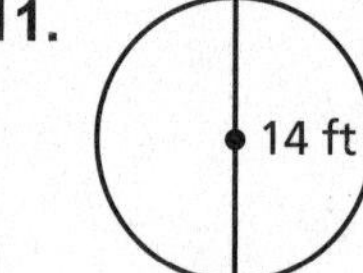

12. 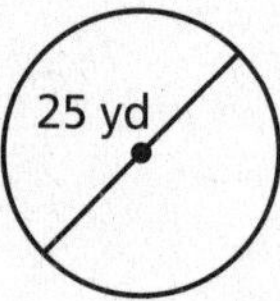

13. 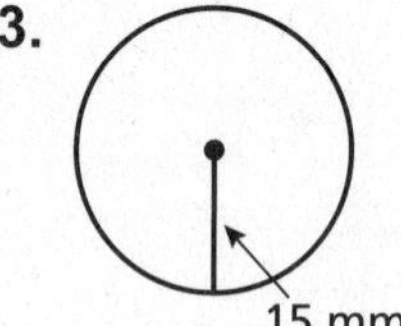

14. Find the area of the shaded region.

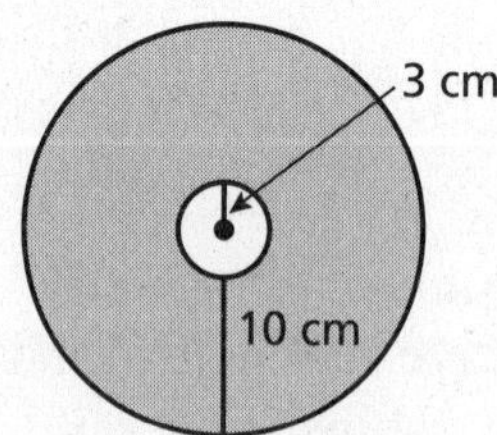

Name____ Date__________

6.1 Drawing 3-Dimensional Figures

For use with Activity 6.1

Essential Question How can you draw three-dimensional figures?

1 ACTIVITY: Finding Surface Area and Volumes

Work with a partner.

Draw the front, side, and top views of each stack of cubes. Then find the surface area and volume. Each small cube has side lengths of 1 unit.

a. 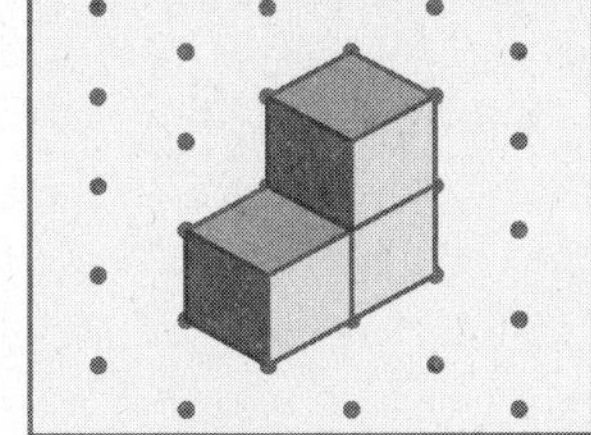

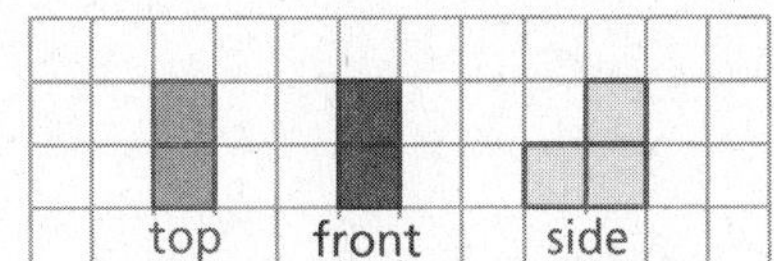

b. 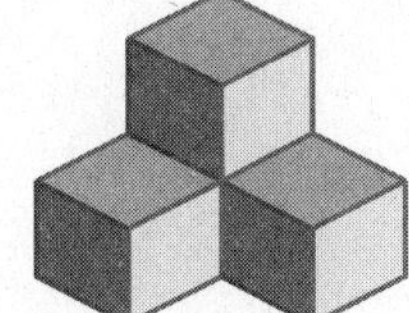

c. 

d. 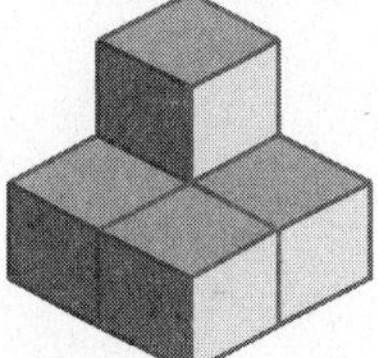

e. 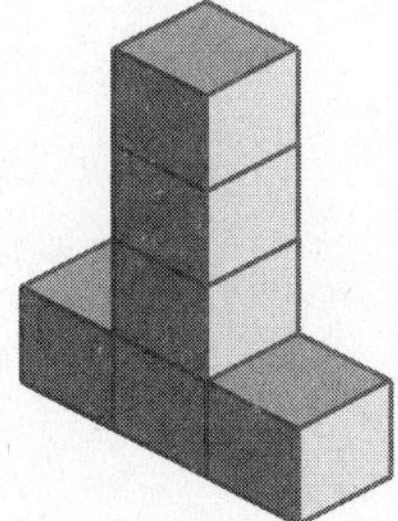

f. 

g. 

2 ACTIVITY: Drawing Solids

Work with a partner.

a. Draw all the different solids you can make by joining four cubes. (Two have been drawn.) Cubes must be joined on faces, not on edges only. Translations, reflections, and rotations do not count as different solids.

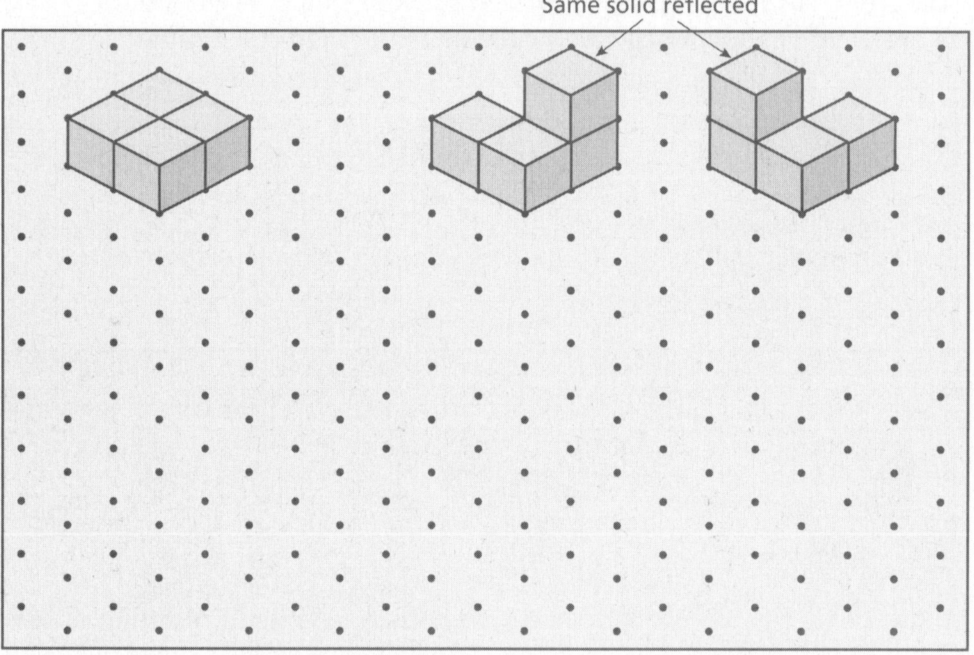

b. Do all the solids have the same surface area? Do all the solids have the same volume? Explain your reasoning.

Name ______________________________ Date __________

What Is Your Answer?

3. **IN YOUR OWN WORDS** How can you draw three-dimensional figures? Draw and shade two prisms that have the same volume but different surface areas.

4. Maurits Escher (1898–1972) was a popular artist who drew optical illusions.

   a. What is the illusion in Escher's drawing?

   b. Why is the cartoon funny? What is the illusion in the cartoon?

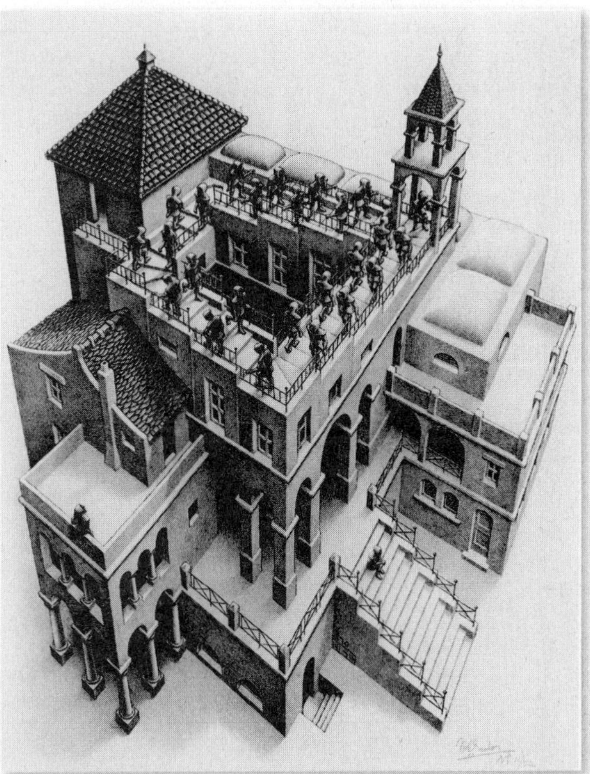

© 2010 M.C. Escher's "Ascending and Descending"

Name ______________________________ Date __________

6.1 Practice
For use after Lesson 6.1

Draw the solid.

1. Pentagonal pyramid

2. Square prism

Draw the front, side, and top views of the solid.

3.

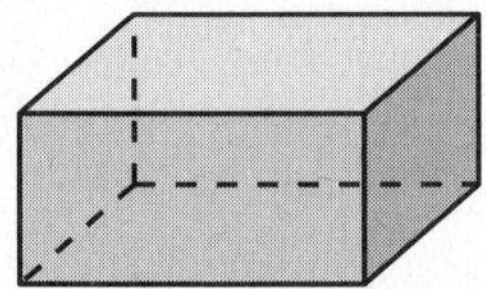

4.

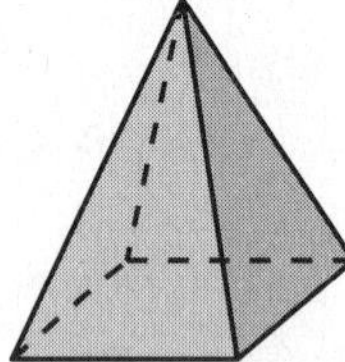

5. Two of the three views of a solid are shown.

Front Side

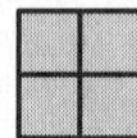

a. What is the greatest number of unit cubes in the solid?

b. Draw the top view of the solid in part (a).

6. Draw a solid with the following front, side, and top views.

Front Side Top

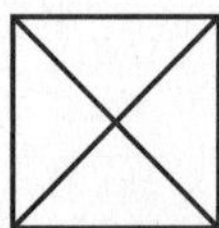

Name____ Date__________

6.2 Surface Areas of Prisms
For use with Activity 6.2

Essential Question How can you use a net to find the surface area of a prism?

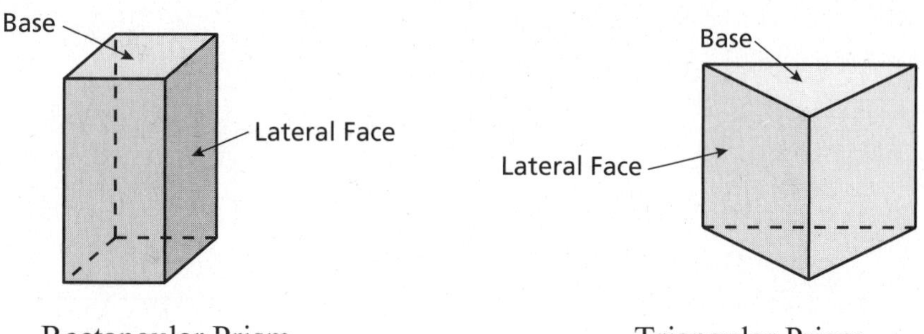

Rectangular Prism Triangular Prism

The **surface area** of a prism is the sum of the areas of all its faces. A two-dimensional representation of a solid is called a **net**.

1 ACTIVITY: Surface Area of a Right Rectangular Prism

Work with a partner.

a. Use the net for the rectangular prism to find its surface area.

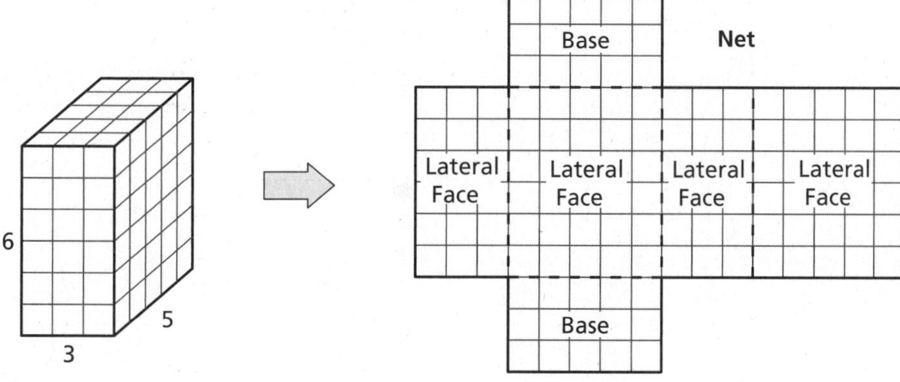

Name ______________________________ Date __________

6.2 Surface Areas of Prisms (continued)

b. Use the net for a rectangular prism. Label each side as h, w, or ℓ. Then write a formula for the surface area of a rectangular prism.

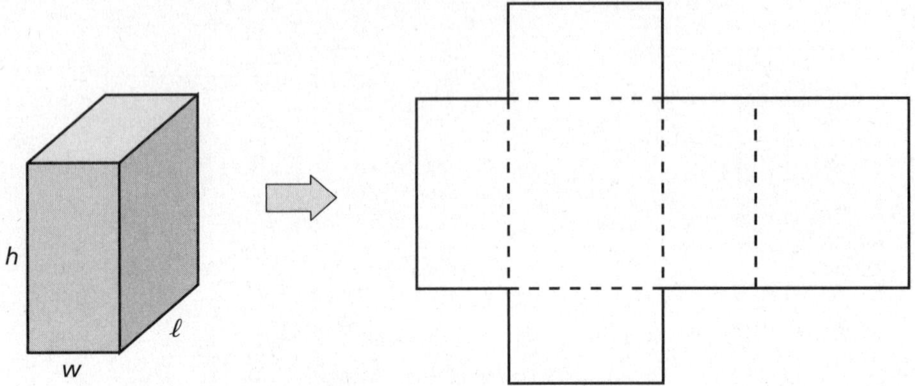

2 ACTIVITY: Finding Surface Area

Work with a partner. Find the surface area of the solid shown by the net. Use a cut-out of the net.* Fold it to form a solid. Identify the solid.

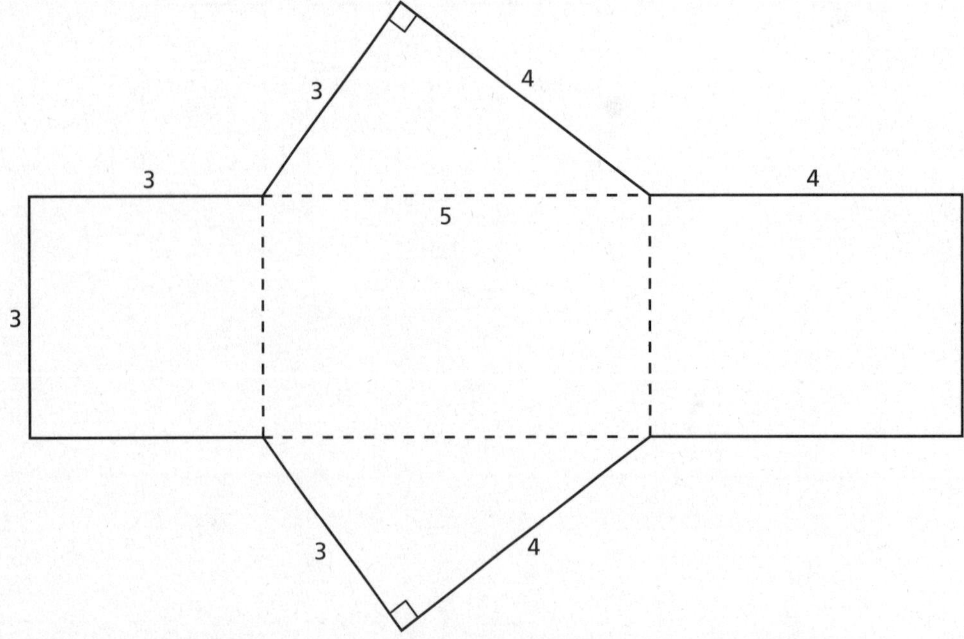

*Cut-outs are available in the back of the Record and Practice Journal.

What Is Your Answer?

3. **IN YOUR OWN WORDS** How can you use a net to find the surface area of a prism? Draw a net, cut it out, and fold it to form a prism.

4. The greater the surface area of an ice block, the faster it will melt. Which will melt faster, the bigger block or the three smaller blocks? Explain your reasoning.

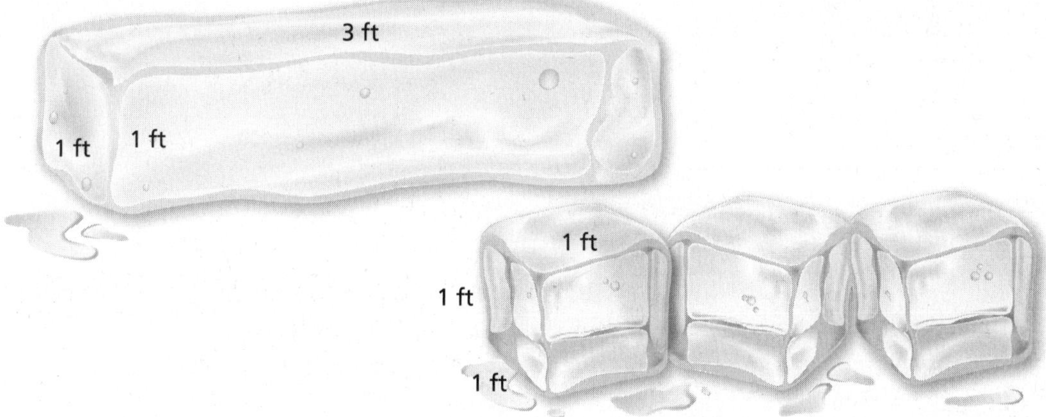

Name ______________________________ Date __________

6.2 Practice
For use after Lesson 6.2

Draw a net for the prism. Then find the surface area.

1.

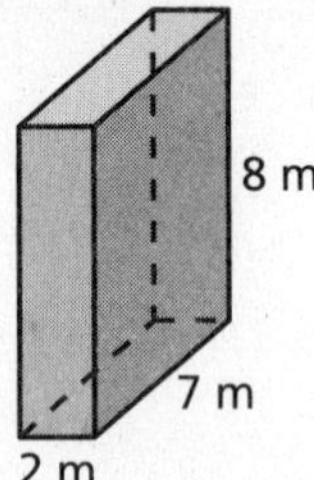

2.

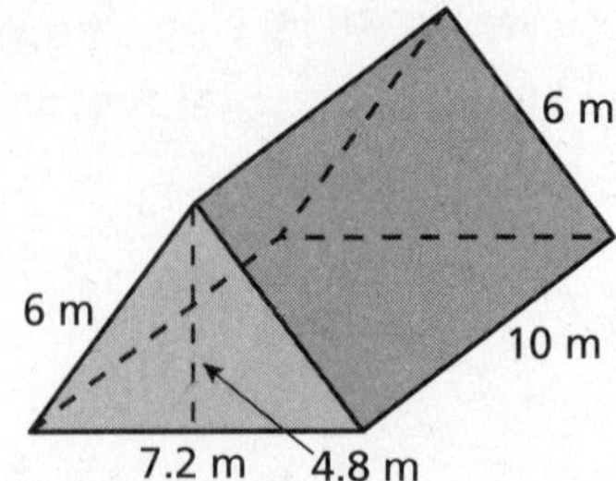

Find the surface area of the prism.

3.

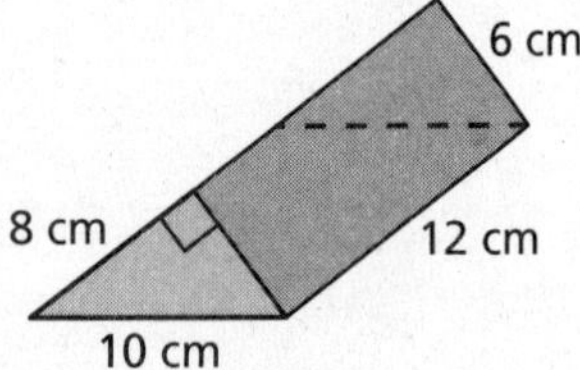

4.

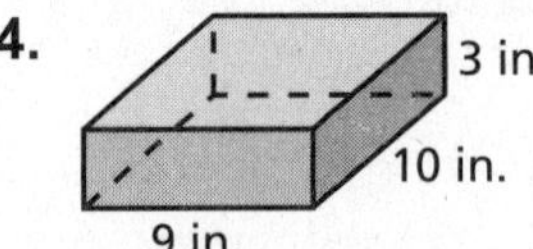

5. You bake a 9-inch by 13-inch by 2-inch cake. Your frosting recipe makes enough to cover 250 square inches of cake. Do you have enough frosting? (Assume you do not need to frost the bottom of the cake.) Explain your reasoning.

6. You buy a ring box as a birthday gift that is in the shape of a triangular prism. What is the least amount of wrapping paper needed to wrap the box?

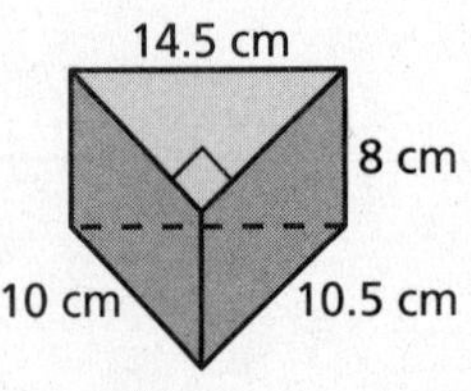

Name______________________________ Date__________

6.2b Practice

For use after Lesson 6.2b

Find the radius of the circle.

1.

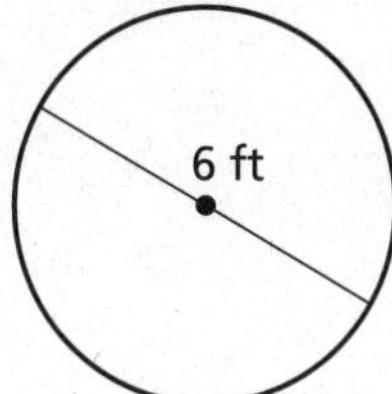

2.

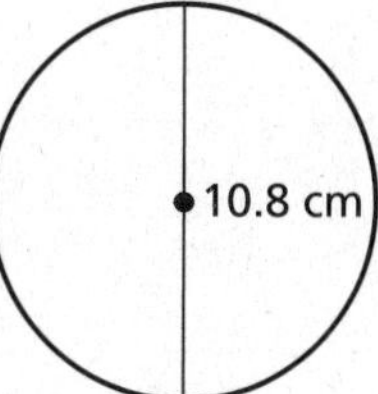

3.

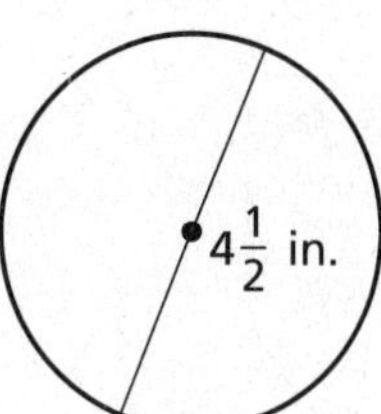

Find the diameter of the circle.

4.

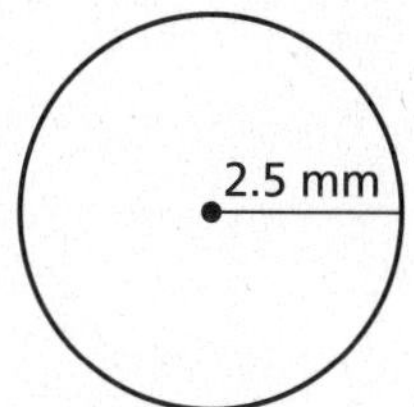

5.

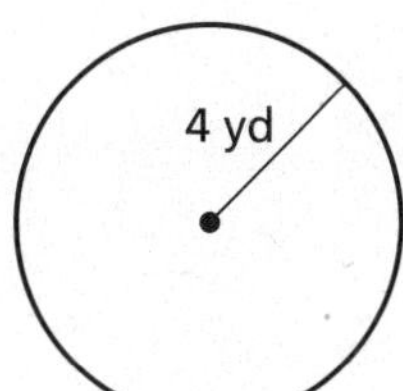

6.

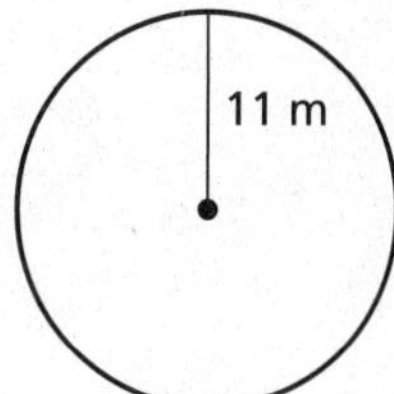

Name ______________________________ Date __________

6.2b Practice (continued)

Find the circumference of the circle. Use 3.14 or $\frac{22}{7}$ for π.

7.

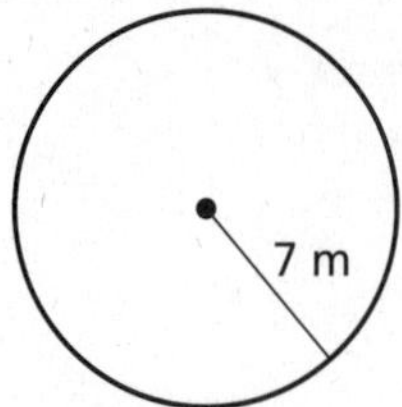

8.

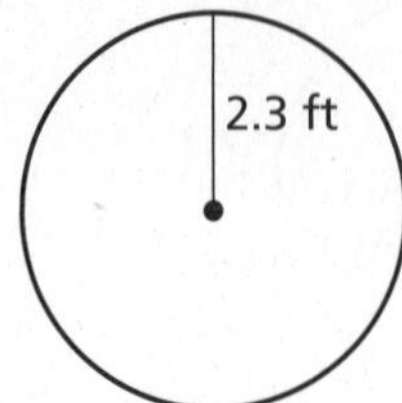

9.

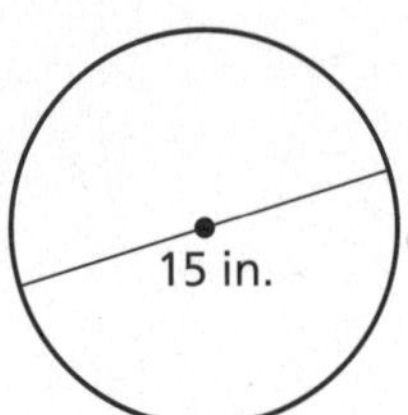

Find the area of the circle. Use 3.14 or $\frac{22}{7}$ for π.

10.

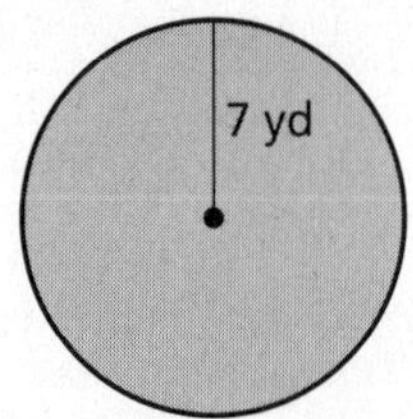

11.

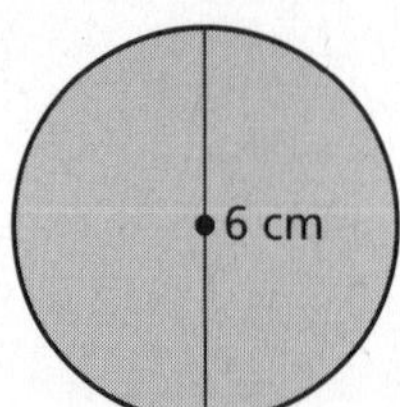

12.

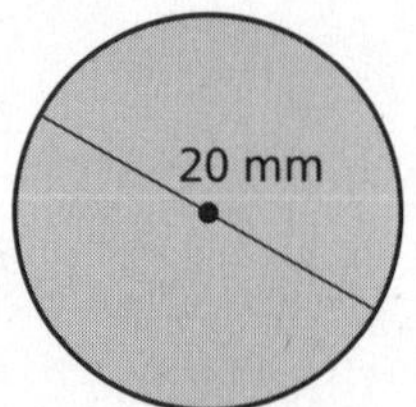

13. The center of a circular garden is at the end of a deck as shown in the diagram. How much area do you have to plant flowers? Explain how you found your answer.

Name____ Date__________

6.3 Surface Areas of Cylinders

For use with Activity 6.3

Essential Question How can you find the surface area of a cylinder?

1 ACTIVITY: Finding Area

Work with a partner. Use a cardboard cylinder.

- **Talk about how you can find the area of the outside of the roll.**
- **Use a ruler to estimate the area of the outside of the roll.**
- **Cut the roll and press it out flat. Then find the area of the flattened cardboard. How close is your estimate to the actual area?**

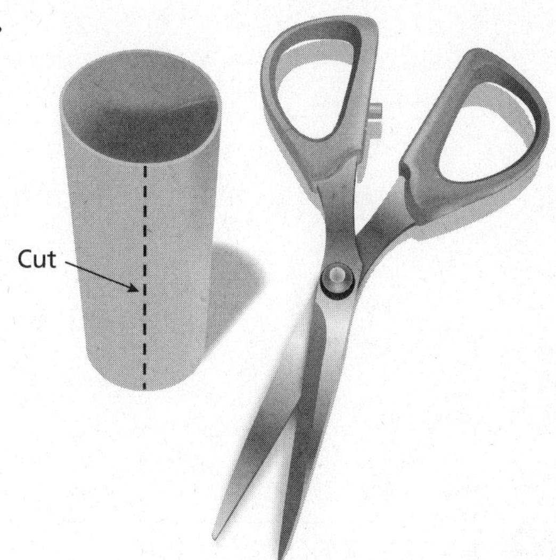

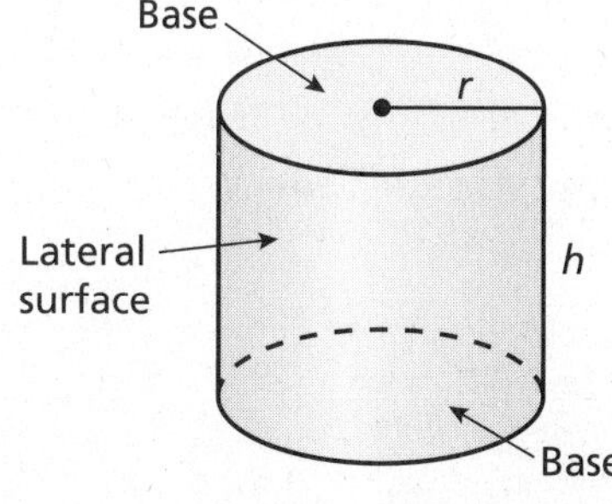

The surface area of a cylinder is the sum of the areas of the bases and the lateral surface.

2 ACTIVITY: Finding Surface Area

Work with a partner.

- **Trace the top and bottom of a can on paper. Cut out the two shapes.**
- **Cut out a long paper rectangle. Make the width the same as the height of the can. Wrap the rectangle around the can. Cut off the excess paper so the edges just meet.**
- **Make a net for the can. Name the shapes in the net.**

- **How are the dimensions of the rectangle related to the dimensions of the can?**

- **Explain how to use the net to find the surface area of the can.**

3 ACTIVITY: Estimation

Work with a partner. From memory, estimate the dimensions of the real-life items in parts (a)–(d) in inches. Then use the dimensions to estimate the surface area of each item in square inches.

a.

b.

Name ____ Date __________

c.

d.

What Is Your Answer?

4. **IN YOUR OWN WORDS** How can you find the surface area of a cylinder? Give an example with your description. Include a drawing of the cylinder.

5. To eight decimal places, $\pi \approx 3.14159265$. Which of the following is closest to π?

a. 3.14 **b.** $\frac{22}{7}$ **c.** $\frac{355}{113}$

"To approximate the irrational number $\pi \approx 3.141593$, I simply remember 1, 1, 3, 3, 5, 5."

"Then I compute the rational number $\frac{355}{113} \approx 3.141593$."

Name ______________________________ Date __________

6.3 Practice

For use after Lesson 6.3

Find the surface area of the cylinder. Round your answer to the nearest tenth.

1.

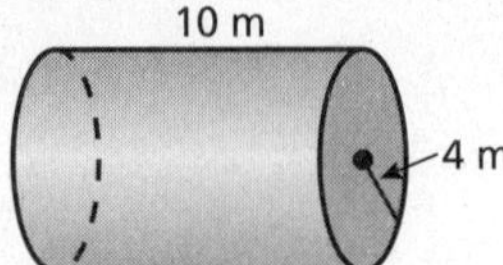

2.

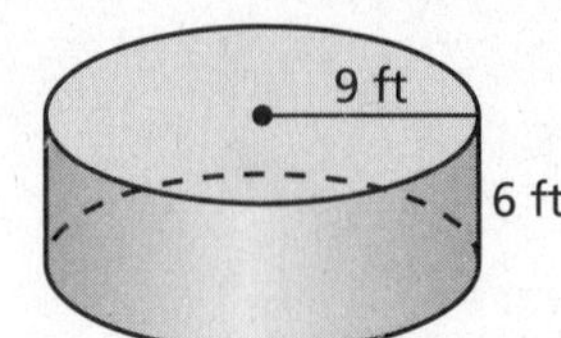

Find the lateral surface area of the cylinder. Round your answer to the nearest tenth.

3.

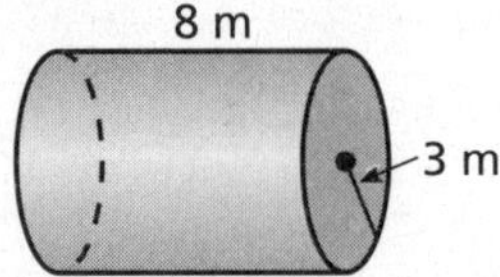

4.

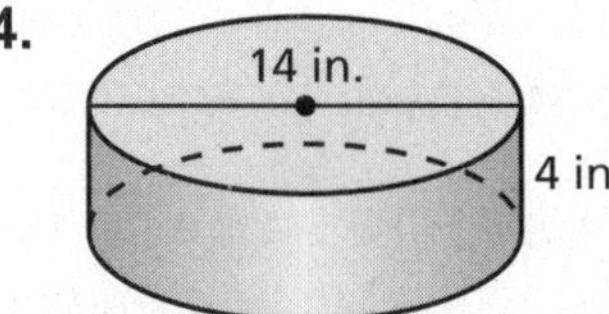

5. How much paper is used in the label for the can of cat food? Round your answer to the nearest whole number.

6. The circumference of a base of a cylinder is 33.3 inches and the height of the cylinder is 7.7 inches. What is the surface area of the cylinder?

Name____ Date__________

6.4 Surface Areas of Pyramids

For use with Activity 6.4

Essential Question How can you find the surface area of a pyramid?

Even though many well-known **pyramids** have square bases, the base of a pyramid can be any polygon.

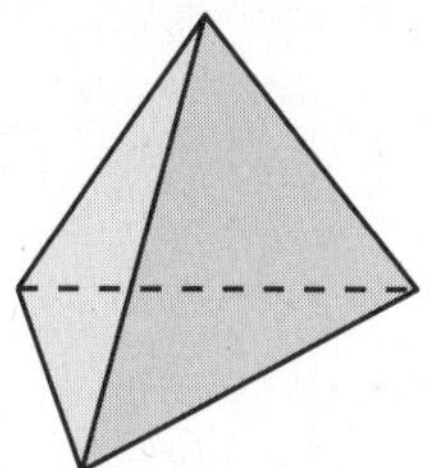

Triangular Base

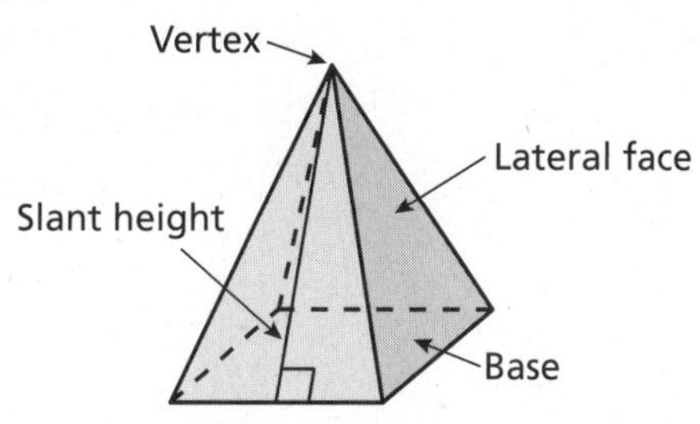

Square Base

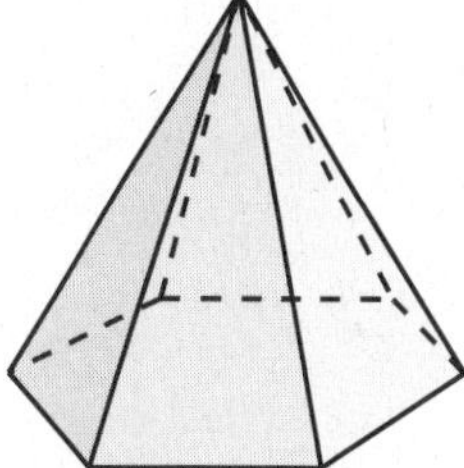

Hexagonal Base

1 ACTIVITY: Making a Scale Model

Work with a partner. Each pyramid has a square base.

- **Draw a net for a scale model of one of the pyramids. Describe your scale.**
- **Cut out the net and fold it to form a pyramid.**
- **Find the lateral surface area of the real-life pyramid.**

a. Cheops Pyramid in Egypt
Side = 230 m, Slant height ≈ 186 m

b. Muttart Conservatory in Edmonton
Side = 26 m, Slant height ≈ 27 m

c. Louvre Pyramid in Paris
Side = 35 m, Slant height ≈ 28 m

d. Pyramid of Caius Cestius in Rome
Side = 22 m, Slant height ≈ 29 m

Name ______________________ Date __________

6.4 Surface Areas of Pyramids (continued)

2 ACTIVITY: Estimation

Work with a partner. There are many different types of gemstone cuts. Here is one called a brilliant cut.

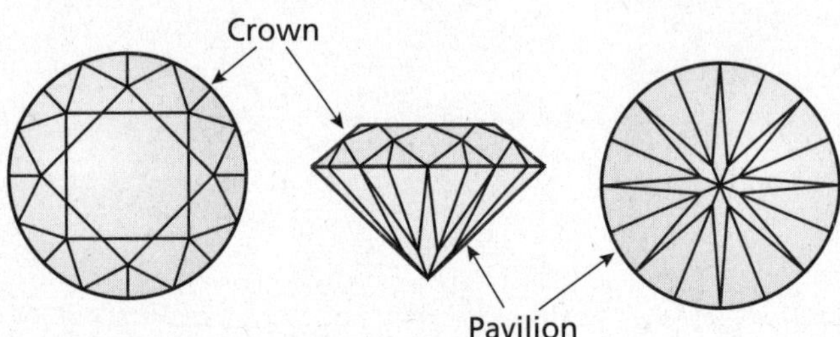

The size and shape of the pavilion can be approximated by an octagonal pyramid.

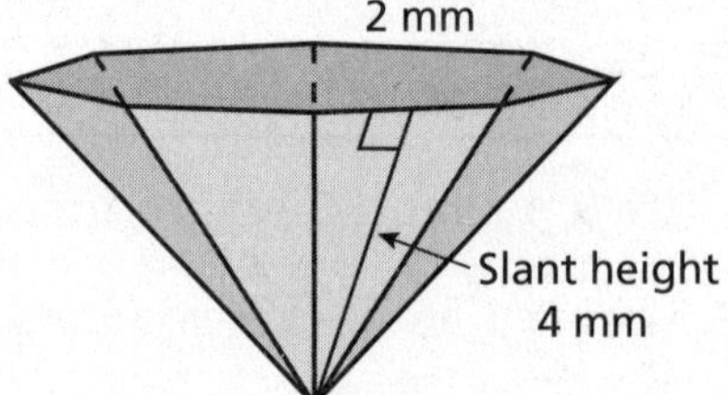

a. What does octagonal mean?

b. Draw a net for the pyramid.

c. Find the lateral surface area of the pyramid.

Name______________________________ Date__________

6.4 Surface Areas of Pyramids (continued)

3 ACTIVITY: Building a Skylight

Work with a partner. The skylight has 12 triangular pieces of glass. Each piece has a base of 1 foot and a slant height of 3 feet.

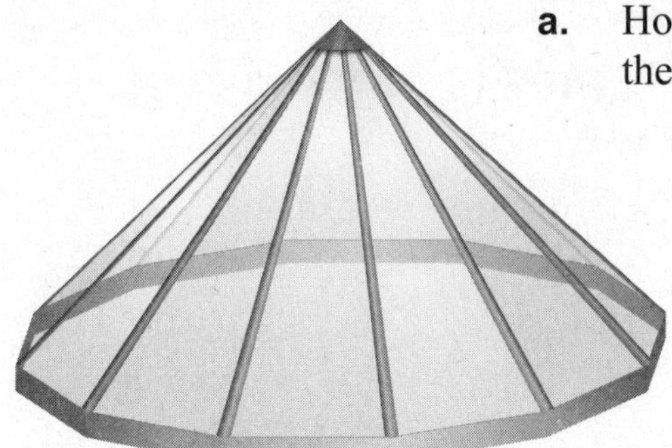

a. How much glass will you need to make the skylight?

b. Can you cut the 12 glass triangles from a sheet of glass that is 4 feet by 8 feet? If so, draw a diagram showing how this can be done.

What Is Your Answer?

4. IN YOUR OWN WORDS How can you find the surface area of a pyramid? Draw a diagram with your explanation.

Name ______________________________ Date __________

6.4 Practice
For use after Lesson 6.4

Find the surface area of the regular pyramid.

1.

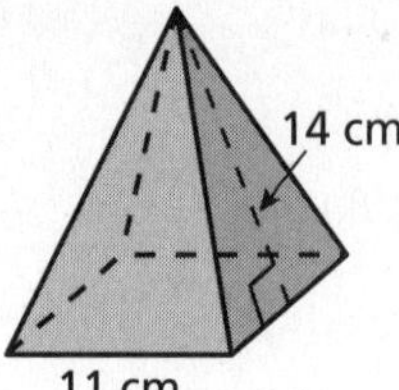

2.

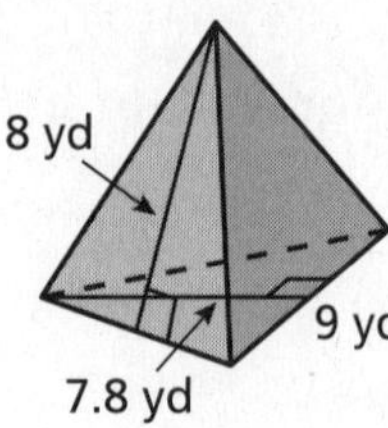

3.

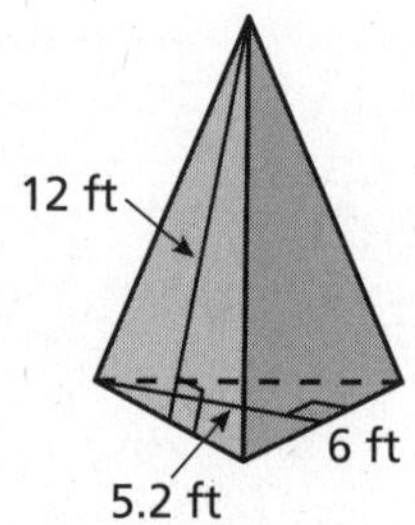

4.

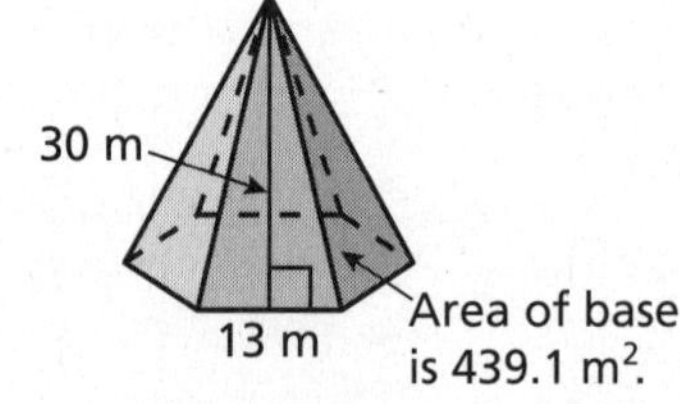

5. The surface area of a triangular pyramid is 305 square inches. The area of the base is 35 square inches. Each face has a base of 9 inches. What is the slant height?

6. A candle shaped like a square pyramid needs wrapped in paper. How much paper is needed to cover a candle that has a base side of 6 centimeters and a slant height of 10 centimeters?

Name____ Date__________

6.5 Surface Areas of Cones

For use with Activity 6.5

Essential Question How can you find the surface area of a cone?

A cone is a solid with one circular base and one vertex.

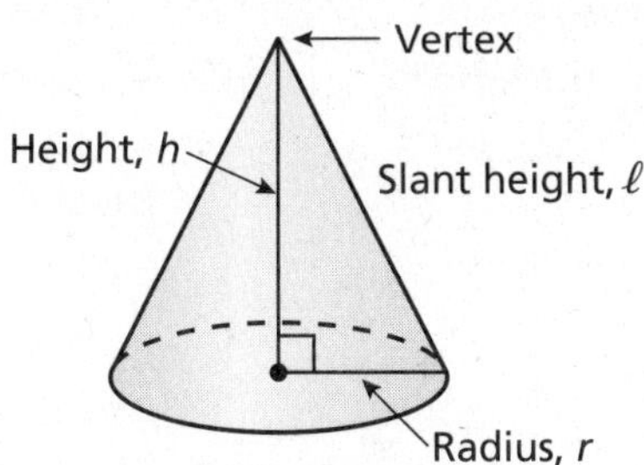

1 ACTIVITY: Finding the Surface Area of a Cone

Work with a partner.

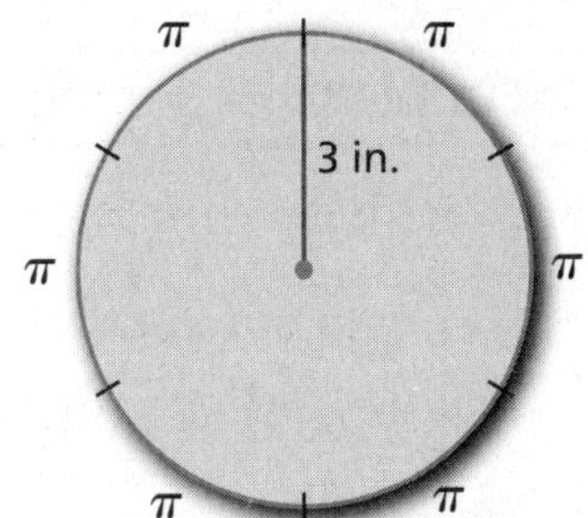

- **Draw a circle with a radius of 3 inches.***
- **Mark the circumference of the circle into six equal parts.**
- **The circumference of the circle is $2(\pi)(3) = 6\pi$. So each of the six parts on the circle has a length of π. Label each part.**
- **Cut one part as shown. Then, make a cone.**

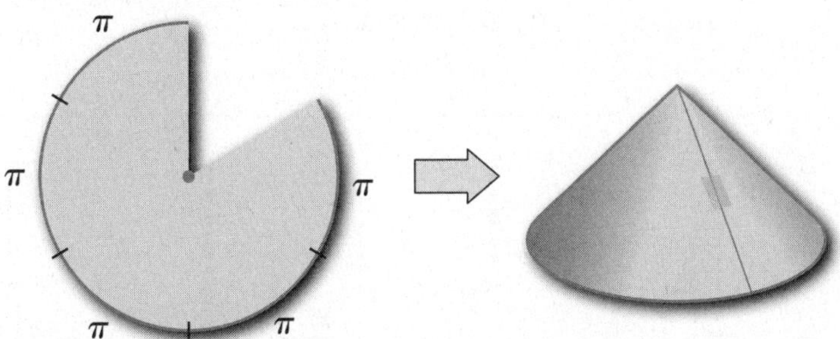

a. The base of the cone should be a circle. Explain why the circumference of the base is 5π.

b. Find the radius of the base.

*Cut-outs are available in the back of the Record and Practice Journal.

Name ______________________________ Date __________

6.5 Surface Areas of Cones (continued)

c. What is the area of the original circle?

d. What is the area of the circle with one part missing?

e. Describe the surface area of the cone. Use your description to find the surface area, including the base.

2 ACTIVITY: Experimenting with Surface Area

Work with a partner.

- **Cut out another part from the circle in Activity 1 and make a cone.**
- **Find the radius of the base and the surface area of the cone.**
- **Record your results in the table.**
- **Repeat this three times.**
- **Describe the pattern.**

Shape					
Radius of Base					
Slant Height					
Surface Area					

Name____ Date__________

3 ACTIVITY: Writing a Story

Write a story that uses real-life cones. Include a diagram and label the dimensions. In your story, explain why you would want to know the surface area of the cone. Then estimate the surface area.

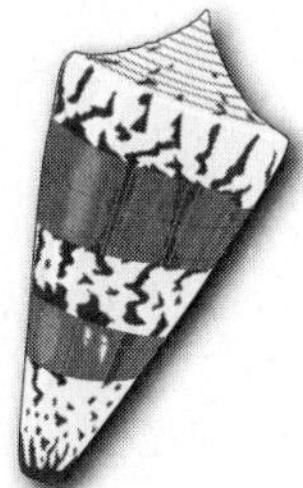

What Is Your Answer?

4. **IN YOUR OWN WORDS** How can you find the surface area of a cone? Draw a diagram with your explanation.

Name ______________________________ Date __________

6.5 Practice
For use after Lesson 6.5

Find the surface area of the cone. Round your answer to the nearest tenth.

1. 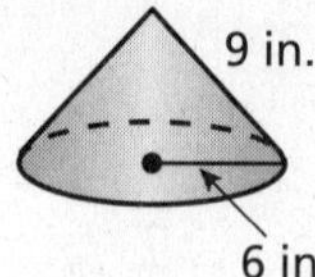

2. 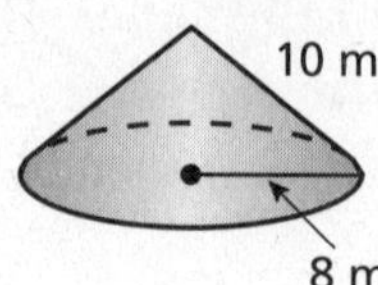

Find the slant height ℓ of the cone.

3. $S = 112\pi \text{ ft}^2$

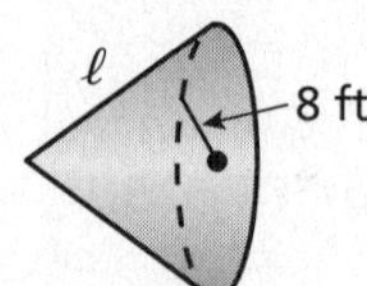

4. $S = 108\pi \text{ in.}^2$

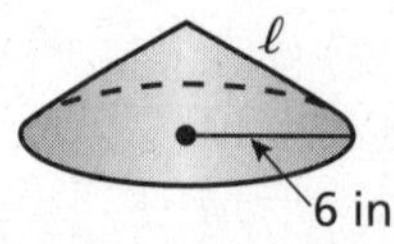

5. A cone-shaped container to hold balloons has a diameter of 2 inches and a slant height of 4 inches. How much paper is needed to wrap the container? Round your answer to the nearest tenth.

6. For a children's play, you design a hat shaped like a cone for a princess. The hat has a radius of 4 inches and a slant height of 2 feet. How much material do you need to make the hat? Round your answer to the nearest tenth.

Name______________________________ Date__________

6.6 Surface Areas of Composite Solids

For use with Activity 6.6

Essential Question How can you find the surface area of a composite solid?

1 ACTIVITY: Finding a Surface Area

Work with a partner. You are manufacturing scale models of old houses.

a. Name the four basic solids in this composite figure.

b. Determine a strategy for finding the surface area of this model. Would you use a scale drawing? Would you use a net? Explain.

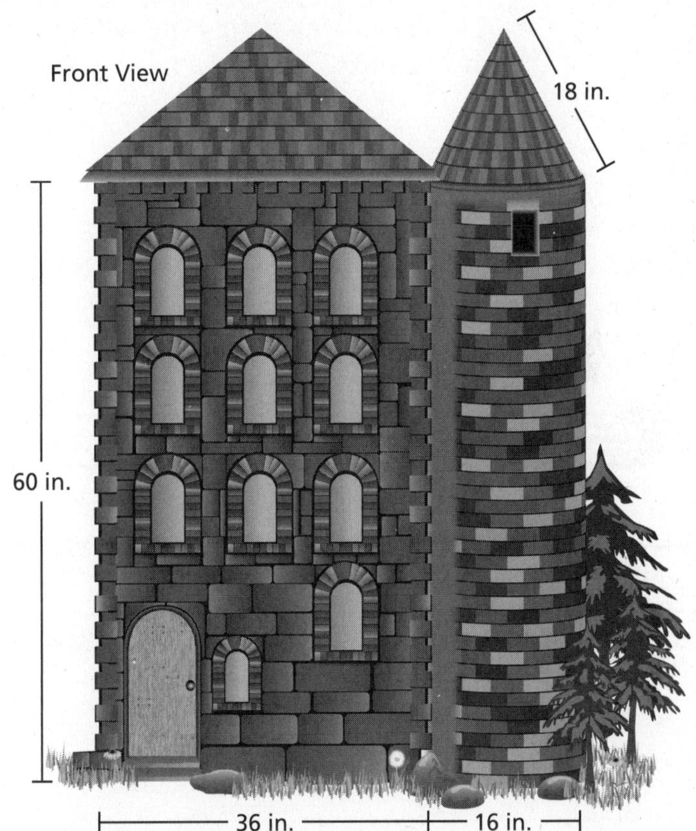

Many castles have cylindrical towers with conical roofs. These are called turrets.

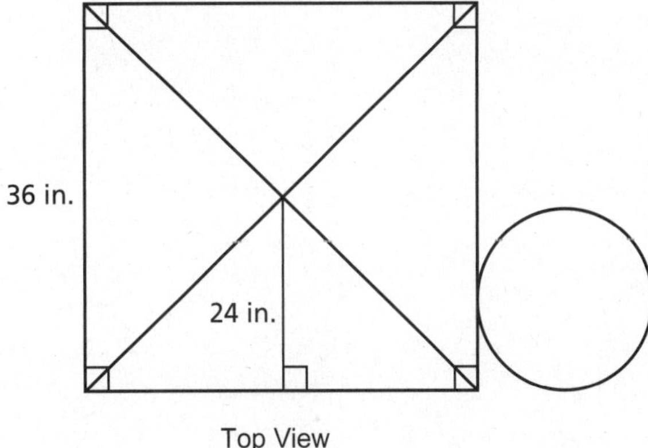

Top View

Name ______________________________ Date __________

6.6 Surface Areas of Composite Solids (continued)

2 ACTIVITY: Finding and Using a Pattern

Work with a partner.

- **Find the surface area of each figure.**
- **Use a table to organize your results.**
- **Describe the pattern in the table.**
- **Use the pattern to find the surface area of the figure that has a base of 10 blocks.**

3 ACTIVITY: Finding and Using a Pattern

Work with a partner. You own a roofing company. Each building has the same base area. Which roof would be cheapest? Which would be the most expensive? Explain your reasoning.

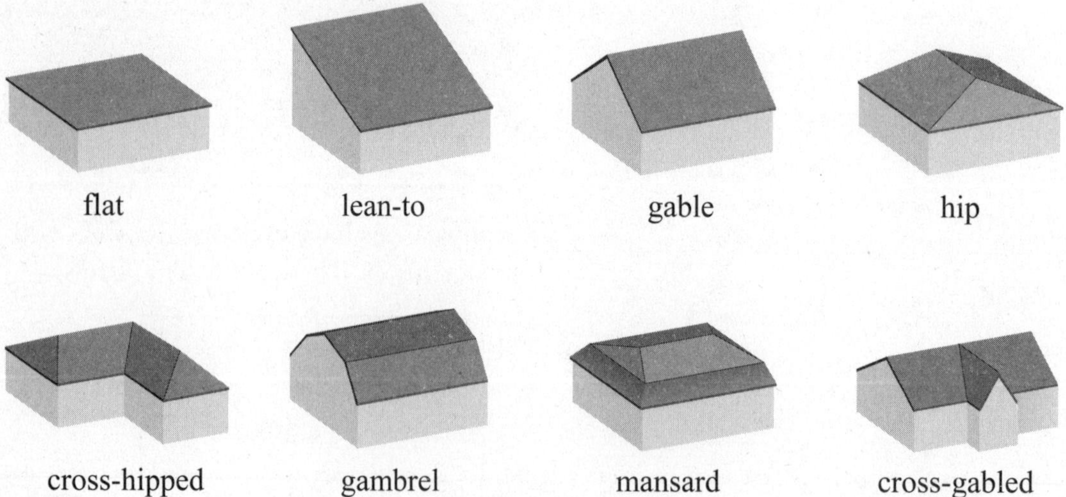

What Is Your Answer?

4. **IN YOUR OWN WORDS** How can you find the surface area of a composite solid?

5. Design a building that has a turret and also has a mansard roof. Find the surface area of the roof.

Name ______________________________ Date __________

6.6 Practice

For use after Lesson 6.6

Identify the solids that form the composite solid. Then find the surface area. Round your answer to the nearest tenth.

1.

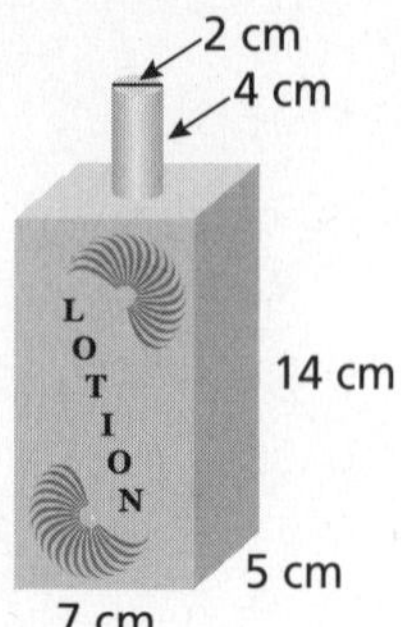

2.

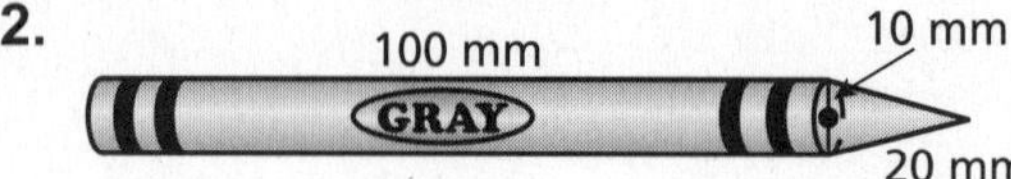

3.

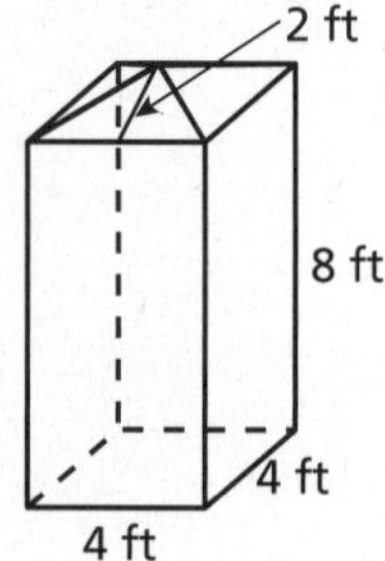

4.

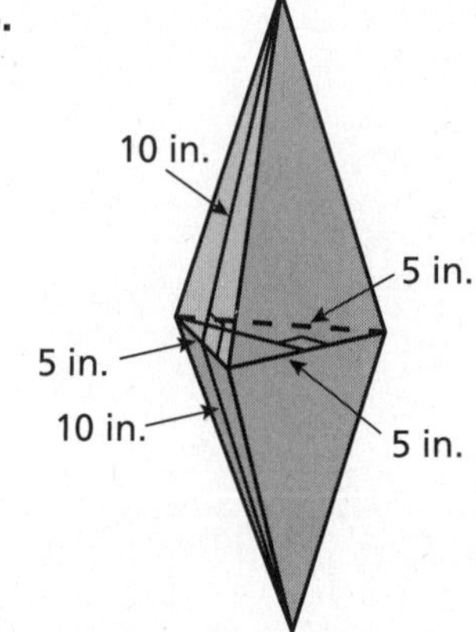

5. The block is made up of a cylinder and a prism. What is the surface area of the block? Round your answer to the nearest tenth.

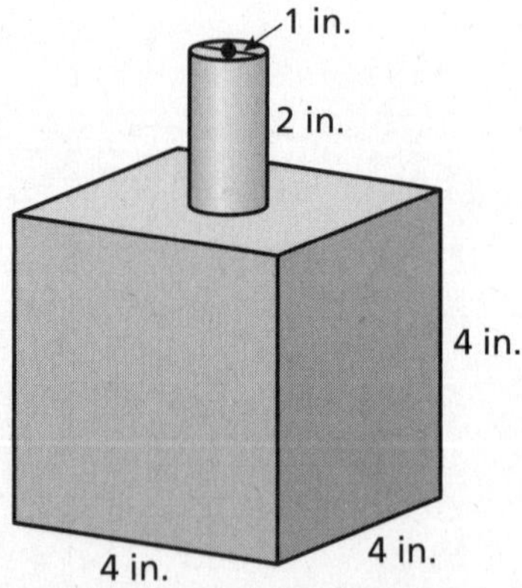

Name______________________________ Date__________

Chapter 7 Fair Game Review

Tell whether the figures are similar. Explain your reasoning.

1.

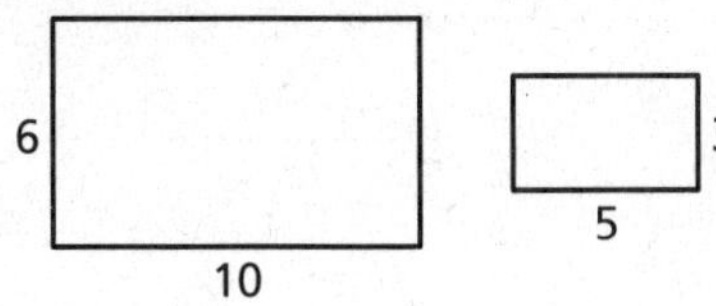

2.

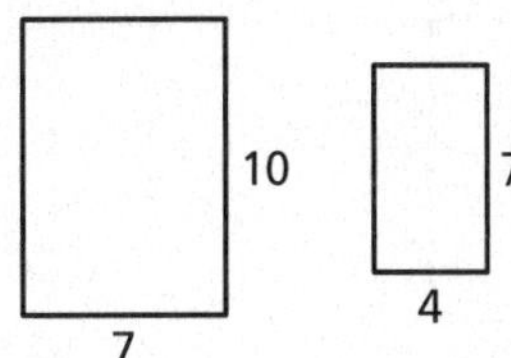

3.

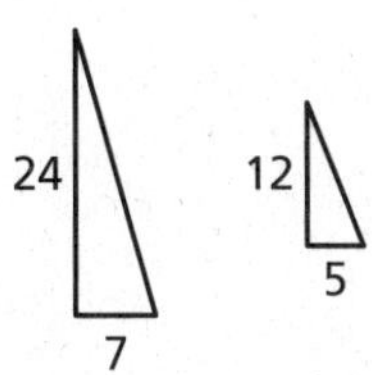

4.

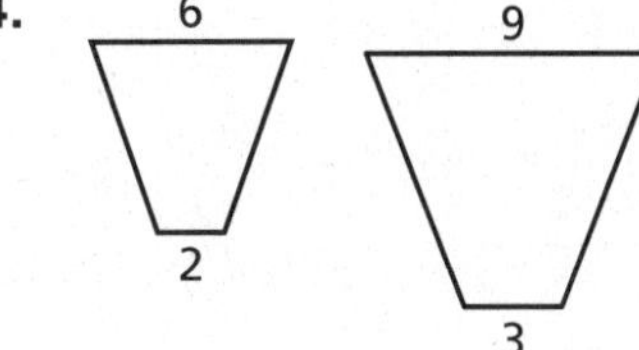

5.

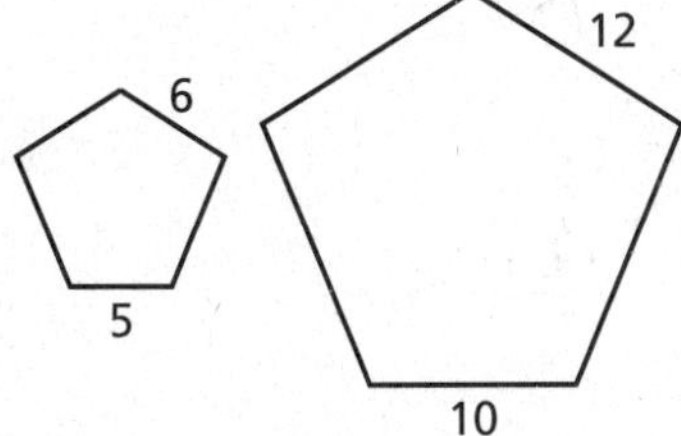

6.

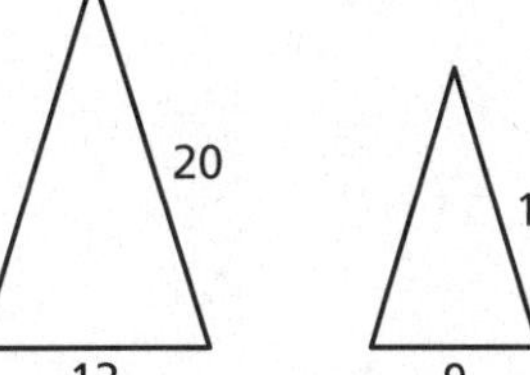

7. Two mirrors are hung on a wall. The large mirror has a length of 3 feet and width of 2 feet. The smaller mirror has a length of 1 foot and width of 6 inches. Are the figures similar? Explain your reasoning.

Name ____ Date __________

Chapter 7 Fair Game Review (continued)

The figures are similar. Find the value of *x*.

8.

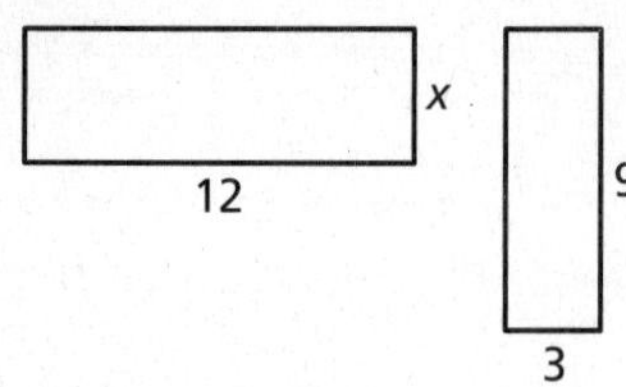

9.

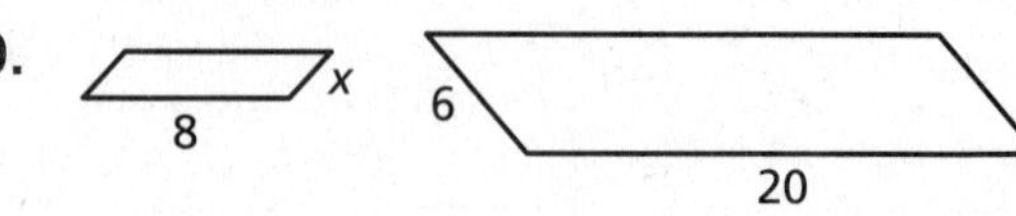

10.

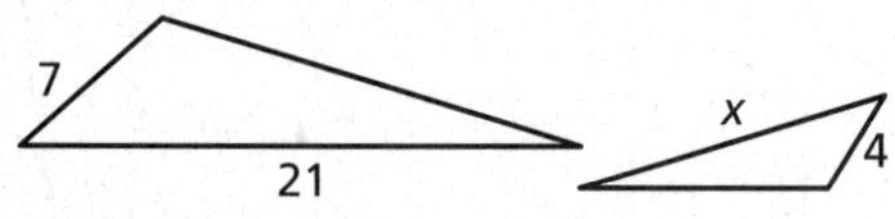

11.

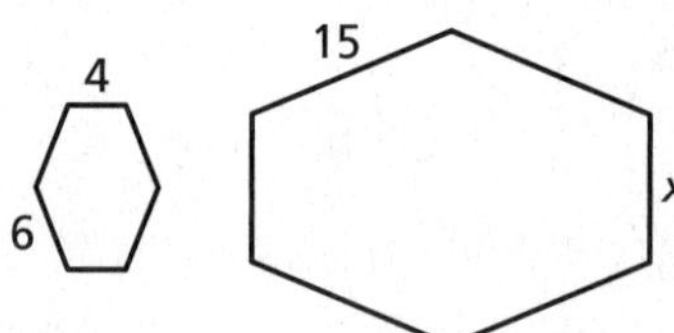

12.

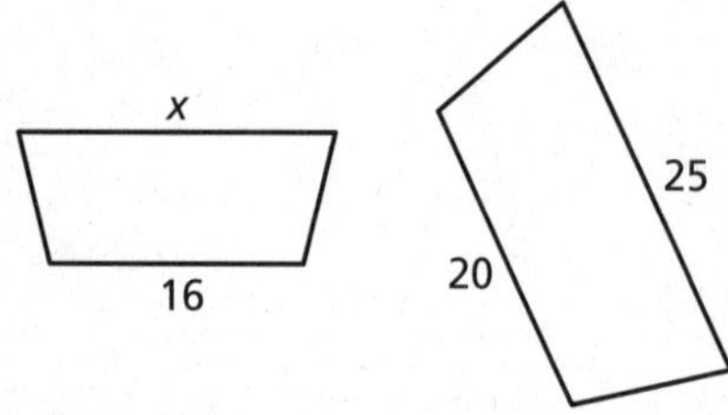

13.

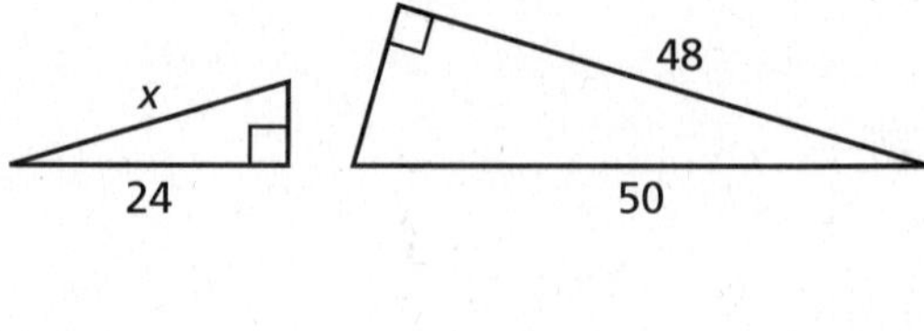

14. The front door of your house is similar to the front door of a dollhouse. The door to your house is 8 feet long and 3.5 feet wide. The dollhouse door is 6 inches long. How wide is the dollhouse door?

Name____ Date__________

7.1 Volumes of Prisms

For use with Activity 7.1

Essential Question How can you find the volume of a prism?

1 ACTIVITY: Pearls in a Treasure Chest

Work with a partner. A treasure chest is filled with valuable pearls. Each pearl is about 1 centimeter in diameter and is worth about $80.

Use the diagrams below to describe two ways that you can estimate the number of pearls in the treasure chest.

a.

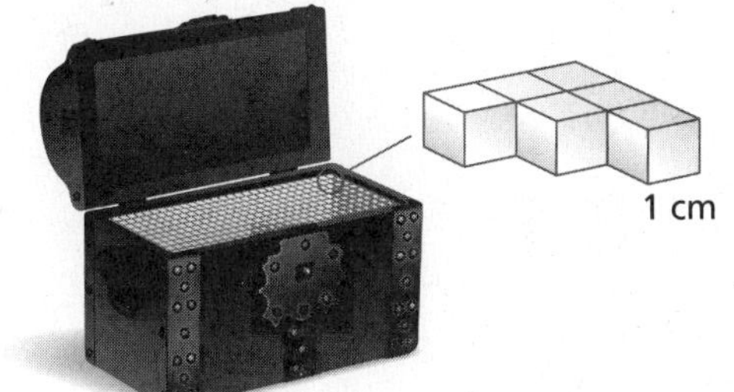

b.

c. Use the method in part (a) to estimate the value of the pearls in the chest.

7.1 Volumes of Prisms (continued)

2 ACTIVITY: Finding a Formula for Volume

Work with a partner. You know that the formula for the volume of a rectangular prism is $V = \ell wh$.

a. Find a new formula that gives the volume in terms of the area of the base B and the height h.

b. Use both formulas to find the volume of each prism. Do both formulas give you the same volumes?

3 ACTIVITY: Finding a Formula for Volume

Work with a partner. Use the concept in Activity 2 to find a formula that gives the volume of any prism.

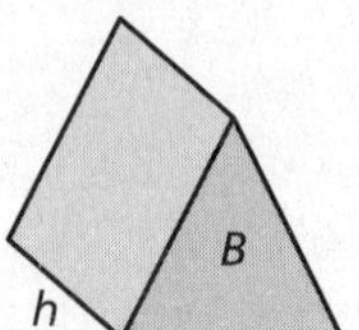

Triangular Prism

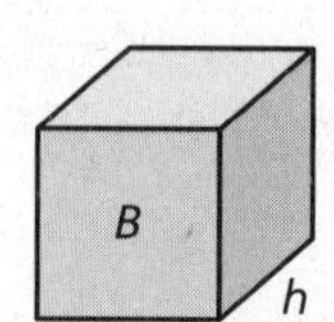

Rectangular Prism

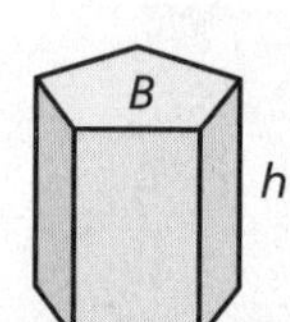

Pentagonal Prism

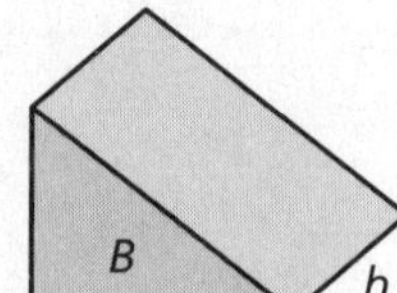

Triangular Prism

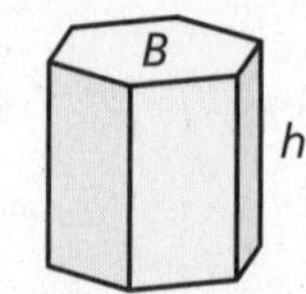

Hexagonal Prism

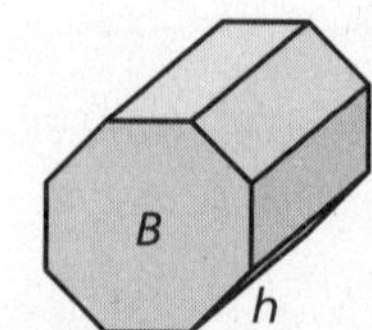

Octagonal Prism

Name______________________________ Date__________

7.1 Volumes of Prisms (continued)

4 ACTIVITY: Using a Formula

Work with a partner. A ream of paper has 500 sheets.

a. Does a single sheet of paper have a volume? Why or why not?

b. If so, explain how you can find the volume of a single piece of paper.

What Is Your Answer?

5. IN YOUR OWN WORDS How can you find the volume of a prism?

6. Draw a prism that has a trapezoid as its base. Use your formula to find the volume of the prism.

Name ______________________________ Date __________

7.1 Practice

For use after Lesson 7.1

Find the volume of the prism.

1.

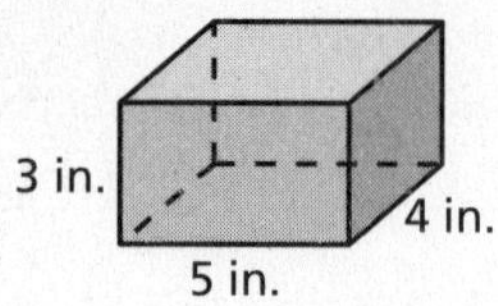

2.

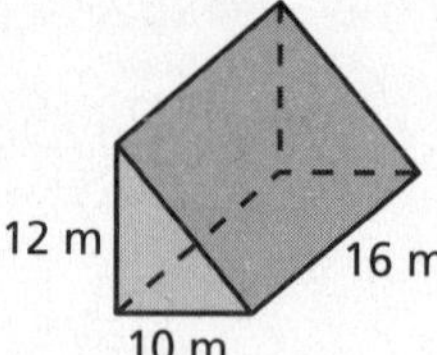

3.

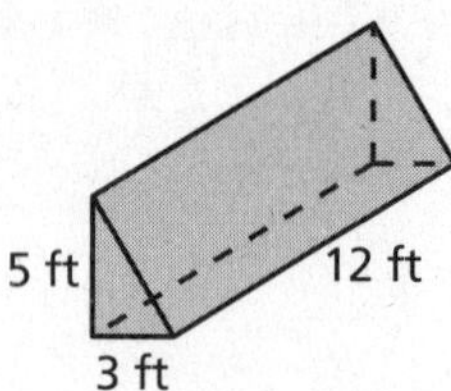

4.

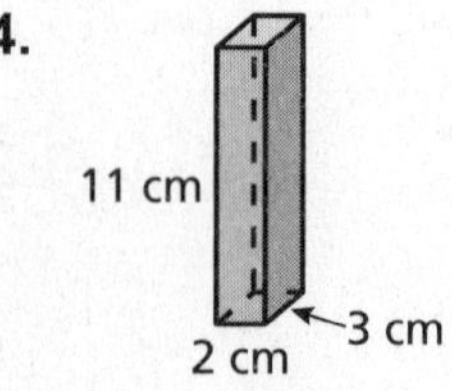

5.

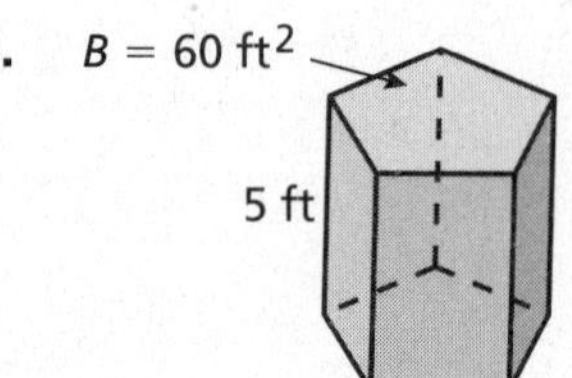

6. $B = 80\ m^2$

11 m

7. Each box is shaped like a rectangular prism. Which has more storage space? Explain.

Box 1

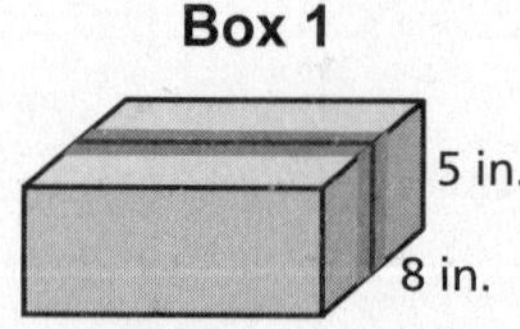

Box 2

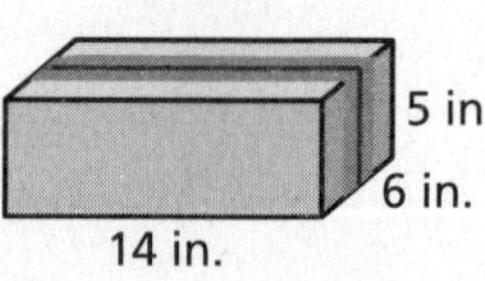

Name____ Date__________

7.2 Volumes of Cylinders

For use with Activity 7.2

Essential Question How can you find the volume of a cylinder?

1 ACTIVITY: Finding a Formula Experimentally

Work with a partner.

a. Find the area of the face of a coin.

b. Find the volume of a stack of a dozen coins.

c. Generalize your results to find the volume of a cylinder.

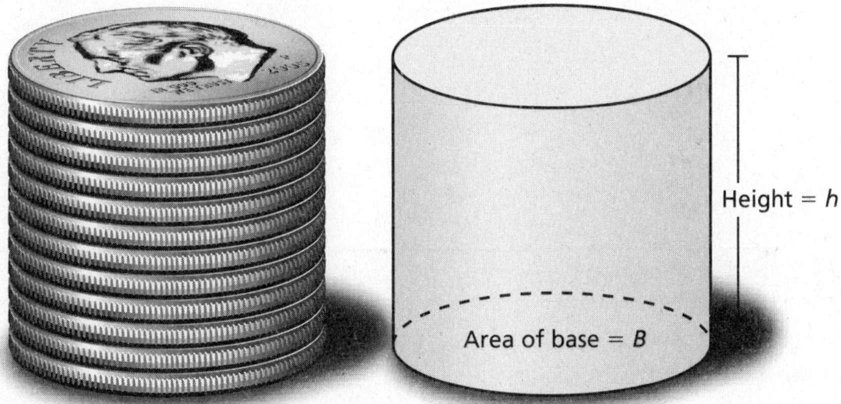

2 ACTIVITY: Making a Business Plan

Work with a partner. You are planning to make and sell 3 different sizes of cylindrical candles. You buy 1 cubic foot of candle wax for $20 to make 8 candles of each size.

a. Design the candles. What are the dimensions of each size?

b. You want to make a profit of $100. Decide on a price for each size.

c. Did you set the prices so that they are proportional to the volume of each size of candle? Why or why not?

3 ACTIVITY: Science Experiment

Work with a partner. Use the diagram to describe how you can find the volume of a small object.

Name_______________________________ Date__________

7.2 Volumes of Cylinders (continued)

4 ACTIVITY: Comparing Cylinders

Work with a partner.

a. Just by looking at two cylinders, which one do you think has the greater volume? Explain your reasoning.

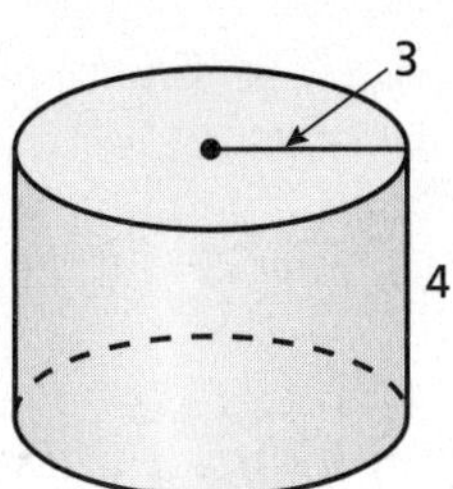

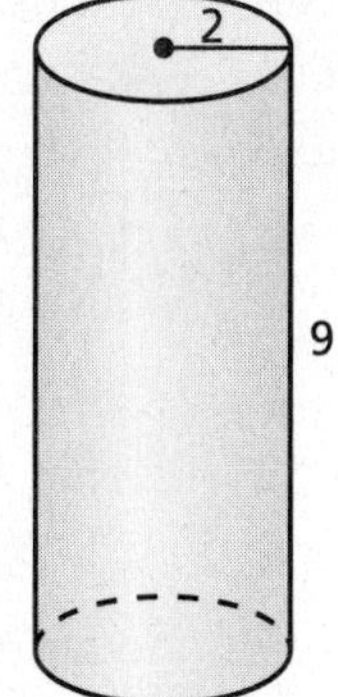

b. Find the volume of each cylinder. Was your prediction in part (a) correct? Explain your reasoning.

What Is Your Answer?

5. IN YOUR OWN WORDS How can you find the volume of a cylinder?

6. Compare your formula for the volume of a cylinder with the formula for the volume of a prism. How are they the same?

Name ______________________________ Date __________

7.2 Practice
For use after Lesson 7.2

Find the volume of the cylinder. Round your answer to the nearest tenth.

1. 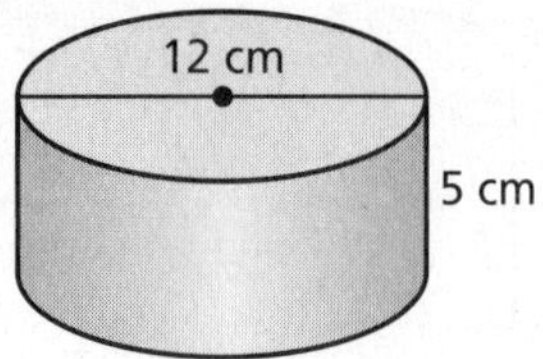

2. 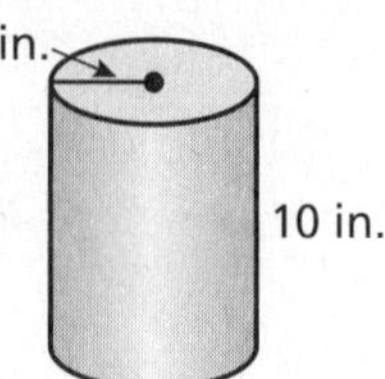

Find the height of the cylinder. Round your answer to the nearest whole number.

3. Volume = 84 in.^{3}

4. Volume = 650 cm^3

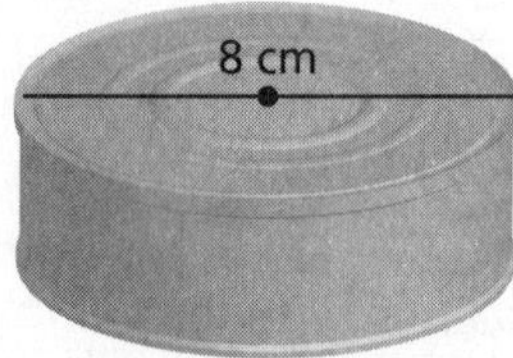

5. What happens to the volume of a cylinder if you double the radius?

6. To make orange juice, the directions call for a can of orange juice concentrate to be mixed with three cans of water. What is the volume of orange juice that you make?

Name____ Date__________

7.3 Volumes of Pyramids

For use with Activity 7.3

Essential Question How can you find the volume of a pyramid?

1 ACTIVITY: Finding a Formula Experimentally

Work with a partner.

- **Draw the two nets on cardboard and cut them out.***

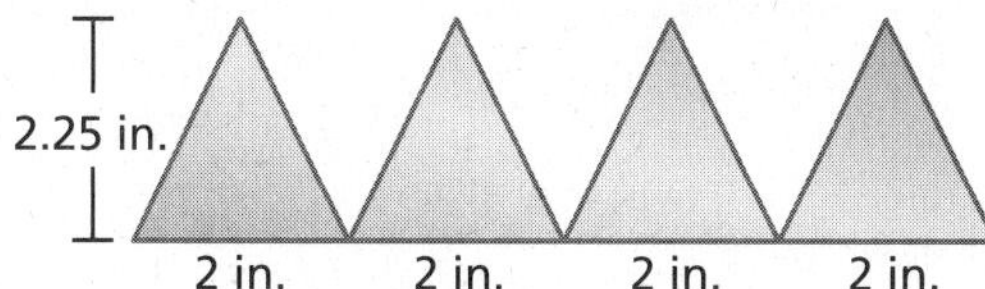

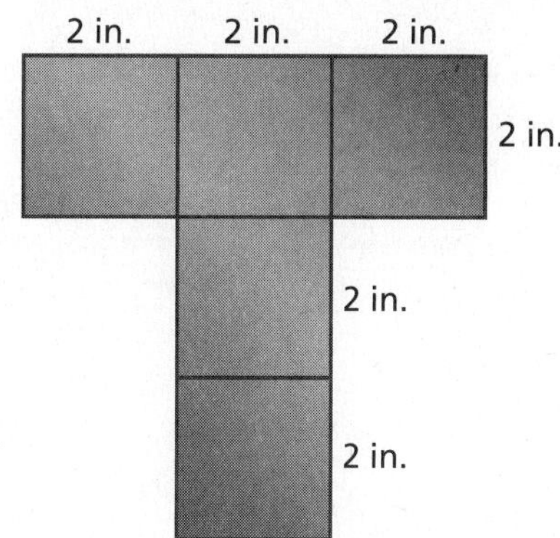

- **Fold and tape the nets to form an open square box and an open pyramid.**
- **Both figures should have the same size square base and the same height.**
- **Fill the pyramid with pebbles. Then pour the pebbles into the box. Repeat this until the box is full. How many pyramids does it take to fill the box?**

- **Use your result to find a formula for the volume of a pyramid.**

2 ACTIVITY: Comparing Volumes

Work with a partner. You are an archeologist studying two ancient pyramids. What factors would affect how long it took to build each pyramid? Given similar conditions, which pyramid took longer to build? Explain your reasoning.

Cholula Pyramid in Mexico
Height: about 217 ft
Base: about 1476 ft by 1476 ft

Cheops Pyramid in Egypt
Height: about 480 ft
Base: about 755 ft by 755 ft

*Cut-outs are available in the back of the Record and Practice Journal.

Name ______________________________ Date __________

3 ACTIVITY: Finding and Using a Pattern

Work with a partner.

- **Find the volumes of the pyramids.**

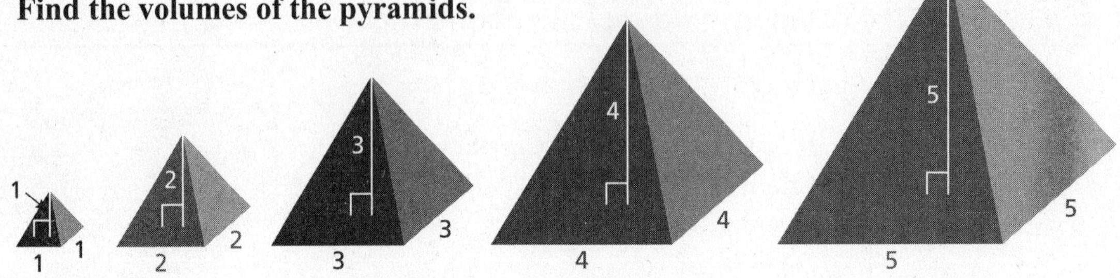

- **Organize your results in a table.**

- **Describe the pattern.**

- **Use your pattern to find the volume of a pyramid with a side length and height of 20.**

4 ACTIVITY: Breaking a Prism into Pyramids

Work with a partner. The rectangular prism can be cut to form three pyramids. Show that the sum of the volumes of the three pyramids is equal to the volume of the prism.

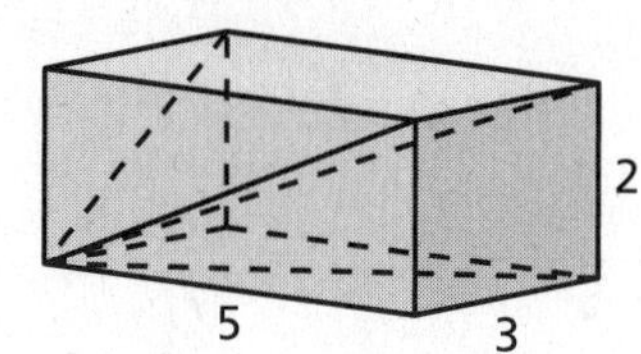

a. 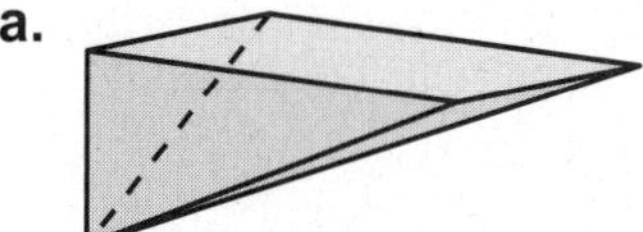

b. 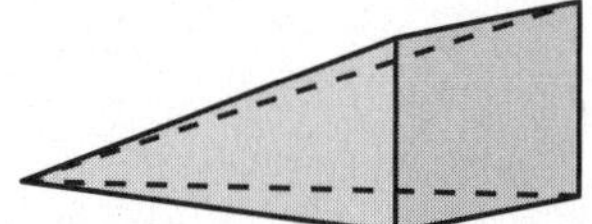

c. 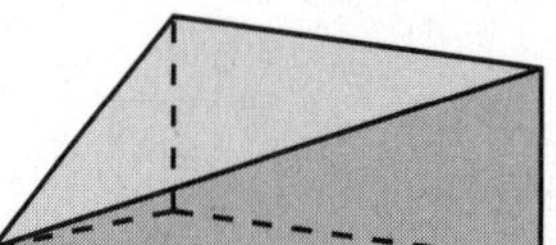

What Is Your Answer?

5. IN YOUR OWN WORDS How can you find the volume of a pyramid?

6. Write a general formula for the volume of a pyramid.

Name ______________________________ Date ________

7.3 Practice

For use after Lesson 7.3

Find the volume of the pyramid.

1.

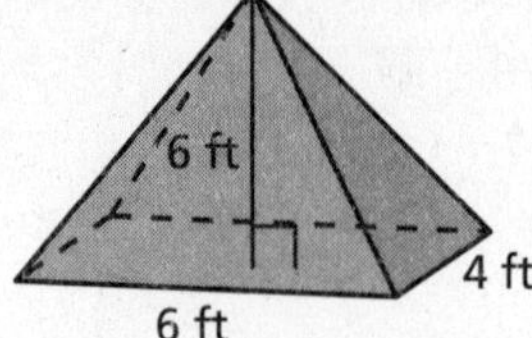

2.

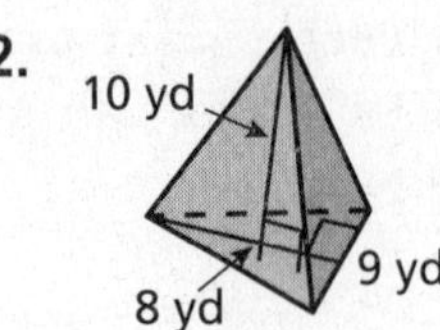

3.

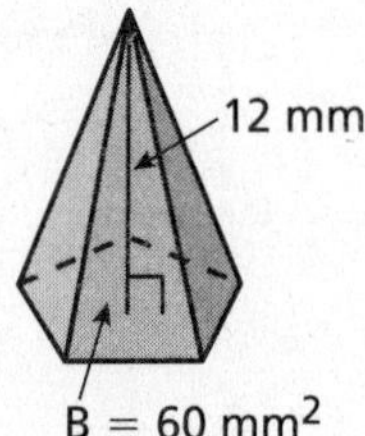

4.

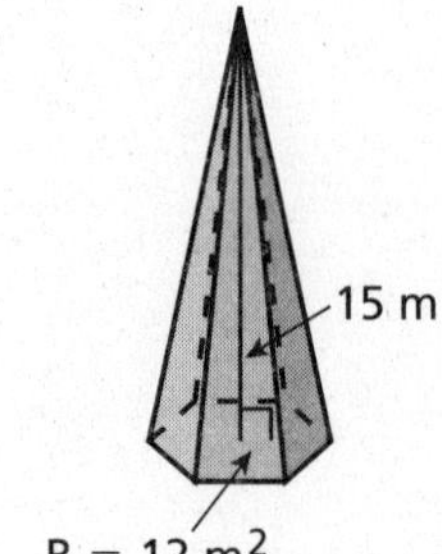

5. You create a simple tent in the shape of a pyramid. What is the volume of the tent?

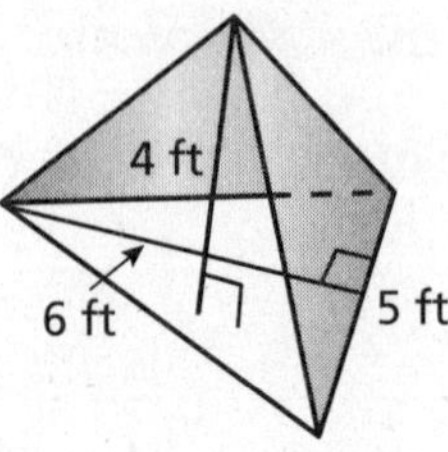

6. You work at a restaurant that has 20 tables. Each table has a set of salt and pepper shakers on it that are in the shape of square pyramids. How much salt do you need to fill all the salt shakers?

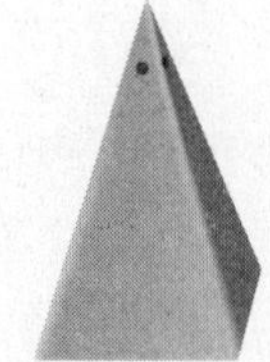
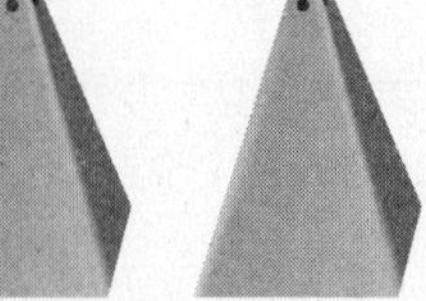

Name____ Date__________

7.4 Volumes of Cones
For use with Activity 7.4

Essential Question How can you remember the formulas for surface area and volume?

You discovered that the volume of a pyramid is one-third the volume of a prism that has the same base and same height. You can use a similar activity to discover that the volume of a cone is one-third the volume of a cylinder that has the same base and height.

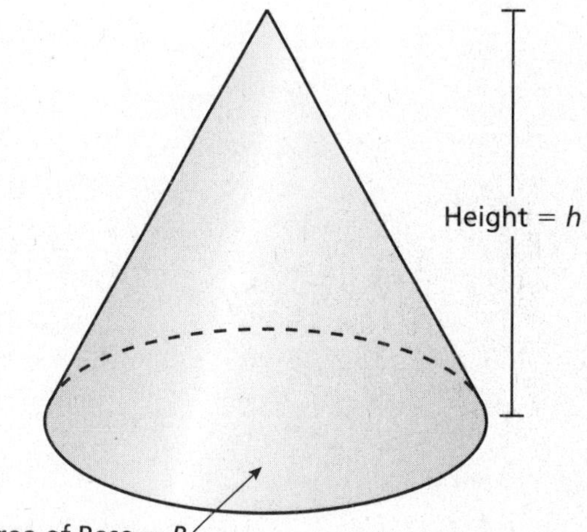

$$\text{Volume of a Cone} = \frac{1}{3}(\text{Area of Base}) \times (\text{Height})$$

1 ACTIVITY: Summarizing Volume Formulas

Work with a partner. You can remember the volume formulas for all of the solids shown with just two concepts.

Volumes of Prisms and Cylinders

$$\text{Volume} = (\text{Area of Base}) \times (\text{Height})$$

Volumes of Pyramids and Cones

$$\text{Volume} = \frac{1}{3}(\text{Volume of Prism or Cylinder with same base and height})$$

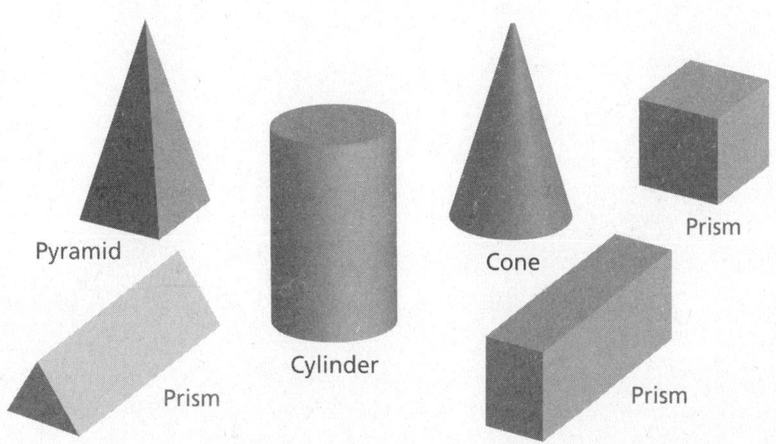

Make a list of all the formulas you need to remember to find the area of a base. Talk about strategies for remembering these formulas.

2 ACTIVITY: Volumes of Oblique Solids

Work with a partner. Think of a stack of paper. If you adjust the stack so that the sides are oblique (slanted), do you change the volume of the stack? If the volume of the stack does not change, then the formulas for volumes of right solids also apply to oblique solids.

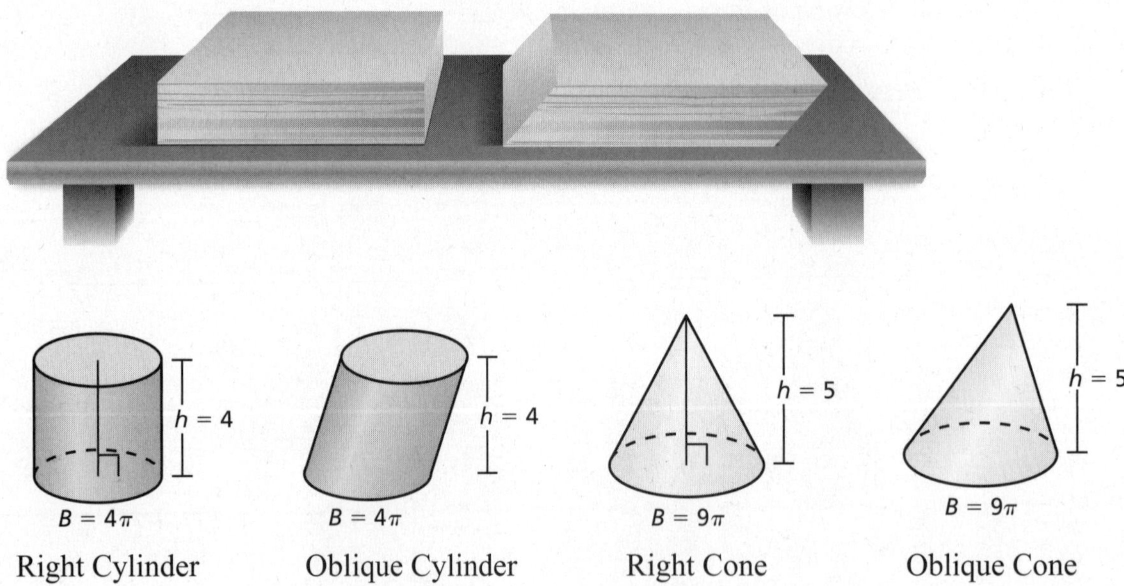

3 ACTIVITY: Summarizing Surface Area Formulas

Work with a partner. Make a list of the formulas for surface area that you studied in Chapter 6. Organize these formulas in a way similar to what you did in Activity 1.

Surface Area of a Right Prism =

Surface Area of a Right Pyramid =

Surface Area of a Right Cylinder =

Surface Area of a Right Cone =

What Is Your Answer?

4. **IN YOUR OWN WORDS** How can you remember the formulas for surface area and volume? Write all of the surface area and volume formulas on a summary sheet. Make the list short so that you do not have to memorize many formulas.

Name ______________________________ Date __________

7.4 Practice

For use after Lesson 7.4

Find the volume of the cone. Round your answer to the nearest tenth.

1.

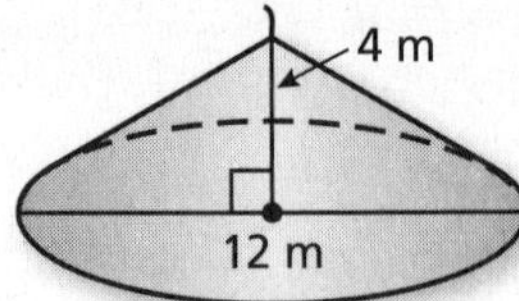

2.

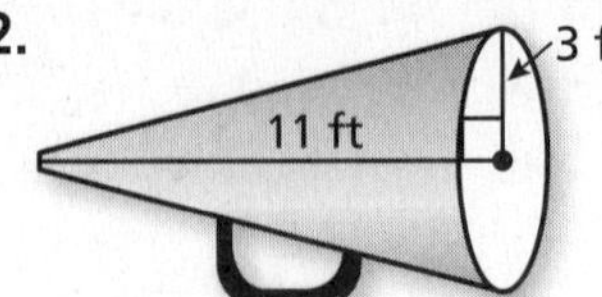

3.

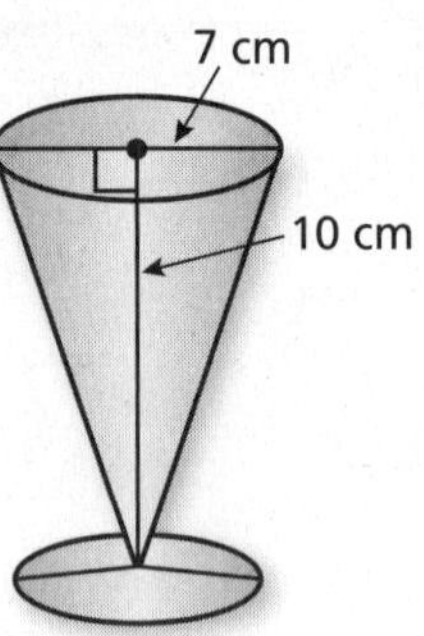

Find the height of the cone. Round your answer to the nearest tenth.

4. Volume $= 300\pi$ mm^3

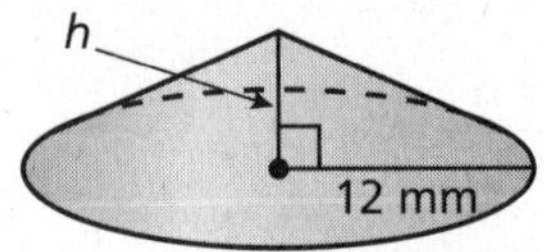

5. Volume $= 78.5$ cm^3

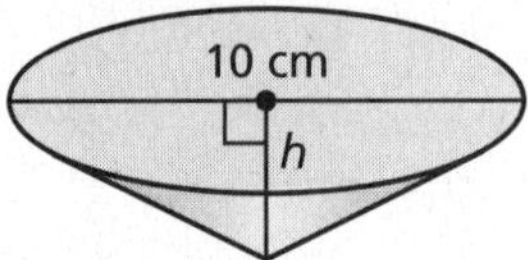

6. What is the volume of the catch and click cone?

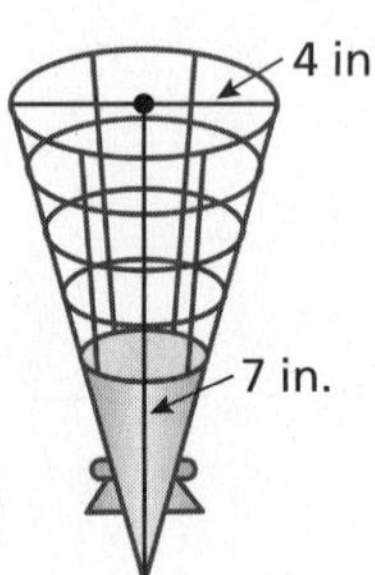

7. You have a candle mold that creates candles like the one shown. How many candles can you make with 170 cubic inches of candle wax?

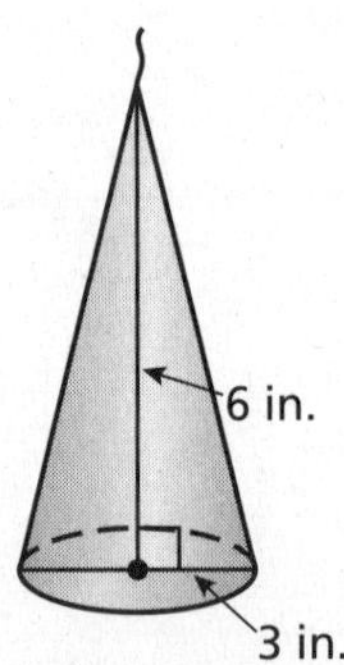

Name____ Date__________

7.5 Volumes of Composite Solids

For use with Activity 7.5

Essential Question How can you estimate the volume of a composite solid?

1 ACTIVITY: Estimating Volume

Work with a partner. You work for a toy company and need to estimate the volume of a Minifigure that will be modeled out of plastic.

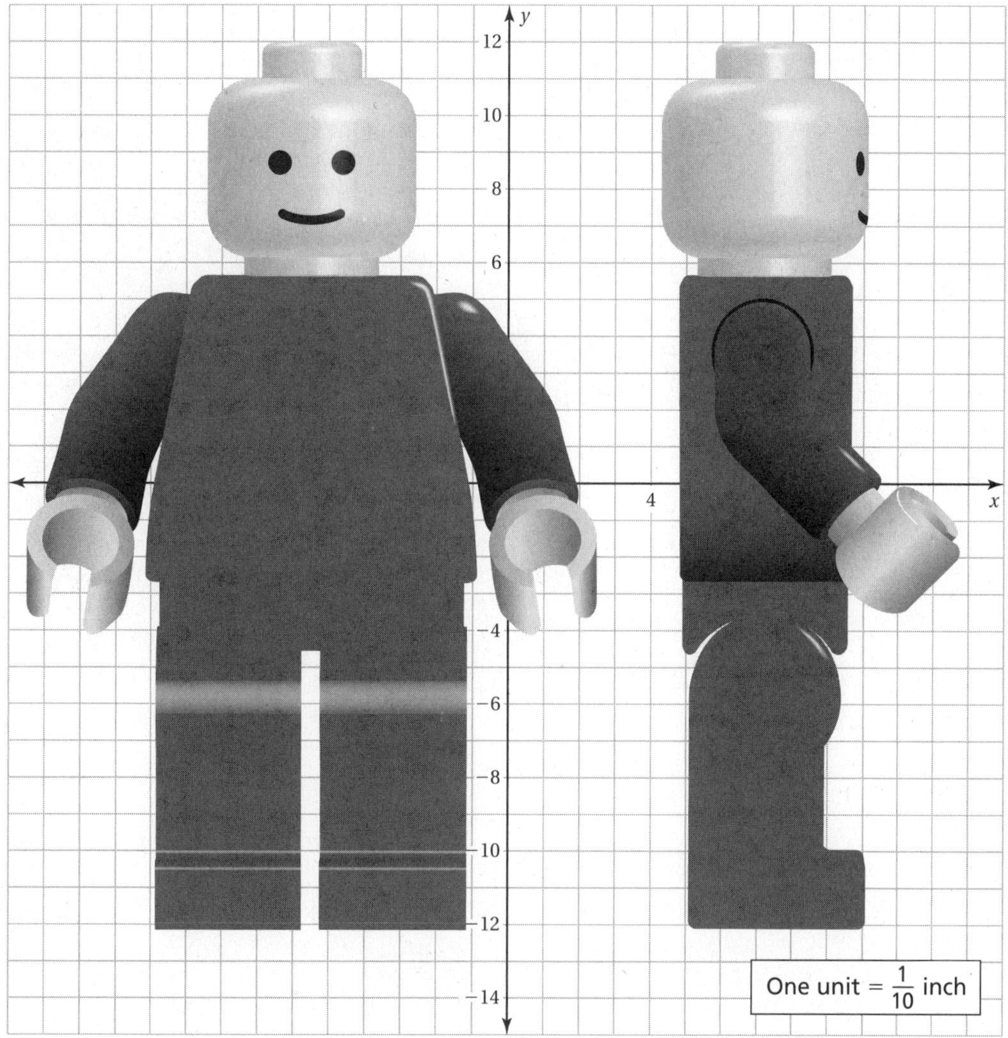

a. Estimate the number of cubic inches of plastic that is needed to mold the Minifigure's head. Show your work.

b. Estimate the number of cubic inches of plastic that is needed to mold one of the Minifigure's legs. Show your work.

2 ACTIVITY: Finding the Volumes of Composite Solids

Work with a partner.

a. Make a plan for estimating the amount of plastic it takes to make a standard eight-stud LEGO® Brick.

$\frac{3}{16}$ in.

$\frac{5}{8}$ in.

$\frac{5}{4}$ in.

$\frac{1}{16}$ in.

$\frac{3}{8}$ in.

b. How much water, in cubic inches, would it take to make ten LEGO® Brick ice cubes?

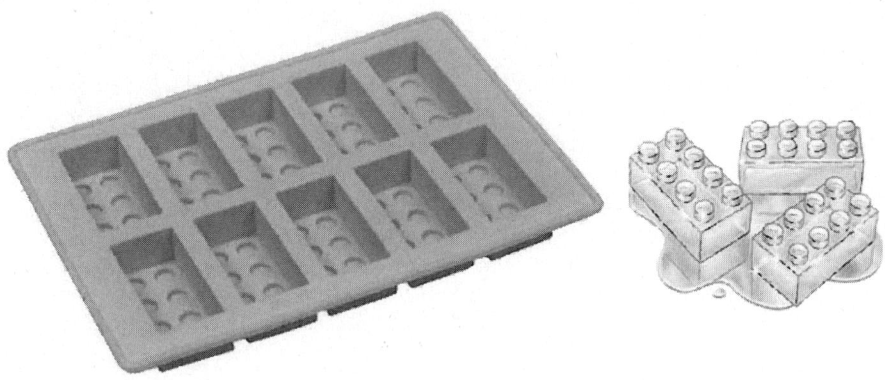

What Is Your Answer?

3. IN YOUR OWN WORDS How can you estimate the volume of a composite solid? Try thinking of some alternative strategies.

Name ____________________ Date __________

7.5 Practice

For use after Lesson 7.5

Find the volume of the composite solid. Round your answer to the nearest tenth.

1. 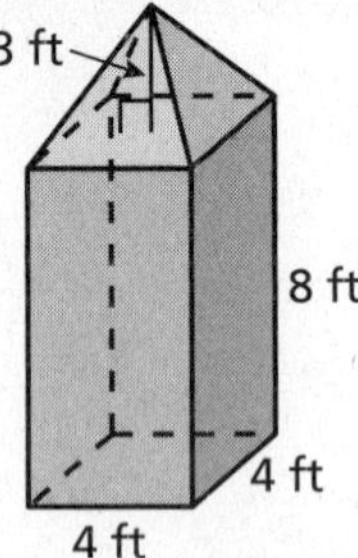

2. 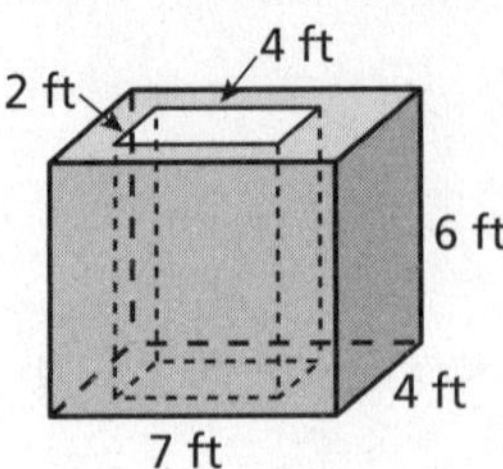

3. 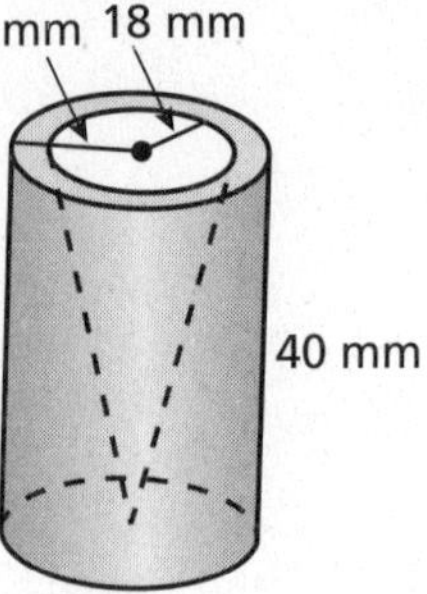

4. An ornament is made up of two identical square pyramids. Find the volume of the ornament.

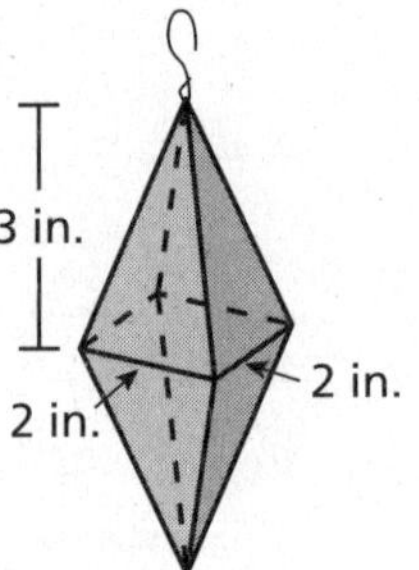

5. An angel food cake pan is shown. What is the volume of the pan? Round your answer to the nearest tenth.

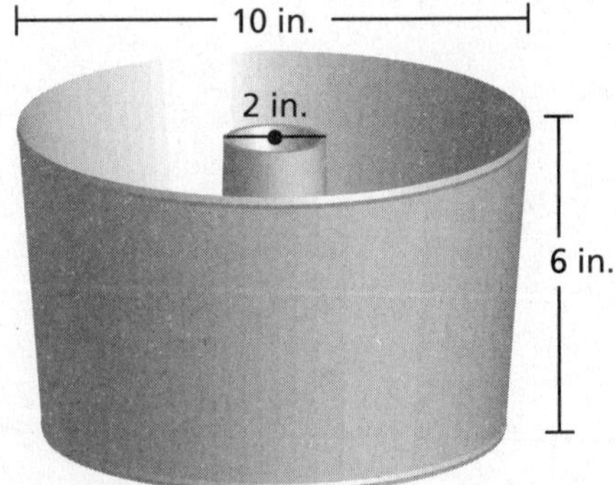

Name____ Date__________

7.6 Surface Areas and Volumes of Similar Solids

For use with Activity 7.6

Essential Question When the dimensions of a solid increase by a factor of k, how does the surface area change? How does the volume change?

1 ACTIVITY: Comparing Volumes and Surface Areas

Work with a partner. Complete the table. Describe the pattern. Are the solids similar? Explain your reasoning.

a.

Radius	1	1	1	1	1
Height	1	2	3	4	5
Surface Area					
Volume					

Name ______________________________ Date __________

b.

Radius	1	2	3	4	5
Height	1	2	3	4	5
Surface Area					
Volume					

2 ACTIVITY: Comparing Volumes and Surface Areas

Work with a partner. Complete the table. Describe the pattern. Are the solids similar? Explain.

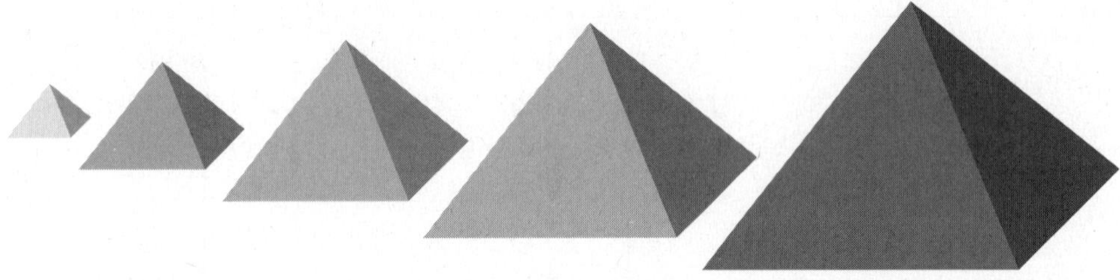

Base Side	6	12	18	24	30
Height	4	8	12	16	20
Slant Height	5	10	15	20	25
Surface Area					
Volume					

What Is Your Answer?

3. **IN YOUR OWN WORDS** When the dimensions of a solid increase by a factor of k, how does the surface area change?

4. **IN YOUR OWN WORDS** When the dimensions of a solid increase by a factor of k, how does the volume change?

5. All the dimensions of a cone increase by a factor of 5.

   a. How many times greater is the surface area? Explain.

5	10	25	125

   b. How many times greater is the volume? Explain.

5	10	25	125

Name ______________________________ Date __________

7.6 Practice
For use after Lesson 7.6

Determine whether the solids are similar.

1\.

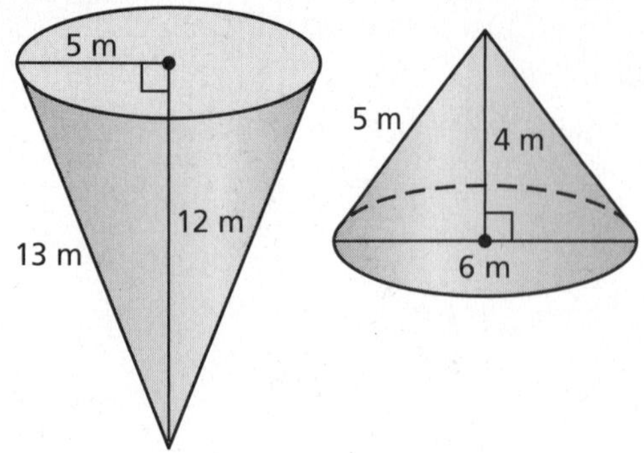

2\.

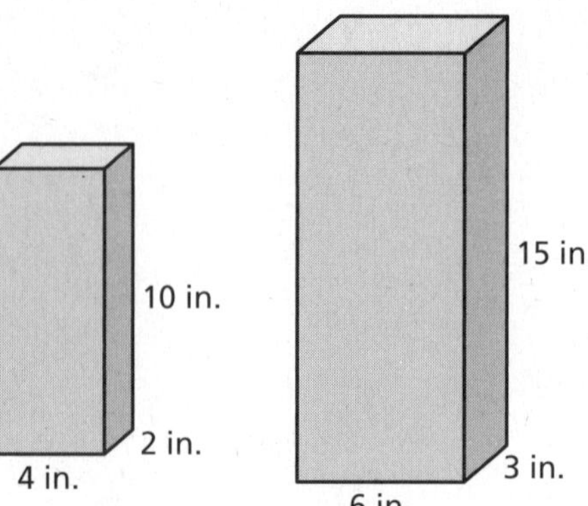

The solids are similar. Find the missing dimension(s).

3\.

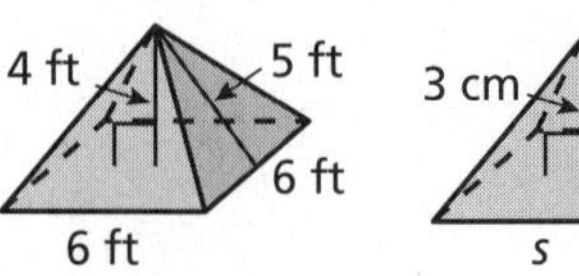

4\.

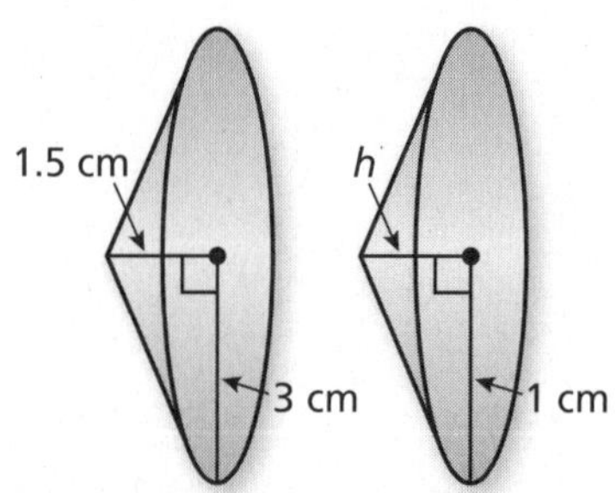

The solids are similar. Find the surface area S or volume V of the shaded solid.

5\.

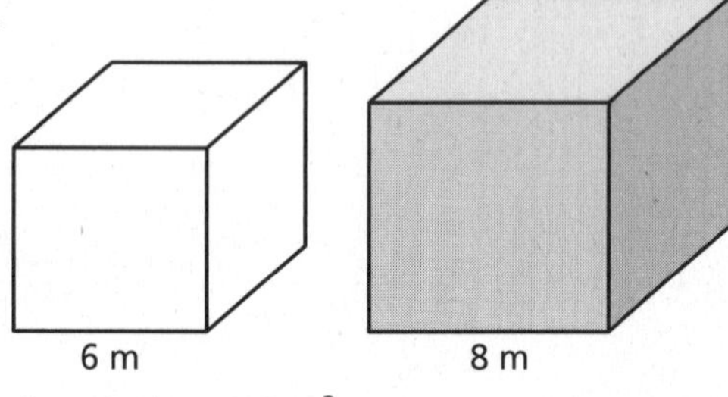

Surface Area = 198 m^2

6\.

Volume = 54 mm^3

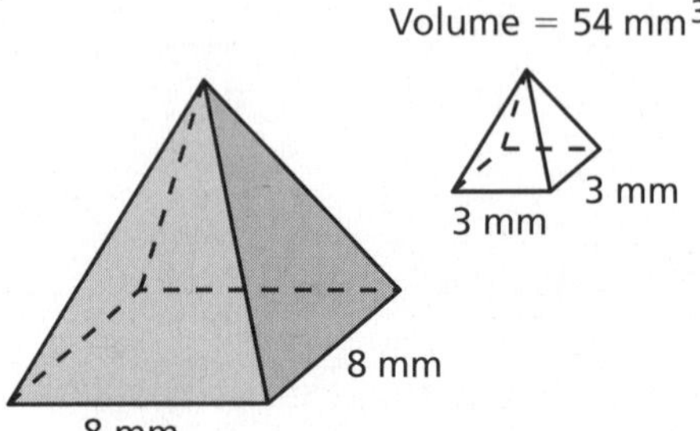

7\. A type of tomato sauce is offered in two sizes. Are the cans similar? Explain.

3 in.
5 in.
4 in.
6 in.

Name_______________________________ Date__________

Fair Game Review

Use the data set to find the (a) mean, (b) median, (c) mode(s), and (d) range.

1.

Player	A	B	C	D
Blocks	8	3	6	3

2.

Phone Plan	A	B	C	D
Minutes	200	400	700	2000

3.

Meeting	Jan	Feb	Mar	Apr	May
People	13	19	24	15	19

4.

Customer	A	B	C	D	E	F
Donation	10	20	25	10	50	20

5.

Day	M	T	W	Th	F
Emails	8	10	6	11	7

6.

Day	Su	M	T	W	Th	F	Sa
Hours	3	3	5	2	3	1	0

Name ______________________ Date ________

Fair Game Review (continued)

7. The data show your bowling scores for four games. What is the mean, median, mode, and range of your scores?

Game	Score
1	89
2	102
3	112
4	109

8. The data in the table shows the scores on a recent test.

Test Scores		
91	96	82
84	84	78
77	72	99
79	95	92
74	71	70
88	83	79

a. Find the mean, median, mode(s), and range.

b. What is the best way to measure the data?

c. Two students have yet to take the test. How can their scores change your answers to parts (a) and (b)?

Name______________________________ Date__________

8.1 Stem-and-Leaf Plots

For use with Activity 8.1

Essential Question How can you use a stem-and-leaf plot to organize a set of numbers?

1 ACTIVITY: Decoding a Graph

Work with a partner. You intercept a secret message that contains two different types of plots. You suspect that each plot represents the same data. The graph with the dots indicates only ranges for the numbers.

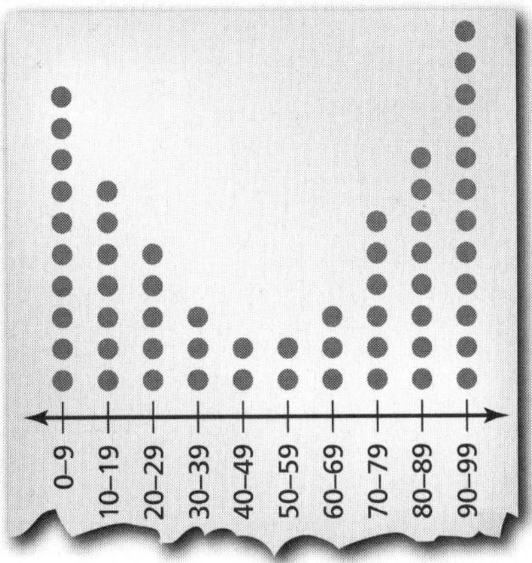

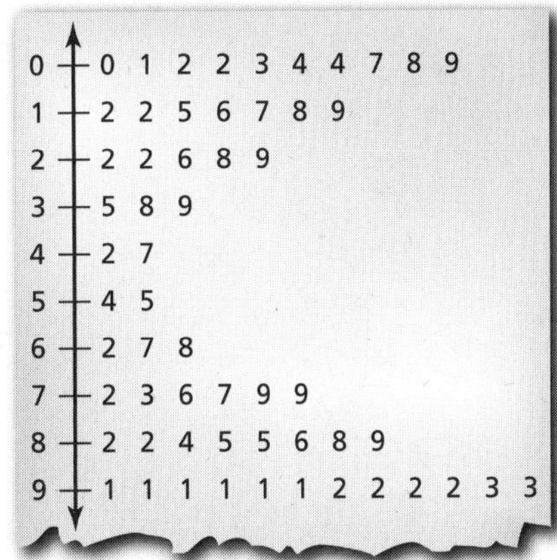

a. How many numbers are in the data set? How can you tell?

b. How many numbers are greater than or equal to 90? How can you tell?

c. Is 91 in the data set? If so, how many times is it in the set? How can you tell?

d. Make a list of all the numbers in the data set.

e. You intercept a new secret message. Use the secret code shown below to decode the message.

Secret Code

A = 29	F = 31	K = 18	P = 4	U = 19
B = 33	G = 8	L = 26	Q = 10	V = 17
C = 7	H = 16	M = 22	R = 21	W = 12
D = 20	I = 5	N = 3	S = 2	X = 25
E = 15	J = 11	O = 9	T = 32	Y = 13
				Z = 1

__ __ __   __ __ __ __   __ __ __ __ __   __ __ __   __ __ __ __
32 16 15   2 32 15 22   2 16 9 12 2   32 16 15   32 15 3 2

__ __ __   __ __ __ __ __ __   __ __ __ __   __ __ __   __ __ __ __
32 16 15   26 15 29 17 15 2   2 16 9 12   32 16 15   9 3 15 2

2 ACTIVITY: Organizing Data

Work with a partner. You are working on an archeological dig. You find several arrowheads. As you find each arrowhead, you measure its length (in millimeters) and record it in a notebook.

18	61	62
42	42	42
23	41	40
45	45	45
37	28	50
35	39	34
37	32	26
63	24	54
58	58	60
52	53	72
17	73	

a. Use a stem-and-leaf plot to organize the lengths.

b. Find the mean length.

c. Find the median length.

d. Describe the distribution of the data.

Name____ Date__________

3 ACTIVITY: Conducting an Experiment

Work with a partner. Use two number cubes to conduct the following experiment.

- **Toss the cubes four times and total the results.**

  Sample: 2 + 3 + 2 + 2 + 3 + 5 + 6 + 3 = 26 (1st toss: 2 + 3; 2nd toss: 2 + 2; 3rd toss: 3 + 5; 4th toss: 6 + 3)

  So, 26 is the first number.

- **Repeat this process 29 more times.**
- **Use a stem-and-leaf plot to organize your results.**
- **Describe your results.**

What Is Your Answer?

4. **IN YOUR OWN WORDS** How can you use a stem-and-leaf plot to organize a set of numbers?

5. **RESEARCH** Find a career in which a person collects and organizes data. Describe how data are collected and organized in that career.

Name ____________________ Date ________

8.1 Practice
For use after Lesson 8.1

Make a stem-and-leaf plot of the data.

1.

Class Sizes			
12	10	21	28
9	16	19	16
25	32	14	21

2.

Minutes Spent on Homework			
75	82	91	68
92	86	79	76
75	81	88	60

3. The number of text messages from eight phones are 8, 11, 14, 22, 5, 15, 7, and 20. Make a stem-and-leaf plot of the data. Describe the distribution of the data.

4. The number of minutes seven members spent at band practice are 57, 49, 55, 62, 78, 72, and 75. Make a stem-and-leaf plot of the data. Describe the distribution of the data.

5. The stem-and-leaf plot shows the number of miles students travel to get to school.

Stem	Leaf
0	5 7
1	2 4 8
2	0 1 5 7
3	3

Key: 1 | 4 = 14 miles

a. How many students travel more than 15 miles?

b. Find the mean, median, mode, and range of the data.

Name____ Date__________

8.2 Histograms
For use with Activity 8.2

Essential Question How do histograms show the differences in distributions of data?

1 ACTIVITY: Analyzing Distributions

Work with a partner. The graphs (histograms) show four different types of distributions.

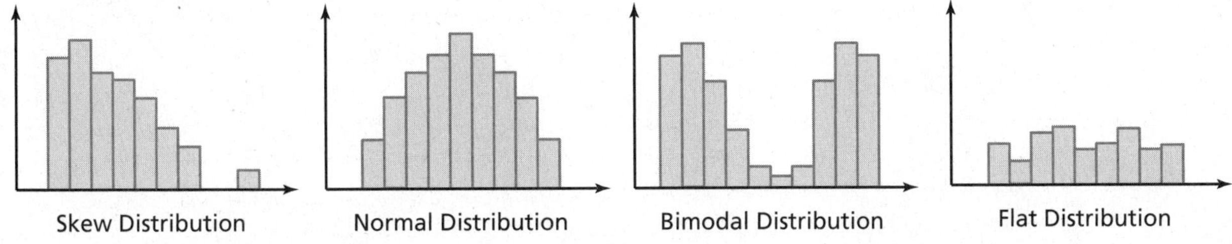

a. Describe a real-life example of each distribution.

b. Describe the mean, median, and mode of each distribution.

c. In which distributions are the mean and median about equal? Explain your reasoning.

d. How did each type of distribution get its name?

Name ______________________________ Date __________

2 ACTIVITY: Analyzing Distributions

Work with a partner. A survey asked 100 adult men and 100 adult women to answer the following questions.

Question 1: What is your ideal weight?

Question 2: What is your ideal age?

Match the histogram to the question.

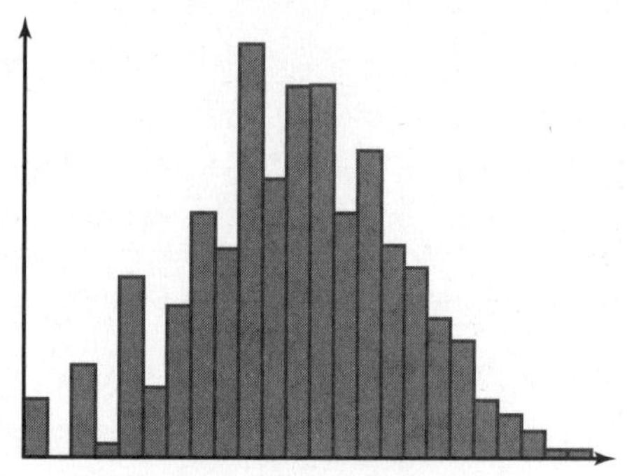

Graph for Question ______

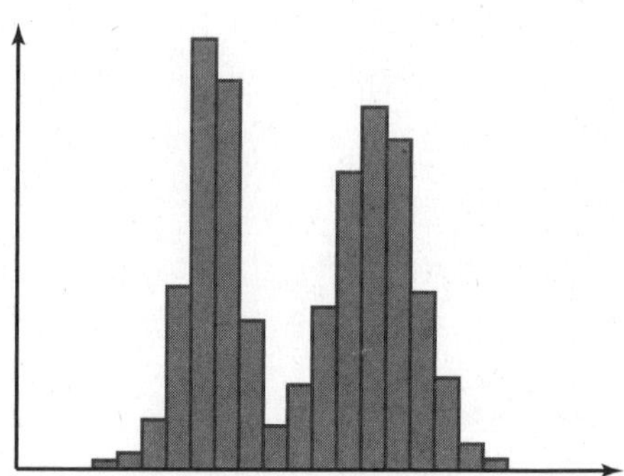

Graph for Question ______

3 ACTIVITY: Conducting Experiments

Work with a partner. Conduct two experiments. Make a frequency table and a histogram for each experiment. Compare and contrast the results of the two experiments.

a. Toss *one* number cube 36 times. Record the numbers.

6	
5	
4	
3	
2	
1	

Frequency Table

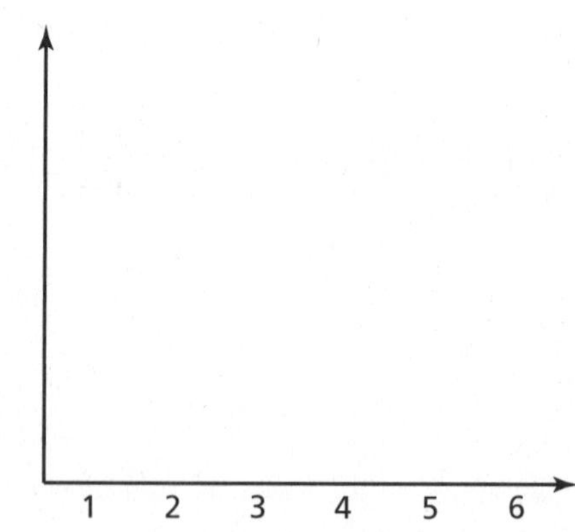

Histogram

Name_______________________________ Date__________

8.2 Histograms (continued)

b. Toss *two* number cubes 36 times. Record the sums of the two numbers.

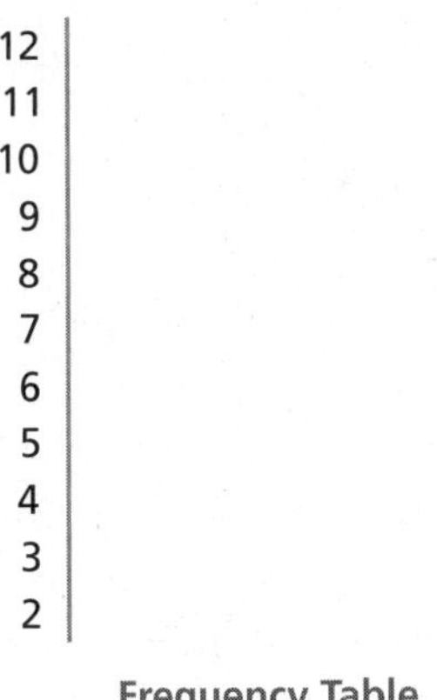

Frequency Table

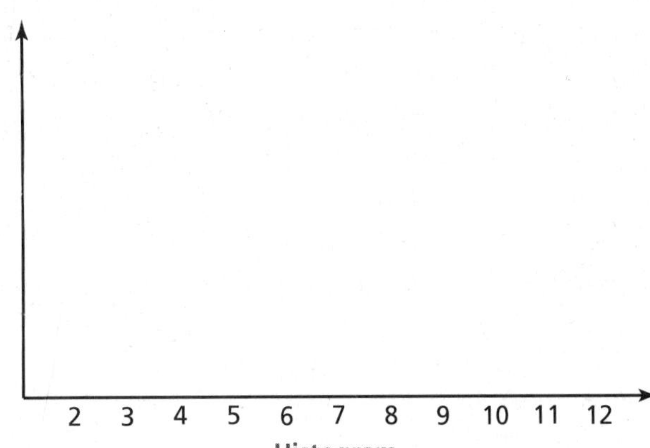

Histogram

What Is Your Answer?

4. **IN YOUR OWN WORDS** How do histograms show the differences in distributions of data?

5. Describe an experiment that you can conduct to collect data. Predict the type of data distribution the results will create.

Name ______________________________ Date __________

8.2 Practice

For use after Lesson 8.2

Display the data in a histogram.

1.

Birthdays	
Months	**Frequency**
Jan–Mar	15
Apr–June	9
Jul–Sept	6
Oct–Dec	12

2.

Goals Scored	
Goals	**Frequency**
0–2	6
3–5	8
6–8	2
9–11	1

3.

Height Jumped	
Inches	**Frequency**
0–11	7
12–23	10
24–35	5
36–47	2

4.

Money Spent	
Dollars	**Frequency**
0–19	3
20–39	8
40–59	8
60–79	15

5. The histogram shows the times students ran the mile in gym class.

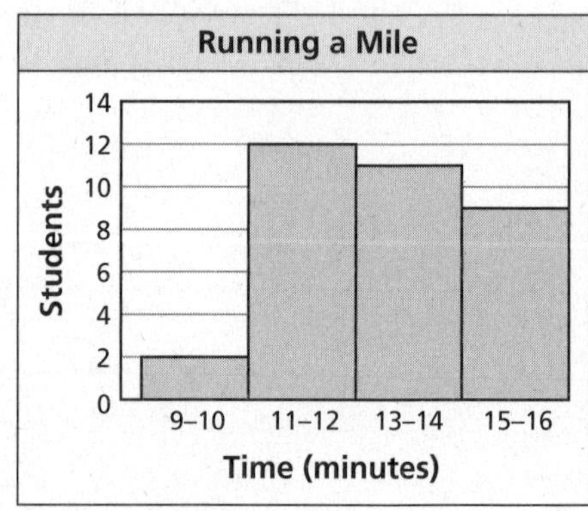

a. Which interval contains the fewest data values?

b. How many students are in the class?

c. What percent of students ran the mile in 12 minutes or less?

Name____ Date__________

8.3 Circle Graphs

For use with Activity 8.3

Essential Question How can you use a circle graph to show the results of a survey?

1 ACTIVITY: Reading a Circle Graph

Work with a partner. Six hundred middle school students were asked "What is your favorite sport?" The circle graph shows the results of the survey.

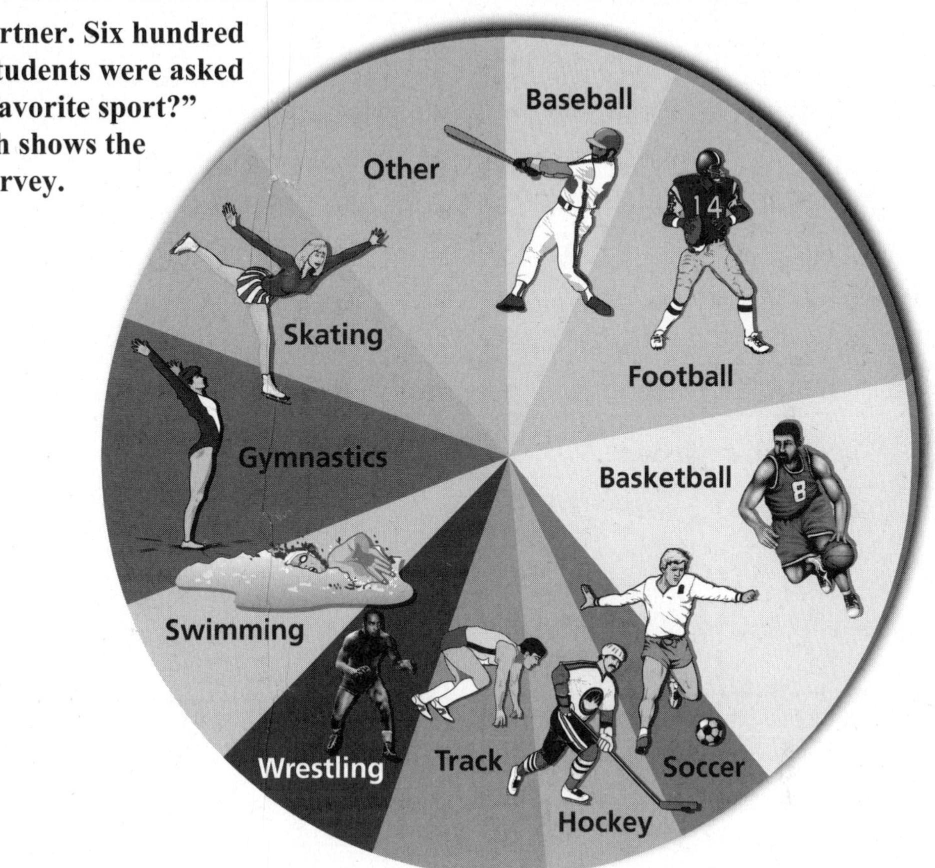

a. Use a protractor to find the angle measure (in degrees) of the section (pie piece) for football.

b. How many degrees are in a full circle?

c. Write and solve a proportion to determine the number of students who said football is their favorite sport.

d. Repeat the process for the other sections of the circle graph.

2 ACTIVITY: Making a Circle Graph

Work with a partner.

a. Conduct a survey in your class. Each student should check his or her favorite sport on a piece of paper similar to the one shown below.

What is your favorite sport?

Baseball	☐	Skating	☐
Basketball	☐	Soccer	☐
Football	☐	Swimming	☐
Gymnastics	☐	Track	☐
Hockey	☐	Wrestling	☐
		Other	☐

b. Organize the results on the board.

c. Display the results in a circle graph.

Name______________________________ Date__________

d. Compare and contrast your class survey with the survey in Activity 1.

What Is Your Answer?

3. IN YOUR OWN WORDS How can you use a circle graph to show the results of a survey?

4. Find a circle graph in a newspaper, in a magazine, or on the Internet. Copy it and describe the results that it shows.

"I conducted a survey and asked 30 people if they would like a million dollars."

"I organized the results in a circle graph."

Name ______________________________ Date __________

8.3 Practice
For use after Lesson 8.3

Find the angle measure that corresponds to the percent of a circle.

1. 50%

2. 65%

3. 9%

Display the data in a circle graph.

4.

Toppings	Pizzas Ordered
Pepperoni	6
Sausage	6
Peppers	3
Extra Cheese	5

5.

Chore	Minutes
Vacuum	15
Dust	20
Make Bed	5
Wash Dishes	20

6. The circle graph shows the results from a class survey on favorite juice.

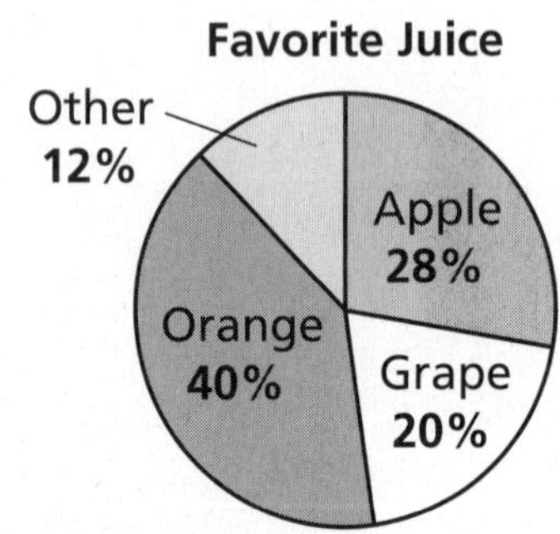

a. Compare the number of students who chose apple juice to the number of students who chose grape juice.

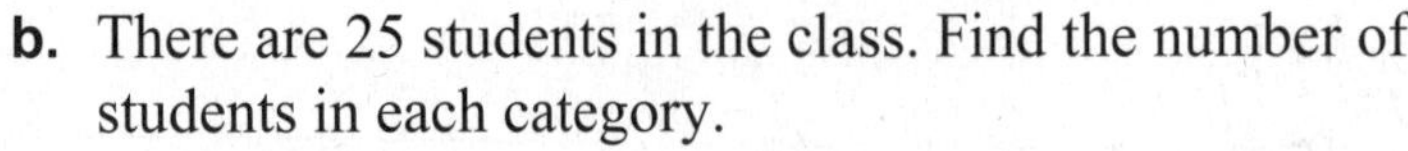

b. There are 25 students in the class. Find the number of students in each category.

Name____ Date__________

8.4 Samples and Populations

For use with Activity 8.4

Essential Question How can you use a survey to make conclusions about the general population?

1 ACTIVITY: Interpreting a Survey

Work with a partner. Read the newspaper article. Analyze the survey by answering the following questions.

The Daily Ti

VOL 01 No. 279 WEDNESDAY, OCTOBER 6, 2010

TEXT MESSAGING SURVEY RESULTS

A survey reports that almost one-third of teens and young adults believe that their text messaging plans are restrictive.

About 40% say their plans lead to higher cell phone bills. According to those participating in the survey, the average number of text messages sent per day is between 6 and 7.

The majority of survey participants say they would send more text messages if their cell phone plans were not as restrictive.

a. The article does not say how many "teens and young adults" were surveyed. How many do you think need to be surveyed so that the results can represent all teens and young adults in your state? in the United States? Explain your reasoning.

b. Outline the newspaper article. List all of the important points.

c. Write a questionnaire that could have been used for the survey. Do not include leading questions. For example, "Do you think your cell phone plan is restrictive?" is a leading question.

Name ______________________________ Date __________

2 ACTIVITY: Conducting a Survey

Work with a partner. The newspaper article in Activity 1 states that the average number of text messages sent per day is between 6 and 7.

a. Does this statement seem correct to you? Explain your reasoning.

b. Plan a survey to check this statement. How will you conduct the survey?

c. Survey your classmates. Organize your data using one of the types of graphs you have studied in this chapter.

d. Write a newspaper article summarizing the results of your survey.

3 ACTIVITY: Conducting and Summarizing a Survey

Work with a partner.

- Plan a survey to determine how many of the following texting shortcuts people know.

Texting Shortcuts

R	Are	U	You
4	For	L8R	Later
SUP	What's up	TTYL	Talk to you later
PLZ	Please	BRB	Be right back
C	See	LOL	Laugh out loud
IDK	I don't know	BFF	Best friends forever
JK	Just kidding	THX	Thanks
2NITE	Tonight	GR8	Great
QPSA?	Que Pasa?	4COL	For crying out loud

Name______________________________ Date__________

8.4 **Samples and Populations (continued)**

- Write a questionnaire to use in your survey.
- In the survey, try to determine whether *teenagers* or *people over 30* know more of the short cuts.

- Conduct your survey. What can you conclude from the results? Do the results confirm your prediction?

What Is Your Answer?

4. **IN YOUR OWN WORDS** How can you use a survey to make conclusions about the general population?

5. Find a survey in a newspaper, in a magazine, or on the Internet. Decide whether you think the conclusion of the survey is correct. Explain your reasoning.

"I'm sending my Mom a text message for Mother's Day."

"2 GR8 2 ME 2 EVR B 4GOT10. XXOO"

Name ______________________________ Date __________

8.4 Practice
For use after Lesson 8.4

Identify the population and the sample.

1. 
Members of the soccer team

All sports players

2. 
8 crayons

A box of crayons

Which sample is better for making a prediction? Explain.

3. Predict the average age of students in your school.
Sample A: A random sample of 50 students in your school.
Sample B: A random sample of 50 students in your class.

4. Predict the number of male dogs in the pet shop.
Sample A: A random sample of 3 dogs in the pet shop.
Sample B: A random sample of 15 dogs in the pet shop.

5. A survey asked 56 randomly chosen students if they play basketball. Seven said yes. There are 24 students who play basketball in your grade. Predict the number of students in your grade.

Name____ Date__________

8.4b Practice

For use after Lesson 8.4b

1. You want to know if students at a school are in favor of building a new computer lab. You conduct two surveys. For Survey 1, you randomly ask 70 students in the hallways before homeroom. For Survey 2, you randomly ask 70 academic club members. There are 1400 students in the school.

Response	Survey 1	Survey 2
Yes	21	34
No	31	15
Not Sure	18	21

a. Use the results of each survey to predict the number n of students in the school that are in favor of building a new computer lab.

b. Which prediction is more reliable? Explain.

Name ______________________________ Date __________

2. The double box-and-whisker plot shows the shoe sizes of random samples of high school students. Compare the shoe sizes of girls to the shoe sizes of boys.

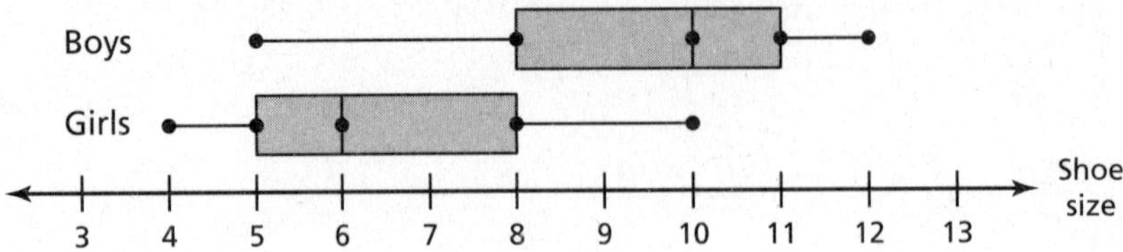

3. Each table shows a random sample of project grades in a class. Create a double box-and-whisker plot of the data. Compare the two data sets.

Grades in Mrs. Arnold's Class			
79	84	75	76
77	68	85	78
90	83	79	72
81	75	84	88
76	85	86	76

Grades in Mrs. Pizker's Class			
83	90	80	75
87	74	92	85
92	85	79	90
78	90	88	74
86	79	85	93

Name____ Date__________

Chapter 9 Fair Game Review

Simplify the fraction.

1. $\frac{10}{12}$

2. $\frac{36}{72}$

3. $\frac{14}{28}$

4. $\frac{18}{26}$

5. $\frac{32}{48}$

6. $\frac{65}{91}$

7. There are 90 students involved in the mentoring program. Of these students, 60 are girls. Write and simplify a fraction showing the number of girls in the mentoring program.

8. There are 56 rows of vegetables planted in a field. Fourteen of the rows are corn. Write and simplify a fraction showing the number of rows of corn in the field.

Name ______________________________ Date __________

Chapter 9 Fair Game Review (continued)

Write the ratio in simplest form.

9. Bats to baseballs

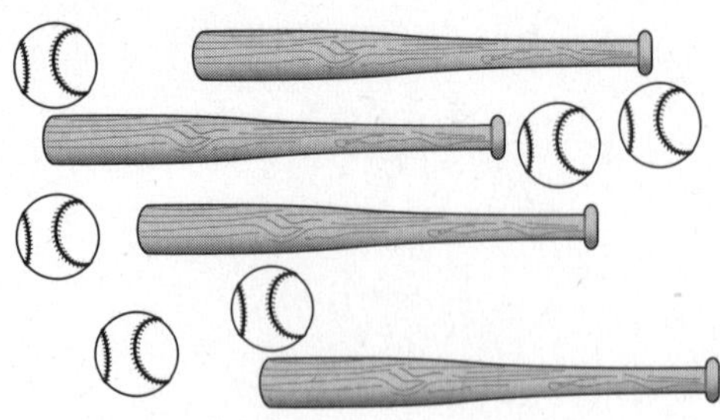

10. Bows to gift boxes

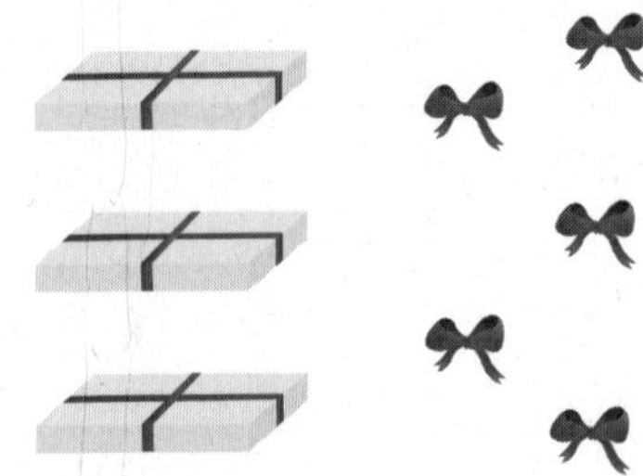

11. Hammers to screwdrivers

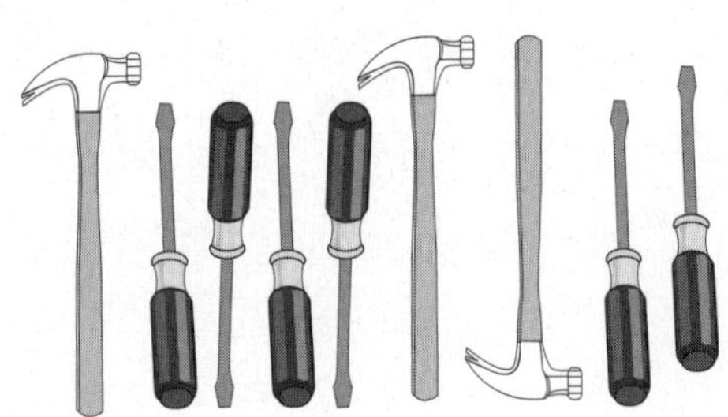

12. Apples to bananas

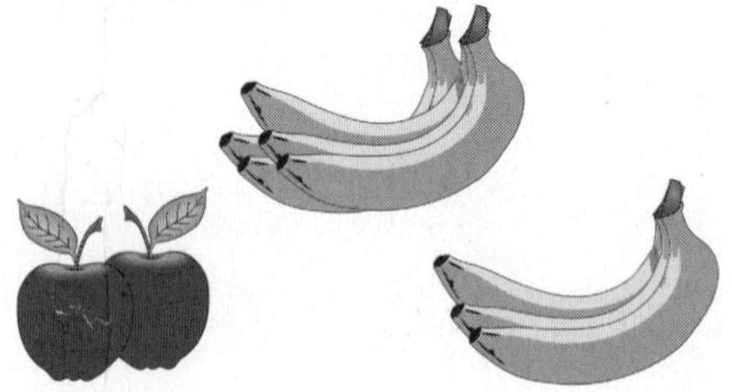

13. Flowers to vases

14. Cars to trucks

15. There are 100 students in the seventh grade. There are 15 seventh grade teachers. What is the ratio of teachers to students?

Name____ Date__________

9.1 Introduction to Probability

For use with Activity 9.1

Essential Question How can you predict the results of spinning a spinner?

1 ACTIVITY: Helicopter Flight

Play with a partner.

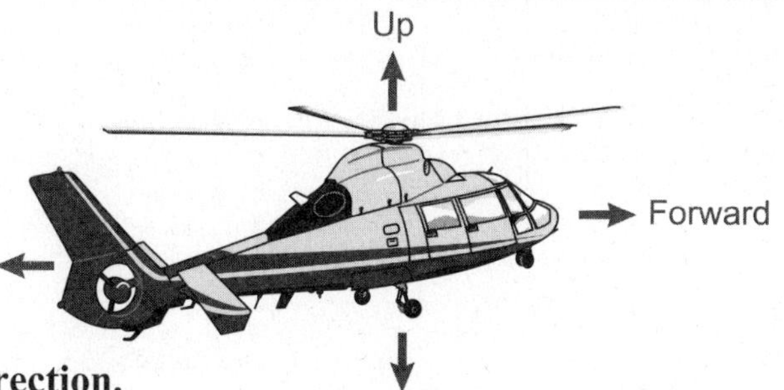

- **You begin flying the helicopter at (0, 0) on the coordinate plane. Your goal is to reach the cabin at (20, 14).**
- **Spin any one of the spinners. Move one unit in the indicated direction.**
- **If the helicopter encounters any obstacles, you must start over.**
- **Record the number of moves it takes to land exactly on (20, 14).**
- **After you have played once, it is your partner's turn to play.**
- **The player who finishes in the fewest moves wins.**

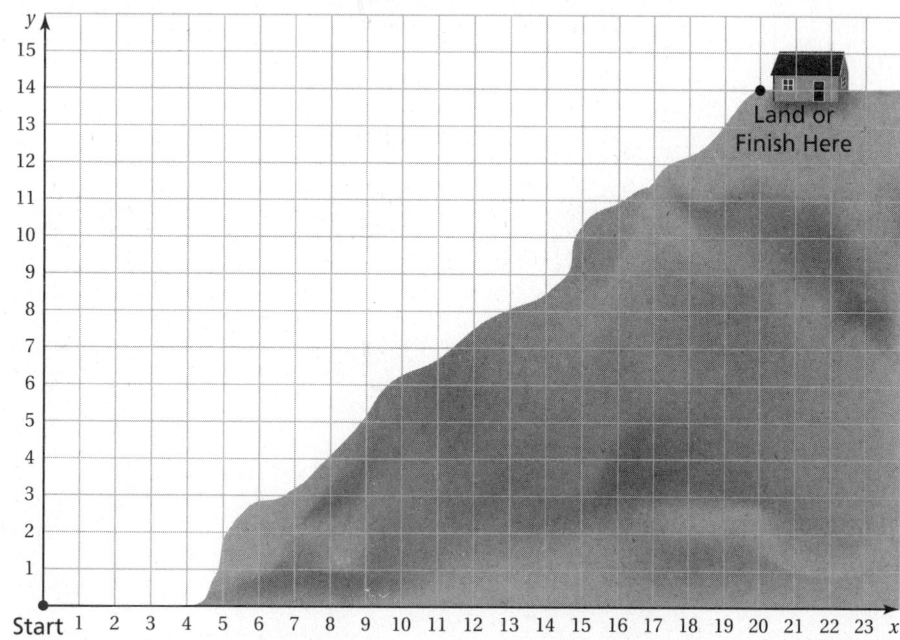

Spinner A

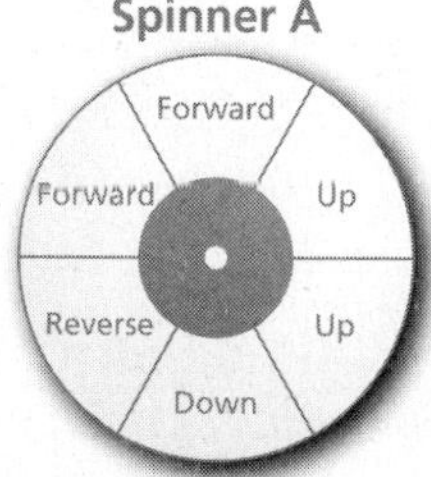

Spinner B

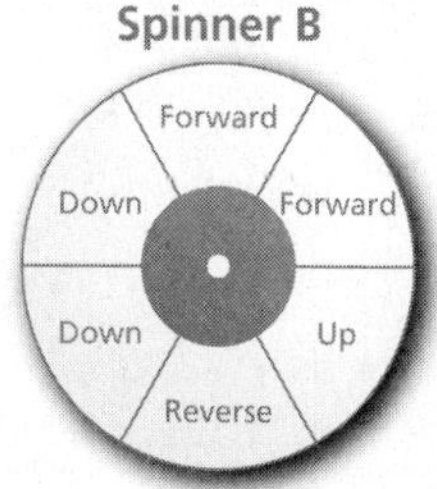

Spinner C

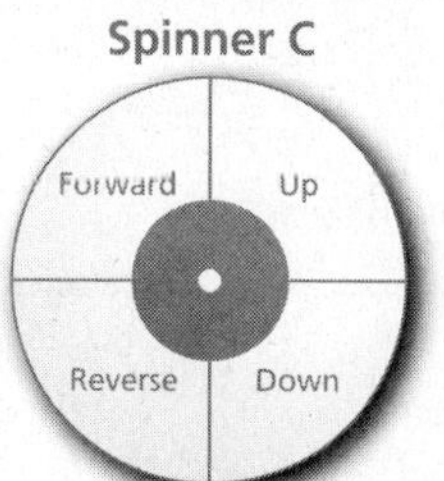

Spinner D

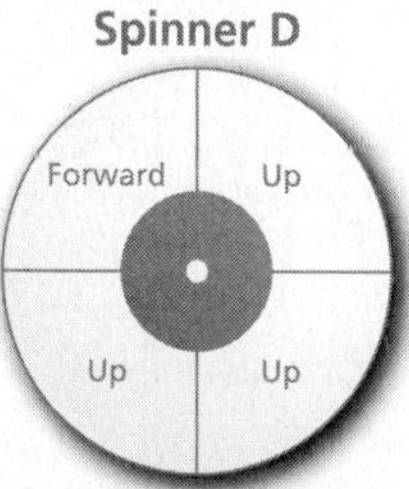

Name ______________________________ Date __________

2 ACTIVITY: Analyzing the Spinners

Work with a partner.

a. How are the spinners in Activity 1 alike? How are they different?

b. Which spinner will advance the helicopter to the finish faster? Why?

c. If you want to move up, which spinner should you spin? Why?

d. Spin each spinner 50 times and record the results.

Spinner A

Up	
Down	
Reverse	
Forward	

Spinner B

Up	
Down	
Reverse	
Forward	

Spinner C

Up	
Down	
Reverse	
Forward	

Spinner D

Up	
Down	
Reverse	
Forward	

Name______________________ Date__________

9.1 Introduction to Probability (continued)

e. Organize the results from part (d) in a bar graph for each spinner.

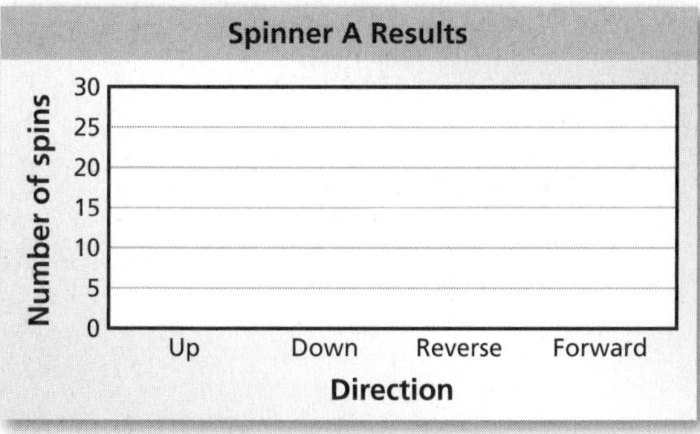

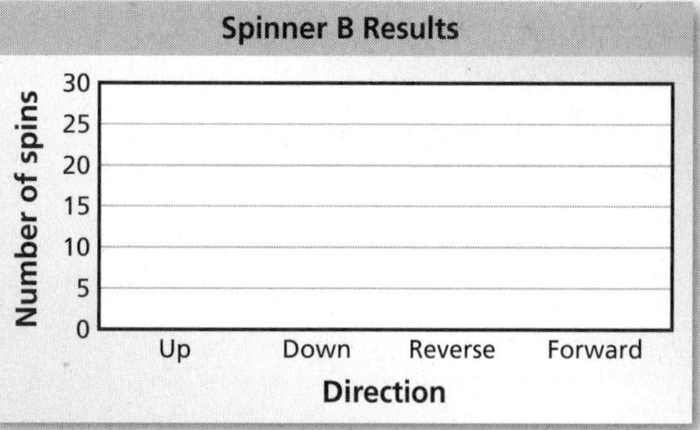

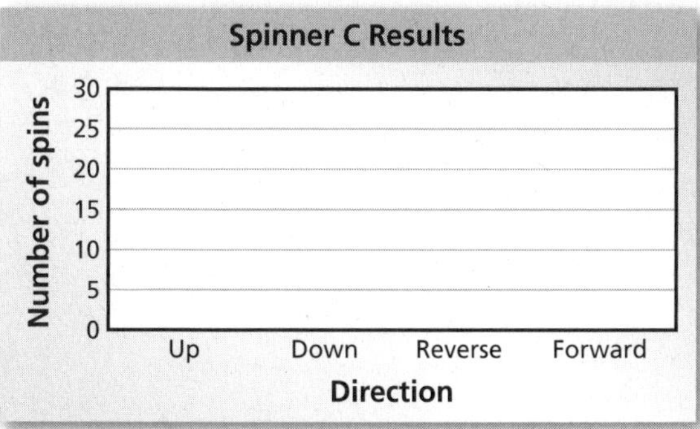

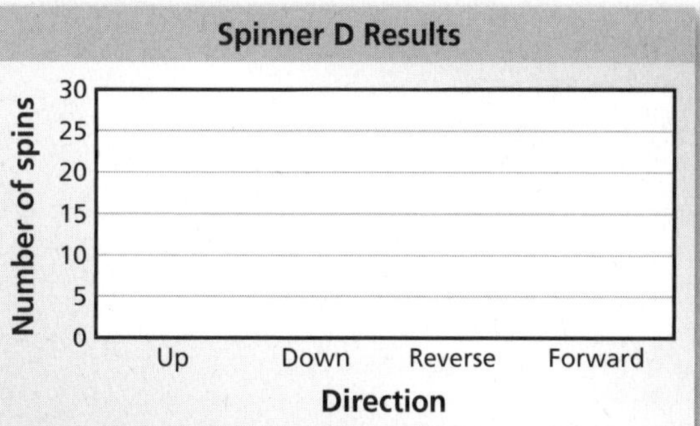

f. After analyzing the results, would you change your strategy in the helicopter flight game? Explain why or why not.

What Is Your Answer?

3. IN YOUR OWN WORDS How can you predict the results of spinning a spinner?

Name ______________________________ Date ________

9.1 Practice

For use after Lesson 9.1

A bag is filled with 4 red marbles, 3 blue marbles, 3 yellow marbles, and 2 green marbles. You randomly choose one marble from the bag. (a) Find the number of ways the event can occur. (b) Find the favorable outcomes of the event.

1. Choosing red

2. Choosing green

3. Choosing yellow

4. Choosing *not* blue

5. In order to figure out who will go first in a game, your friend asks you to pick a number between 1 and 25.

a. What are the possible outcomes?

b. What are the favorable outcomes of choosing an even number?

c. What are the favorable outcomes of choosing a number less than 20?

Name____ Date__________

9.2 Theoretical Probability

For use with Activity 9.2

Essential Question How can you find a theoretical probability?

1 ACTIVITY: Black and White Spinner Game

Work with a partner. You work for a game company. You need to create a game that uses the spinner below.

a. Write rules for a game that uses the spinner. Then play it.

b. After playing the game, do you want to revise the rules? Explain.

c. Each pie-shaped section of the spinner is the same size. What is the measure of the central angle of each section?

d. What is the probability that the spinner will land on 1? Explain.

Name ______________________________ Date __________

2 ACTIVITY: Changing the Spinner

Work with a partner. For each spinner, find the probability of landing on each number. Do your rules for Activity 1 make sense for these spinners? Explain.

a.

b.

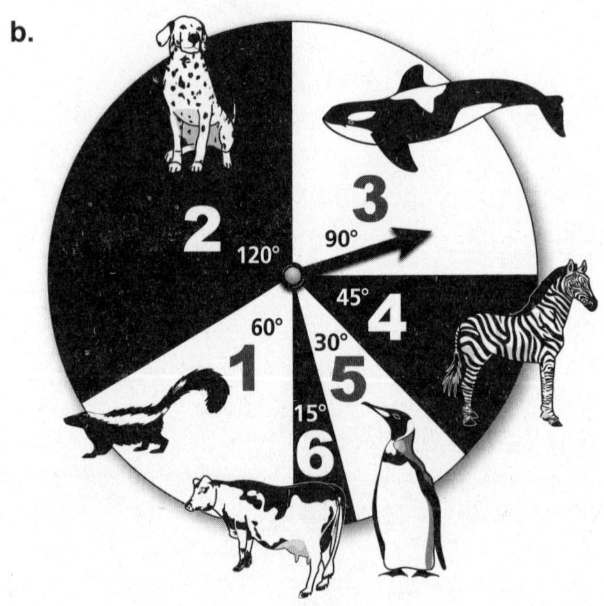

3 ACTIVITY: Is This Game Fair?

Work with a partner. Apply the following rules to each spinner in Activities 1 and 2. Is the game fair? If not, who has the better chance of winning?

- **Take turns spinning the spinner.**
- **If the spinner lands on an odd number, Player 1 wins.**
- **If the spinner lands on an even number, Player 2 wins.**

What Is Your Answer?

4. **IN YOUR OWN WORDS** How can you find a theoretical probability?

5. Find and describe a career in which probability is used. Explain why probability is used in that career.

6. Two people play the following game.

   Each player has 6 cards numbered 1, 2, 3, 4, 5, and 6. At the same time, each player holds up one card. If the product of the two numbers is odd, Player 1 wins. If the product is even, Player 2 wins. Continue until both players are out of cards. Which player is more likely to win? Why?

Name ______________________ Date ________

9.2 Practice

For use after Lesson 9.2

Use a number cube to determine the theoretical probability of the event.

1. Rolling a 2

2. Rolling a 5

3. Rolling an even number

4. Rolling a number greater than 1

A spinner is used for a game. Determine if the game is fair. If it is *not* fair, who has the greater probability of winning?

5. You win if the number is less than 4. If it is not less than 4, your friend wins.

6. You win if the number is a multiple of 2. If it is not a multiple of 2, your friend wins.

7. At a carnival, you pick a duck out of a pond that designates a prize. You want to win a large prize and the theoretical probability of winning it is $\frac{9}{25}$. There are 50 ducks. How many ducks will win a large prize?

Name________________________________ Date__________

9.3 Experimental Probability

For use with Activity 9.3

Essential Question What is meant by experimental probability?

1 ACTIVITY: Throwing Sticks

Play with a partner. This game is based on an Apache game called "Throw Sticks."

- **Take turns throwing three sticks into the center of the circle and moving around the circle according to the chart.**
- **If your opponent lands on or passes your playing piece, you must start over.**
- **The first player to pass his or her starting point wins.**

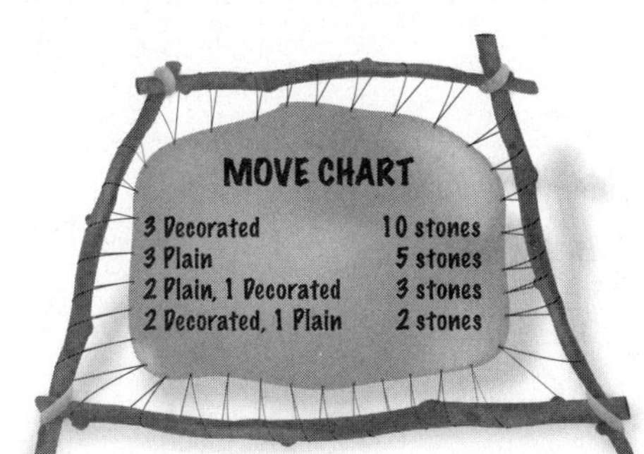

Each stick has one plain side and one decorated side.

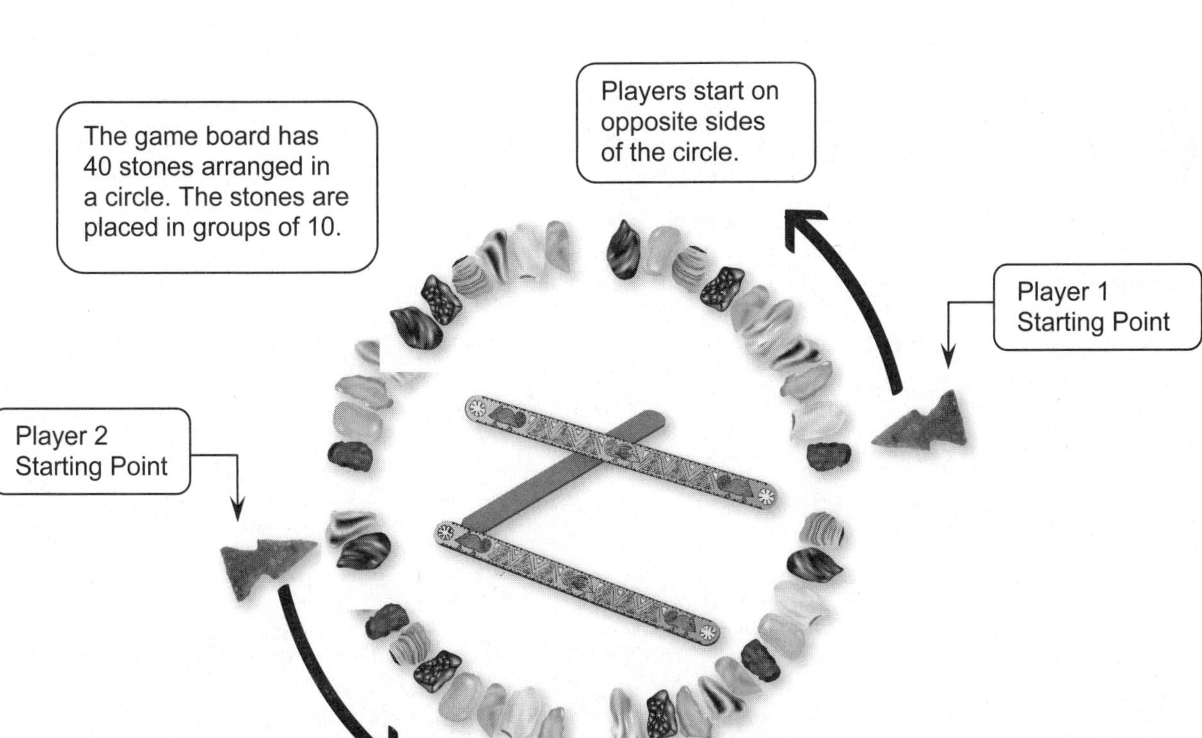

Name ____ Date __________

2 ACTIVITY: Conducting an Experiment

Work with a partner. Throw the 3 sticks 32 times. Tally the results using the outcomes listed below. A "P" represents the plain side landing up and a "D" represents the decorated side landing up. Organize the results in a bar graph. Use the bar graph to estimate the probability of each outcome. These are called experimental probabilities.

a. PPP

b. DPP

c. DDP

d. DDD

3 ACTIVITY: Analyzing the Possibilities

Work with a partner. A tree diagram helps you see different ways that the same outcome can occur.

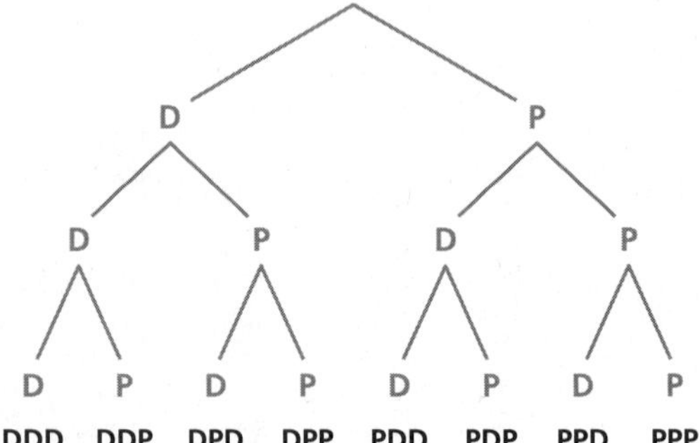

a. Find the number of ways that each outcome can occur.

- Three Ps
- One D and two Ps
- Two Ds and one P
- Three Ds

b. Find the theoretical probability of each outcome.

c. Compare and contrast your experimental and theoretical probabilities.

What Is Your Answer?

4. IN YOUR OWN WORDS What is meant by experimental probability?

5. Give a real-life example of experimental probability.

Name ______________________________ Date ________

9.3 Practice
For use after Lesson 9.3

Use the bar graph to find the experimental probability.

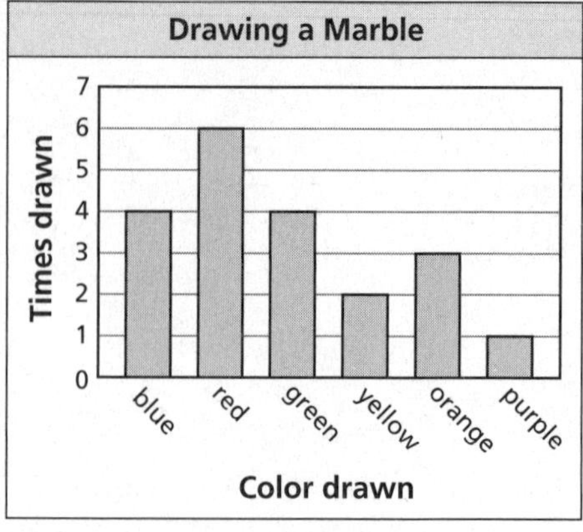

1. Drawing red

2. Drawing orange

3. Drawing *not* yellow

4. Drawing a color with more than 4 letters in its name

5. There are 25 students' names in a hat. You choose 5 names. Three are boys' names and two are girls' names. How many of the 25 names would you expect to be boys' names?

6. You must stop at 3 of 5 stoplights on a stretch of road. If this trend continues, how many times will you stop if the road has 10 stoplights?

7. Your teacher has a large box containing an equal number of red and blue folders. There are 24 students in your class. The teacher passes out the folders at random. Ten students receive a red folder. Compare the experimental probability of receiving a red folder with the theoretical probability of receiving a red folder.

Name______________________________ Date__________

9.4 Independent and Dependent Events

For use with Activity 9.4

Essential Question What is the difference between dependent and independent events?

1 ACTIVITY: Dependent Events

Work with a partner. You have three marbles in a bag. There are two green marbles (G) and one purple marble (P). You randomly draw two marbles from the bag.

a. Use the tree diagram to find the probability that both marbles are green.

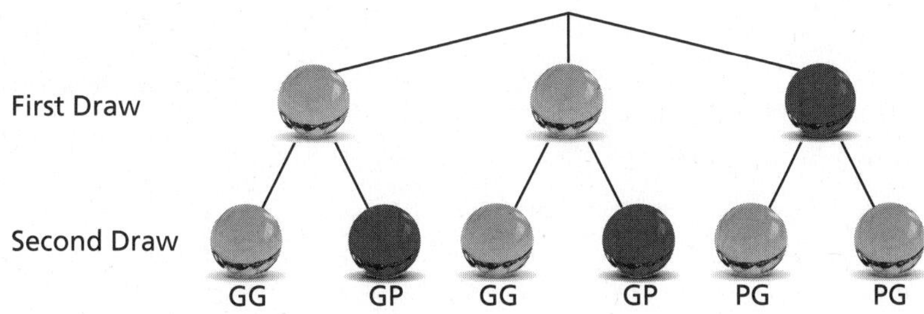

b. In the tree diagram, does the probability of getting a green marble on the second draw *depend* on the color of the first marble? Explain.

2 ACTIVITY: Independent Events

Work with a partner. Using the same marbles from Activity 1, randomly draw a marble from the bag. Then put the marble back in the bag and draw a second marble.

a. Use the tree diagram to find the probability that both marbles are green.

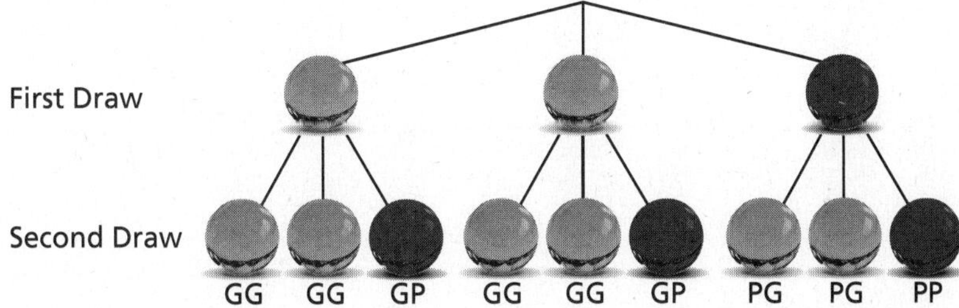

Name ______________________________ Date __________

9.4 Independent and Dependent Events (continued)

b. In the tree diagram, does the probability of getting a green marble on the second draw *depend* on the color of the first marble? Explain.

3 ACTIVITY: Conducting an Experiment

Work with a partner. Conduct two experiments using two green marbles (G) and one purple marble (P).

a. In the first experiment, randomly draw two marbles from the bag 36 times. Record each result as GG or GP. Make a bar graph of your results.

GG	
GP	

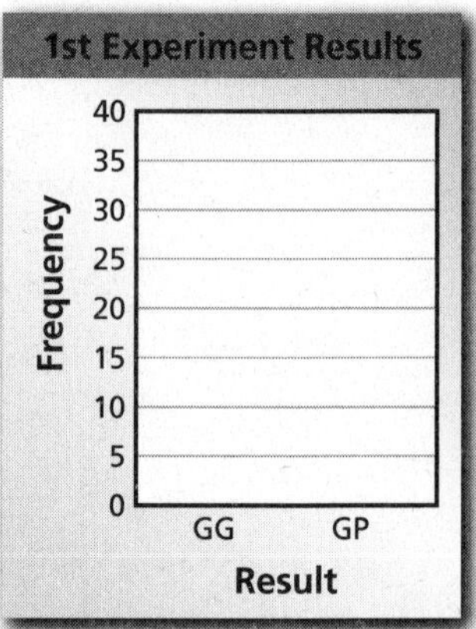

b. What is the experimental probability of drawing two green marbles? Does this answer seem reasonable? Explain.

Name______________________________ Date__________

9.4 Independent and Dependent Events (continued)

c. In the second experiment, randomly draw one marble from the bag. Put it back. Draw a second marble. Repeat this 36 times. Record each result as GG, GP, or PP. Make a bar graph of your results.

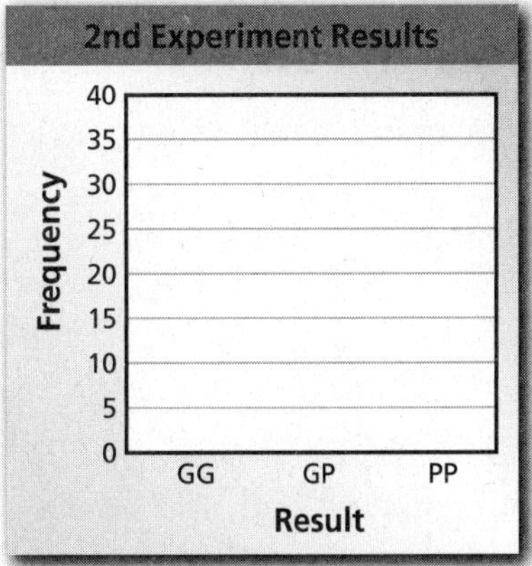

GG	
GP	
PP	

d. What is the experimental probability of drawing two green marbles? Does this answer seem reasonable? Explain.

What Is Your Answer?

4. **IN YOUR OWN WORDS** What is the difference between dependent and independent events? Describe a real-life example of each.

Name ______________________________ Date __________

9.4 Practice
For use after Lesson 9.4

Tell whether the events are *independent* or *dependent*. Explain.

1. You spin a game spinner twice.
First Spin: blue
Second Spin: yellow

2. You roll a number cube twice
First Roll: You roll a 6.
Second Roll: You roll an odd number.

3. You and a friend are playing a game. You both randomly draw a playing piece and you get to draw first.
Your Draw: red piece   Friend's Draw: blue piece

You roll a number cube twice. Use the tree diagram to find the probability of the events.

4. Rolling a 5 and then a 3

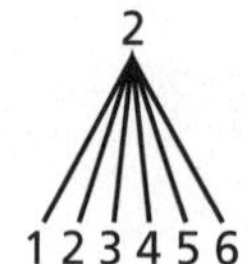

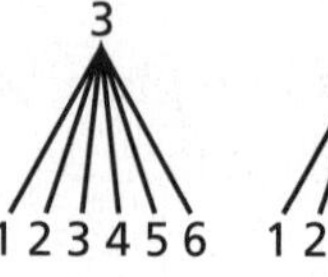

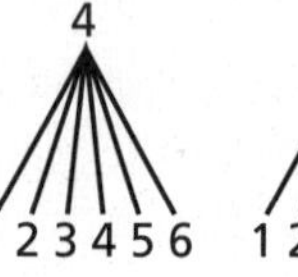

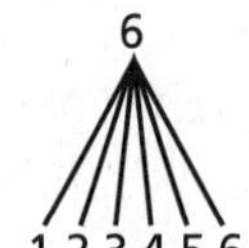

5. Rolling an even number on each roll

6. During a card trick, your friend asks you to pick two cards. A deck of cards has 52 cards and is divided evenly into four suits: hearts, diamonds, clubs, and spades. What is the probability that the first pick is a heart and the second is a diamond?

Name______________________________ Date__________

Chapter 10 Fair Game Review

Solve the equation.

1. $x + 2 = 13$

2. $x - 7 = 10$

3. $3x = 18$

4. $\frac{x}{5} = 6$

5. You have seven new emails in your inbox. The total number of emails in your inbox is 22. Write and solve an equation to find the number of emails e in your inbox that have already been read.

6. You have completed one-fourth of a bike race. Write and solve an equation to find the total distance d of the race if you have already biked 6 miles.

Name ______________________________ Date __________

Chapter 10 Fair Game Review (continued)

Write the ordered pair that corresponds to the point.

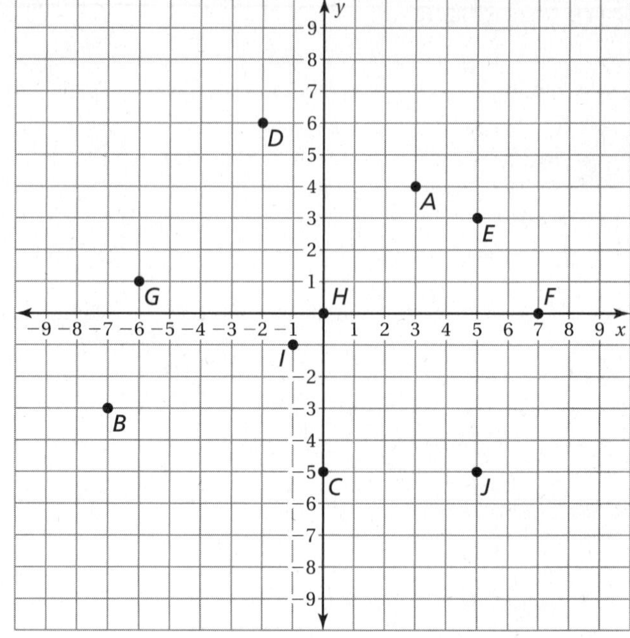

7. Point A

8. Point B

9. Point C

10. Point D

11. Which point is located at $(-6, 1)$?

12. Which point is located in Quadrant IV?

13. Which point is located at the origin?

14. Which point is located on the y-axis?

Name______________________________ Date__________

10.1 Solving Multi-Step Equations

For use with Activity 10.1

Essential Question How can you convert temperatures between the Fahrenheit and Celsius scales?

1 ACTIVITY: Comparing Fahrenheit and Celsius

Work with a partner. The temperature scales show the relationship between the Fahrenheit and Celsius scales. Use the two scales to complete the table.

F	0°	32°	70°	80°	90°	100°	212°
C							

Name ____ Date __________

10.1 Solving Multi-Step Equations (continued)

2 ACTIVITY: Comparing Fahrenheit and Celsius

Work with a partner.

a. Plot the points from the table in Activity 1.

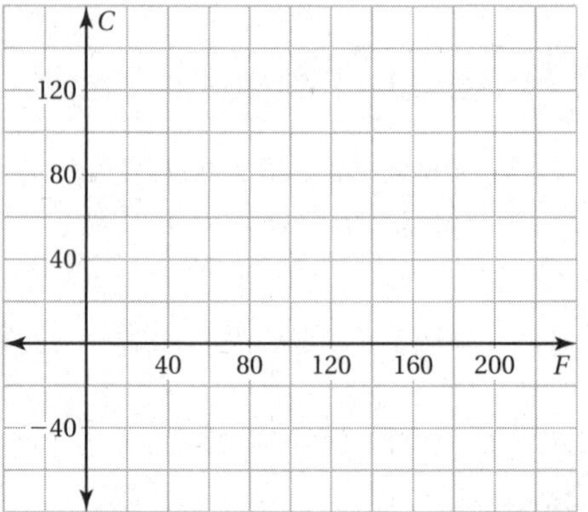

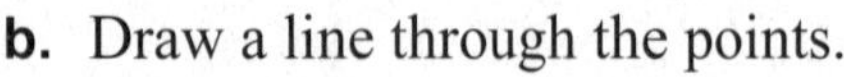

b. Draw a line through the points.

c. Find the slope of the line. Write the slope as a fraction in simplest form.

d. Which of the following shows the relationship between C and F?

$C = \frac{5}{9}(F + 32)$	$C = \frac{5}{9}(F - 32)$
$C = \frac{9}{5}(F + 32)$	$C = \frac{9}{5}(F - 32)$

3 ACTIVITY: Converting Temperatures

Work with a partner. You have email pals in four countries that use the Celsius scale. Write each temperature in degrees Fahrenheit. Then use the scale in Activity 1 to check that your answer is reasonable.

a. Canada: 19°C

b. Mexico: 35°C

c. Japan: 28°C

d. Russia: 6°C

What Is Your Answer?

4. IN YOUR OWN WORDS How can you convert temperatures between the Fahrenheit and Celsius scales? Give two examples.

Name ____ Date __________

10.1 Practice

For use after Lesson 10.1

Solve the equation. Check your solution.

1. $-2x + 8x = 9 + 3$

2. $-5w + 10w - 18 = 12$

3. $6k + 7 - 3k + 7k = 27$

4. $9(b - 2) + 1 = 19$

5. $4 + 5(c - 6) + 8c = -13$

6. $\frac{1}{2}(y - 18) = -2$

7. The length of a rectangular prism is 5 feet and its height is 6 feet. Find the width of the prism if the surface area is 126 square feet.

8. You receive x dollars an hour for babysitting. You babysit 3 hours on Friday and 5 hours on Saturday. You receive $40 for the two days. Write and solve an equation to find how much you earn per hour.

Name______________________________ Date__________

10.2 Solving Equations with Variables on Both Sides
For use with Activity 10.2

Essential Question How can you solve an equation that has variables on both sides?

1 ACTIVITY: Using a Table, Graph, and Algebra

Work with a partner. You have an email pal in Antarctica. Your email pal tells you the temperature in McMurdo. You ask whether he gave the temperature in Celsius or Fahrenheit. He says "It's the same on both scales." What is the temperature?

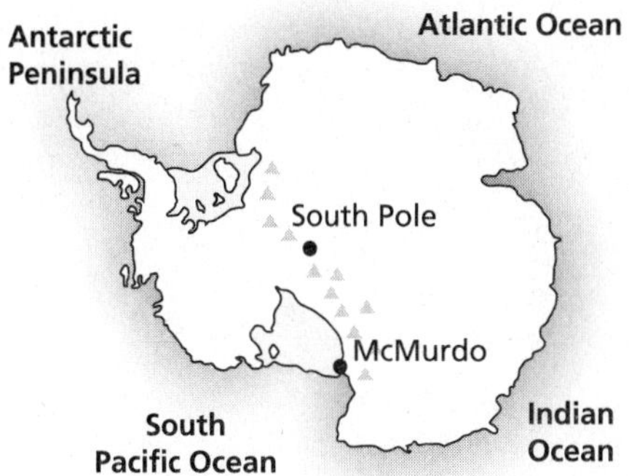

a. TABLE Use "Guess, Check, and Revise" with a table to find the only temperature that is the same on both scales.

F							
C							

b. GRAPH Draw the line given by $C = F$ in the coordinate plane. Locate the point at which the graph of $C = F$ intersects the graph of $C = \frac{5}{9}(F - 32)$.

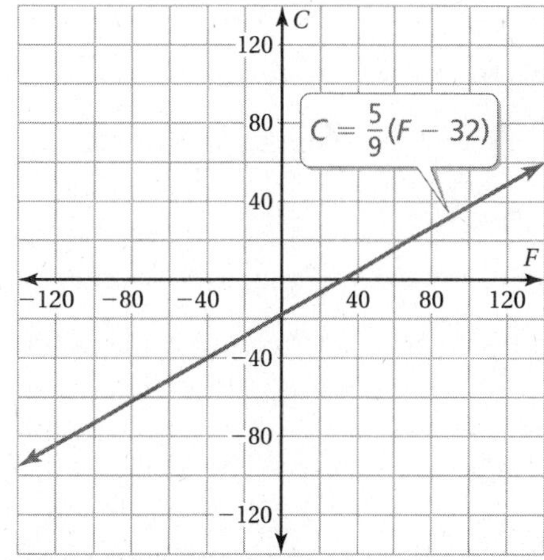

c. ALGEBRA Let x be the temperature that is the same on both scales. Substitute x for C and F in the equation $C = \frac{5}{9}(F - 32)$. Then solve for x.

d. Compare your solutions from parts (a)–(c). Did you get the same solution with each method? Which method do you prefer? Why?

2 GAME: Race to the South Pole

Play with a partner.

- Write each expression on a scrap of brown or blue paper. Place the brown pieces of paper in one bag and the blue pieces of paper in another bag.
- Draw an expression from each bag and set them equal to each other.
- If you can solve the equation, you move one space on the game board on the next page. If you cannot solve the equation, your partner gets a chance to solve it and move one space.
- Put the expressions back into their bags.
- Take turns. The first person to reach the South Pole wins.

Brown Papers	Blue Papers
x	$2x$
$x + 1$	$2x + 4$
$x - 1$	$-2x$
$x + 2$	$-2x + 4$
$x - 2$	$3x$
$x + 3$	$3x + 6$
$x - 3$	$-3x$
	$-3x + 6$

$x + 1$ = $3x$

Name________________________________ Date__________

What Is Your Answer?

3. **IN YOUR OWN WORDS** How can you solve an equation that has variables on both sides? Give an example and solve it.

Name ______________________________ Date __________

10.2 Practice

For use after Lesson 10.2

Solve the equation. Check your solution.

1. $x = -2x - 21$

2. $-3x = 4x - 14$

3. $5p - 11 = 9p + 17$

4. $3.8d + 7 = -8.2d + 70$

5. $-7n + 6 = -3(3n + 10)$

6. $6(y - 5) = -2(5y - 1)$

7. You start a business making painted flower containers. You spend \$300 on paint and \$5 on each container. You charge \$20 for each container. How many containers do you have to sell to break even?

8. There are 322 students in the seventh grade at your school. There are 48 more girls than boys. How many of each are in the seventh grade?

Name____ Date__________

10.2b Practice

For use after Lesson 10.2b

Solve the equation.

1. $2x - 8 = 2x$

2. $3x - 5 = 3x + 7$

3. $6 - x = x + 6$

4. $5x - 3 = 10\left(\frac{1}{2}x + \frac{1}{5}\right)$

5. $7(x - 2) = 4(2x + 1)$

6. $2(2 - 3x) = -6(x + 2)$

7. You and your friend go to an amusement park. You buy t tickets and spend \$8 on food. Your friend buys t tickets and spends \$12 on food. Is it possible that you and your friend spend the same amount at the amusement park? Explain.

Name ______________________________ Date __________

10.2b Practice (continued)

Solve the equation.

8. $\frac{1}{2}(x + 4) = 2 + \frac{1}{2}x$

9. $3(x + 4) = 4(x + 3)$

10. $3x - 6 - 2x = 3x + 6$

11. $\frac{1}{3}(18x - 12) = 2(3x - 2)$

12. $12 - x = -(x + 12)$

13. $\frac{3}{2}x - \frac{1}{2} = -\frac{1}{4}(2 - 6x)$

14. Are there any values of x for which the areas of the figures are the same? Explain.

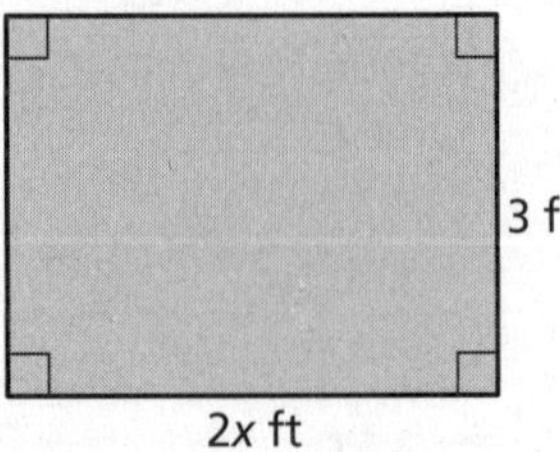

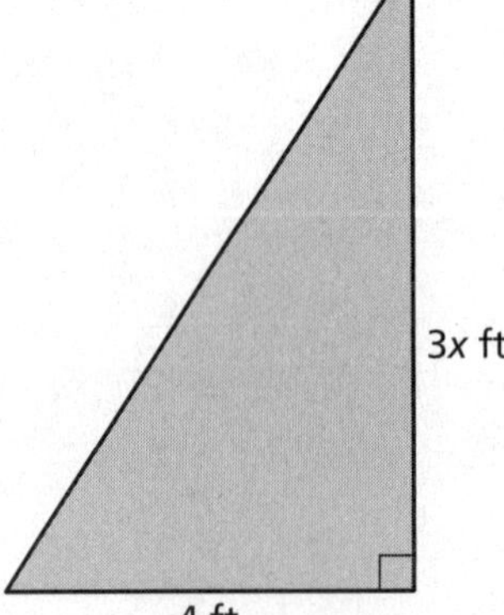

Name______________________________ Date__________

10.3 Solving Equations Using Tables and Graphs

For use with Activity 10.3

Essential Question How can you use tables and graphs to solve equations?

1 ACTIVITY: Using a Table, Graph, and Algebra

Work with a partner. You start a website design company. How many sites must you design before you start making a profit?

- **You pay \$4000 for a new computer and software.**
- **It costs you \$100 to design each website.**
- **You charge \$500 to design each website.**

Let x represent the number of sites you design.

$C = 4000 + 100x$ Cost of designing x sites

$R = 500x$ Income for designing x sites

You will start making a profit when $C = R$. That is, when you have designed enough websites to cover your start-up cost of \$4000 and \$100 for each site.

a. TABLE Use "Guess, Check, and Revise" with a table to find the value of x for which $C = R$.

x							
C							
R							

b. GRAPH Graph $C = 4000 + 100x$ and $R = 500x$ in the same coordinate plane. Find the value of x for which the two lines intersect.

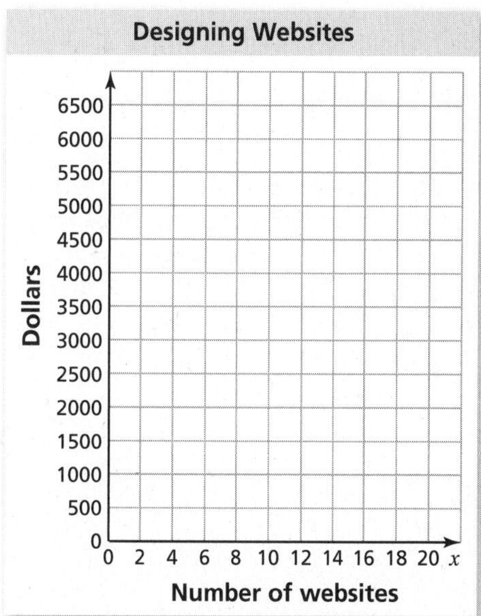

c. ALGEBRA Set C equal to R. Solve for x.

d. The point at which the two lines intersect is called the "break-even" point. Why is it called this?

2 ACTIVITY: Planning Your Own Business

Make a plan to start your own business.

- Describe your business.
- Are you providing a product or a service?
- Make a list of the things you need to start the business. Find the cost of each item or service.
- Write an equation that represents the cost of making x items. Write an equation that represents the income for selling x items.

10.3 Solving Equations Using Tables and Graphs (continued)

- Use a table to compare the cost and income for several values of x.

x							
C							
R							

- Draw a graph that shows when your company will reach the break-even point.

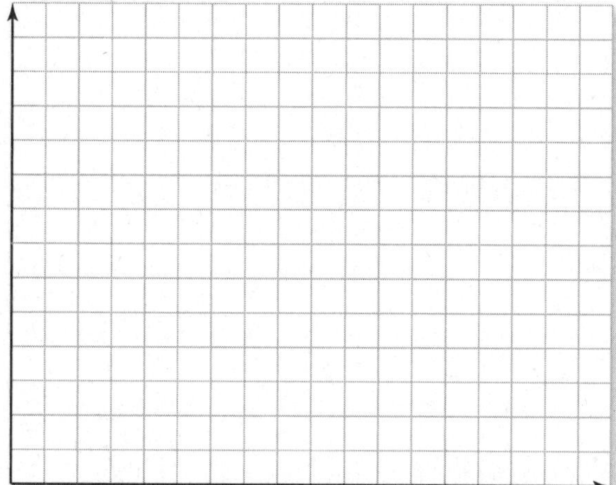

- Organize all of your planning in a folder. Include your company name, logo, and a plan for advertising and selling your product or service.

What Is Your Answer?

3. **IN YOUR OWN WORDS** How can you use tables and graphs to solve equations? Describe a real-life example.

Name ______________________________ Date __________

10.3 Practice

For use after Lesson 10.3

Use a table to solve the equation. Check your solution.

1. $2p + 8 = -2p$

2. $-4y - 7 = 10y$

3. $5p - 20 = 3p + 8$

4. $-6d + 15 = -10d - 9$

Use the graph to solve the equation. Check your solution.

5. $x + 2 = 2x + 1$

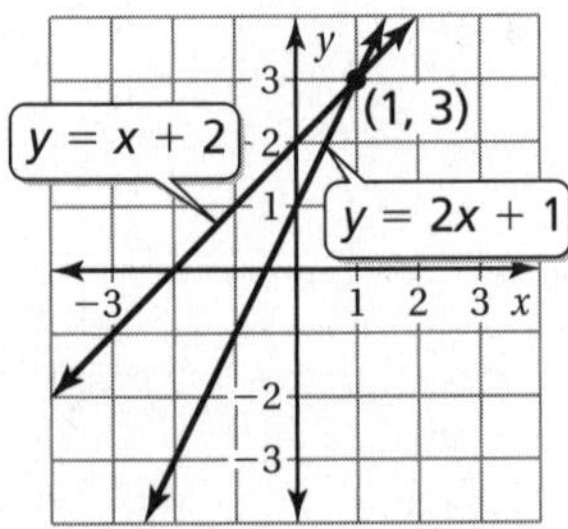

6. $4x - 4 = -2x + 2$

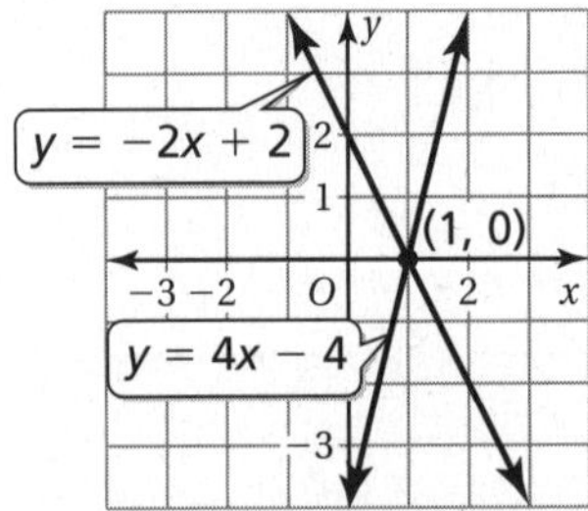

7. Company A sells a satellite radio for \$300 and the music package for \$10 per month. Company B sells a satellite radio for \$200 and the music package for \$15 per month.

a. Use a graph to find the number of months it takes for the cost of Company A's products to equal the cost of Company B's products.

b. If you are signing a two-year contract, which company should you buy from? Why?

Name______________________________ Date__________

10.4 Slope of a Line

For use with Activity 10.4

Essential Question How can the slope of a line be used to describe the line?

You studied the following definition of the slope of a line.

Slope is the rate of change between any two points on a line. It is a measure of the *steepness* of a line. To find the slope of a line, find the ratio of the change in y (vertical change) to the change in x (horizontal change).

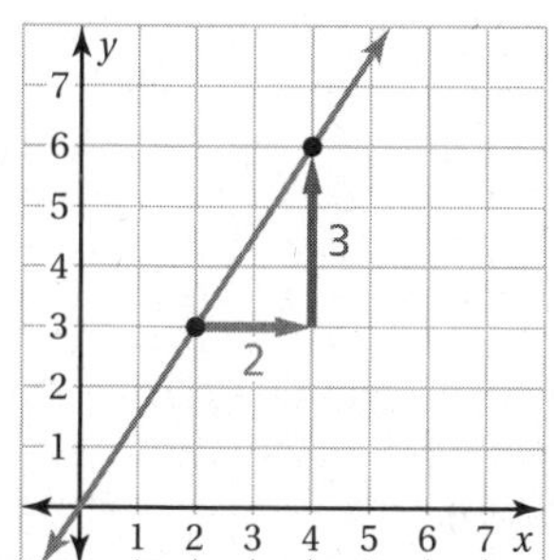

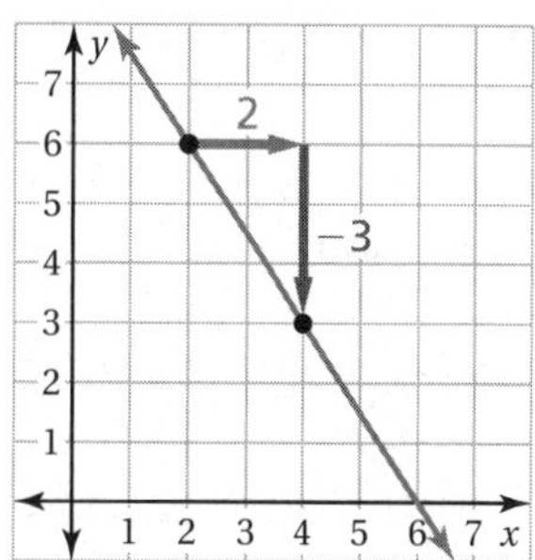

$$\textbf{slope} = \frac{\text{change in } y}{\text{change in } x} = \frac{3}{2}$$

$$\textbf{slope} = \frac{\text{change in } y}{\text{change in } x} = \frac{-3}{2} = -\frac{3}{2}$$

1 ACTIVITY: Extending the Concept of a Slope

Work with a partner. Find the slope of each line.

a. 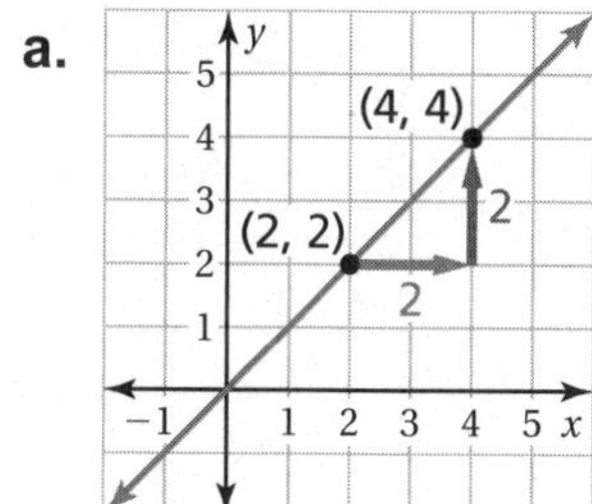

b. 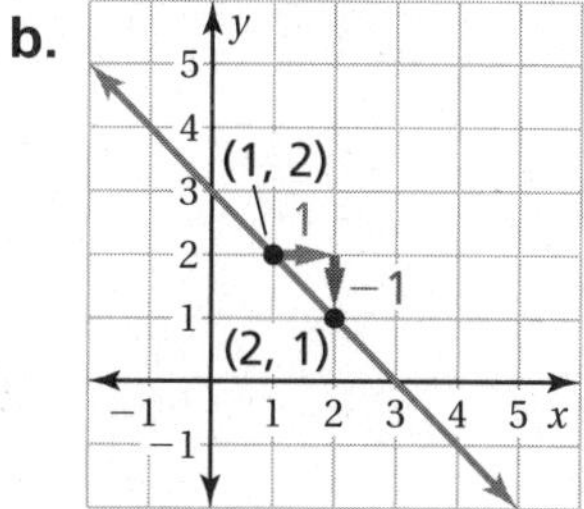

c. 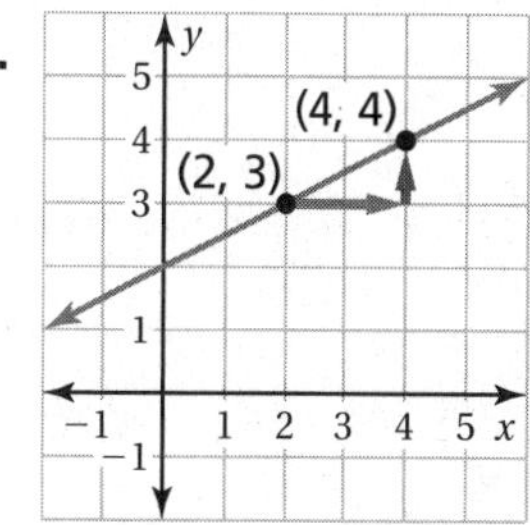

Name ____________________ Date __________

10.4 Slope of a Line (continued)

d. 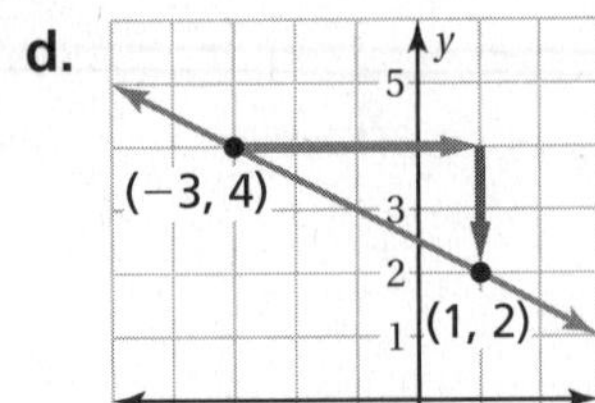

e. 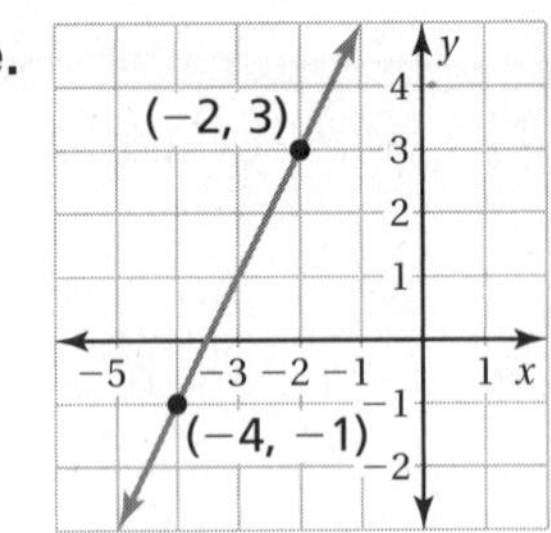

f. 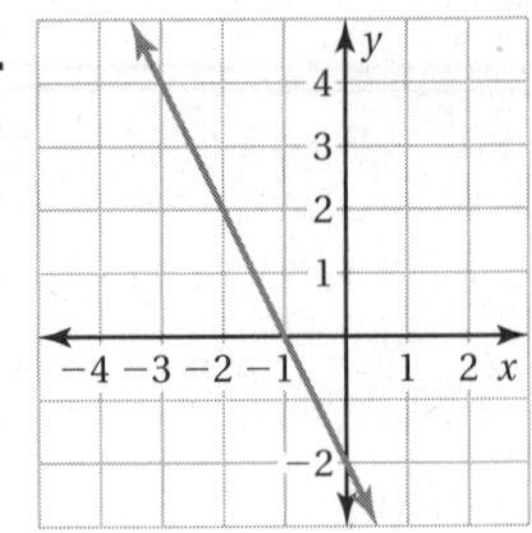

Inductive Reasoning

Work with a partner. Complete the table.

	Two Points	Change in *y*	Change in *x*	Slope of Line
1a	**2.** (2, 2), (4, 4)			
1b	**3.** (1, 2), (2, 1)			
1c	**4.** (2, 3), (4, 4)			
1d	**5.** (−3, 4), (1, 2)			
1e	**6.** (−4, −1), (−2, 3)			
1f	**7.**			
	8. (−4, 0), (0, 1)			
	9. (−3, 4), (6, −2)			
	10. (−4, 2), (8, −1)			
	11. (−6, −1), (3, 5)			
	12. (−5, 7), (10, −5)			
	13. (0, 1), (4, 1)			
	14. (−4, −2), (−3, −6)			

Name____________________ Date__________

What Is Your Answer?

15. IN YOUR OWN WORDS How can the slope of a line be used to describe the line?

a. Draw three lines that have positive slopes.

b. Draw three lines that have negative slopes.

16. Compare a slope of 1 with a slope of 2. Show your comparison on a graph.

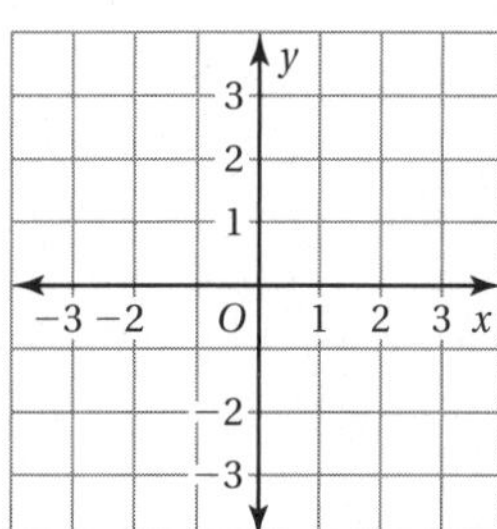

17. Compare a slope of –1 to a slope of −2. Show your comparison on a graph.

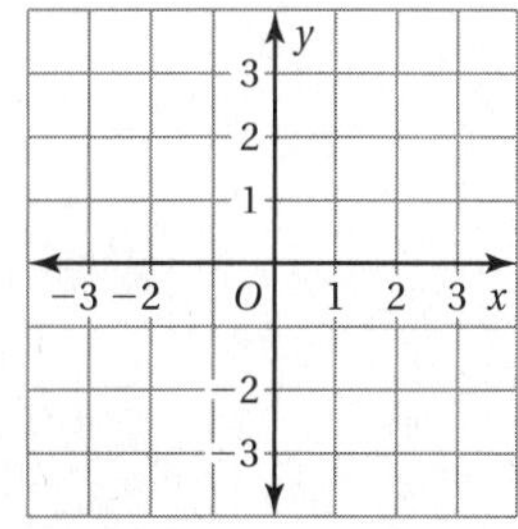

Name ______________________________ Date __________

10.4 Practice

For use after Lesson 10.4

Find the slope of the line.

1.

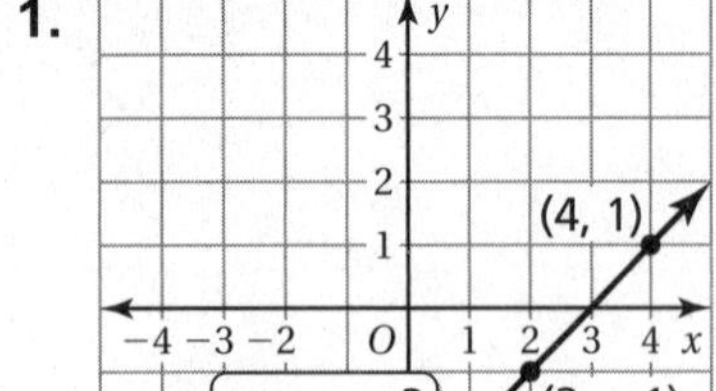

2.

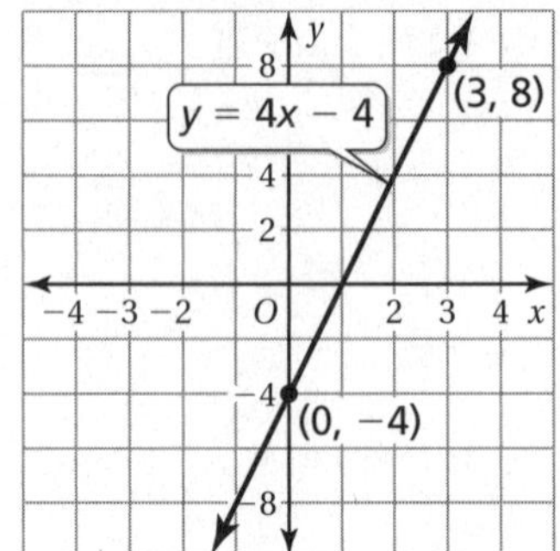

Graph the line with the given slope that passes through the given point.

3. slope $= -1$; $(2, 3)$

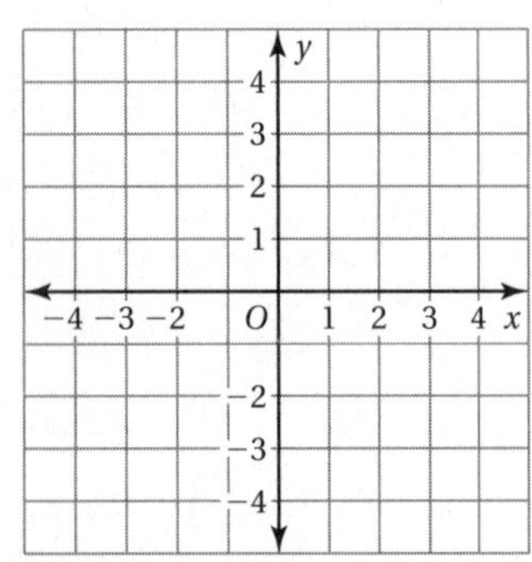

4. slope $= \dfrac{2}{3}$; $(-1, 3)$

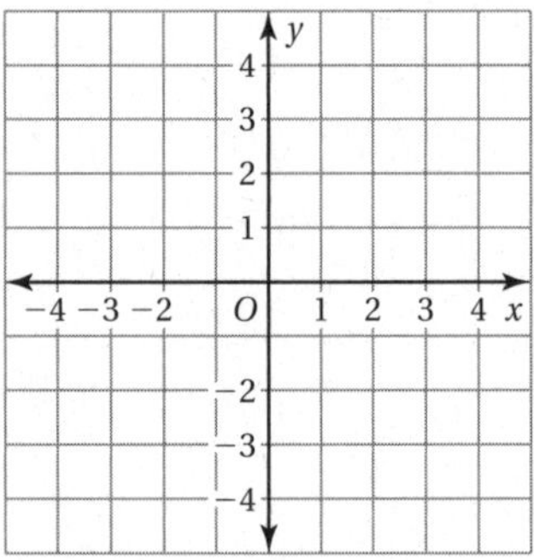

5. slope $= 4$; $(-2, -4)$

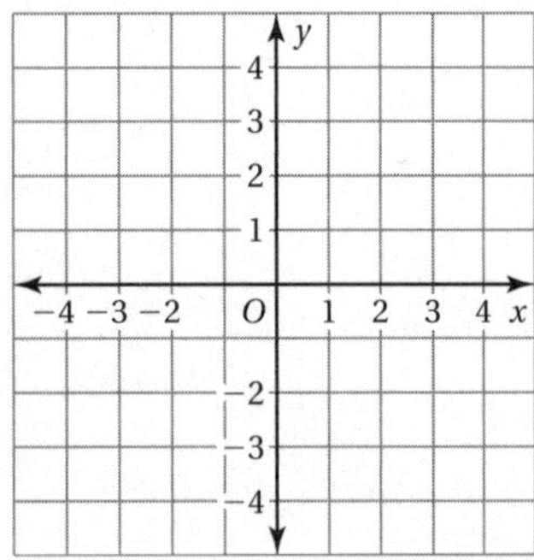

6. slope $= -\dfrac{1}{5}$; $(3, -2)$

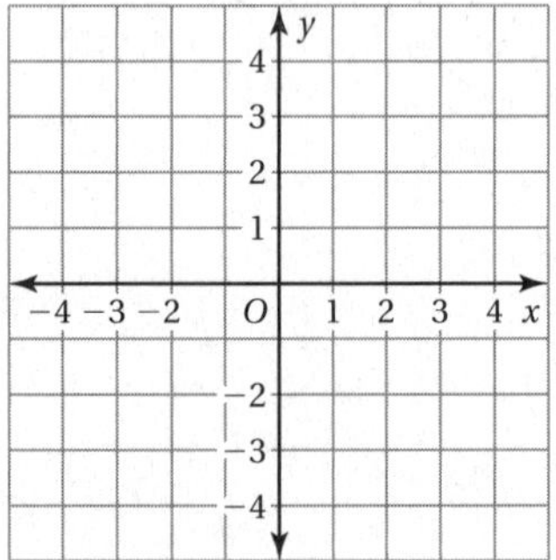

7. What is the slope of the ramp?

Name____ Date__________

10.5 Linear Functions
For use with Activity 10.5

Essential Question How can you describe the graph of an equation of the form $y = mx + b$?

1 ACTIVITY: Using an Input-Output Table

Work with a partner.

a. Complete the input-output table for the equation $y = -\frac{1}{2}x + 2$.

Input, x	−3	−2	−1	0	1	2	3
Output, y							

b. Plot the points from the table.

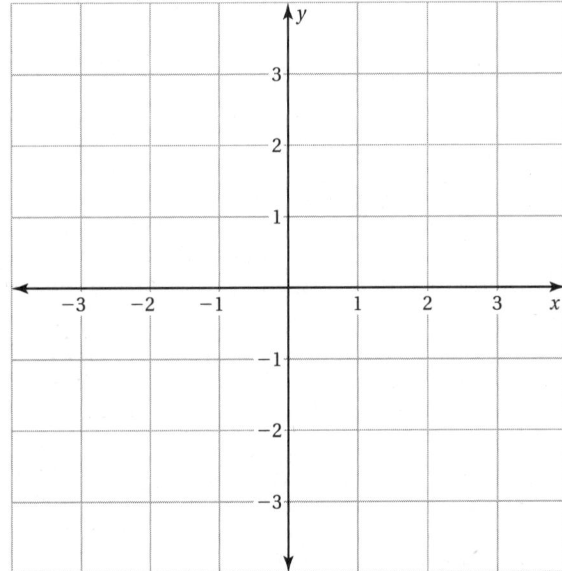

c. Describe the pattern of the points. Draw a graph that represents the pattern.

d. Choose three values of x that are not in the table. Find their corresponding y-values and plot the points on your graph from part (b). Do the points lie on the graph you made in part (c)?

Inductive Reasoning

Work with a partner. Sketch the graph of each equation. Then complete the table.

	Equation	Description of Graph	Point of Intersection with y-axis	Slope of Graph
1	**2.** $y = -\frac{1}{2}x + 2$			
	3. $y = -x + 2$			
	4. $y = -x + 1$			
	5. $y = -\frac{1}{2}x + 1$			
	6. $y = x + 1$			
	7. $y = x - 1$			
	8. $y = \frac{1}{2}x - 1$			
	9. $y = \frac{1}{2}x + 1$			
	10. $y = 2x + 1$			
	11. $y = 2x - 2$			
	12. $y = -2x + 3$			

What Is Your Answer?

13. IN YOUR OWN WORDS How can you describe the graph of an equation of the form $y = mx + b$?

a. How does the value of m affect the graph?

b. How does the value of b affect the graph?

c. Test your answers to parts (a) and (b) with three equations that are not in the table.

14. Why is an equation of the form $y = mx + b$ called a linear function? What does the word *linear* mean? What does the word *function* mean?

Name ______________________________ Date __________

10.5 Practice

For use after Lesson 10.5

Find the slope and *y*-intercept of the graph of the linear function.

1. $y = \frac{5}{8}x - 6$ **2.** $y = -7x + 5$ **3.** $2x + 4y = 10$

Graph the linear function using slope-intercept form.

4. $y = 4x - 2$

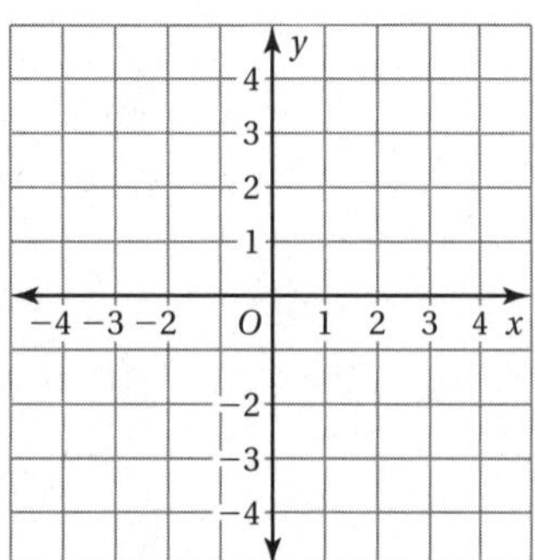

5. $3x + 5y = 20$

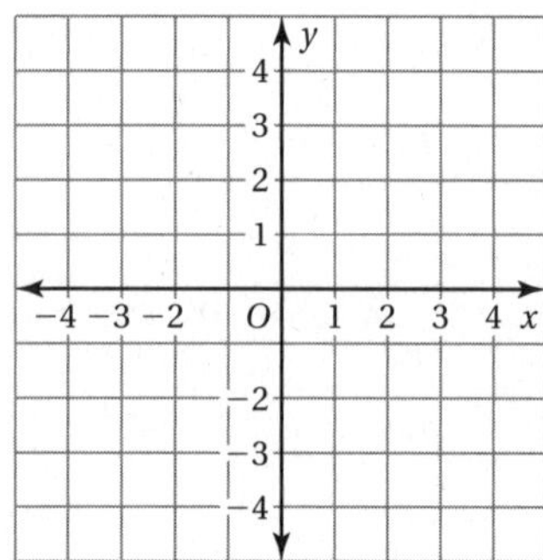

Write an equation of the linear function in slope-intercept form.

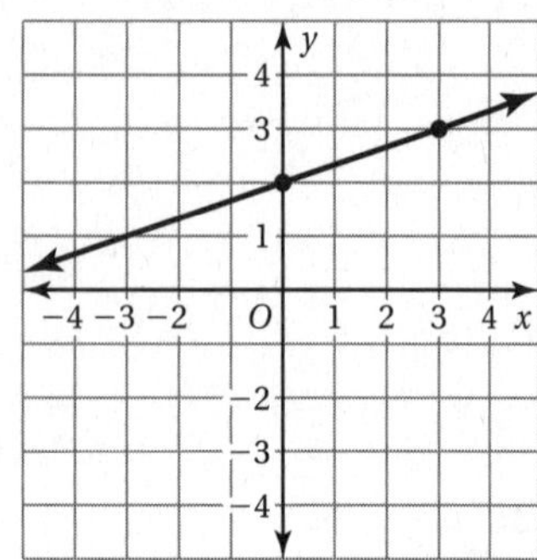

7.

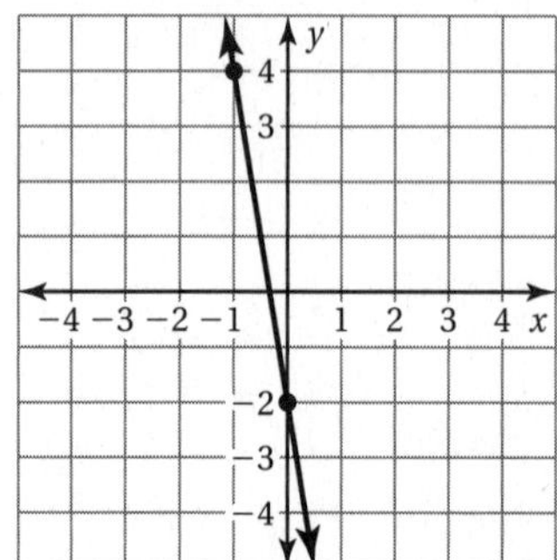

8. The number of songs s that you can learn to play on the piano after n weeks is given by $s = 8 + 3n$. What does the y-intercept represent? What does the slope represent?

Name____ Date__________

Chapter 11

Fair Game Review

The polygons are similar. Find the value of *x*.

1.

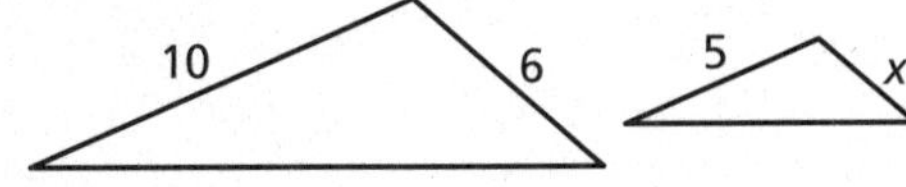

2.

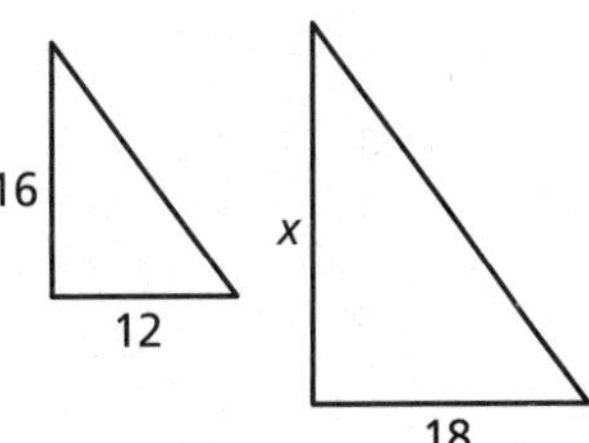

3.

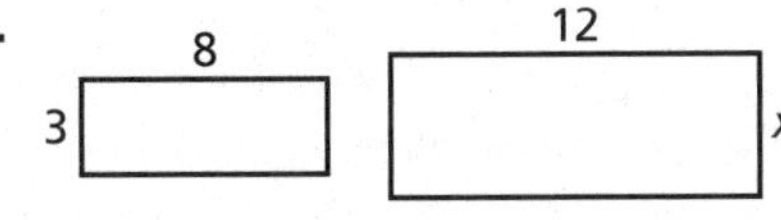

4.

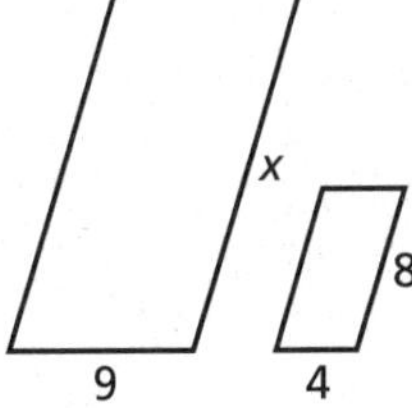

5. The two peaks of a house are similar triangles. What is the value of x?

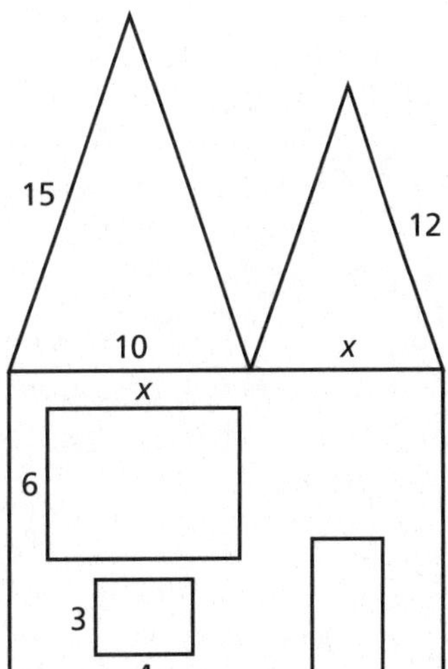

6. The two windows on the house are also similar. What is the value of x?

Name ______________________________ Date ________

Chapter 11 Fair Game Review (continued)

The polygons are similar. Find the value of *x*.

7. The ratio of the perimeters is 2 : 1.

8. The ratio of the perimeters is 2 : 5.

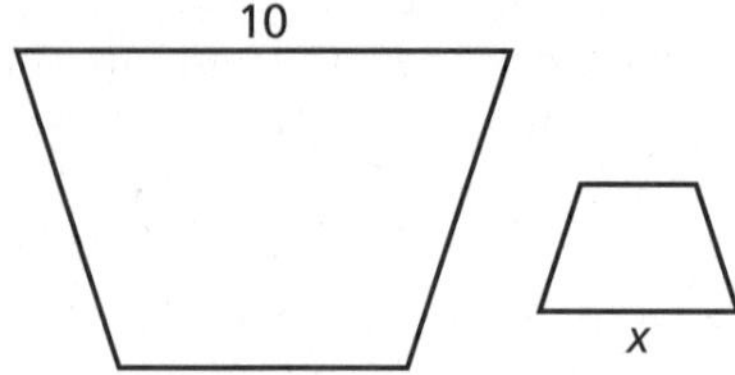

9. The ratio of the perimeters is 4 : 3.

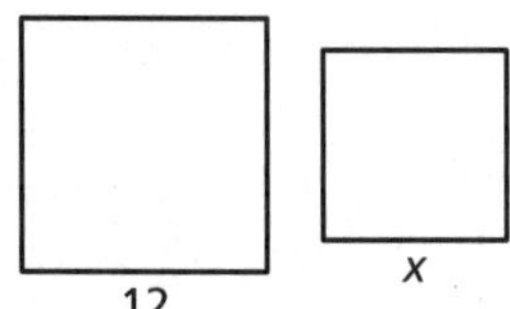

10. The ratio of the perimeters is 3 : 5.

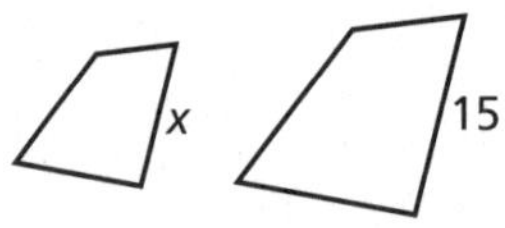

11. Your school builds a new gymnasium that is similar to the old one. The ratio of the perimeters is 2 : 3. The new gymnasium has a length of 90 feet. What was the length of the old gymnasium?

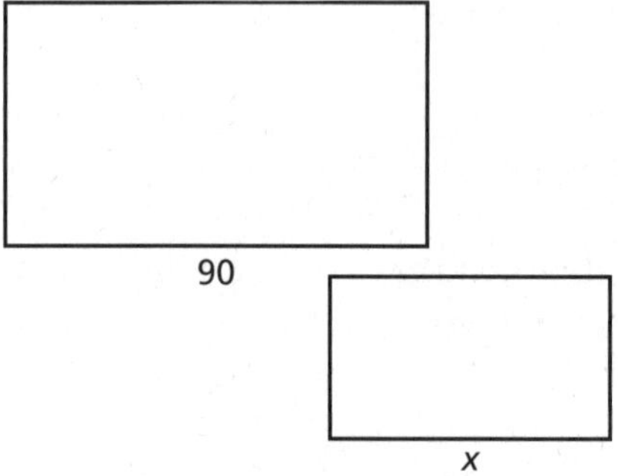

Name______________________________ Date__________

11.1 Classifying Angles

For use with Activity 11.1

Essential Question How can you classify two angles as complementary or supplementary?

Classification of Angles

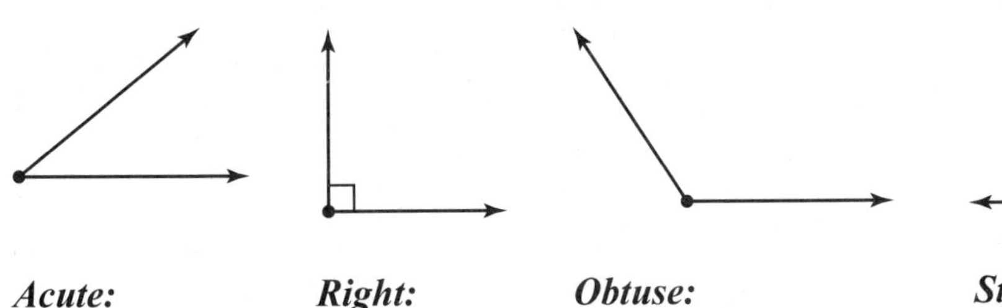

Acute: Less than 90°

Right: Equal to 90°

Obtuse: Greater than 90° and less than 180°

Straight: Equal to 180°

1 ACTIVITY: Complementary and Supplementary Angles

Work with a partner.

- **Complete each table.**
- **Graph each function. Is the function linear?**
- **Write an equation for *y* as a function of *x*.**
- **Describe the values of *x* that make sense for each function.**

a. Two angles are **complementary** if the sum of their measures is 90°. In the table, *x* and *y* are complementary.

x	15°	30°	45°	60°	75°
y					

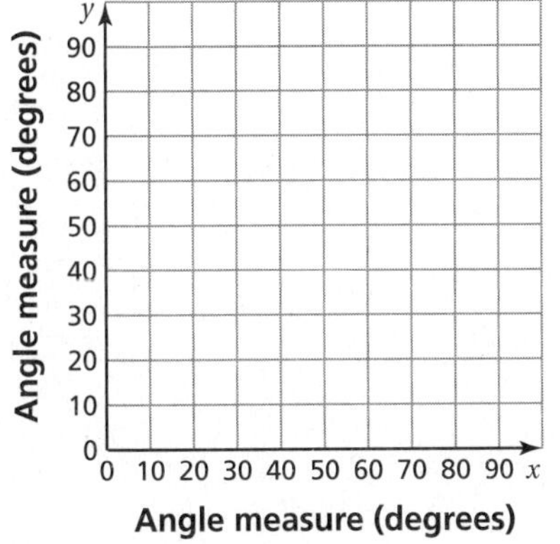

b. Two angles are **supplementary** if the sum of their measures is 180°. In the table, *x* and *y* are supplementary.

x	30°	60°	90°	120°	150°
y					

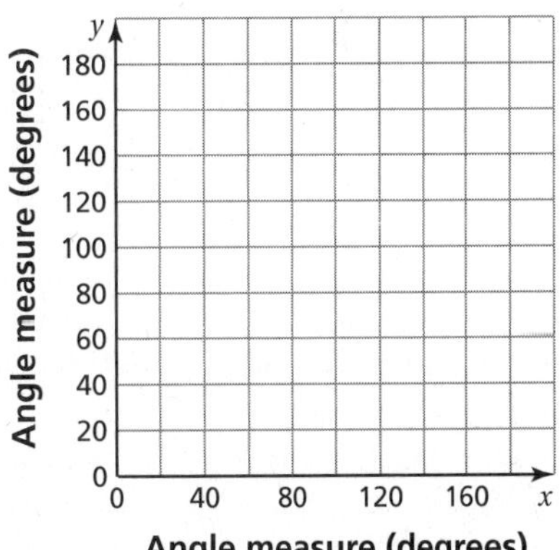

Name ____ Date __________

11.1 Classifying Angles (continued)

2 ACTIVITY: Exploring Rules About Angles

Work with a partner. Complete each sentence with *always*, *sometimes*, or *never*.

a. If x and y are complementary angles, then both x and y are ____________ acute.

b. If x and y are supplementary angles, then x is ____________ acute.

c. If x is a right angle, then x is ____________ acute.

3 ACTIVITY: Naming Angles

Some angles, such as $\angle A$, can be named by a single letter. When this does not clearly identify an angle, you should use three letters, as follows.

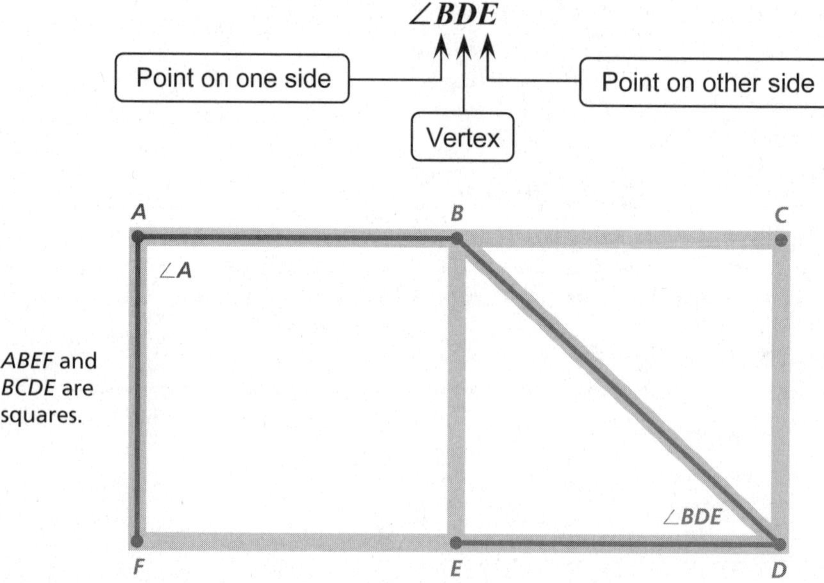

Work with a partner.

a. Name all pairs of complementary angles in the diagram above.

b. Name all pairs of supplementary angles in the diagram above.

What Is Your Answer?

4. **IN YOUR OWN WORDS** How can you classify two angles as complementary or supplementary? Give examples of each type.

5. Find examples of real-life objects that use complementary and supplementary angles. Make a drawing of each object and approximate the degree measure of each angle.

Name ______________________________ Date __________

11.1 Practice
For use after Lesson 11.1

Tell whether the angles are *complementary*, *supplementary*, or *neither*.

1.
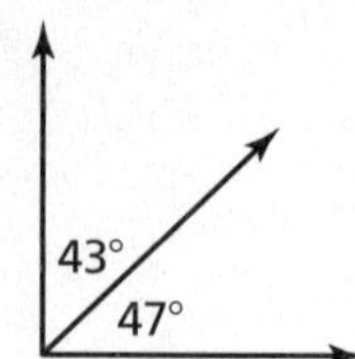

2.
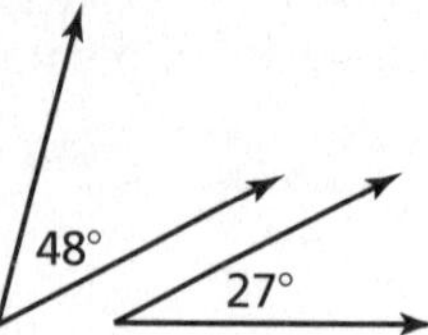

3.
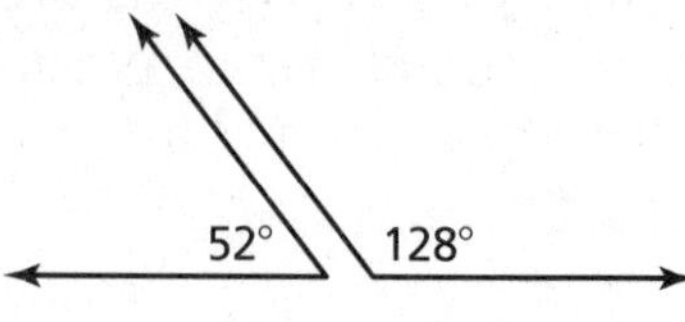

Find the value of *x*.

4.
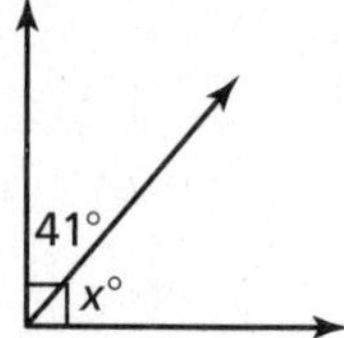

5.
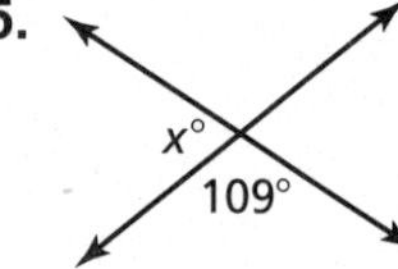

6.
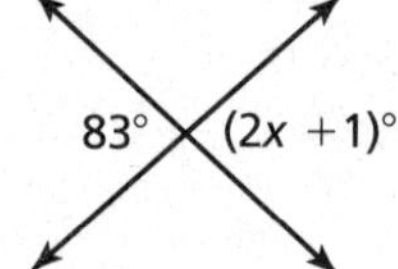

7.
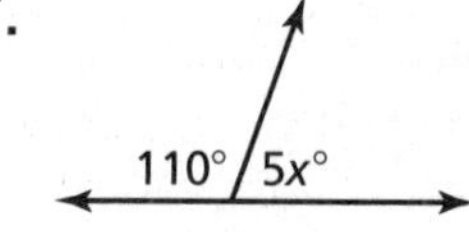

8. Find the value of x needed to hit the ball in the hole.

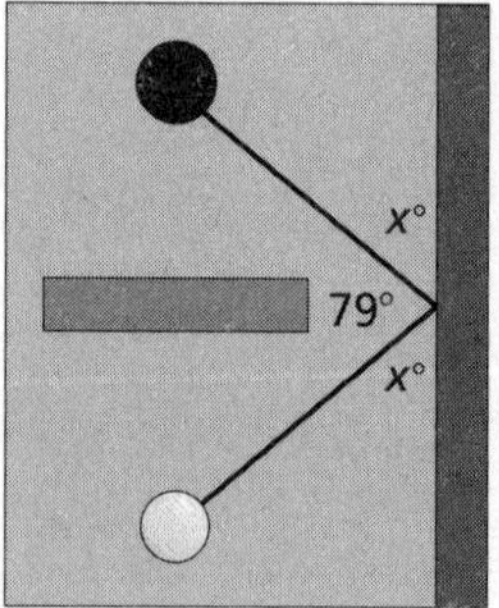

Name____ Date__________

11.2 Angles and Sides of Triangles

For use with Activity 11.2

Essential Question How can you classify triangles by their angles?

1 ACTIVITY: Exploring the Angles of a Triangle

Work with a partner.

a. Draw a large triangle that has an obtuse angle on a separate piece of paper. Label the angles *A*, *B*, and *C*.

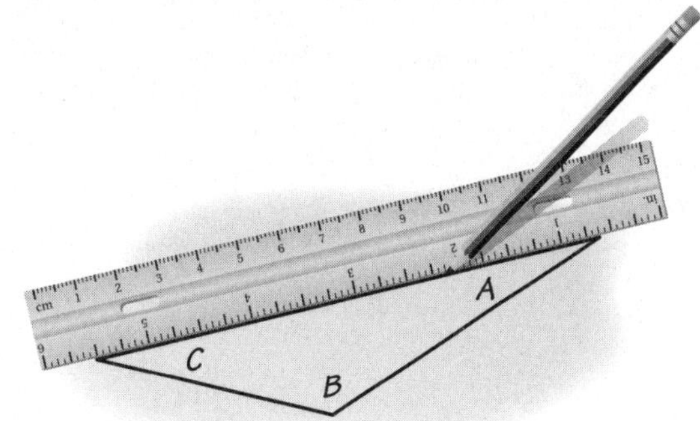

b. Carefully cut out the triangle. Tear off the three corners of the triangle.

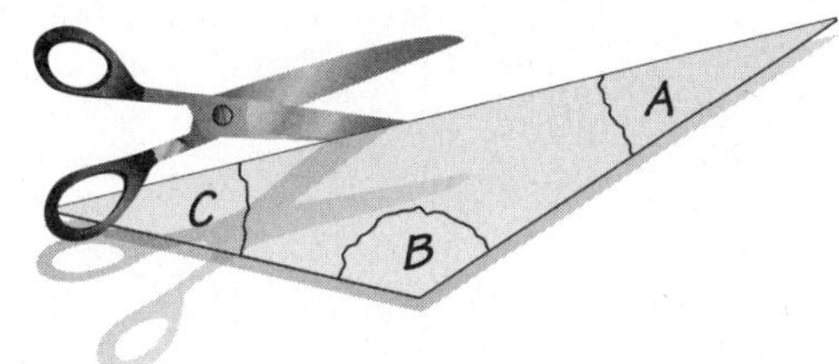

c. Draw a straight line on a piece of paper. Arrange angles *A* and *B* as shown.

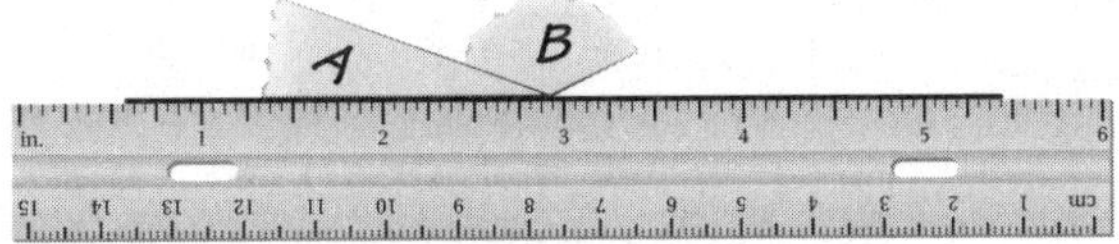

d. Place the third angle as shown. What does this tell you about the sum of the measures of the angles?

e. Draw three other triangles that have different shapes. Repeat parts (b)–(d) for each one. Do you get the same results as in part (d)? Explain.

f. Write a rule about the sum of the measures of the angles of a triangle.

Name ____ Date _________

11.2 Angles and Sides of Triangles (continued)

2 ACTIVITY: Thinking About Vocabulary

Work with a partner. Talk about the meaning of each name. Use reasoning to define each name. Then match each name with a triangle.

Note: Each triangle has at least one name, but some have more than one name.

a. Right triangle

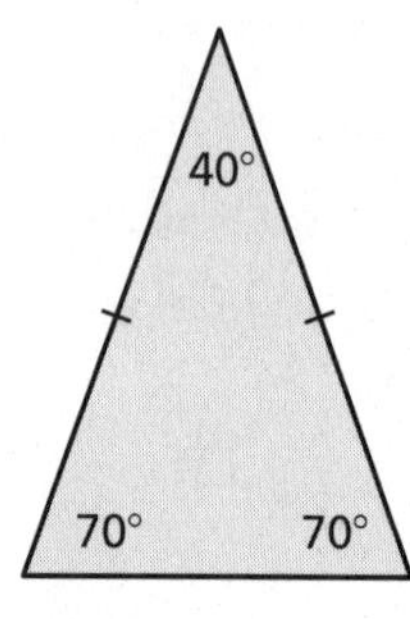

b. Acute triangle

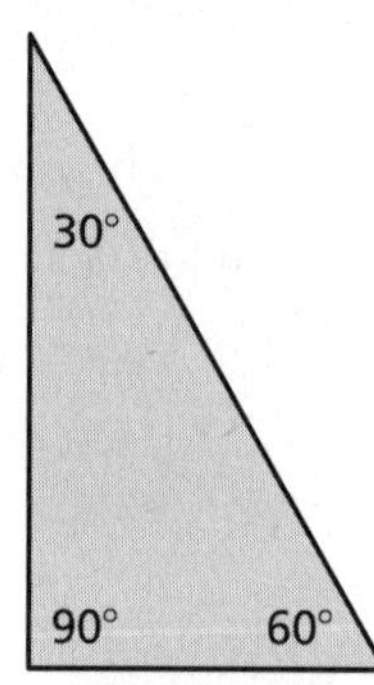

c. Obtuse triangle

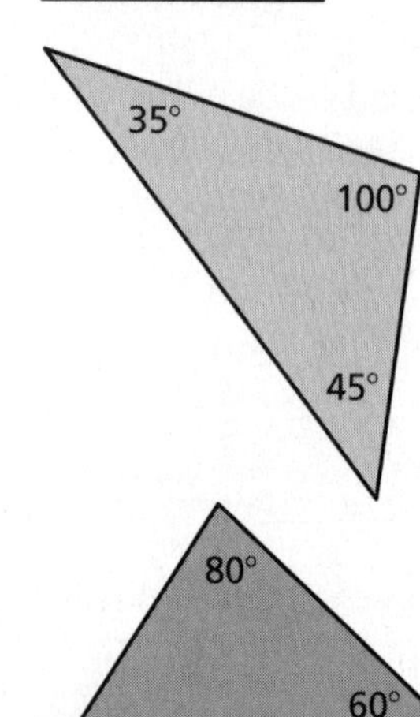

d. Equiangular triangle

e. Equilateral triangle

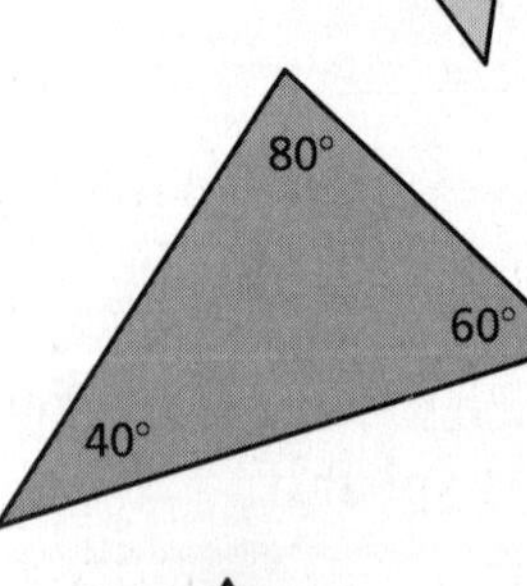

f. Isosceles triangle

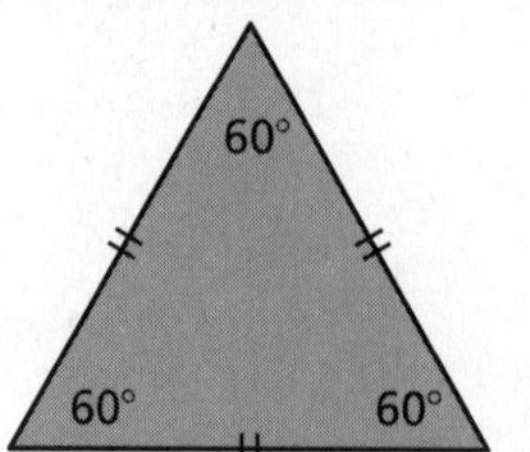

Name________________________________ Date__________

11.2 Angles and Sides of Triangles (continued)

3 ACTIVITY: Triangles in Art

Work with a partner.

a. Trace four triangles in the painting. Classify each triangle using the names in Activity 2.

Abstract II by Linda Bahner

b. Design your own abstract art painting. How many different types of triangles did you use in your painting?

What Is Your Answer?

4. IN YOUR OWN WORDS How can you classify triangles by their angles?

5. Find examples of real-life triangles in architecture. Name each type of triangle that you find.

Name ______________________________ Date ________

11.2 Practice

For use after Lesson 11.2

Find the value of x. Then classify the triangle in as many ways as possible.

1.

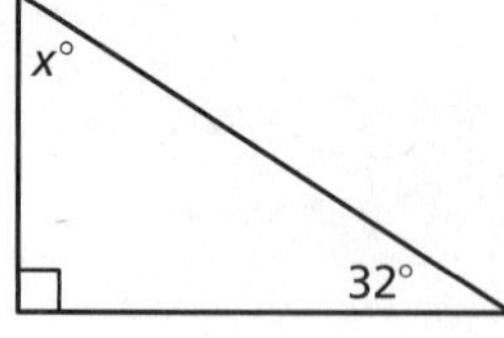

2.

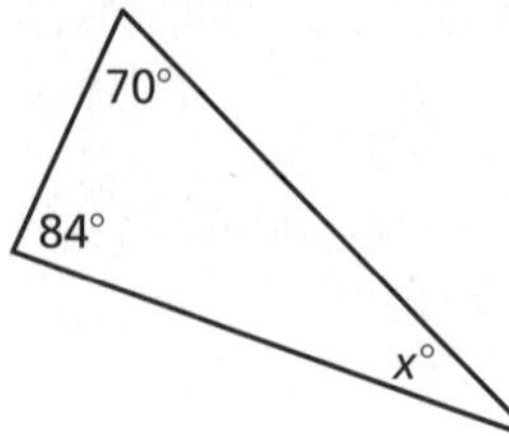

3.

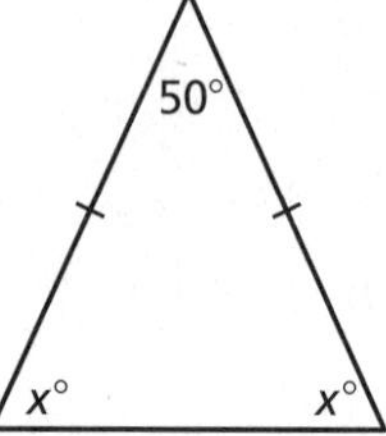

4.

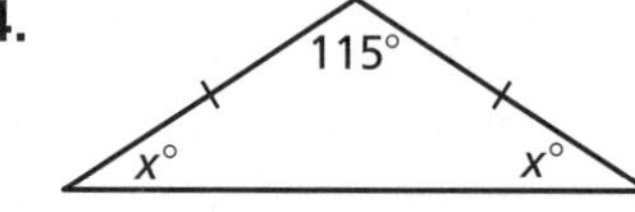

Tell whether a triangle can have the given angle measures. If not, change the first angle measure so that the angle measures form a triangle.

5. 28°, 42°, 110°

6. 77°, 98°, 15°

7. 31°, 59°, 60°

8. Find the value of x on the clothes hanger. What type of triangle must the hanger be to hang clothes evenly?

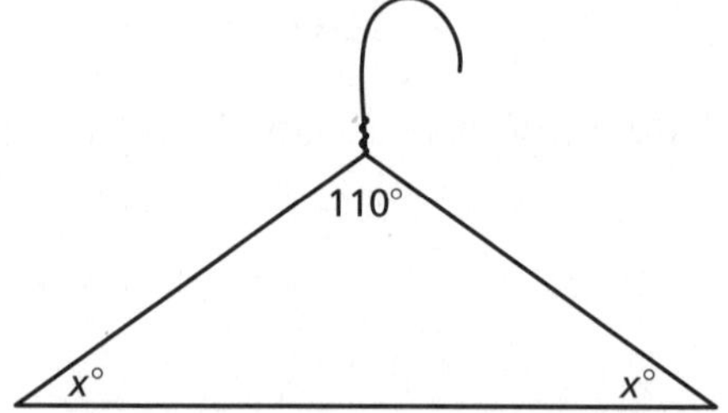

Name ______________________ Date __________

11.3 Angles of Polygons

For use with Activity 11.3

Essential Question How can you find a formula for the sum of the angle measures of any polygon?

1 ACTIVITY: The Sum of the Angle Measures of a Polygon

Work with a partner. Find the sum of the angle measures of each polygon with *n* sides.

a. Sample: Quadrilateral: $n = 4$
Draw a line that divides the quadrilateral into two triangles.

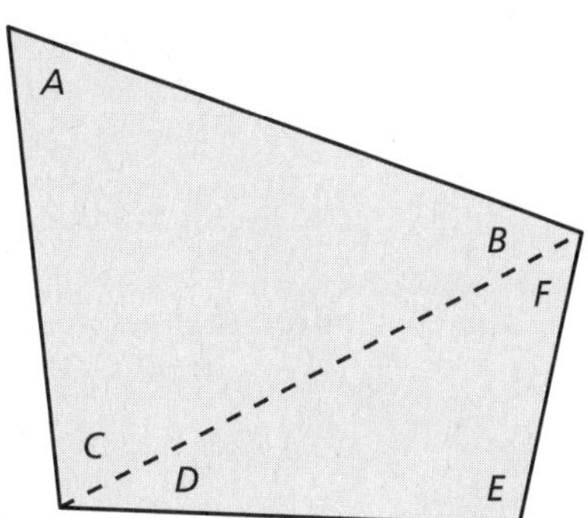

Because the sum of the angle measures of each triangle is $180°$, the sum of the angle measures of the quadrilateral is $360°$.

$$(A + B + C) + (D + E + F) = 180° + 180°$$
$$= 360°$$

b. Pentagon: $n = 5$

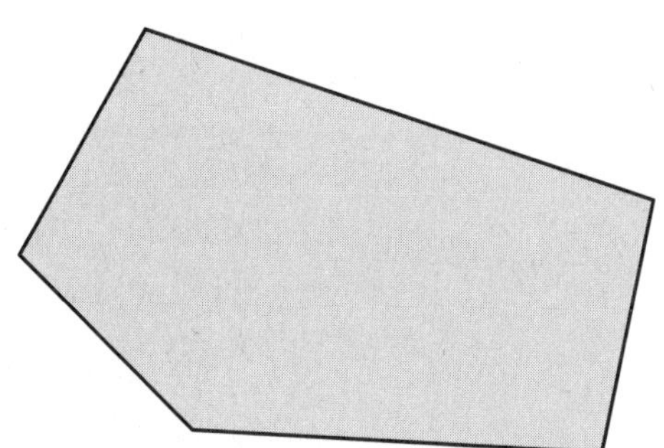

c. Hexagon: $n = 6$

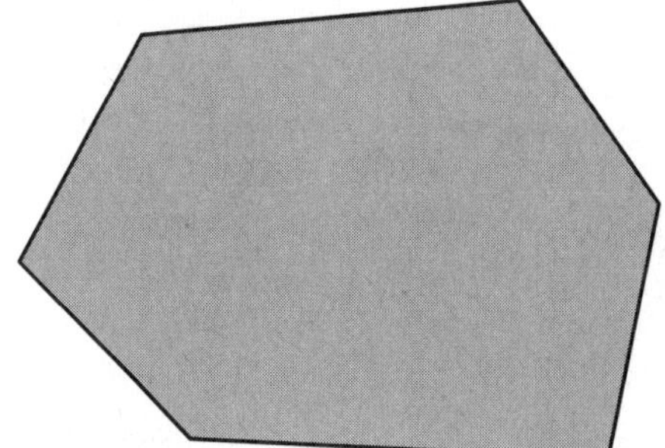

d. Heptagon: $n = 7$

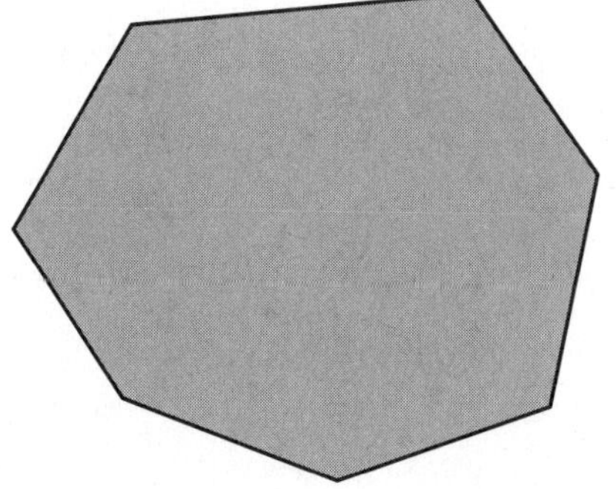

e. Octagon: $n = 8$

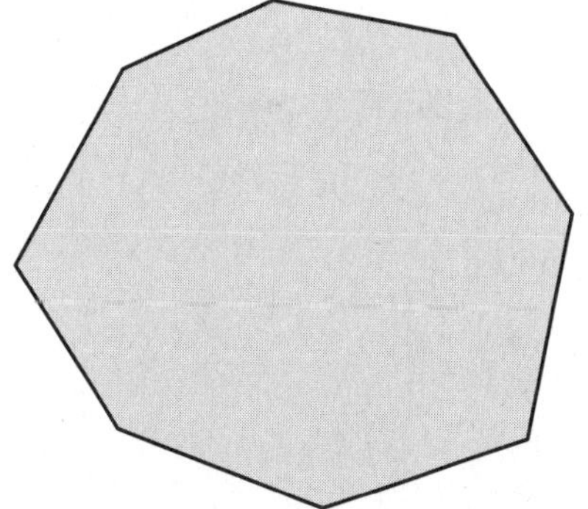

Name ______________________________ Date __________

11.3 Angles of Polygons (continued)

2 ACTIVITY: The Sum of the Angle Measures of a Polygon

Work with a partner.

a. Use the table to organize your results from Activity 1.

Sides, n	3	4	5	6	7	8
Angle Sum, S						

b. Plot the points in the table in a coordinate plane.

c. Write a linear equation that relates S to n.

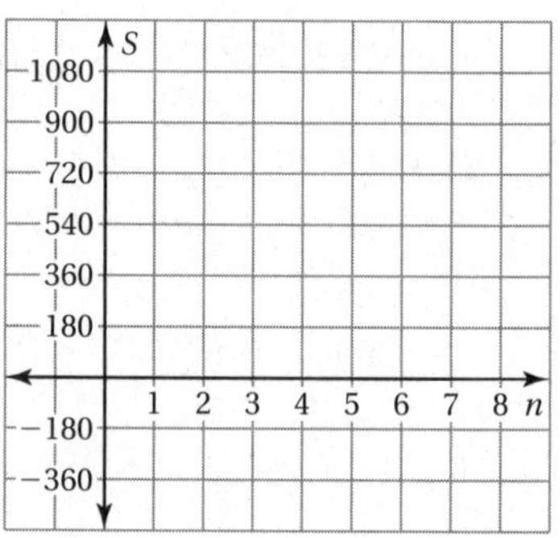

d. What values of n make sense for the function? Explain your reasoning.

e. Use the function to find the sum of the angle measures of a polygon with 10 sides.

Name____ Date__________

11.3 Angles of Polygons (continued)

3 ACTIVITY: The Sum of the Angle Measures of a Polygon

Work with a partner.

A polygon is **convex** if the line segment connecting any two vertices lies entirely inside the polygon. A polygon that is not convex is called **concave**.

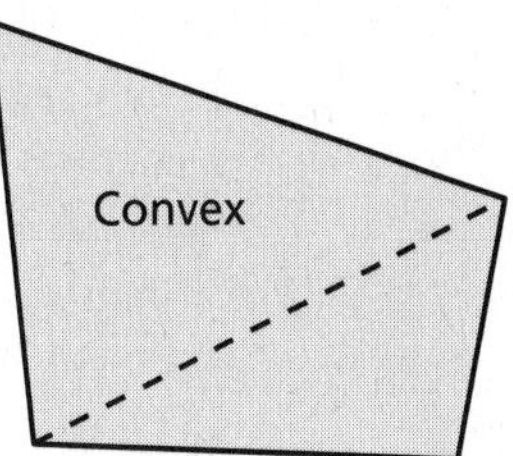

Does the equation you found in Activity 2 apply to concave polygons? Explain.

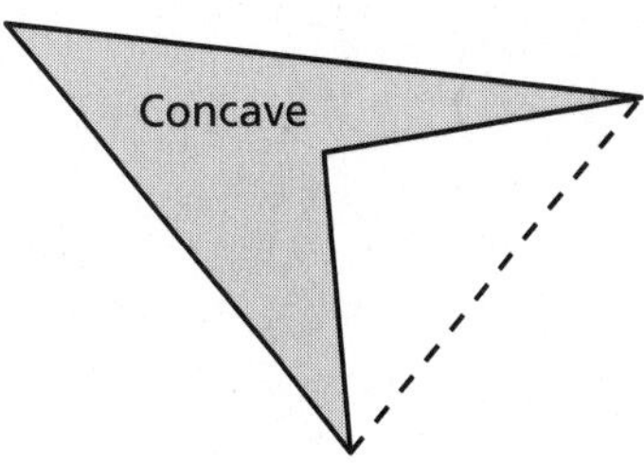

How can you define the measure of an angle so that your equation applies to *any* polygon?

What Is Your Answer?

4. **IN YOUR OWN WORDS** How can you find a formula for the sum of the angle measures of any polygon?

Name ______________________________ Date __________

11.3 Practice

For use after Lesson 11.3

Find the sum of the angle measures of the polygon.

1. 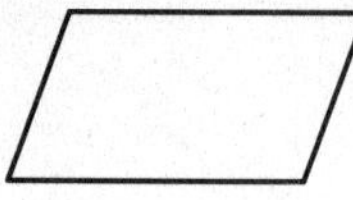

2. 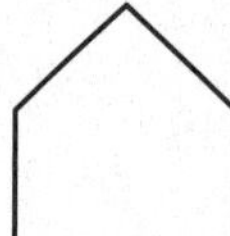

3. 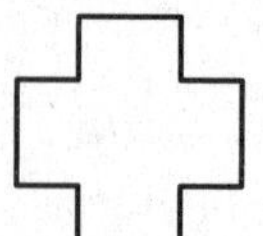

Find the value of *x*.

4. 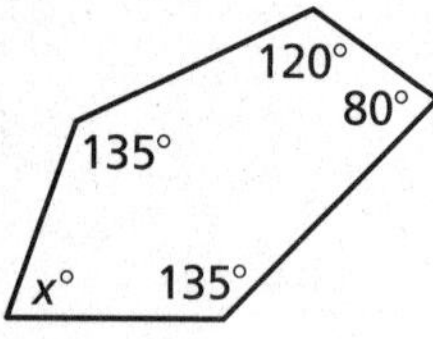

5. 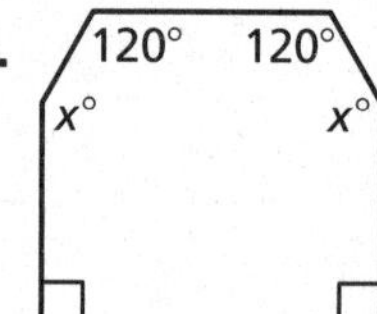

Find the measure of each angle of the regular polygon.

6. 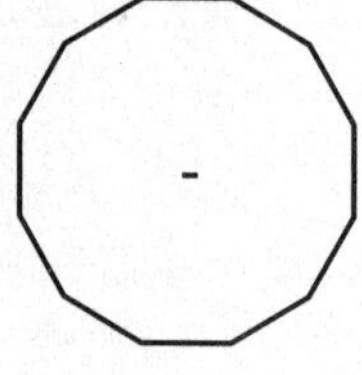

7. 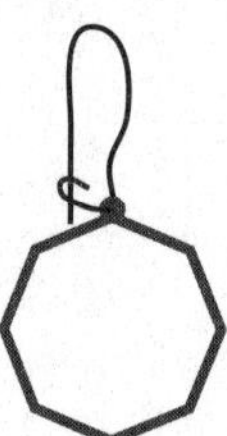

Tell whether the polygon is *convex* or *concave*.

8. 

9. 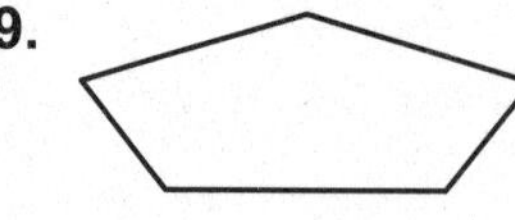

10. In pottery class, you are making a pot that is shaped as a regular hexagon. What is the measure of each angle in the regular hexagon?

Name______________________________ Date__________

11.4 Using Similar Triangles

For use with Activity 11.4

Essential Question Which properties of triangles make them special among all other types of polygons?

You already know that two triangles are **similar** if and only if the ratios of their corresponding side lengths are equal.

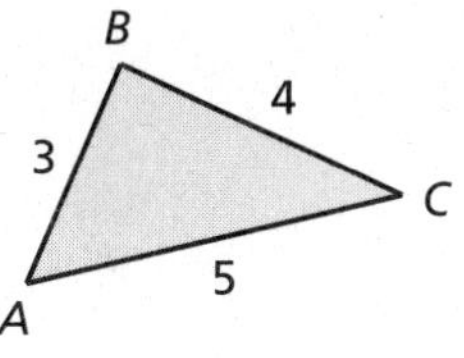

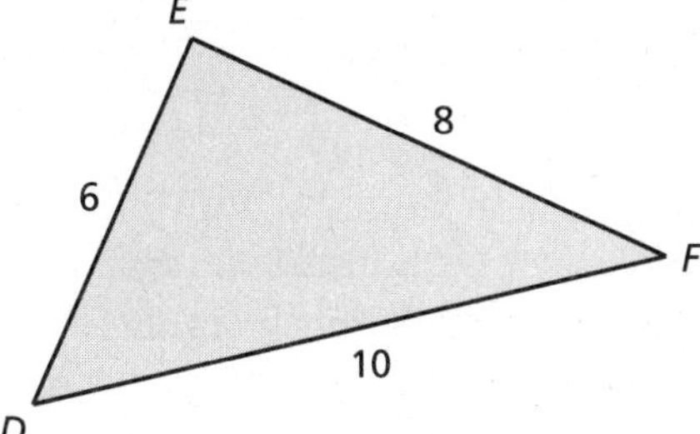

For example, ΔABC is similar to ΔDEF because the ratios of their corresponding side lengths are equal.

$$\frac{6}{3} = \frac{10}{5} = \frac{8}{4}$$

1 ACTIVITY: Angles of Similar Triangles

Work with a partner.

- **Discuss how to make a triangle that is larger than ΔXYZ and has the *same* angle measures as ΔXYZ.**

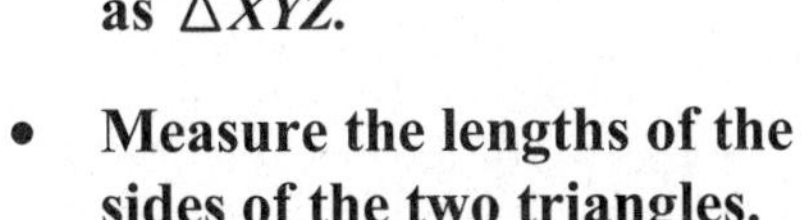

- **Measure the lengths of the sides of the two triangles.**
- **Find the ratios of the corresponding side lengths. Are they all the same? What can you conclude?**

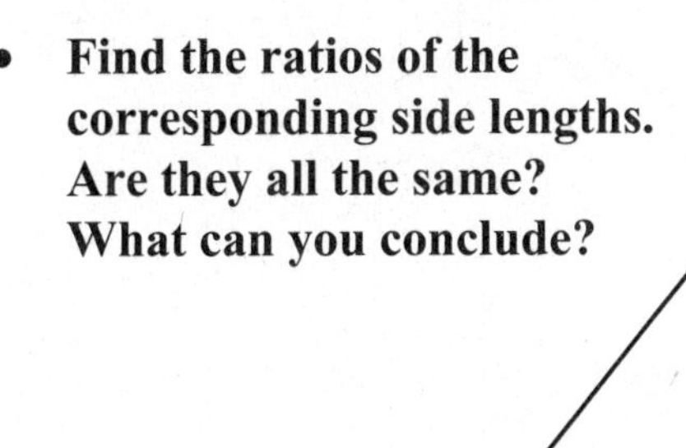

2 ACTIVITY: Amazing Triangles

Work with a partner. Use what you know about polygons to decide whether each statement is true. In each case, explain your reasoning.

a. If two *triangles* are similar, then the ratios of their corresponding side lengths are equal.

If two *quadrilaterals* are similar, then the ratios of their corresponding side lengths are equal.

b. If the ratios of the corresponding side lengths of two *triangles* are equal, then the triangles are similar.

If the ratios of the corresponding side lengths of two *quadrilaterals* are equal, then the quadrilaterals are similar.

c. If two *triangles* are similar, then their corresponding angles are congruent.

If two *quadrilaterals* are similar, then their corresponding angles are congruent.

11.4 Using Similar Triangles (continued)

d. 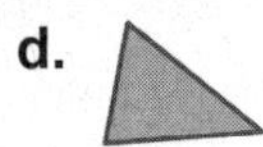 If the corresponding angles in two *triangles* are congruent, then the triangles are similar.

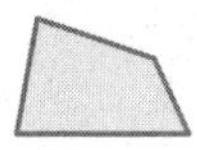 If the corresponding angles in two *quadrilaterals* are congruent, then the quadrilaterals are similar.

e. 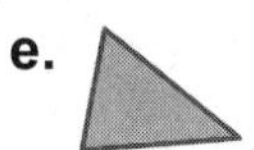 If the corresponding sides of two *triangles* are congruent, then the two triangles have identical shapes.

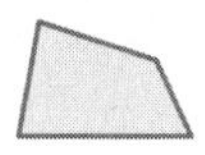 If the corresponding sides of two *quadrilaterals* are congruent, then the two quadrilaterals have identical shapes.

What Is Your Answer?

3. IN YOUR OWN WORDS Which properties of triangles make them special among all other types of polygons? Describe two careers in which the special properties of triangles are used.

Name ______________________________ Date __________

11.4 Practice

For use after Lesson 11.4

Tell whether the triangles are similar. Explain.

1.

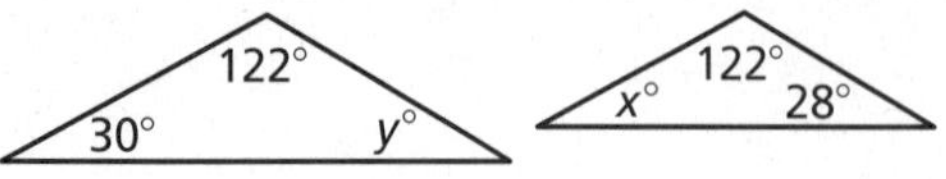

2.

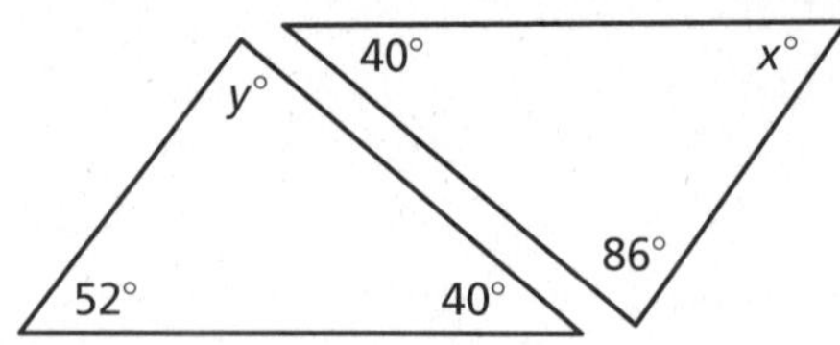

The triangles are similar. Find the value of *x*.

3.

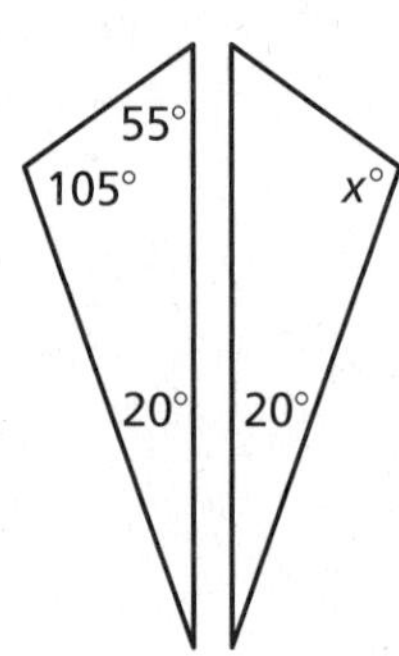

4.

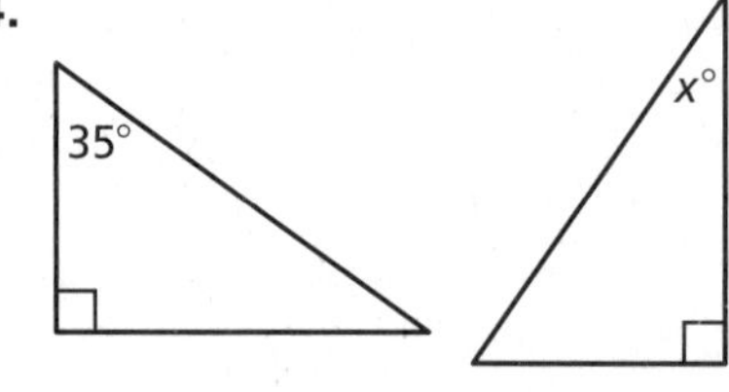

5. You can use similar triangles to find the height of a tree. Triangle ABC is similar to triangle DEC. What is the height of the tree?

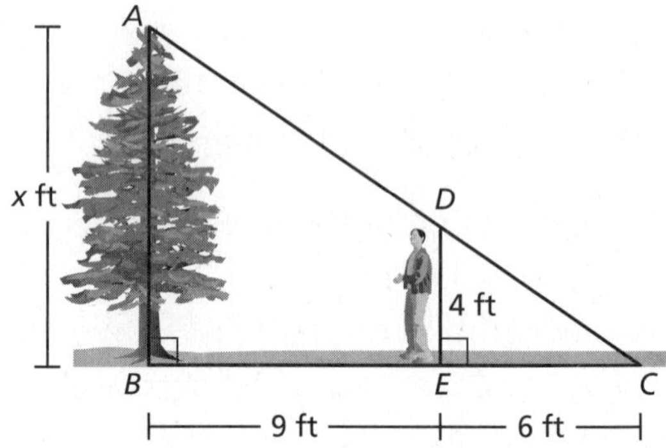

Name____ Date__________

11.5 Parallel Lines and Transversals

For use with Activity 11.5

Essential Question How can you use properties of parallel lines to solve real-life problems?

1 ACTIVITY: A Property of Parallel Lines

Work with a partner.

- Talk about what it means for two lines to be parallel. Decide on a strategy for drawing two parallel lines.
- Use your strategy to carefully draw two lines that are parallel in the space below.
- Now, draw a third line that intersects the two parallel lines. This line is called a **transversal**.
- The two parallel lines and the transversal form eight angles. Which of these angles have equal measures? Explain your reasoning.

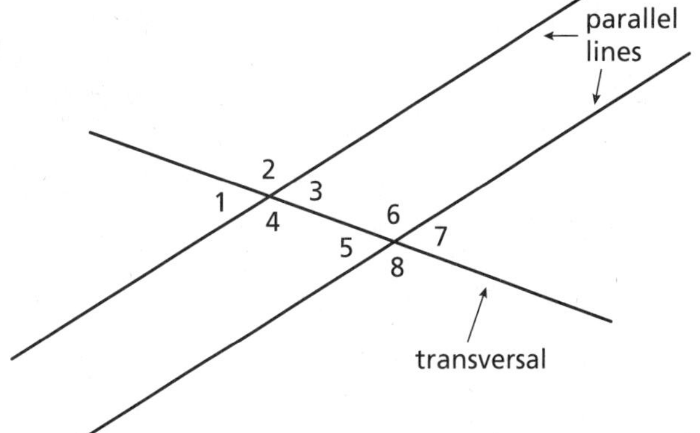

Name ______________________________ Date ________

11.5 Parallel Lines and Transversals (continued)

2 ACTIVITY: Creating Parallel Lines

Work with a partner.

a. If you were building the house in the photograph, how could you make sure that the studs are parallel to each other?

b. Identify sets of parallel lines and transversals in the photograph.

3 ACTIVITY: Indirect Measurement

Work with a partner.

a. Use the fact that two rays from the sun are parallel to explain why $\triangle ABC$ and $\triangle DEF$ are similar.

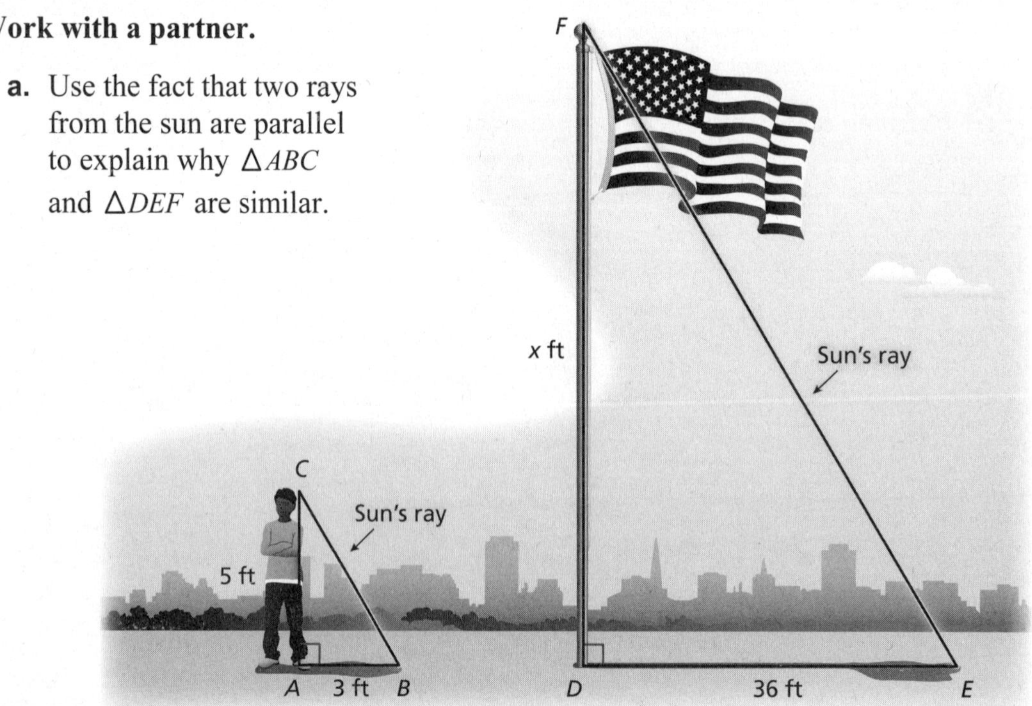

11.5 Parallel Lines and Transversals (continued)

b. Explain how to use similar triangles to find the height of the flagpole.

What Is Your Answer?

4. IN YOUR OWN WORDS How can you use properties of parallel lines to solve real-life problems? Describe some examples.

5. INDIRECT MEASUREMENT PROJECT Work with a partner or in a small group.

a. Explain why the process in Activity 3 is called "indirect" measurement.

b. Use indirect measurement to measure the height of something outside your school (a tree, a building, a flagpole). Before going outside, decide what you need to take with you to do the measurement.

c. Draw a diagram of the indirect measurement process you used. In the diagram, label the lengths that you actually measured and also the lengths that you calculated.

Name ______________________________ Date __________

11.5 Practice
For use after Lesson 11.5

Use the figure to find the measures of the numbered angles.

1.

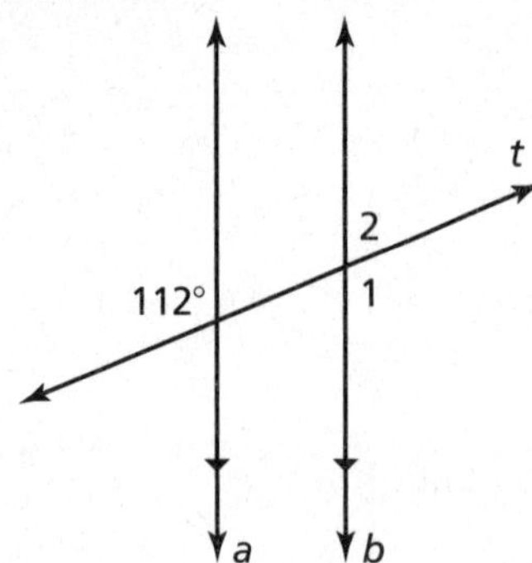

2.

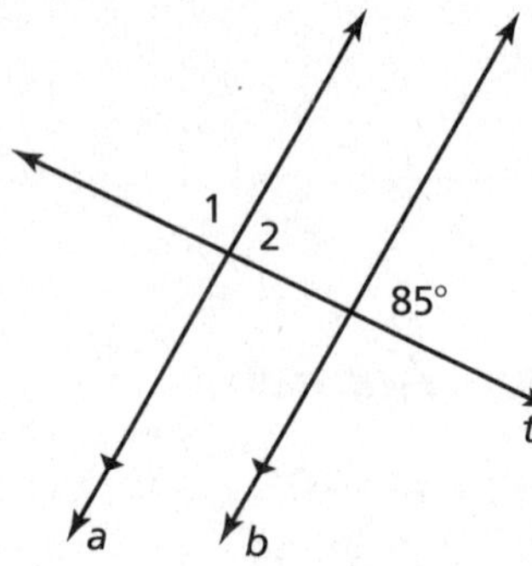

3.

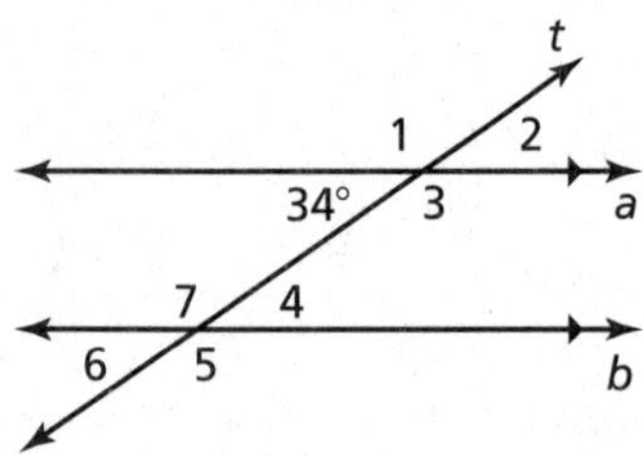

4.

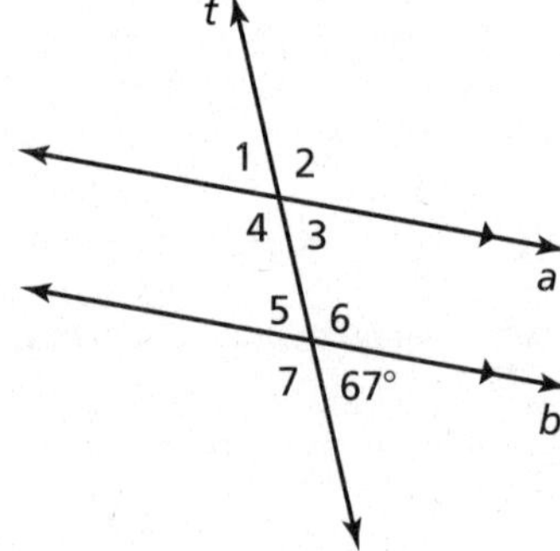

Complete the statement. Explain your reasoning.

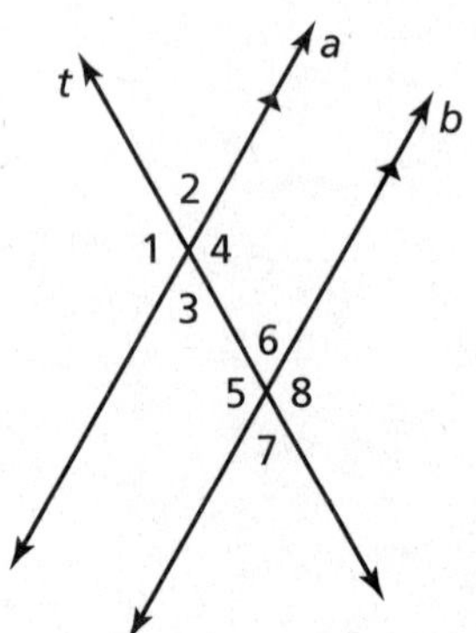

5. If the measure of $\angle 1 = 150°$, then the measure of $\angle 6 =$ ______.

6. If the measure of $\angle 3 = 42°$, then the measure of $\angle 5 =$ ______.

7. If the measure of $\angle 6 = 28°$, then the measure of $\angle 3 =$ ______.

8. You paint a border around the top of the walls in your room. What angle does x need to be to repeat the pattern?

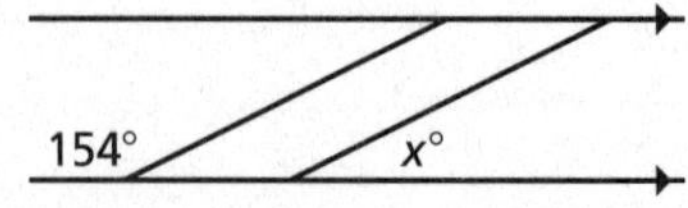

Name________________________________ Date__________

Chapter 12 Fair Game Review

Complete the number sentence with <, >, or =.

1. 3.4 ______ 3.45

2. −6.01 ______ −6.1

3. 3.50 ______ 3.5

4. −0.84 ______ −0.91

Find three decimals that make the number sentence true.

5. $-5.2 \geq$ ______

6. $2.65 >$ ______

7. $-3.18 \leq$ ______

8. $0.03 <$ ______

9. The table shows the times of a 100-meter dash. Order the runners from first place to fifth place.

Runner	Time (seconds)
A	12.60
B	12.55
C	12.49
D	12.63
E	12.495

Name ________________________________ Date ________

Chapter 12 Fair Game Review (continued)

Evaluate the expression.

10. $10^2 - 48 \div 6 + 25 \bullet 3$

11. $8\left(\frac{16}{4}\right) + 2^2 - 11 \bullet 3$

12. $\left(\frac{6}{3} + 4\right)^2 \div 4 \bullet 7$

13. $5(9 - 4)^2 - 3^2$

14. $5^2 - 2^2 \bullet 4^2 - 12$

15. $\left(\frac{50}{5^2}\right)^2 \div 4$

16. The table shows the numbers of students in 4 classes. The teachers are combining the classes and dividing the students in half to form two groups for a project. Write an expression to represent this situation. How many students are in each group?

Class	Students
1	24
2	32
3	30
4	28

Name____ Date__________

12.1 Finding Square Roots

For use with Activity 12.1

Essential Question How can you find the side length of a square when you are given the area of the square?

When you multiply a number by itself, you square the number.

Symbol for squaring is 2nd power. → $4^2 = 4 \bullet 4$

$= 16$

4 squared is 16.

To "undo" this, take the **square root** of the number.

Symbol for square root is a radical sign. → $\sqrt{16} = \sqrt{4^2} = 4$ The square root of 16 is 4.

1 ACTIVITY: Finding Square Roots

Work with a partner. Use a square root symbol to write the side length of the square. Then find the square root. Check your answer by multiplying.

a. Sample: $s = \sqrt{121} =$ **Check:**

Area = 121 ft^2

s

s

The length of each side of the square is ______________________.

b. Area = 81 yd^2

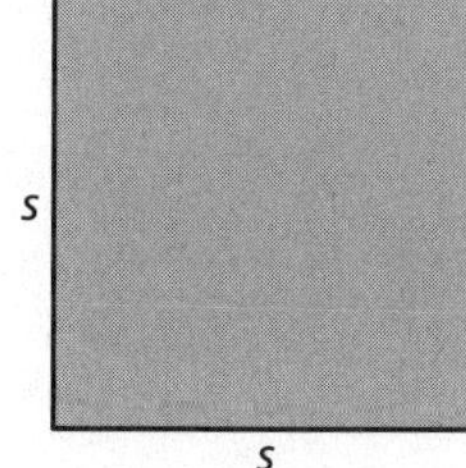

s

s

c. Area = 324 cm^2

s

s

d. Area = 361 mi^2

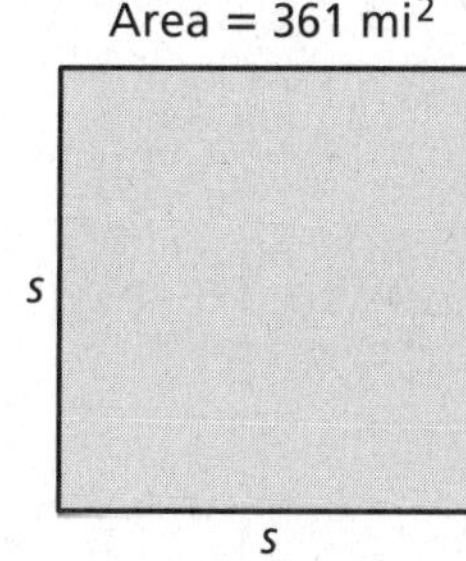

s

s

Name ________________________________ Date __________

12.1 Finding Square Roots (continued)

e. Area = 2.89 in.^{2}

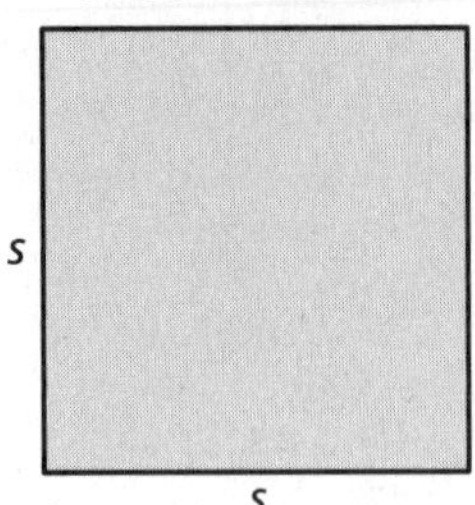

f. Area = 4.41 m^2

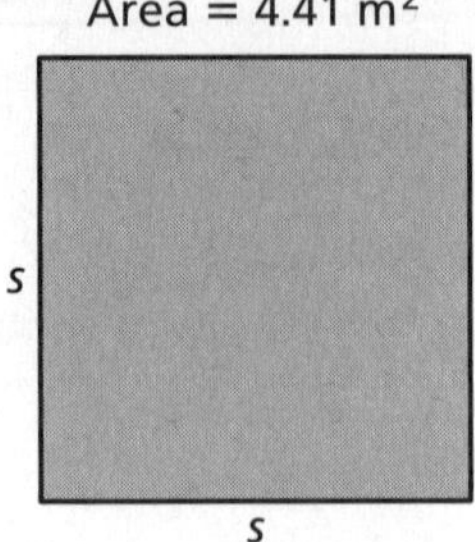

g. Area = $\frac{4}{9}$ ft^2

s

s

2 ACTIVITY: The Period of a Pendulum

Work with a partner.

The period of a pendulum is the time (in seconds) it takes the pendulum to swing back *and* forth.

The period T is represented by $T = 1.1\sqrt{L}$, where L is the length of the pendulum (in feet).

Complete the table. Then graph the function on the next page. Is the function linear?

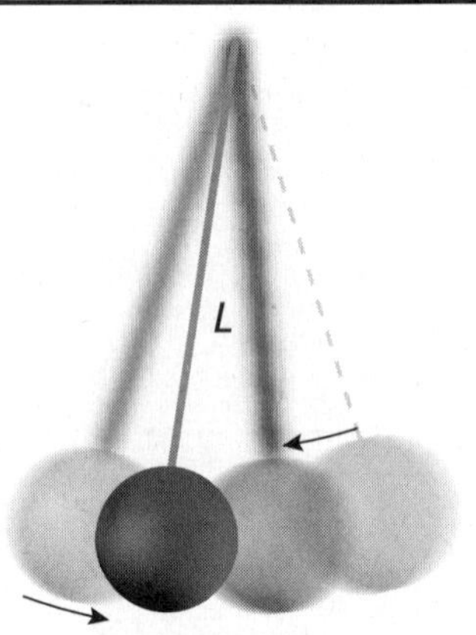

L	1.00	1.96	3.24	4.00	4.84	6.25	7.29	7.84	9.00
T									

12.1 Finding Square Roots (continued)

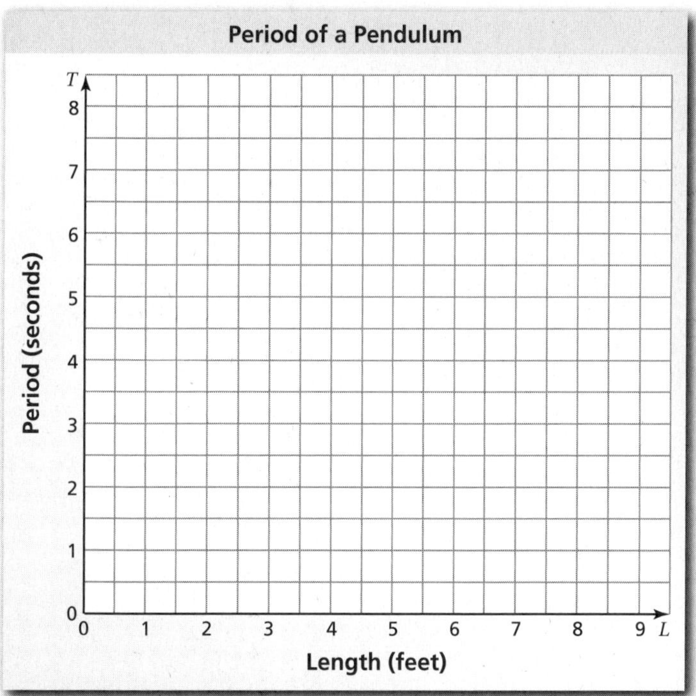

What Is Your Answer?

3. **IN YOUR OWN WORDS** How can you find the side length of a square when you are given the area of a square? Give an example. How can you check your answer?

Name ______________________________ Date __________

12.1 Practice

For use after Lesson 12.1

Find the two square roots of the number.

1. 16

2. 100

3. 196

Find the square root(s).

4. $\sqrt{169}$

5. $\sqrt{\dfrac{4}{225}}$

6. $-\sqrt{12.25}$

Evaluate the expression.

7. $2\sqrt{36} + 9$

8. $8 - 11\sqrt{\dfrac{25}{121}}$

9. $3\left(\sqrt{\dfrac{125}{5}} - 8\right)$

10. A trampoline has an area of 49π square feet. What is the diameter of the trampoline?

11. The volume of a cylinder is 75π cubic inches. The cylinder has a height of 3 inches. What is the radius of the base of the cylinder?

Name____ Date__________

12.2 The Pythagorean Theorem

For use with Activity 12.2

Essential Question How are the lengths of the sides of a right triangle related?

Pythagoras was a Greek mathematician and philosopher who discovered one of the most famous rules in mathematics. In mathematics, a rule is called a **theorem**. So, the rule that Pythagoras discovered is called the Pythagorean Theorem.

Pythagoras
(c. 570 B.C.–c. 490 B.C.)

1 ACTIVITY: Discovering the Pythagorean Theorem

Work with a partner.

a. On grid paper, draw any right triangle. Label the lengths of the two shorter sides (the **legs**) a and b.

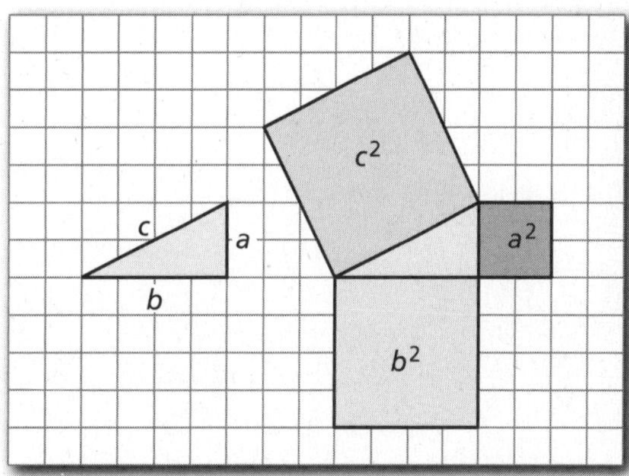

b. Label the length of the longest side (the **hypotenuse**) c.

c. Draw squares along each of the three sides. Label the areas of the three squares a^2, b^2, and c^2.

d. Cut out the three squares. Make eight copies of the right triangle and cut them out. Arrange the figures to form two identical larger squares.

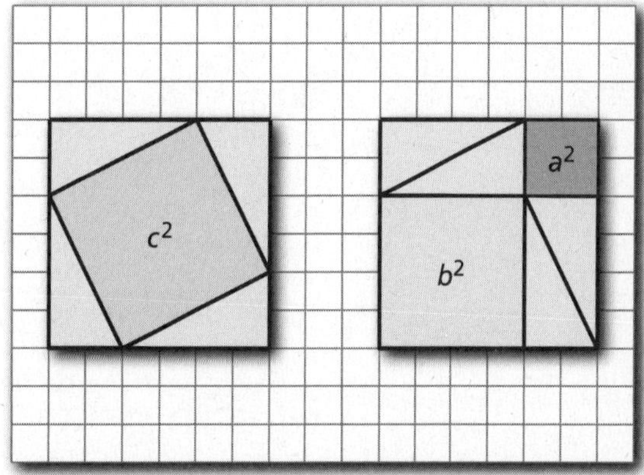

e. What does this tell you about the relationship among a^2, b^2, and c^2?

Name ______________________________ Date __________

12.2 The Pythagorean Theorem (continued)

2 ACTIVITY: Finding the Length of the Hypotenuse

Work with a partner. Use the result of Activity 1 to find the length of the hypotenuse of each right triangle.

a.

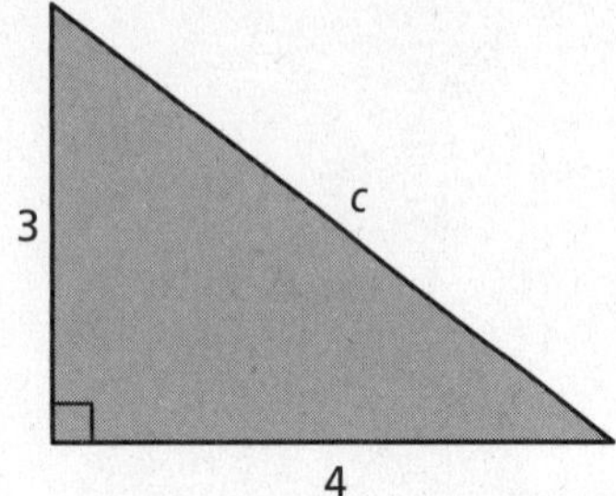

b.

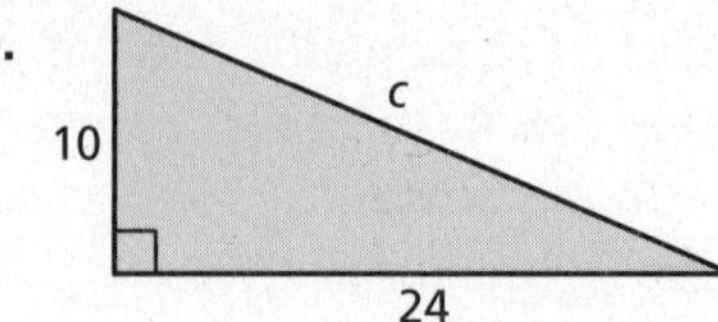

c.

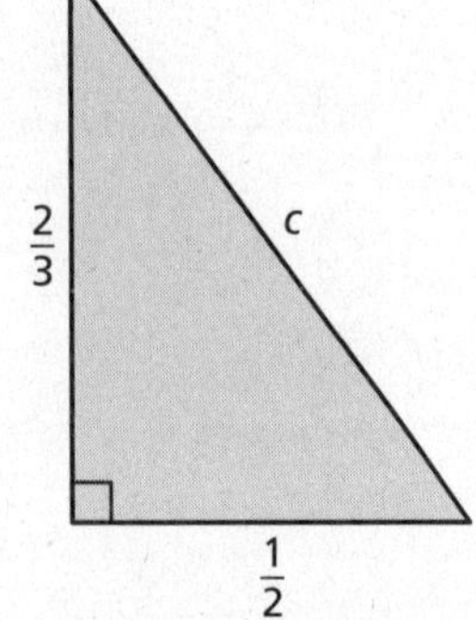

d.

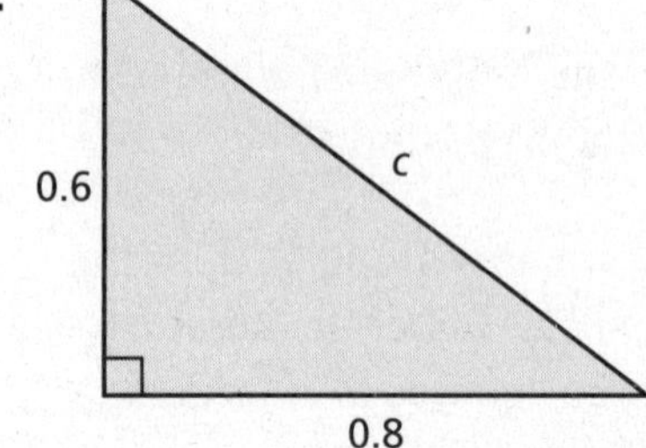

Name____ Date__________

12.2 The Pythagorean Theorem (continued)

3 ACTIVITY: Finding the Length of a Leg

Work with a partner. Use the result of Activity 1 to find the length of the leg of each right triangle.

a.

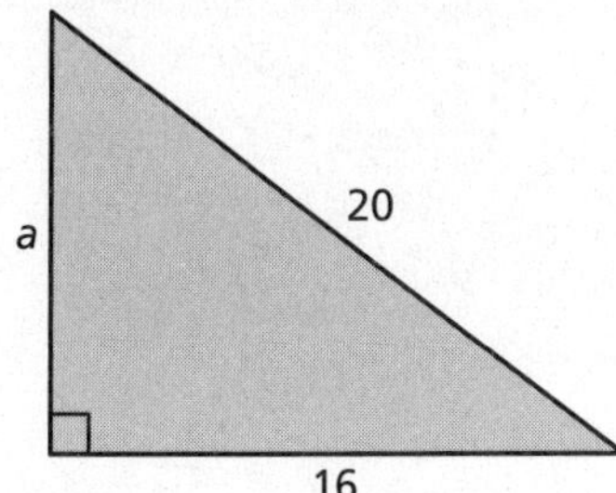

b.

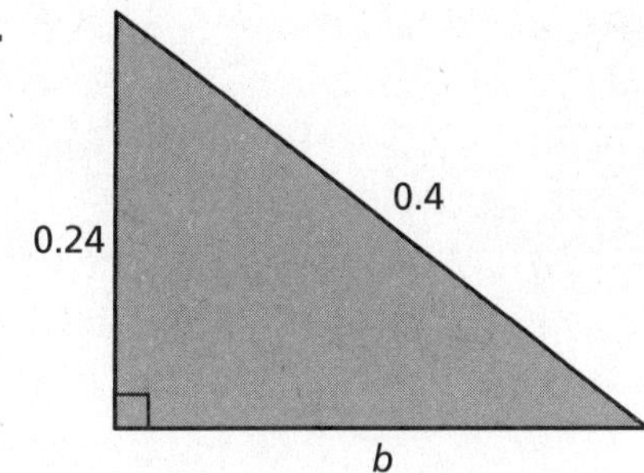

What Is Your Answer?

4. **IN YOUR OWN WORDS** How are the lengths of the sides of a right triangle related? Give an example using whole numbers.

Name ______________________________ Date __________

12.2 Practice

For use after Lesson 12.2

Find the missing length of the triangle.

1.

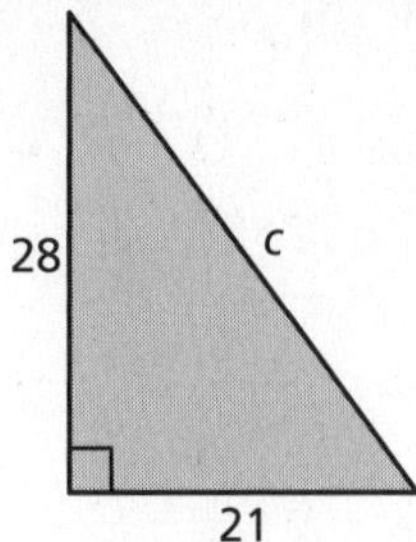

2.

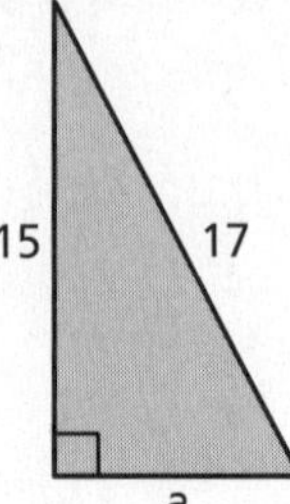

3.

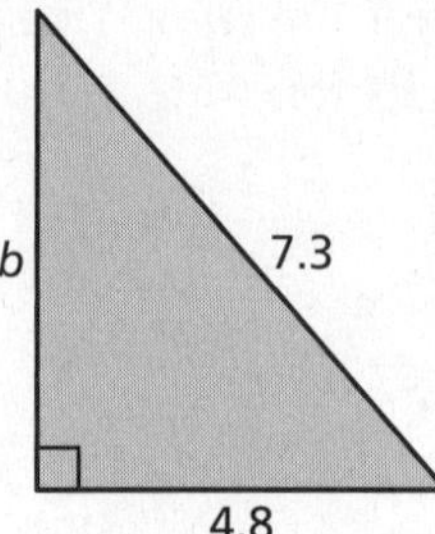

Find the value of *x*.

4.

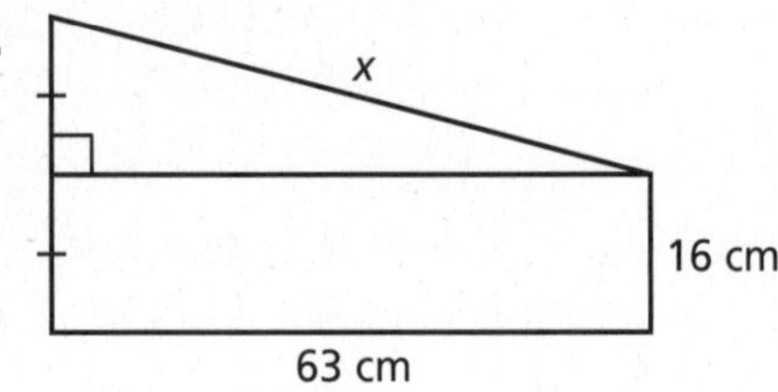

5.

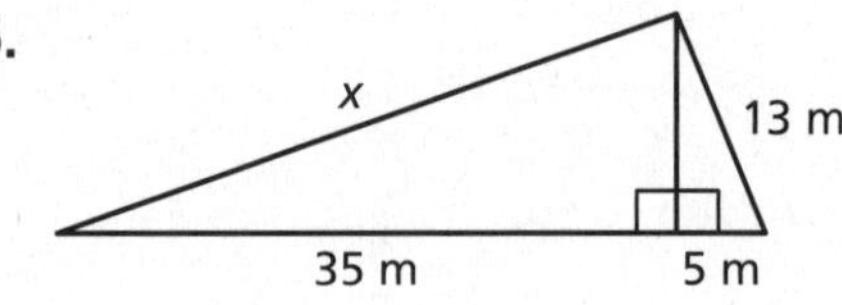

6. In wood shop, you make a bookend that is in the shape of a right triangle. What is the base *b* of the bookend?

8 in.
10 in.
b

Name________________________________ Date__________

12.3 Approximating Square Roots

For use with Activity 12.3

Essential Question How can you find decimal approximations of square roots that are irrational?

You already know that a rational number is a number that can be written as the ratio of two integers. Numbers that cannot be written as the ratio of two integers are called **irrational**.

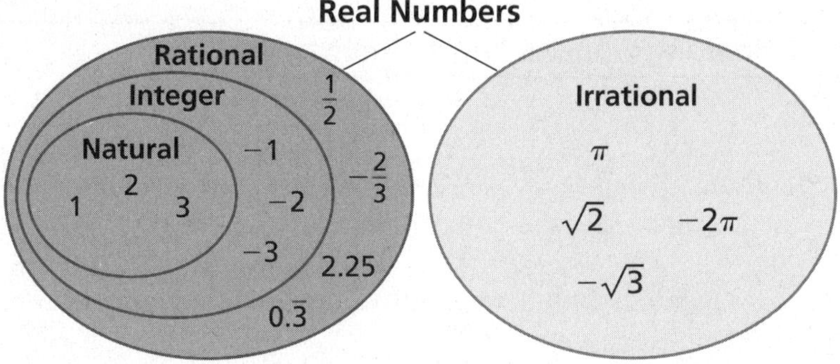

1 ACTIVITY: Approximating Square Roots

Work with a partner.

Archimedes was a Greek mathematician, physicist, engineer, inventor, and astronomer.

a. Archimedes tried to find a rational number whose square is 3. Here are two that he tried.

$$\frac{265}{153} \text{ and } \frac{1351}{780}$$

Are either of these numbers equal to $\sqrt{3}$? How can you tell?

b. Use a calculator with a square root key to approximate $\sqrt{3}$.

Write the number on a piece of paper. Then enter it into the calculator and square it. Then subtract 3. Do you get 0? Explain.

Name ______________________________ Date __________

12.3 Approximating Square Roots (continued)

c. Calculators did not exist in the time of Archimedes. How do you think he might have approximated $\sqrt{3}$?

2 ACTIVITY: Approximating Square Roots Geometrically

Work with a partner.

a. Use grid paper and the given scale to draw a horizontal line segment 1 unit in length. Draw your segment near the bottom of the grid. Label this segment *AC*.

b. Draw a vertical line segment 2 units in length. Draw your segment near the left edge of the grid. Label this segment *DC*.

c. Set the point of a compass on *A*. Set the compass to 2 units. Swing the compass to intersect segment *DC*. Label this intersection as *B*.

d. Use the Pythagorean Theorem to show that the length of segment *BC* is $\sqrt{3}$ units.

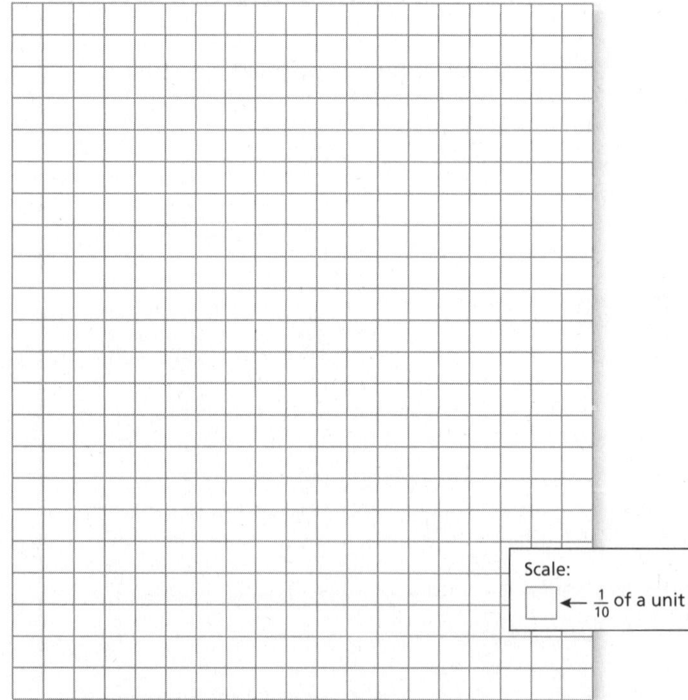

e. Use the grid paper to approximate $\sqrt{3}$.

Name____ Date__________

What Is Your Answer?

3. Repeat Activity 2 for a triangle in which segment CA is 2 units and segment BA is 3 units. Use the Pythagorean Theorem to show that segment BC is $\sqrt{5}$ units. Use the grid paper to approximate $\sqrt{5}$.

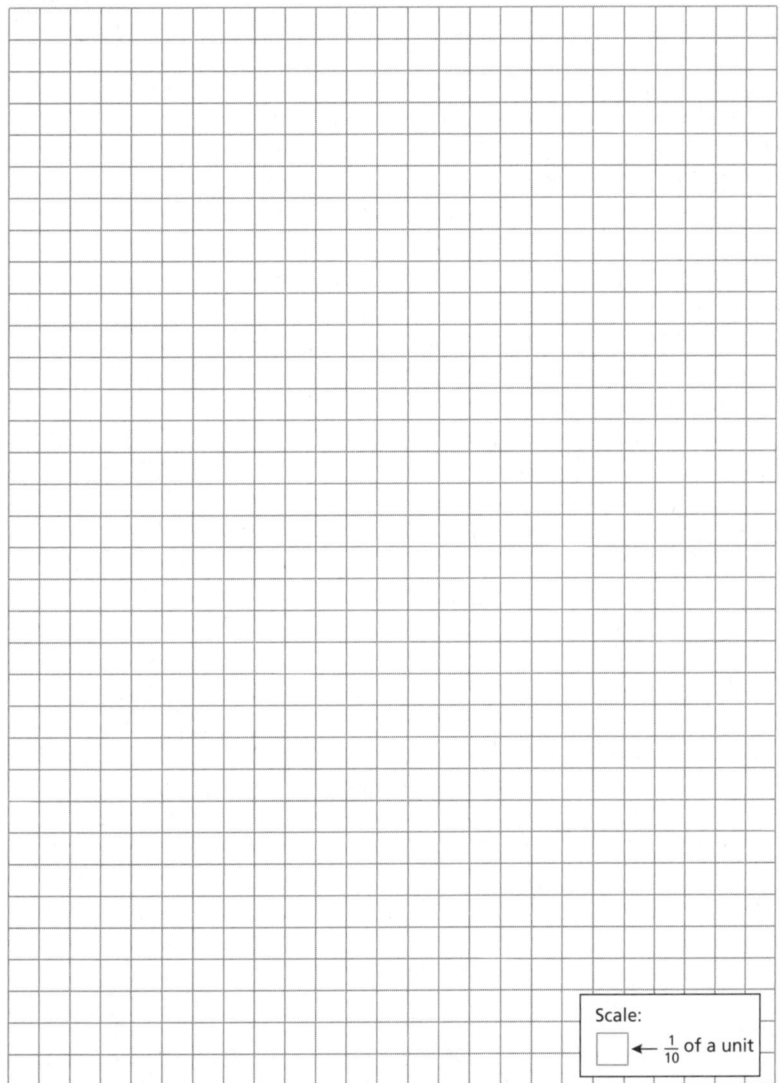

4. **IN YOUR OWN WORDS** How can you find decimal approximations of square roots that are irrational?

Name ______________________________ Date __________

12.3 Practice

For use after Lesson 12.3

Tell whether the number is *rational* or *irrational*. Explain.

1. $\sqrt{12}$

2. $-\frac{3}{7}$

3. $0.4\overline{89}$

Estimate to the nearest integer.

4. $\sqrt{8}$

5. $\sqrt{60}$

6. $-\sqrt{\frac{172}{25}}$

Which number is greater? Explain.

7. $\sqrt{88}$, 12

8. $-\sqrt{18}$, -6

9. 14.5, $\sqrt{220}$

10. The velocity in meters per second of a ball that is dropped from a window at a height of 10.5 meters is represented by the equation $v = \sqrt{2(9.8)(10.5)}$. Estimate the velocity of the ball. Round your answer to the nearest tenth.

11. The area of a square table cloth is 30 square feet. Estimate the length of one side of the tablecloth. Round your answer to the nearest tenth.

Name________________________________ Date__________

12.4 Simplifying Square Roots
For use with Activity 12.4

Essential Question How can you use a square root to describe the golden ratio?

Two quantities are in the *golden ratio* if the ratio between the sum of the quantities and the greater quantity is the same as the ratio between the greater quantity and the lesser quantity.

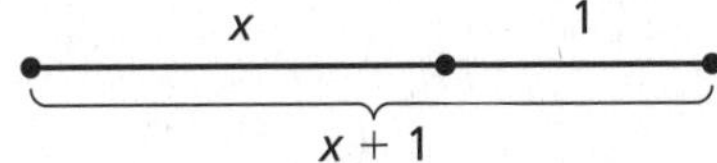

$$\frac{x+1}{x} = \frac{x}{1}$$

In a future algebra course, you will be able to prove that the golden ratio is

$$\frac{1+\sqrt{5}}{2}.$$

1 ACTIVITY: Constructing a Golden Ratio

Work with a partner.

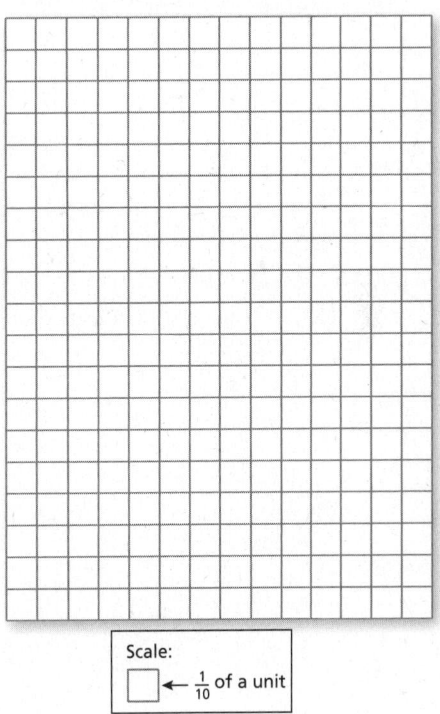

a. Use grid paper and the given scale to draw a square that is 1 unit by 1 unit. Label the midpoint of the right side of the square *C*. Label the bottom left corner of the square *A*, the bottom right corner *B*, and the top left corner *D*.

b. Draw a line from midpoint *C* of one side of the square to the opposite corner *D*.

c. Use the Pythagorean Theorem to find the length of segment *CD*.

d. Set the point of a compass on *C*. Set the compass radius to the length of segment *CD*. Swing the compass to intersect line *BC*. Label the point of intersection *E*. Form rectangle *ABEF*.

e. The rectangle *ABEF* is called the *golden rectangle* because the ratio of its side lengths is the golden ratio.

f. Use a calculator to find a decimal approximation of the golden ratio. Round your answer to two decimal places.

2 ACTIVITY: The Golden Ratio and the Human Body

Work with a partner.

Leonardo da Vinci was one of the first to notice that there are several ratios in the human body that approximate the golden ratio.

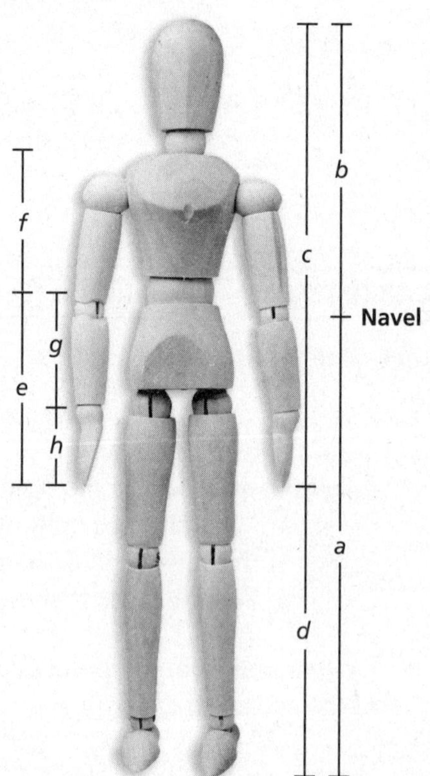

a. Use a tape measure or two yardsticks to measure the lengths shown in the diagram for both you and your partner. (Take your shoes off before measuring.)

b. Record your results in the first two columns of the tables on the next page.

c. Calculate the ratios shown in the tables.

d. Leonardo da Vinci stated that for many people, the ratios are close to the golden ratio. How close are your ratios?

Name____________________ Date__________

You		
$a =$	$b =$	$\frac{a}{b} =$
$c =$	$d =$	$\frac{c}{d} =$
$e =$	$f =$	$\frac{e}{f} =$
$g =$	$h =$	$\frac{g}{h} =$

Partner		
$a =$	$b =$	$\frac{a}{b} =$
$c =$	$d =$	$\frac{c}{d} =$
$e =$	$f =$	$\frac{e}{f} =$
$g =$	$h =$	$\frac{g}{h} =$

What Is Your Answer?

3. **IN YOUR OWN WORDS** How can you use a square root to describe the golden ratio? Use the Internet or some other reference to find examples of the golden ratio in art and architecture.

Name ________________________________ Date ________

12.4 Practice

For use after Lesson 12.4

Simplify the expression.

1. $\frac{\sqrt{3}}{8} + \frac{1}{8}$

2. $\frac{2}{9} - \frac{\sqrt{11}}{9}$

3. $7\sqrt{7} + 3\sqrt{7}$

4. $\frac{3}{2}\sqrt{15} + \frac{1}{2}\sqrt{15}$

5. $12\sqrt{42} - 5\sqrt{42}$

6. $16.4\sqrt{21} - 15.1\sqrt{21}$

7. $\sqrt{20}$

8. $\sqrt{32}$

9. $\sqrt{75}$

10. $\sqrt{\frac{29}{81}}$

11. $\sqrt{\frac{17}{a^2}}$

12. $\sqrt{40} + 3\sqrt{10}$

13. You build a shed in your backyard.

a. What is the perimeter of the shed?

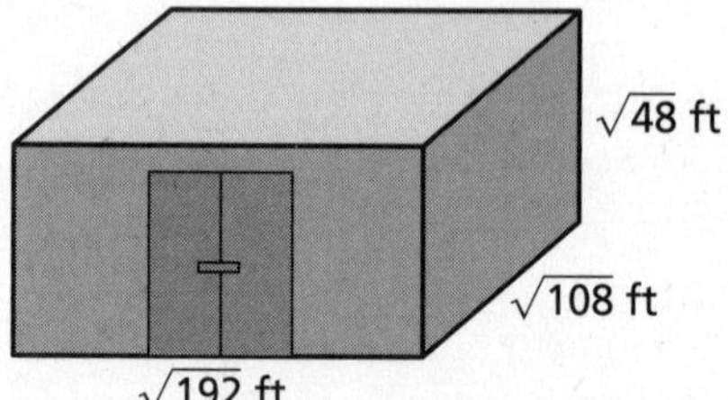

b. What is the volume of the shed?

Name______________________________ Date__________

12.4b Practice

For use after Lesson 12.4b

Find the cube root.

1. $\sqrt[3]{-64}$

2. $\sqrt[3]{27}$

3. $\sqrt[3]{-216}$

4. $\sqrt[3]{512}$

5. $\sqrt[3]{\frac{1}{125}}$

6. $\sqrt[3]{-0.064}$

Simplify the expression.

7. $7\sqrt[3]{12} + 3\sqrt[3]{12}$

8. $3 + 2\sqrt[3]{-343}$

9. $6\sqrt[3]{10} - 12\sqrt[3]{10}$

10. $8\sqrt[3]{125} - 3\sqrt[3]{125}$

11. $4\sqrt[3]{80} - 5\sqrt[3]{80}$

12. $-1 + 2\sqrt[3]{-\frac{1}{8}}$

Name ______________________________ Date __________

12.4b Practice (continued)

Which is greater? Explain.

13. $4.3, \sqrt[3]{8}$

14. $\sqrt[3]{81}, 5$

15. $-4, \sqrt[3]{-12}$

16. The volume of the moving box is 64 cubic feet. Find the surface area of the box.

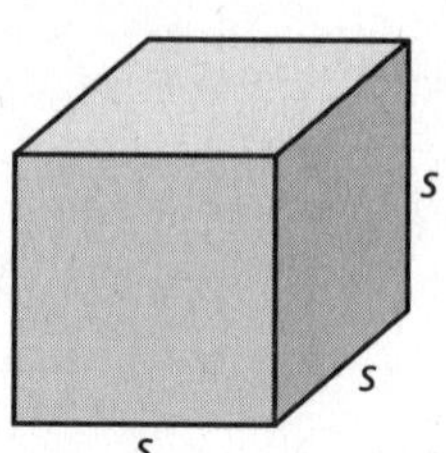

17. A plastic container is in the shape of a cube. The volume of the container is 343 cubic inches. Find the area of the top of the container.

Name______________________________ Date__________

12.5 Using the Pythagorean Theorem

For use with Activity 12.5

Essential Question How can you use the Pythagorean Theorem to solve real-life problems?

1 ACTIVITY: Using the Pythagorean Theorem

Work with a partner.

a. A baseball player throws a ball from second base to home plate. How far does the player throw the ball? Include a diagram showing how you got your answer. Decide how many decimal points of accuracy are reasonable. Explain your reasoning.

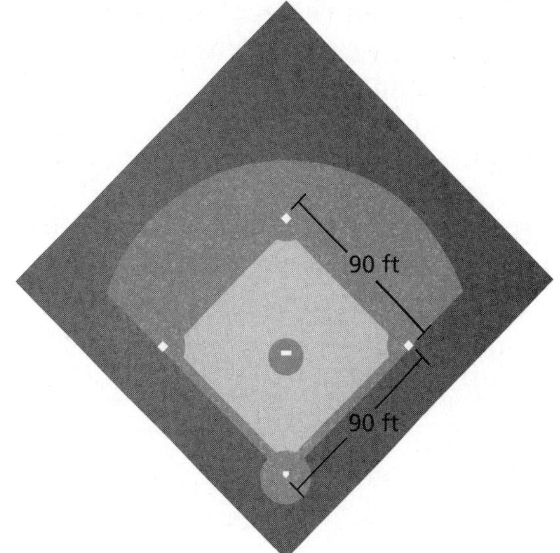

b. The distance from the pitcher's mound to home plate is 60.5 feet. Does this form a right triangle with first base? Explain your reasoning.

12.5 Using the Pythagorean Theorem (continued)

2 ACTIVITY: Firefighting and Ladders

Work with a partner.

The recommended angle for a firefighting ladder is 75°.

When a 110-foot ladder is put up against a building at this angle, the base of the ladder is about 28 feet from the building.

The base of the ladder is 8 feet above the ground.

How high on the building will the ladder reach? Round your answer to the nearest tenth.

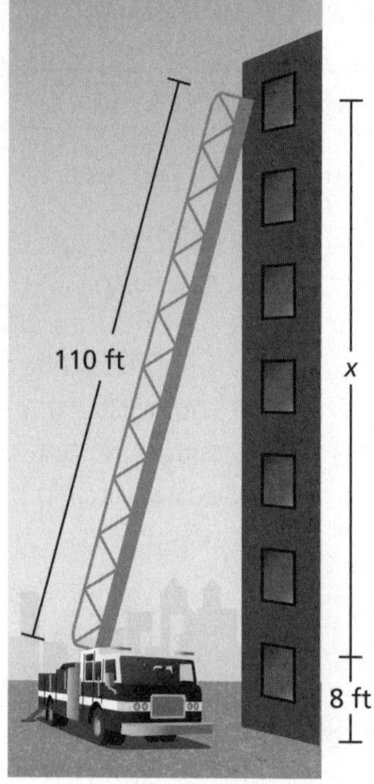

3 ACTIVITY: Finding Perimeters

Work with a partner.

Find the perimeter of each figure. Round your answer to the nearest tenth. Did you use the Pythagorean Theorem? If so, explain.

a. Right triangle

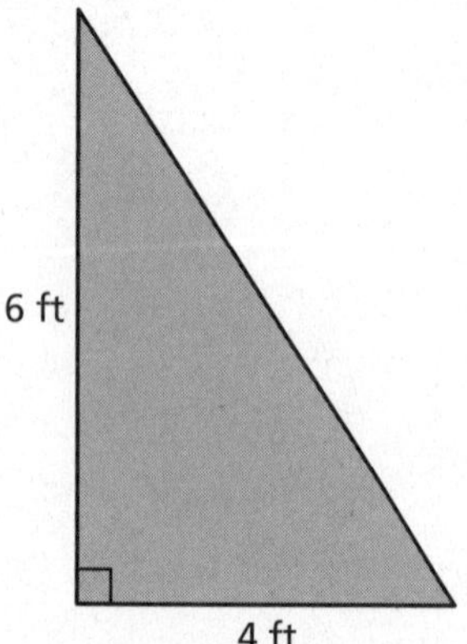

b. Trapezoid

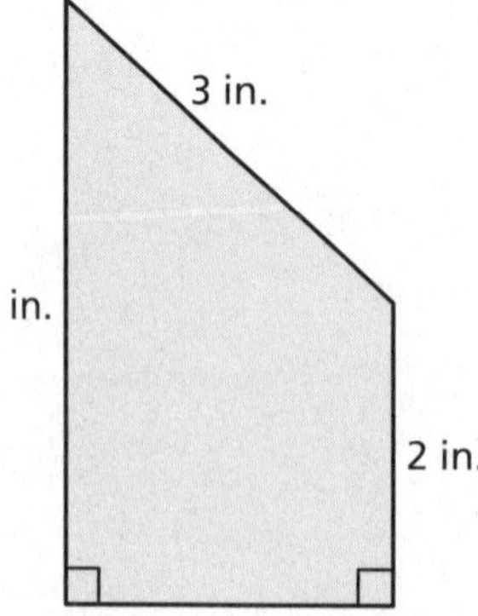

c. Parallelogram

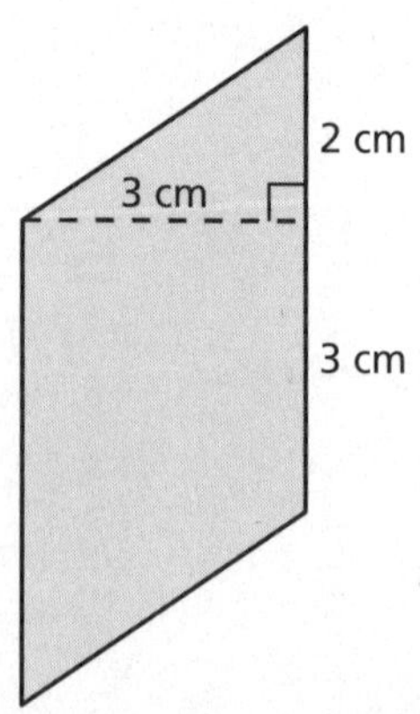

Name____ Date__________

12.5 Using the Pythagorean Theorem (continued)

4 ACTIVITY: Writing a Formula

Work with a partner.

a. Write a formula for the area of an equilateral triangle with side length s.

b. Use your formula to find the area of an equilateral triangle with a side length of 10 inches.

s s

s

What Is Your Answer?

5. IN YOUR OWN WORDS How can you use the Pythagorean Theorem to solve real-life problems?

6. Describe a situation in which you could use the Pythagorean Theorem to help make decisions. Give an example of a real-life problem.

Name ______________________________ Date __________

12.5 Practice

For use after Lesson 12.5

Find the distance *d*. Round your answer to the nearest tenth.

1.

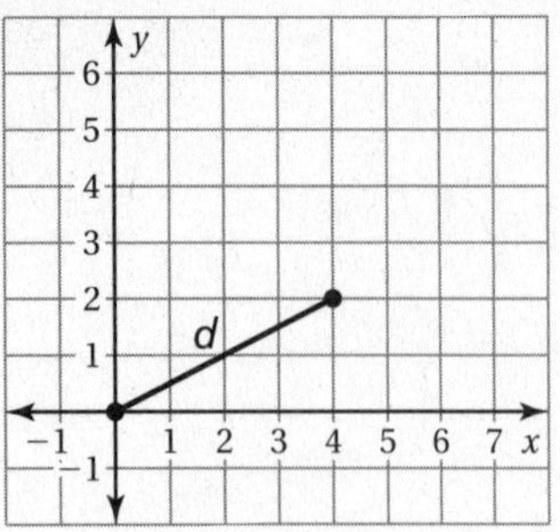

2.

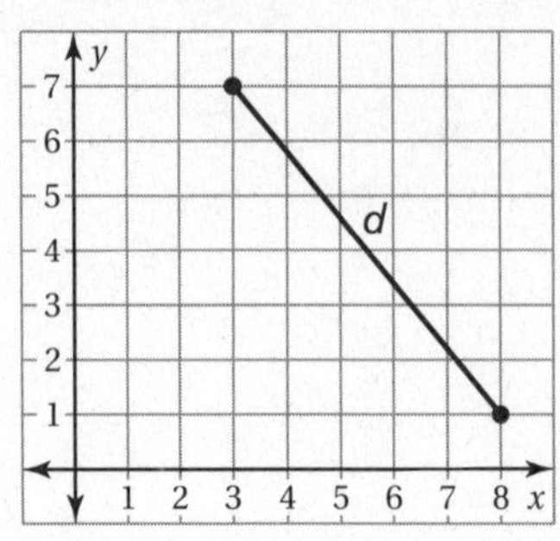

3.

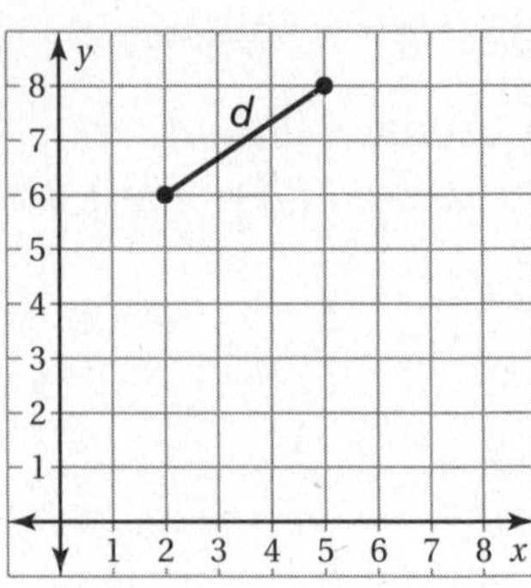

Find the height *x*. Round your answer to the nearest tenth.

4.

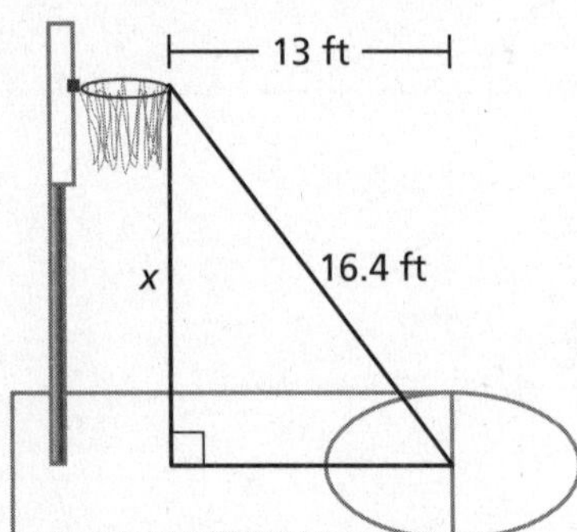

5.

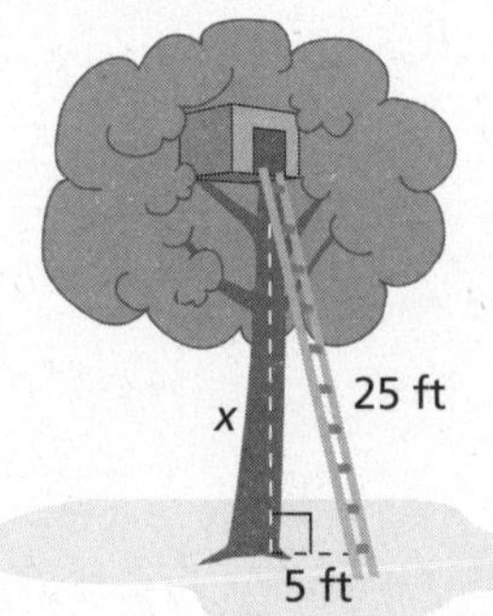

Tell whether the triangle with the given side lengths is a right triangle.

6.

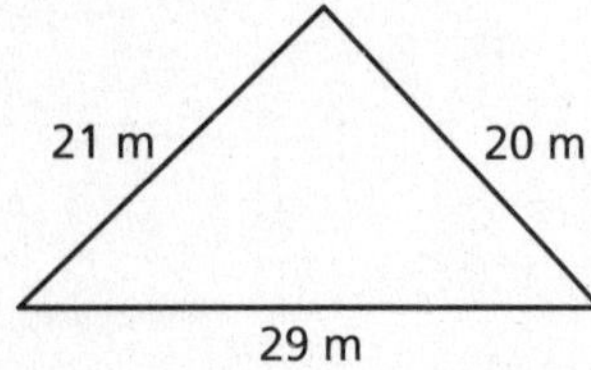

7.

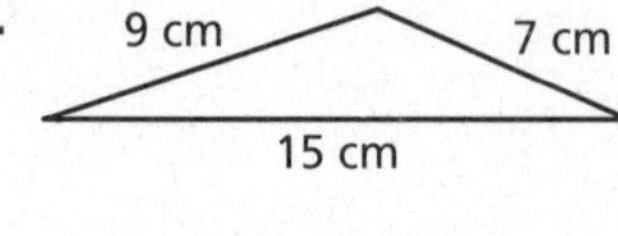

8. You set up a badminton net in your backyard. About how long is the rope used to secure the net?

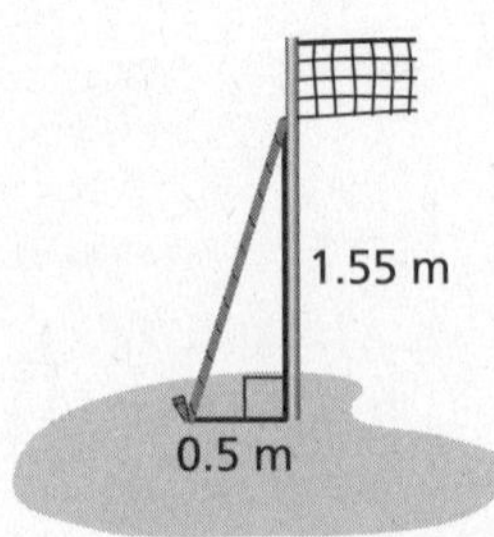

Name____ Date__________

Chapter 13 Fair Game Review

Find the sum or difference.

1. 8.01 + 4.2

2. 9.736 + 10.922

3. 4.81 + 0.755

4. 10.6 − 2.18

5. 6.75 − 5.9

6. 3.874 − 0.06

7. You bring $20 on a shopping trip. You buy a shirt for $7.62.

a. How much money do you have after you buy the shirt?

b. Later, you buy a hat for $5.18. How much money do you have after you buy the hat?

8. You have 3.85 yards of fleece and 2.6 yards of silk for your design supplies. How many total yards of fabric do you have?

Name ______________________ Date __________

Chapter 13 Fair Game Review (continued)

Find the product or quotient.

9. $3.92 \bullet 0.6$

10. $0.78 \bullet 0.13$

11. $\begin{array}{r} 5.004 \\ \times \quad 1.2 \\ \hline \end{array}$

12. $6.3 \div 0.7$

13. $2.25 \div 1.5$

14. $0.003\overline{)8.1}$

15. Grapes cost $1.98 per pound. You buy 3.5 pounds of grapes. How much do you pay for the grapes?

16. A box of cereal costs $3.69. The box has 13.7 ounces of cereal. About how much does each ounce cost?

Name____ Date__________

13.1 Exponents

For use with Activity 13.1

Essential Question How can you use exponents to write numbers?

The expression 3^5 is called a **power.** The base is 3. The **exponent** is 5.

Base → 3^5 ← Exponent

1 ACTIVITY: Using Exponent Notation

Work with a partner.

a. Complete the table.

Power	Repeated Multiplication Form	Value
$(-3)^1$		
$(-3)^2$		
$(-3)^3$		
$(-3)^4$		
$(-3)^5$		
$(-3)^6$		
$(-3)^7$		

b. Describe what is meant by the expression $(-3)^n$. How can you find the value of $(-3)^n$?

Name ____ Date ________

2 ACTIVITY: Using Exponent Notation

Work with a partner.

a. The cube at the right has \$3 in each of its small cubes. Write a single power that represents the total amount of money in the large cube.

b. Evaluate the power to find the total amount of money in the large cube.

3 ACTIVITY: Writing Powers as Whole Numbers

Work with a partner. Write each distance as a whole number. Which numbers do you know how to write in words? For instance, in words, 10^3 is equal to *one thousand*.

a. 10^{26} meters: Diameter of observable universe

b. 10^{21} meters: Diameter of Milky Way Galaxy

c. 10^{16} meters: Diameter of Solar System

d. 10^{7} meters: Diameter of Earth

e. 10^{6} meters: Length of Lake Erie Shoreline

f. 10^{5} meters: Width of Lake Erie

Name_______________________________________ Date__________

13.1 Exponents (continued)

4 ACTIVITY: Writing a Power

Work with a partner. Write the number of kits, cats, sacks, and wives as a power.

As I was going to St. Ives
I met a man with seven wives
and every wife had seven sacks
and every sack had seven cats
and every cat had seven kits
Kits, cats, sacks, wives
How many were going to St. Ives?

Nursery Rhyme, 1730

What Is Your Answer?

5. **IN YOUR OWN WORDS** How can you use exponents to write numbers? Give some examples of how exponents are used in real life.

Name ____________________ Date __________

13.1 Practice
For use after Lesson 13.1

Write the product using exponents.

1. $4 \bullet 4 \bullet 4 \bullet 4 \bullet 4$

2. $\left(-\frac{1}{8}\right) \bullet \left(-\frac{1}{8}\right) \bullet \left(-\frac{1}{8}\right)$

3. $5 \bullet 5 \bullet (-x) \bullet (-x) \bullet (-x) \bullet (-x)$

4. $9 \bullet 9 \bullet y \bullet y \bullet y \bullet y \bullet y \bullet y$

Evaluate the expression.

5. 10^3

6. $(-7)^4$

7. $-\left(\frac{1}{6}\right)^5$

8. $3 + 6 \bullet (-5)^2$

9. $\left|-\frac{1}{3}(1^{10} + 9 - 2^3)\right|$

10. A foam toy is 2 inches wide. It doubles in size for every minute it is in water. Write an expression for the width of the toy after 5 minutes. What is the width after 5 minutes?

Name____ Date__________

13.2 Product of Powers Property

For use with Activity 13.2

Essential Question How can you multiply two powers that have the same base?

1 ACTIVITY: Finding Products of Powers

Work with a partner.

a. Complete the table.

Product	Repeated Multiplication Form	Power
$2^2 \bullet 2^4$		
$(-3)^2 \bullet (-3)^4$		
$7^3 \bullet 7^2$		
$5.1^1 \bullet 5.1^6$		
$(-4)^2 \bullet (-4)^2$		
$10^3 \bullet 10^5$		
$\left(\frac{1}{2}\right)^5 \bullet \left(\frac{1}{2}\right)^5$		

b. INDUCTIVE REASONING Describe the pattern in the table. Then write a rule for multiplying two powers that have the same base.

$a^m \bullet a^n = a^{\_\_\_}$

c. Use your rule to simplify the products in the first column of the table above. Does your rule give the results in the third column?

Name ______________________________ Date __________

2 ACTIVITY: Using a Calculator

Work with a partner.

Some calculators have *exponent keys* that are used to evaluate powers.

Use a calculator with an exponent key to evaluate the products in Activity 1.

3 ACTIVITY: The Penny Puzzle

Work with a partner.

- The rows y and columns x of a chess board are numbered as shown.
- Each position on the chess board has a stack of pennies. (Only the first row is shown.)
- The number of pennies in each stack is $2^x \bullet 2^y$.

a. How many pennies are in the stack in location $(3, 5)$?

13.2 Product of Powers Property (continued)

b. Which locations have 32 pennies in their stacks?

c. How much money (in dollars) is in the location with the tallest stack?

d. A penny is about 0.06 inch thick. About how tall (in inches) is the tallest stack?

What Is Your Answer?

4. IN YOUR OWN WORDS How can you multiply two powers that have the same base? Give two examples of your rule.

Name ____________________ Date ________

13.2 Practice

For use after Lesson 13.2

Simplify the expression. Write your answer as a power.

1. $(-6)^5 \bullet (-6)^4$

2. $x^1 \bullet x^9$

3. $\left(\frac{4}{5}\right)^3 \bullet \left(\frac{4}{5}\right)^{12}$

4. $(-1.5)^{11} \bullet (-1.5)^{11}$

5. $\left(y^{10}\right)^{20}$

6. $\left(\left(-\frac{2}{9}\right)^8\right)^7$

Simplify the expression.

7. $(2a)^6$

8. $(-4b)^4$

9. $\left(-\frac{9}{10}p\right)^2$

10. $(xy)^{15}$

11. $10^5 \bullet 10^3 - \left(10^1\right)^8$

12. $7^2\left(7^4 \bullet 7^4\right)$

13. The surface area of the sun is about $4 \times 3.141 \times \left(7 \times 10^5\right)^2$ square kilometers. Simplify the expression.

Name____ Date__________

13.3 Quotient of Powers Property

For use with Activity 13.3

Essential Question How can you divide two powers that have the same base?

1 ACTIVITY: Finding Quotients of Powers

Work with a partner.

a. Complete the table.

Quotient	Repeated Multiplication Form	Power
$\frac{2^4}{2^2}$		
$\frac{(-4)^5}{(-4)^2}$		
$\frac{7^7}{7^3}$		
$\frac{8.5^9}{8.5^6}$		
$\frac{10^8}{10^5}$		
$\frac{3^{12}}{3^4}$		
$\frac{(-5)^7}{(-5)^5}$		
$\frac{11^4}{11^1}$		

b. INDUCTIVE REASONING Describe the pattern in the table. Then write a rule for dividing two powers that have the same base.

$$\frac{a^m}{a^n} = a^{\_\_\_}$$

13.3 Quotient of Powers Property (continued)

c. Use your rule to simplify the quotients in the first column of the table on the previous page. Does your rule give the results in the third column?

2 ACTIVITY: Comparing Volumes

Work with a partner.

How many of the smaller cubes will fit inside the larger cube? Record your results in the table on the next page. Describe the pattern in the table.

a. Sample:

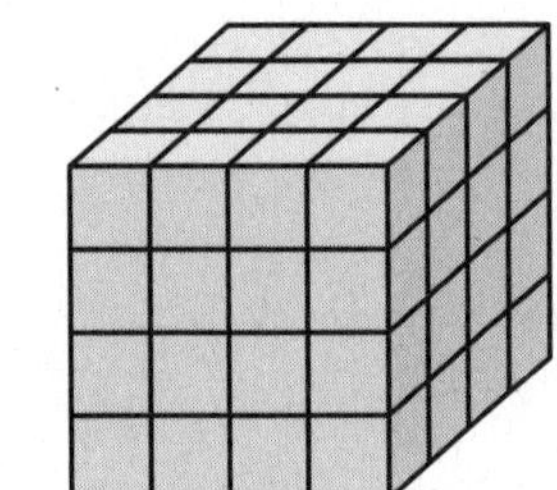

b.

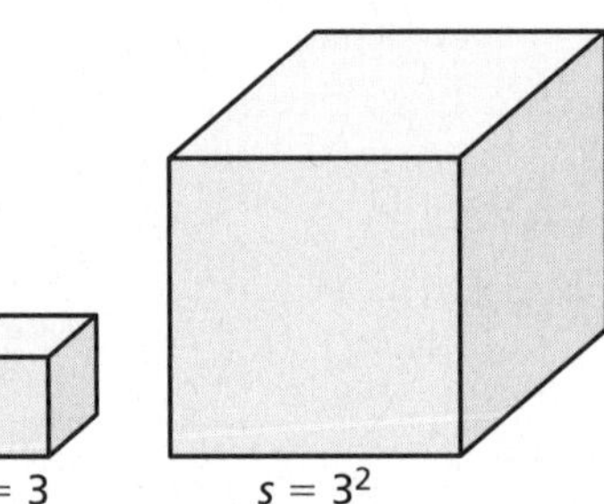

c.

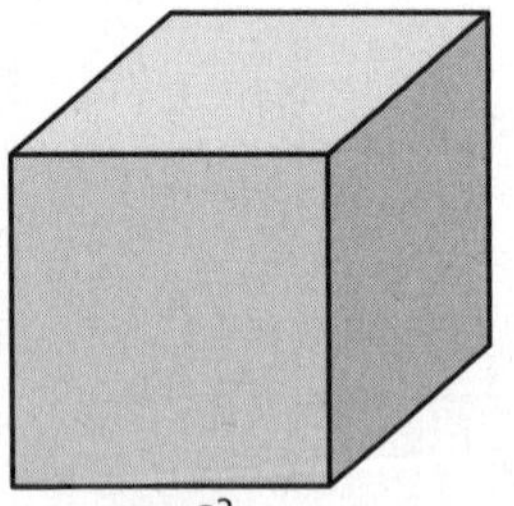

d.

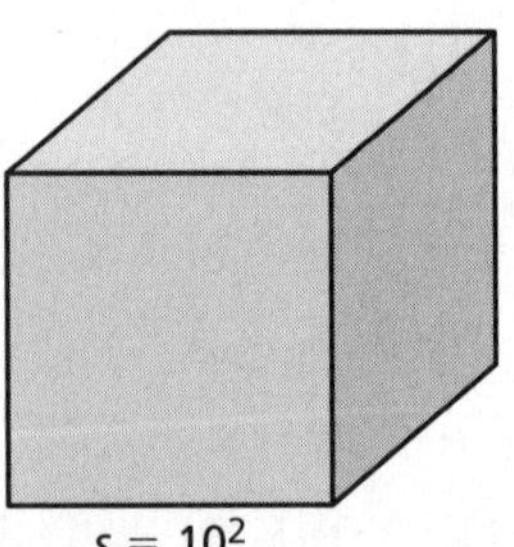

	Volume of Smaller Cube	Volume of Larger Cube	$\frac{\text{Larger Volume}}{\text{Smaller Volume}}$	Answer
a.				
b.				
c.				
d.				

What Is Your Answer?

3. **IN YOUR OWN WORDS** How can you divide two powers that have the same base? Give two examples of your rule.

Name ______________________________ Date __________

13.3 Practice

For use after Lesson 13.3

Simplify the expression. Write your answer as a power.

1. $\frac{7^6}{7^5}$

2. $\frac{(-21)^{15}}{(-21)^9}$

3. $\frac{8.6^{11}}{8.6^4}$

4. $\frac{(3.9)^{20}}{(3.9)^{10}}$

5. $\frac{t^7}{t^3}$

6. $\frac{d^{32}}{d^{16}}$

7. $\frac{8^7 \bullet 8^4}{8^9}$

8. $\frac{(-1.1)^{13} \bullet (-1.1)^{12}}{(-1.1)^{10} \bullet (-1.1)^1}$

9. $\frac{m^{50}}{m^{22}} \bullet \frac{m^{17}}{m^{15}}$

Simplify the expression.

10. $\frac{k \bullet 3^9}{3^5}$

11. $\frac{x^4 \bullet y^{10} \bullet 2^{11}}{y^8 \bullet 2^7}$

12. $\frac{a^{15}b^{19}}{a^6b^{12}}$

13. The radius of a basketball is about 3.6 times greater than the radius of a tennis ball. How many times greater is the volume of a basketball than the volume of a tennis ball? $\left(\text{Note: The volume of a sphere is } V = \frac{4}{3}\pi r^3.\right)$

Name____ Date__________

13.4 Zero and Negative Exponents

For use with Activity 13.4

Essential Question How can you define zero and negative exponents?

1 ACTIVITY: Finding Patterns and Writing Definitions

Work with a partner.

a. Talk about the following notation.

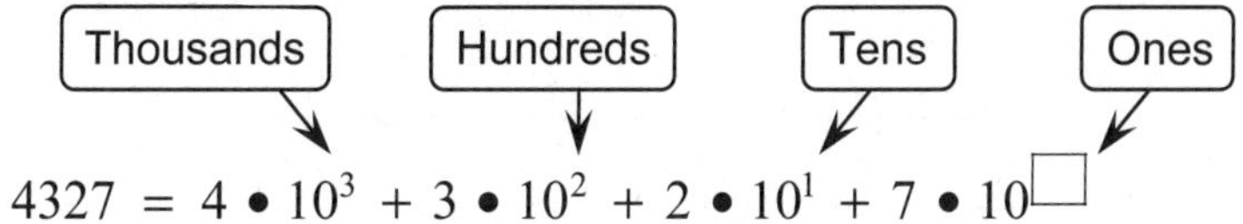

$$4327 = 4 \bullet 10^3 + 3 \bullet 10^2 + 2 \bullet 10^1 + 7 \bullet 10^{\square}$$

What patterns do you see in the first three exponents?

Continue the pattern to find the fourth exponent.

How would you define 10^0? Explain.

b. Complete the table.

n	5	4	3	2	1	0
2^n						

c. Use the Quotient of Powers Property to complete the table.

$\frac{3^5}{3^2} = 3^{5-2} = \qquad = $
$\frac{3^4}{3^2} = 3^{4-2} = \qquad = $
$\frac{3^3}{3^2} = 3^{3-2} = \qquad = $
$\frac{3^2}{3^2} = 3^{2-2} = \qquad = $

What patterns do you see in the first four rows of the table on the previous page? How would you define 3^0? Explain.

2 ACTIVITY: Comparing Volumes

Work with a partner.

The quotients show three ratios of the volumes of the solids. Identify each ratio, find its value, and describe what it means.

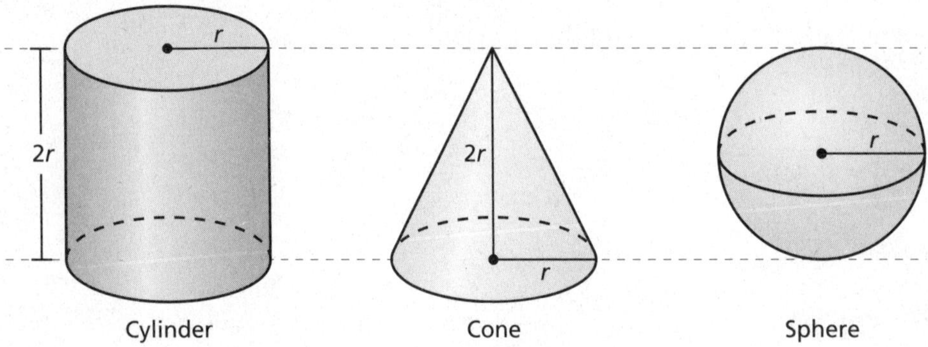

a. $2\pi r^3 \div \frac{2}{3}\pi r^3 =$

b. $\frac{4}{3}\pi r^3 \div \frac{2}{3}\pi r^3 =$

c. $2\pi r^3 \div \frac{4}{3}\pi r^3 =$

3 ACTIVITY: Writing a Definition

Work with a partner.

Compare the two methods used to simplify $\frac{3^2}{3^5}$. Then describe how you can rewrite a power with a negative exponent as a fraction.

Method 1

$$\frac{3^2}{3^5} = \frac{\cancel{3}^1 \bullet \cancel{3}^1}{{}_1\cancel{3} \bullet {}_1\cancel{3} \bullet 3 \bullet 3 \bullet 3}$$

$$= \frac{1}{3^3}$$

Method 2

$$\frac{3^2}{3^5} = 3^{2-5}$$

$$= 3^{-3}$$

What Is Your Answer?

4. **IN YOUR OWN WORDS** How can you define zero and negative exponents? Give two examples of each.

Name ______________________________ Date __________

13.4 Practice

For use after Lesson 13.4

Evaluate the expression.

1. 29^0

2. 12^{-1}

3. $(-15)^{-2} \bullet (-15)^2$

4. $10^{-4} \bullet 10^{-6}$

5. $\dfrac{1}{3^{-3}} \bullet \dfrac{1}{3^5}$

6. $\dfrac{(4.1)^8}{(4.1)^5 \bullet (4.1)^7}$

Simplify. Write the expression using only positive exponents.

7. $19x^{-6}$

8. $\dfrac{14a^{-5}}{a^{-8}}$

9. $\dfrac{16y^4}{4y^{10}}$

10. $3t^6 \bullet 8t^{-6}$

11. $7k^{-2} \bullet 5m^0 \bullet k^9$

12. $\dfrac{12s^{-1} \bullet 4^{-2} \bullet r^3}{s^2 \bullet r^5}$

13. The density of a proton is about $\dfrac{1.64 \times 10^{-24}}{3.7 \times 10^{-38}}$ grams per cubic centimeter. Simplify the expression.

Name______________________________ Date__________

13.5 Reading Scientific Notation

For use with Activity 13.5

Essential Question How can you read numbers that are written in scientific notation?

1 ACTIVITY: Very Large Numbers

Work with a partner.

- Use a calculator. Experiment with multiplying large numbers until your calculator gives an answer that is *not* in standard form.
- When the calculator on the right was used to multiply 2 billion by 3 billion, it listed the result as

  6.0E+18.

- Multiply 2 billion by 3 billion by hand. Use the result to explain what 6.0E+18. means.

- Check your explanation using products of other large numbers.
- Why didn't the calculator show the answer in standard form?

- Experiment to find the maximum number of digits your calculator displays. For instance, if you multiply 1000 by 1000 and your calculator shows 1,000,000, then it can display 7 digits.

Name ______________________________ Date __________

2 ACTIVITY: Very Small Numbers

Work with a partner.

- Use a calculator. Experiment with multiplying very small numbers until your calculator gives an answer that is *not* in standard form.
- When the calculator at the right was used to multiply 2 billionths by 3 billionths, it listed the result as

  6.0E−18.

- Multiply 2 billionths by 3 billionths by hand. Use the result to explain what 6.0E−18. means.

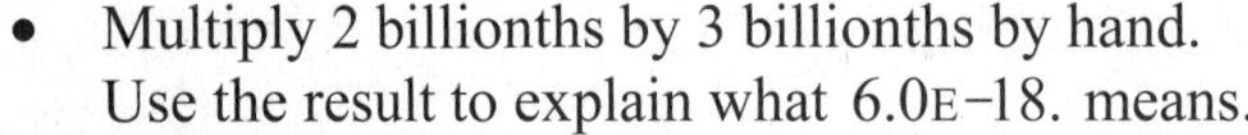

- Check your explanation using products of other very small numbers.

3 ACTIVITY: Reading Scientific Notation

Work with a partner.

Each description gives an example of a number written in scientific notation. Answer the question in the description. Write your answer in standard form.

a. Nearly 1.0×10^5 dust mites can live in 1 square yard of carpet.

How many dust mites can live in 100 square yards of carpet?

b. A micron is about 4.0×10^{-5} inch. The length of a dust mite is 250 microns.

How long is a dust mite in inches?

13.5 Reading Scientific Notation (continued)

c. About 1.0×10^{15} bacteria live in a human body.

How many bacteria are living in the humans in your classroom?

d. A micron is about 4.0×10^{-5} inch. The length of a bacterium is about 0.5 micron.

How many bacteria could lie end-to-end on your finger?

e. Earth has only about 1.5×10^{8} kilograms of gold. Earth has a mass of 6.0×10^{24} kilograms.

What percent of Earth's mass is gold?

f. A gram is about 0.035 ounce. An atom of gold weighs about 3.3×10^{-22} gram.

How many atoms are in an ounce of gold?

What Is Your Answer?

4. **IN YOUR OWN WORDS** How can you read numbers that are written in scientific notation? Why do you think this type of notation is called "scientific notation?" Why is scientific notation important?

Name ______________________________ Date __________

13.5 Practice

For use after Lesson 13.5

Tell whether the number is written in scientific notation. Explain.

1. 14×10^{8}

2. 2.6×10^{12}

3. 4.79×10^{-8}

4. 3.99×10^{16}

5. 0.15×10^{22}

6. 6×10^{3}

Write the number in standard form.

7. 4×10^{9}

8. 2×10^{-5}

9. 3.7×10^{6}

10. 4.12×10^{-3}

11. 7.62×10^{10}

12. 9.908×10^{-12}

13. Light travels at 3×10^{8} meters per second.

a. Write the speed of light in standard form.

b. How far has light traveled after 5 seconds?

Name____________________ Date__________

13.6 Writing Scientific Notation

For use with Activity 13.6

Essential Question How can you write a number in scientific notation?

1 ACTIVITY: Finding pH Levels

Work with a partner. In chemistry, pH is a measure of the activity of dissolved hydrogen ions (H^+). Liquids with low pH values are called acids. Liquids with high pH values are called bases.

Find the pH of each liquid. Is the liquid a base, neutral, or an acid?

a. Lime juice: $[H^+] = 0.01$

b. Egg: $[H^+] = 0.00000001$

c. Distilled water: $[H^+] = 0.0000001$

d. Ammonia water: $[H^+] = 0.0000000001$

e. Tomato juice: $[H^+] = 0.0001$

f. Hydrochloric acid: $[H^+] = 1$

pH	$[H^+]$
14	1×10^{-14}
13	1×10^{-13}
12	1×10^{-12}
11	1×10^{-11}
10	1×10^{-10}
9	1×10^{-9}
8	1×10^{-8}
7	1×10^{-7}
6	1×10^{-6}
5	1×10^{-5}
4	1×10^{-4}
3	1×10^{-3}
2	1×10^{-2}
1	1×10^{-1}
0	1×10^{0}

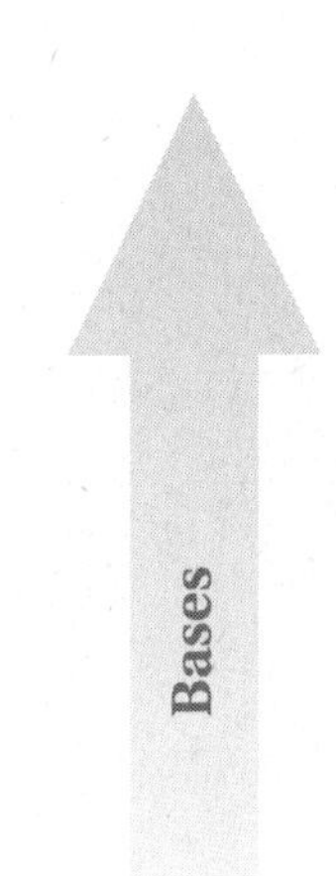

Neutral

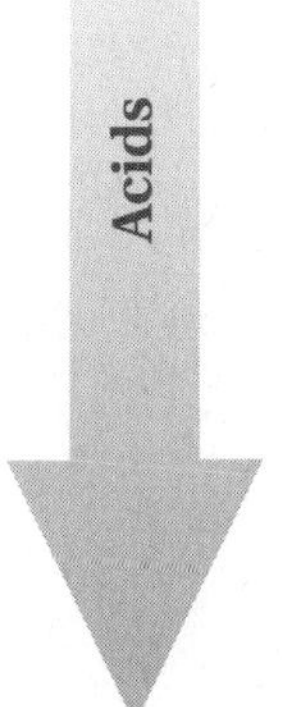

Name ______________________________ Date __________

2 ACTIVITY: Writing Scientific Notation

Work with a partner. Match each planet with its description. Then write each of the following in scientific notation.

- **Distance from the Sun (in miles)**
- **Distance from the Sun (in feet)**
- **Mass (in kilograms)**

a. Distance: 1,800,000,000 miles

Mass: 87,000,000,000,000,000,000,000,000 kg

b. Distance: 67,000,000 miles

Mass: 4,900,000,000,000,000,000,000,000 kg

c. Distance: 890,000,000 miles

Mass: 570,000,000,000,000,000,000,000,000 kg

d. Distance: 93,000,000 miles

Mass: 6,000,000,000,000,000,000,000,000 kg

e. Distance: 140,000,000 miles

Mass: 640,000,000,000,000,000,000,000 kg

f. Distance: 2,800,000,000 miles

Mass: 100,000,000,000,000,000,000,000,000 kg

g. Distance: 480,000,000 miles

Mass: 1,900,000,000,000,000,000,000,000,000 kg

h. Distance: 36,000,000 miles

Mass: 330,000,000,000,000,000,000,000 kg

13.6 Writing Scientific Notation (continued)

3 ACTIVITY: Making a Scale Drawing

Work with a partner. The illustration in Activity 2 is not drawn to scale. Make a scale drawing of the distances in our solar system.

- **Cut a sheet of paper into three strips of equal width. Tape the strips together.**
- **Draw a long number line. Label the number line in hundreds of millions of miles.**
- **Locate each planet's position on the number line.**

What Is Your Answer?

4. **IN YOUR OWN WORDS** How can you write a number in scientific notation?

Name ______________________ Date __________

13.6 Practice

For use after Lesson 13.6

Write the number in scientific notation.

1. 4,200,000

2. 0.038

3. 600,000

4. 0.0000808

5. 0.0007

6. 29,010,000,000

Multiply. Write your answer in scientific notation.

7. $(6 \times 10^{8}) \times (4 \times 10^{6})$

8. $(9 \times 10^{-3}) \times (9 \times 10^{-3})$

9. $(7 \times 10^{-7}) \times (5 \times 10^{10})$

10. $(1.4 \times 10^{-2}) \times (2 \times 10^{-15})$

11. A patient has 0.0000075 gram of iron in 1 liter of blood. The normal level is between 6×10^{-7} gram and 1.6×10^{-5} gram. Is the patient's iron level normal? Write the patient's amount of iron in scientific notation.

Name____________________ Date__________

13.6b Practice

For use after Lesson 13.6b

Add or subtract. Write your answer in scientific notation.

1. $(2 \times 10^4) + (7.2 \times 10^4)$

2. $(3.2 \times 10^{-2}) + (9.4 \times 10^{-2})$

3. $(6.7 \times 10^5) - (4.3 \times 10^5)$

4. $(8.9 \times 10^{-3}) - (1.9 \times 10^{-3})$

5. $(9.3 \times 10^8) + (8.6 \times 10^7)$

6. $(4.2 \times 10^3) + (2.7 \times 10^{-1})$

7. $(1.4 \times 10^6) - (5.5 \times 10^5)$

8. $(1.9 \times 10^{-2}) - (3.1 \times 10^{-3})$

Name ______________________________ Date __________

13.6b Practice (continued)

Divide. Write your answer in scientific notation.

9. $\dfrac{8 \times 10^3}{2 \times 10^2}$

10. $\dfrac{2.34 \times 10^5}{7.8 \times 10^5}$

11. $\dfrac{3.4 \times 10^{-4}}{8.5 \times 10^2}$

12. $\dfrac{6.9 \times 10^{-7}}{4.6 \times 10^{-2}}$

13. How many times greater is the radius of a basketball than the radius of a marble?

Radius = 1.143×10^1 cm

Radius = 5×10^{-1} cm

Name____ Date__________

Additional Topics Fair Game Review

Use a protractor to find the measure of the angle. Then classify the angle as *acute*, *obtuse*, *right*, or *straight*.

1.

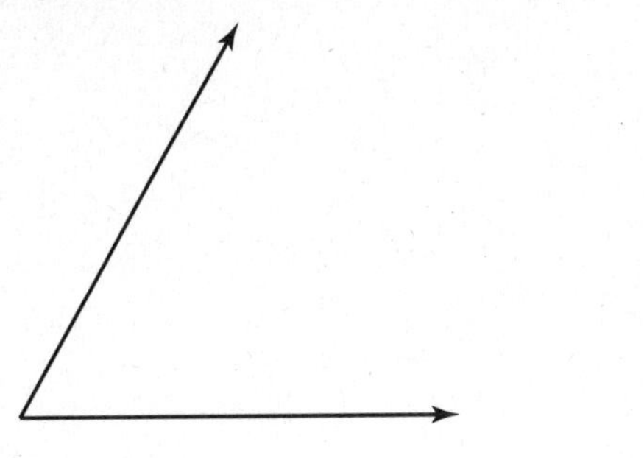

2.

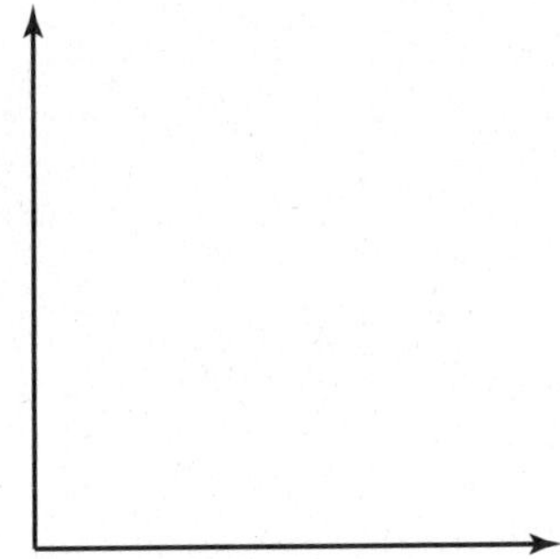

3.

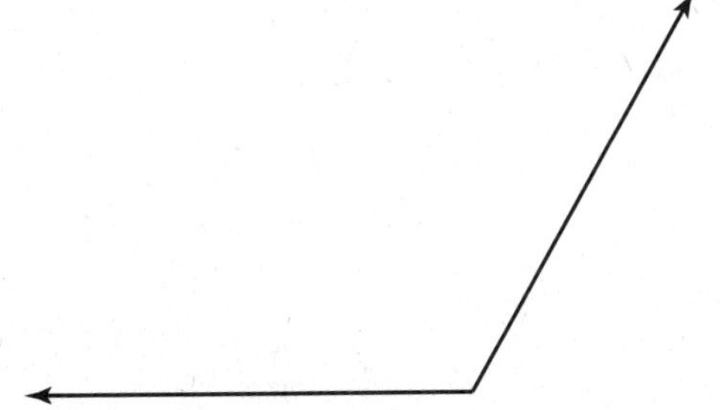

4.

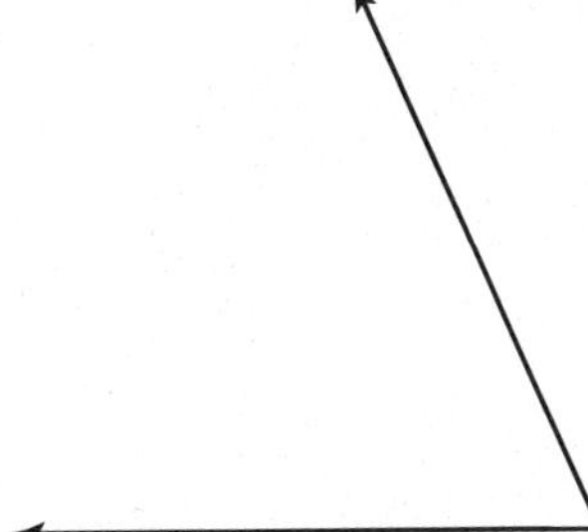

5.

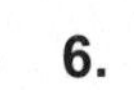

6.

Name ______________________________ Date __________

Fair Game Review (continued)

Use a protractor to draw an angle with the given measure.

7. 80°

8. 35°

9. 100°

10. 175°

11. 57°

12. 122°

Name____ Date__________

Practice

For use after Topic 1

Tell whether the angles are *complementary*, *supplementary*, or *neither*.

1.

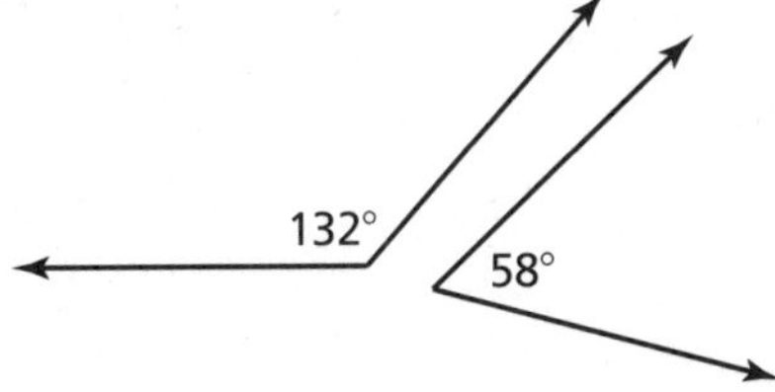

2.

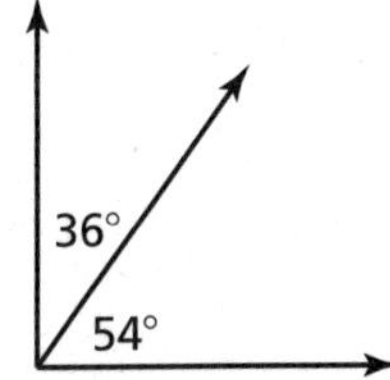

3.

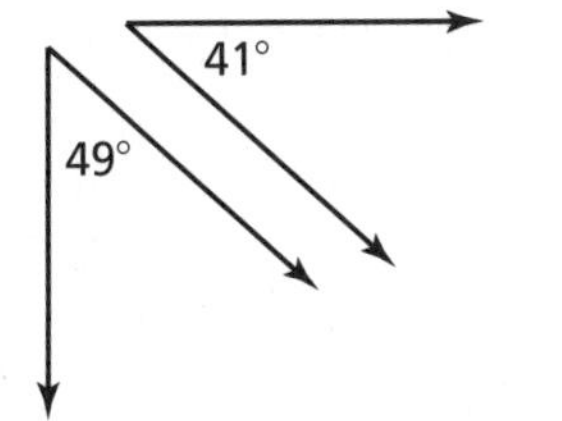

4.

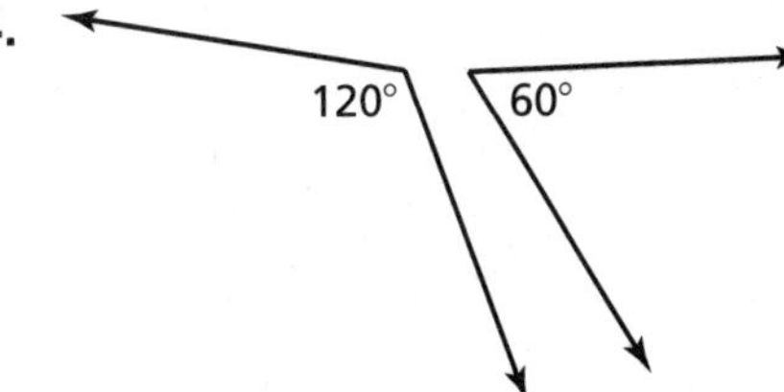

5.

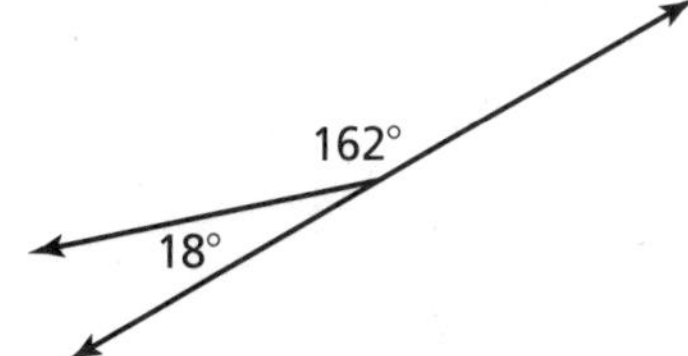

6.

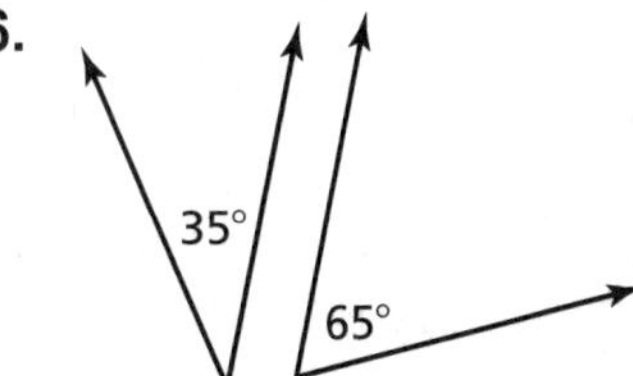

7. Two roads join at an angle. Find the value of x.

$x°$ 130°

Name ______________________________ Date __________

Topic 1 Practice (continued)

Tell whether the angles are *adjacent* or *vertical*. Then find the value of *x*.

8.

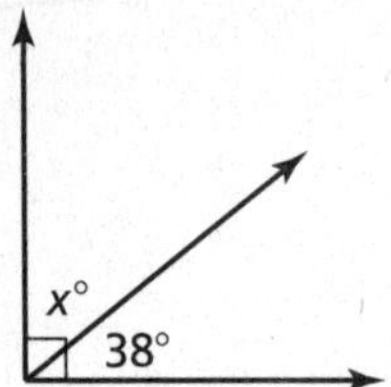

9.

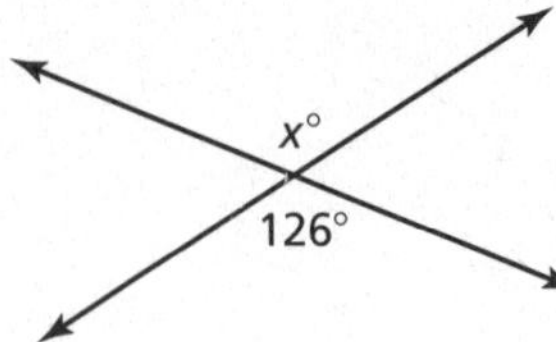

10.

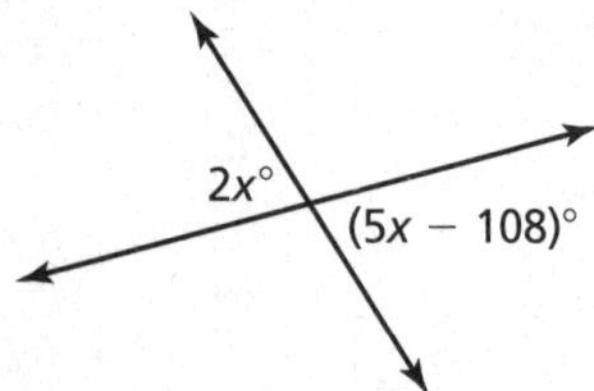

11.

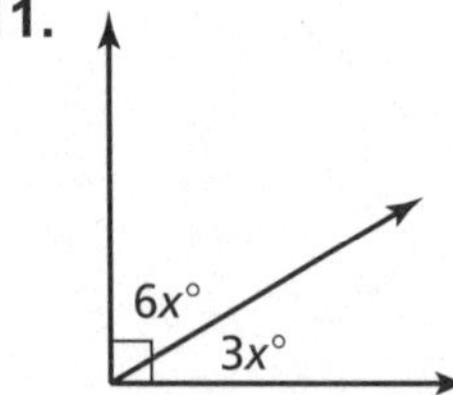

12. What are the measures of the other three angles formed by the intersection of the skis?

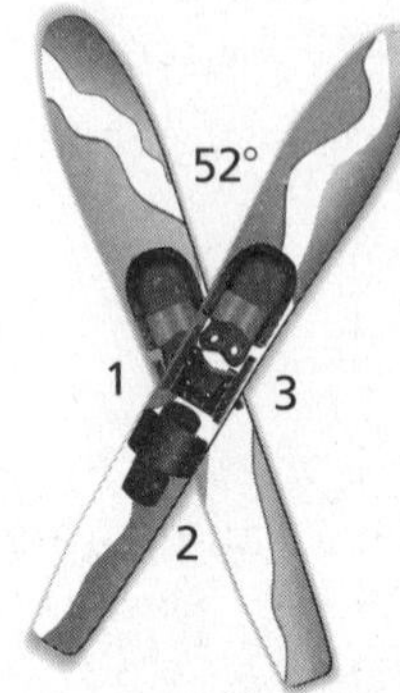

Name____ Date__________

Practice
For use after Topic 2

Construct a triangle with the given side lengths, if possible.

1. 4 cm, 4 cm, 6 cm

2. 3 cm, 4 cm, 8 cm

3. 1.5 in., 3 in., 4 in.

Name ______________________________ Date __________

Topic 2 Practice (continued)

Construct a triangle with the given angle measures, if possible.

4. 50°, 60°, 70°

5. 40°, 50°, 85°

Describe the intersection of the plane and the solid.

6.

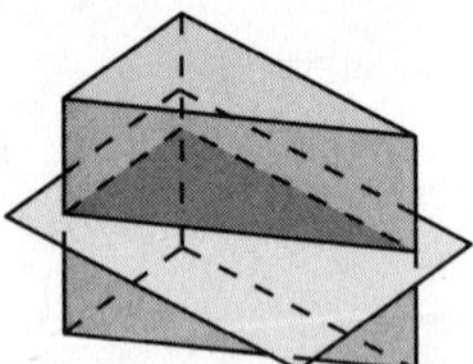

7.

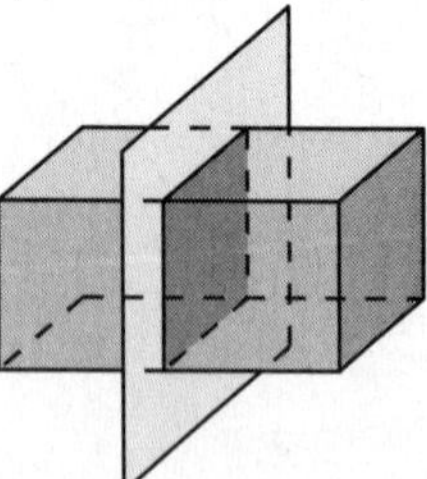

8.

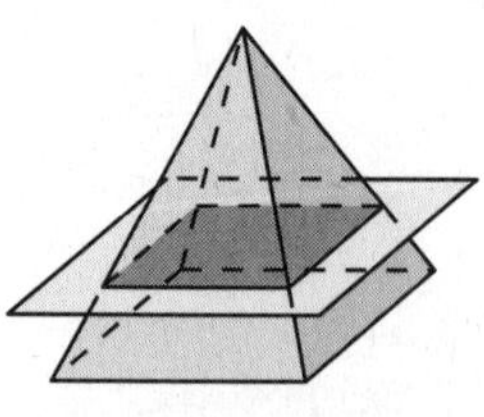

Name________________________________ Date__________

Topic 3 Practice

For use after Topic 3

Complete the statement.

1. $3 \text{ m} \approx \underline{\qquad} \text{ ft}$

2. $32 \text{ cm} \approx \underline{\qquad} \text{ in.}$

3. $16 \text{ qt} \approx \underline{\qquad} \text{ L}$

4. $\dfrac{50 \text{ mi}}{\text{h}} \approx \dfrac{\boxed{} \text{ km}}{\text{h}}$

5. $\dfrac{25 \text{ gal}}{\text{min}} = \dfrac{\boxed{} \text{ qt}}{\text{sec}}$

6. $\dfrac{1000 \text{ m}}{\text{sec}} = \dfrac{\boxed{} \text{ km}}{\text{min}}$

Name ____ Date __________

Topic 3 Practice (continued)

Complete the statement.

7. $20 \text{ in.}^2 \approx$ _____ ft^2

8. $50 \text{ ft}^2 \approx$ _____ yd^2

9. $50 \text{ m}^3 =$ _____ cm^3

10. Your doctor prescribes you to take 400 milligrams of medicine every 8 hours. How many ounces of medicine do you take in a day?

11. In Canada, a speed limit is 100 kilometers per hour. What is the speed limit in miles per hour?

Name____________________ Date__________

Practice

For use after Topic 4

1. The distance y (in miles) traveled by a car in x hours is represented by the equation $y = 70x$. The graph shows the distance traveled by a truck.

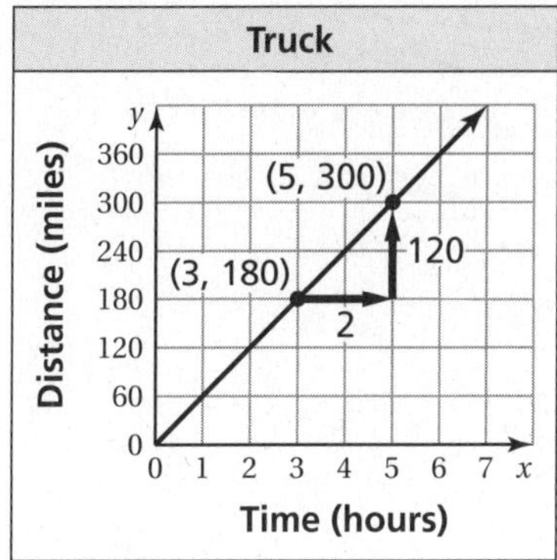

a. Which vehicle is faster?

b. Graph the equation that represents the car in the same coordinate plane as the truck. Compare the steepness of the graphs. What does this mean in the context of the problem?

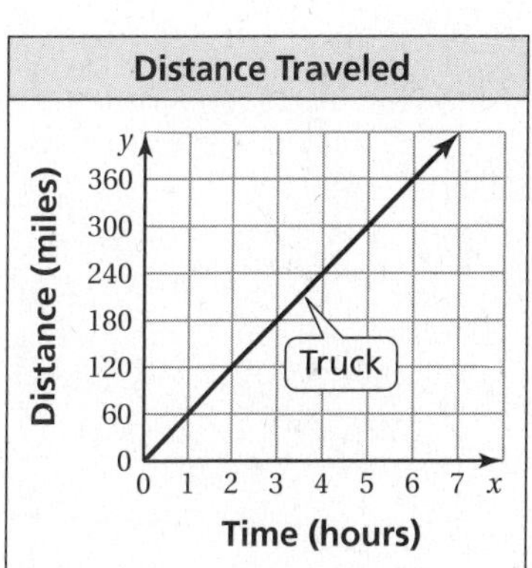

Name ______________________________ Date __________

2. The earnings y (in dollars) of Salesman A working x hours is represented by the function $y = 12.5x + 40$. The table shows the earnings of Salesman B.

Time (hours)	1	2	3	4
Earnings (dollars)	20.50	41.00	61.50	82.00

Time: +1, +1, +1

Earnings: +20.50, +20.50, +20.50

a. Which salesman has a higher hourly wage?

b. Write a function that relates the earnings of Salesman B to the number of hours worked. Graph the functions that represent the earnings of the two salesmen in the same coordinate plane. Interpret the graphs.

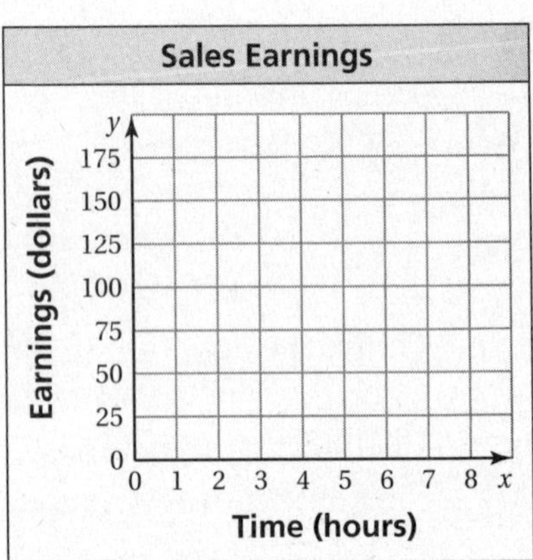

Name____ Date__________

Topic 5

Practice

For use after Topic 5

The vertices of a parallelogram are $A(-6, -1)$, $B(-3, 2)$, $C(3, 2)$, and $D(0, -1)$. Draw the parallelogram and its image after the translation. Find the coordinates of the image.

1. 4 units right and 2 units down

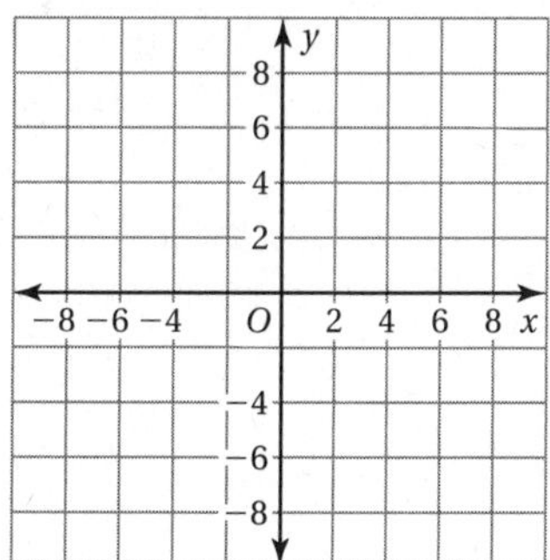

2. 2 units left and 1 unit up

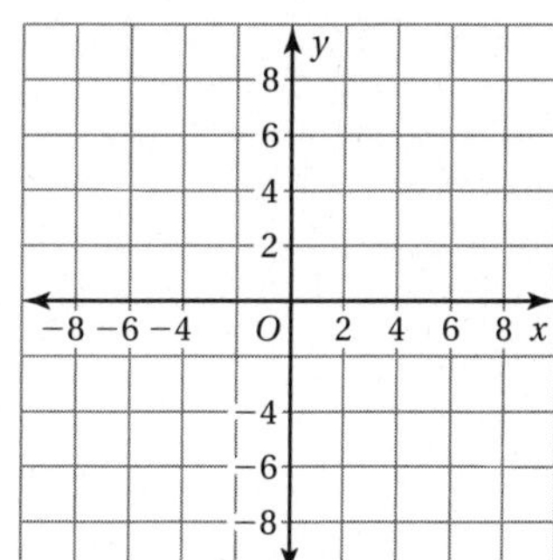

Find the coordinates of the figure after (a) reflecting in the *x*-axis and (b) reflecting in the *y*-axis.

3. $W(-6, 1)$, $X(-6, 4)$, $Y(-2, 4)$, $Z(-2, 1)$

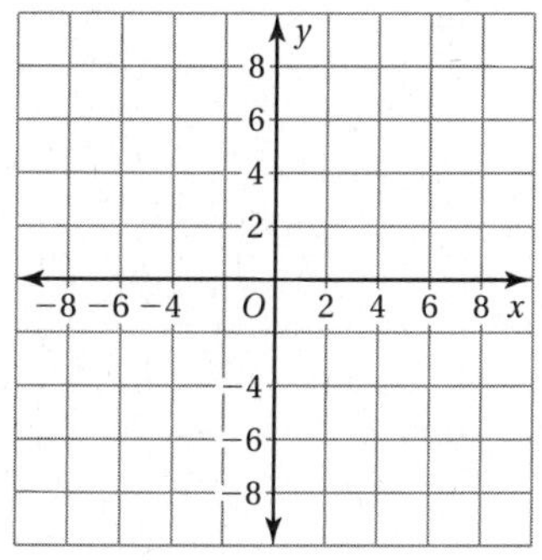

4. $P(4, -6)$, $Q(4, -1)$, $R(9, -6)$

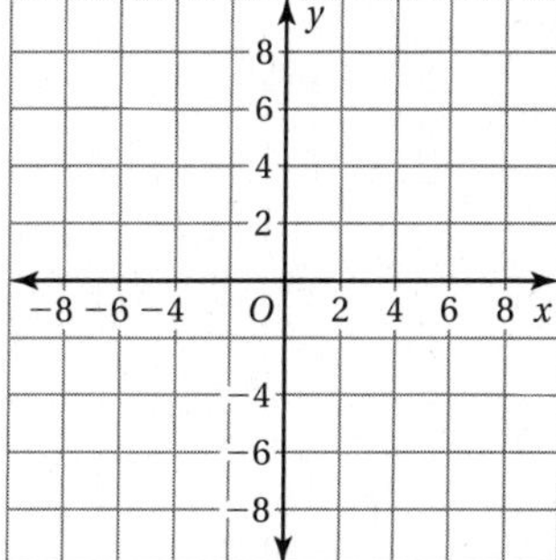

Name ______________________________ Date __________

Topic 5 **Practice (continued)**

The vertices of a triangle are $L(-3, 1)$, $M(-3, 4)$, and $N(-1, 1)$. Rotate the triangle as described. Find the coordinates of the image.

5. 180° clockwise about the origin

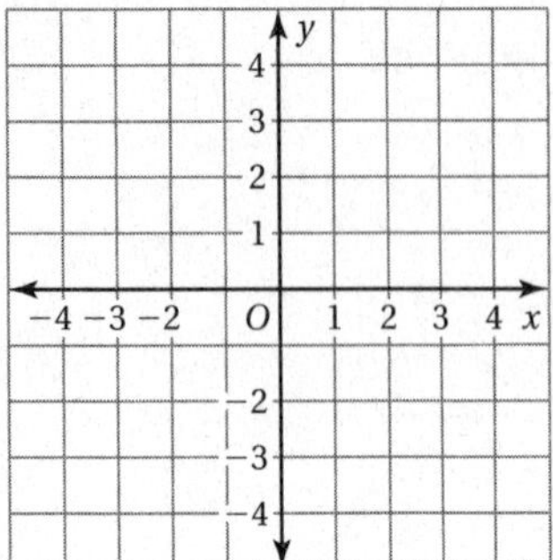

6. 90° counterclockwise about the origin

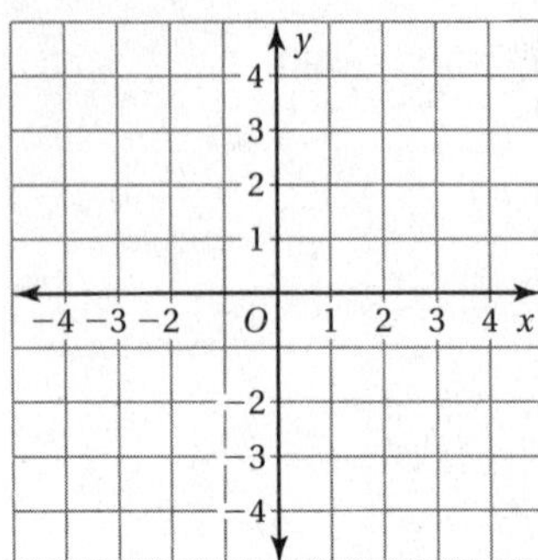

The vertices of a kite are $F(-6, -1)$, $G(-4, 1)$, $H(-2, -1)$, and $J(-4, -5)$. Dilate the kite using the given scale factor. Find the coordinates of the image. Identify the type of dilation.

7. scale factor $= 2$

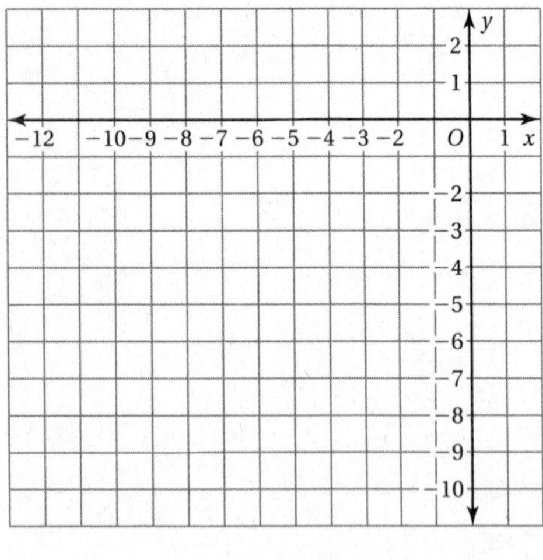

8. scale factor $= \frac{1}{2}$

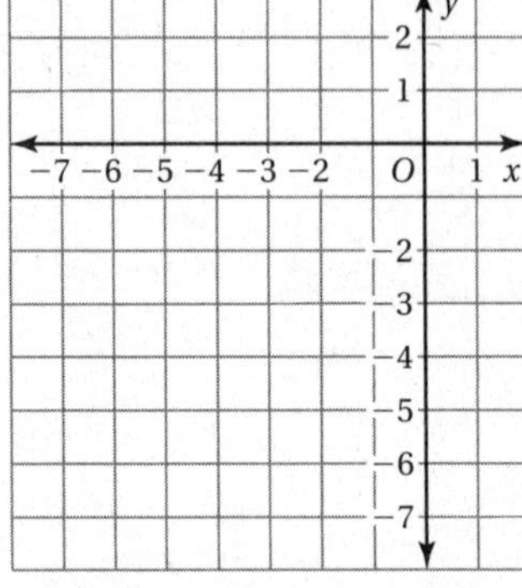

Name____ Date __________

Practice

For use after Topic 6

Find the volume of the solid. Round your answer to the nearest tenth.

1.

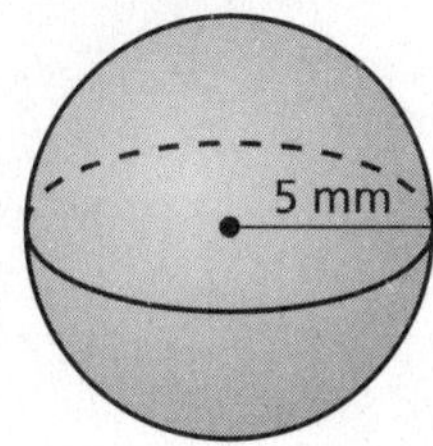

2.

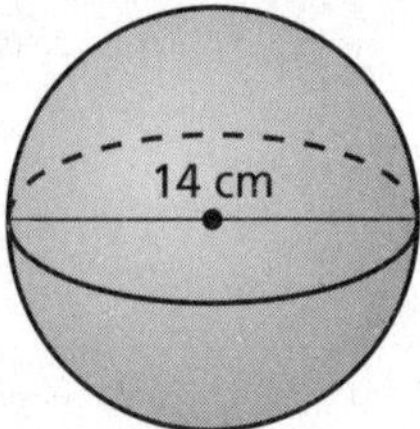

3.

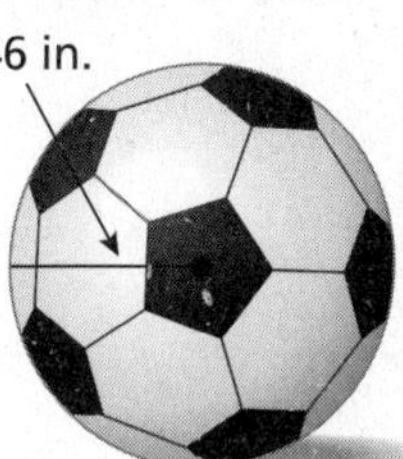

4.

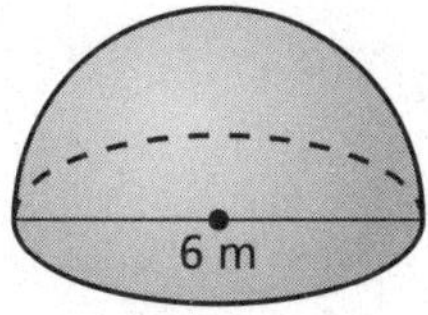

5.

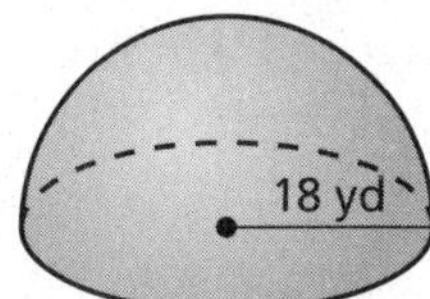

6.

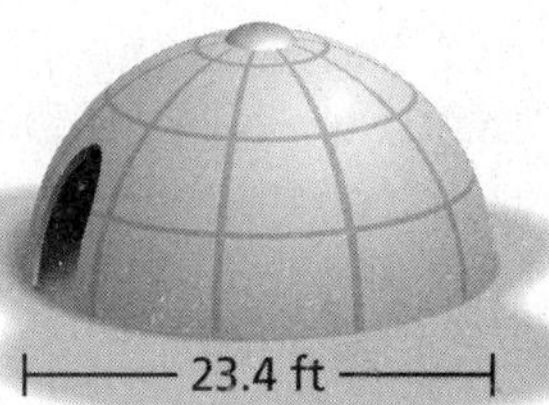

Name ______________________________ Date __________

Topic 6 Practice (continued)

7. Find the volume of the light fixture. Round your answer to the nearest whole number.

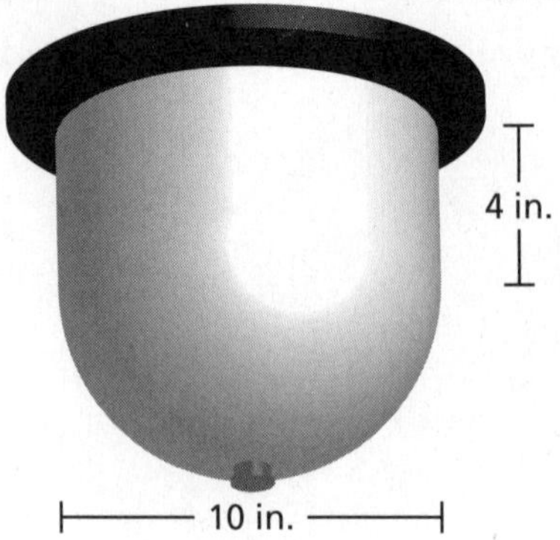

8. A box contains four golf balls. Each ball has a radius of 2.1 centimeters. Find the amount of space in the box that is not occupied by golf balls. Round your answer to the nearest whole number.

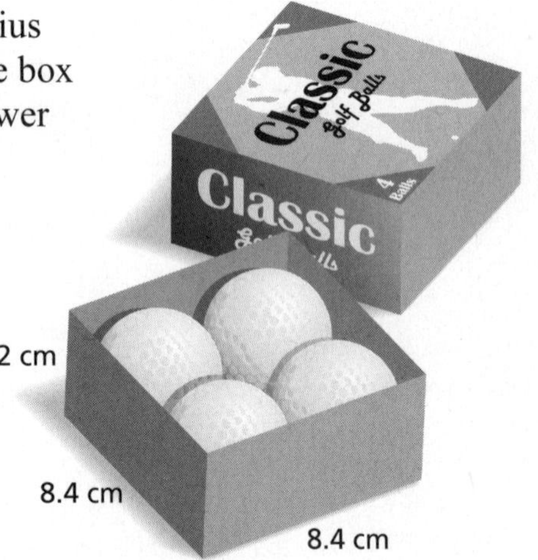

Name____ Date__________

Topic 7 Practice

For use after Topic 7

Tell whether the two right triangles are similar. Explain your reasoning.

1.

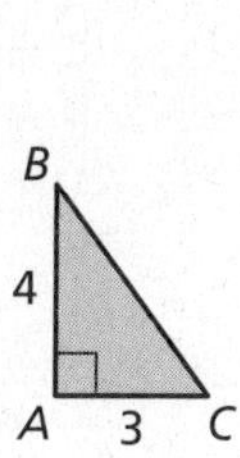

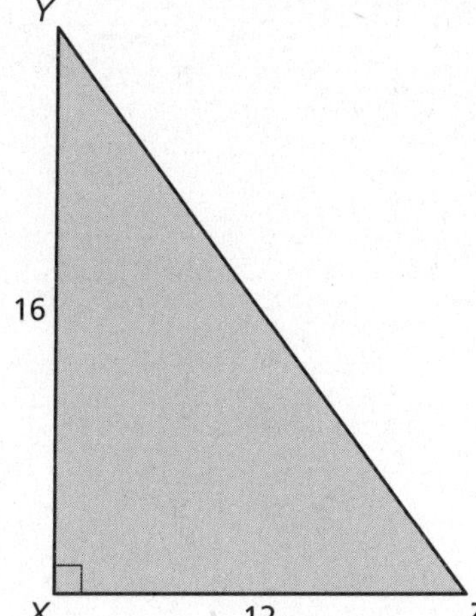

2.

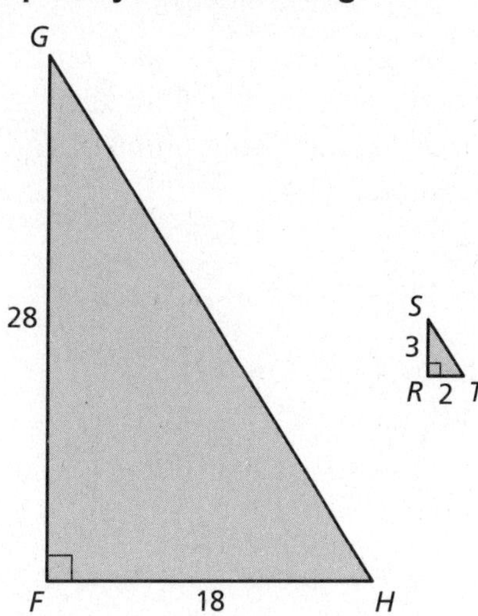

3. The graph shows similar right triangles drawn using pairs of points on a line.

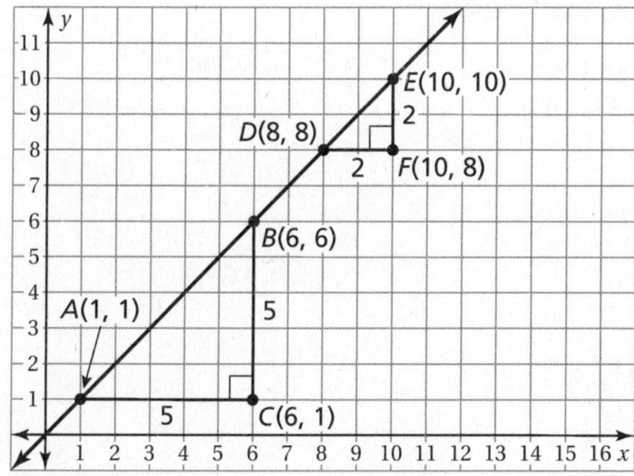

a. For each triangle, find the ratio of the length of the vertical leg to the length of the horizontal leg.

b. Relate the ratios in part (a) to the slope of the line.

Name ______________________________ Date __________

Topic 7 Practice (continued)

4. Consider the line shown in the graph.

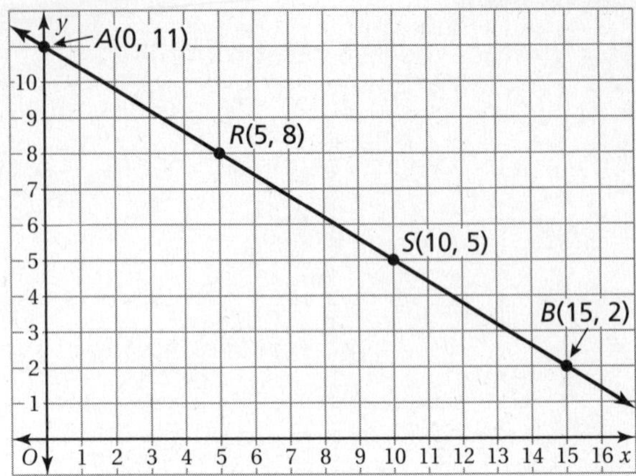

a. Draw two triangles that show the rise and the run of the line using points A and B and points R and S.

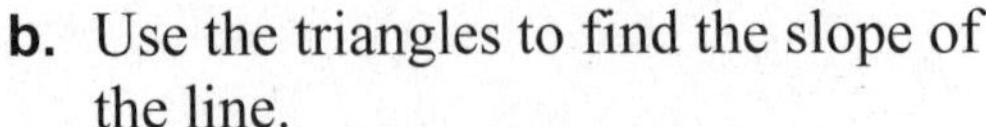

b. Use the triangles to find the slope of the line.

c. Repeat parts (a) and (b) using different pairs of points.

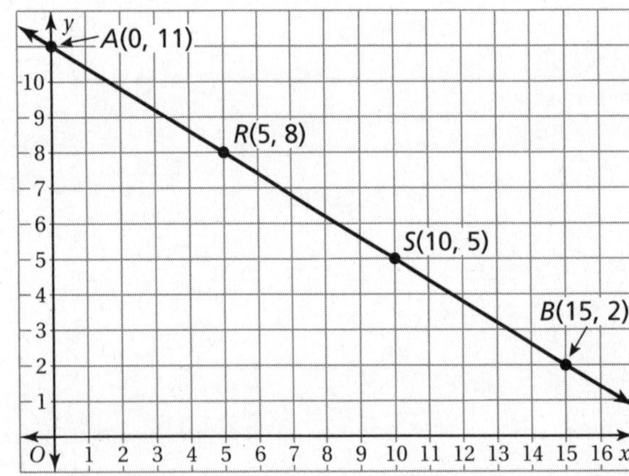

Math Card War – Chapter 2 Section 1*

1.25	0.75	$\frac{3}{4}$	0.6
-0.6	$\frac{19}{10}$	-0.4	$-\frac{2}{5}$
$-\frac{3}{4}$	-1.2	-0.75	1.6
$\frac{3}{10}$	$\frac{8}{5}$	1.9	$-\frac{3}{10}$
$-\frac{3}{2}$	$\frac{3}{20}$	1.5	$\frac{6}{5}$

*Available at *BigIdeasMath.com.*

Math Card War – Chapter 2 Section 1 (continued)*

-0.3	0.3	$-\frac{19}{10}$	$-\frac{8}{5}$
-1.6	1.2	$-\frac{3}{20}$	0.4
$\frac{3}{5}$	$-\frac{3}{5}$	$\frac{2}{5}$	-1.25
$\frac{5}{4}$	$-\frac{6}{5}$	-1.9	$\frac{3}{2}$
-0.15	-1.5	$-\frac{5}{4}$	0.15

*Available at *BigIdeasMath.com.*

Math Card War – Chapter 2 Section 5*

$-9 = 9x$	$x = -6$	$-1 = x + 5$	$x = 3$
$2x = -10$	$\frac{x}{-2} = -2$	$x - 2 = 1$	$-8 = -2x$
$x - 3 = 1$	$-3x = -3$	$-7x = -14$	$\frac{x}{3} = -1$
$x - 1 = 1$	$x = -2$	$-3x = -9$	$9x = -27$
$-4x = -12$	$3 + x = -2$	$6x = -36$	$x = -1$

*Available at *BigIdeasMath.com.*

Math Card War – Chapter 2 Section 5 (continued)*

$-2 = -3 + x$	$x + 13 = 11$	$-4 + x = -2$	$x - 5 = -4$
$x = -4$	$x = 2$	$\frac{x}{2} = -2$	$x + 6 = 2$
$-10 = 10x$	$-16 = 8x$	$x = 1$	$x = 4$
$x = -5$	$x + 9 = 8$	$-8 = 2x$	$-6 = x - 3$
$-7 = -1 + x$	$-20 = 10x$	$x = -3$	$\frac{x}{5} = -1$

*Available at *BigIdeasMath.com*.

For use with Chapter 5 Section 6*

a.

b.

c.

d.

*Available at *BigIdeasMath.com.*

For use with Chapter 5 Section 6 (continued)*

For use with Chapter 5 Section 7*

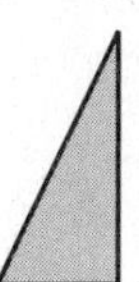

*Available at *BigIdeasMath.com.*

For use with Chapter 6 Section 5*

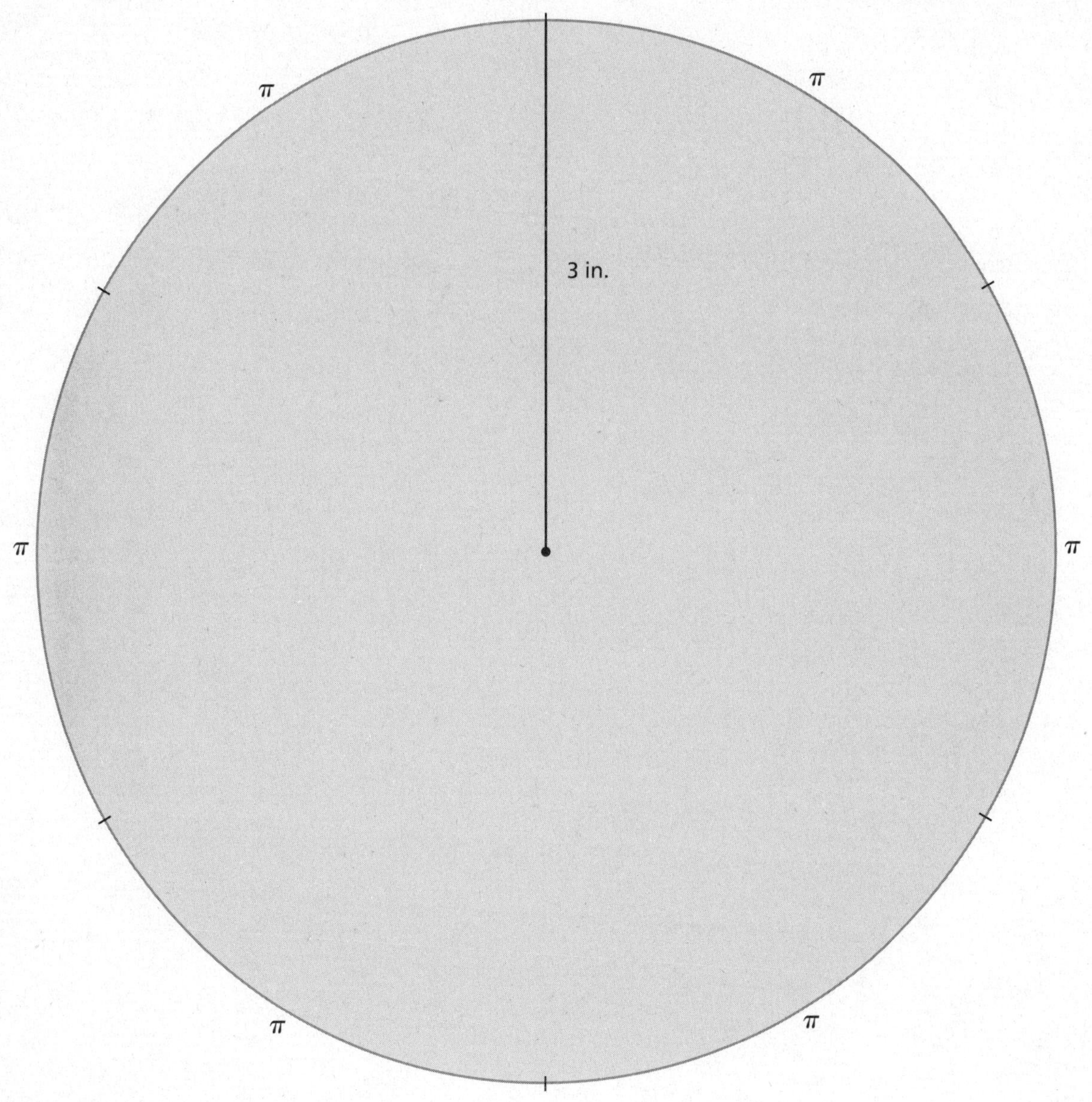

*Available at *BigIdeasMath.com.*

For use with Chapter 7 Section 3*

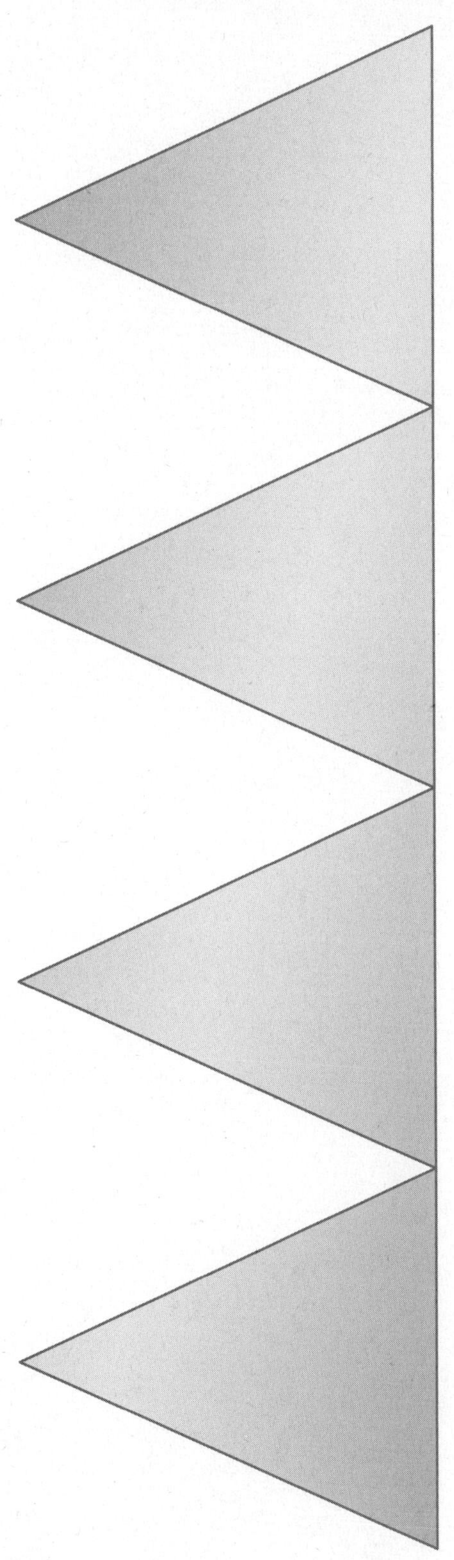

*Available at *BigIdeasMath.com.*

For use with Chapter 7 Section 3 (continued)*

*Available at *BigIdeasMath.com.*

Integer Counters*

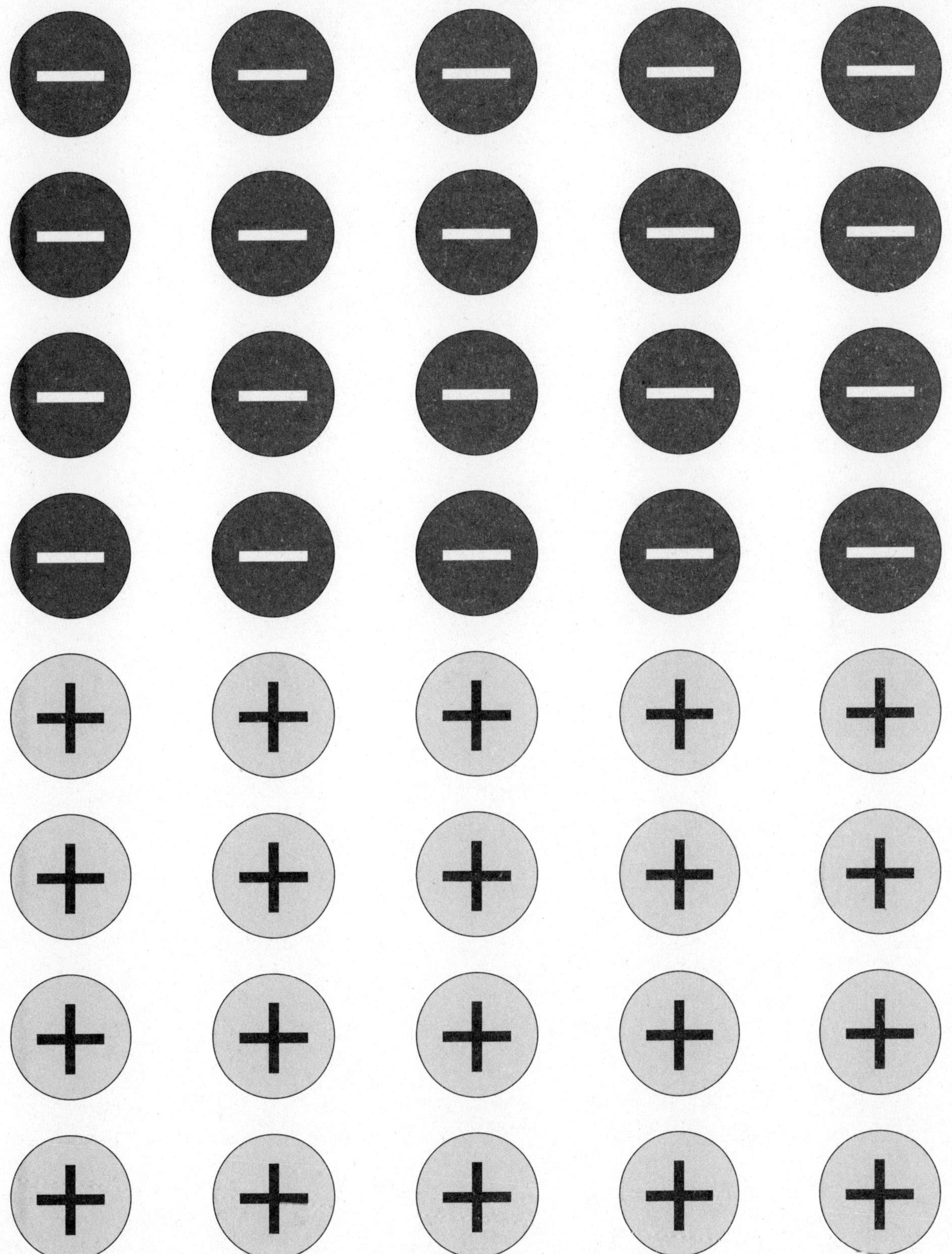

*Available at *BigIdeasMath.com.*

Algebra Tiles*

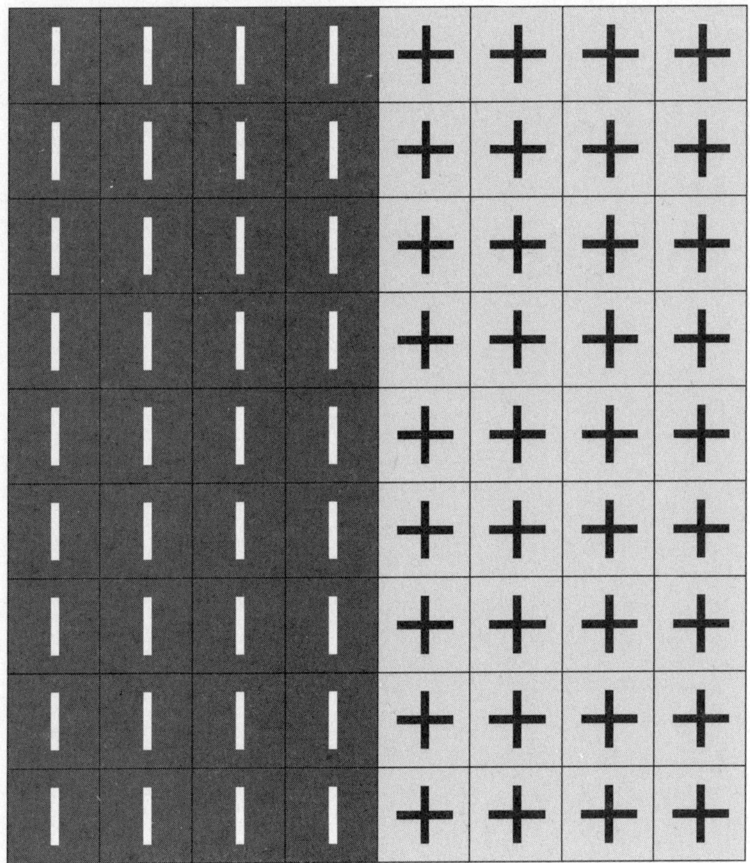

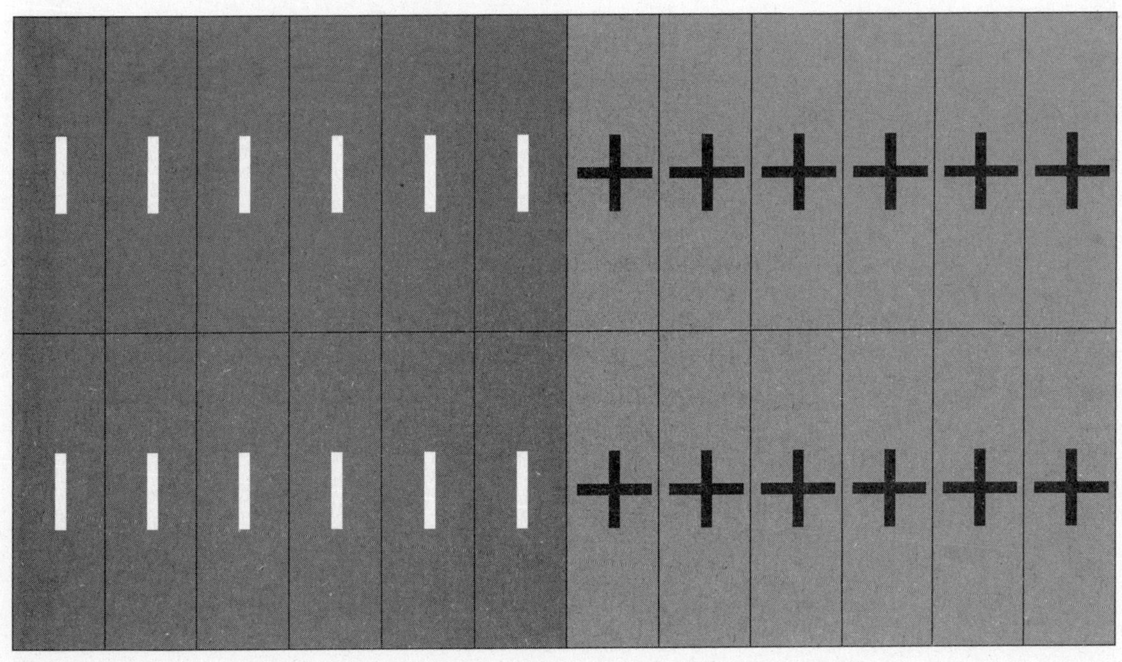

*Available at *BigIdeasMath.com.*

Pattern Blocks*

*Available at *BigIdeasMath.com.*

Pattern Blocks*

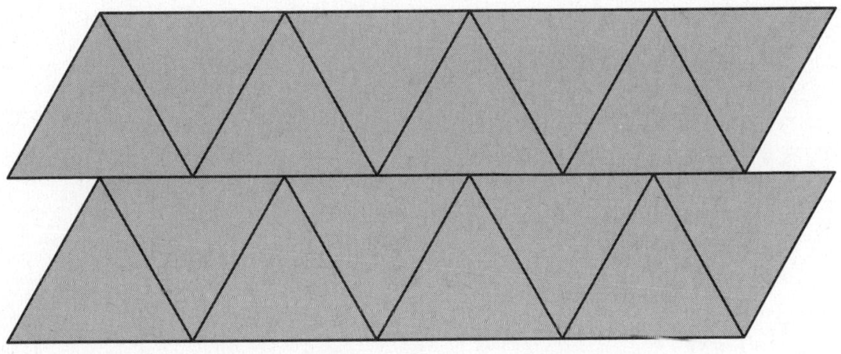

*Available at *BigIdeasMath.com.*